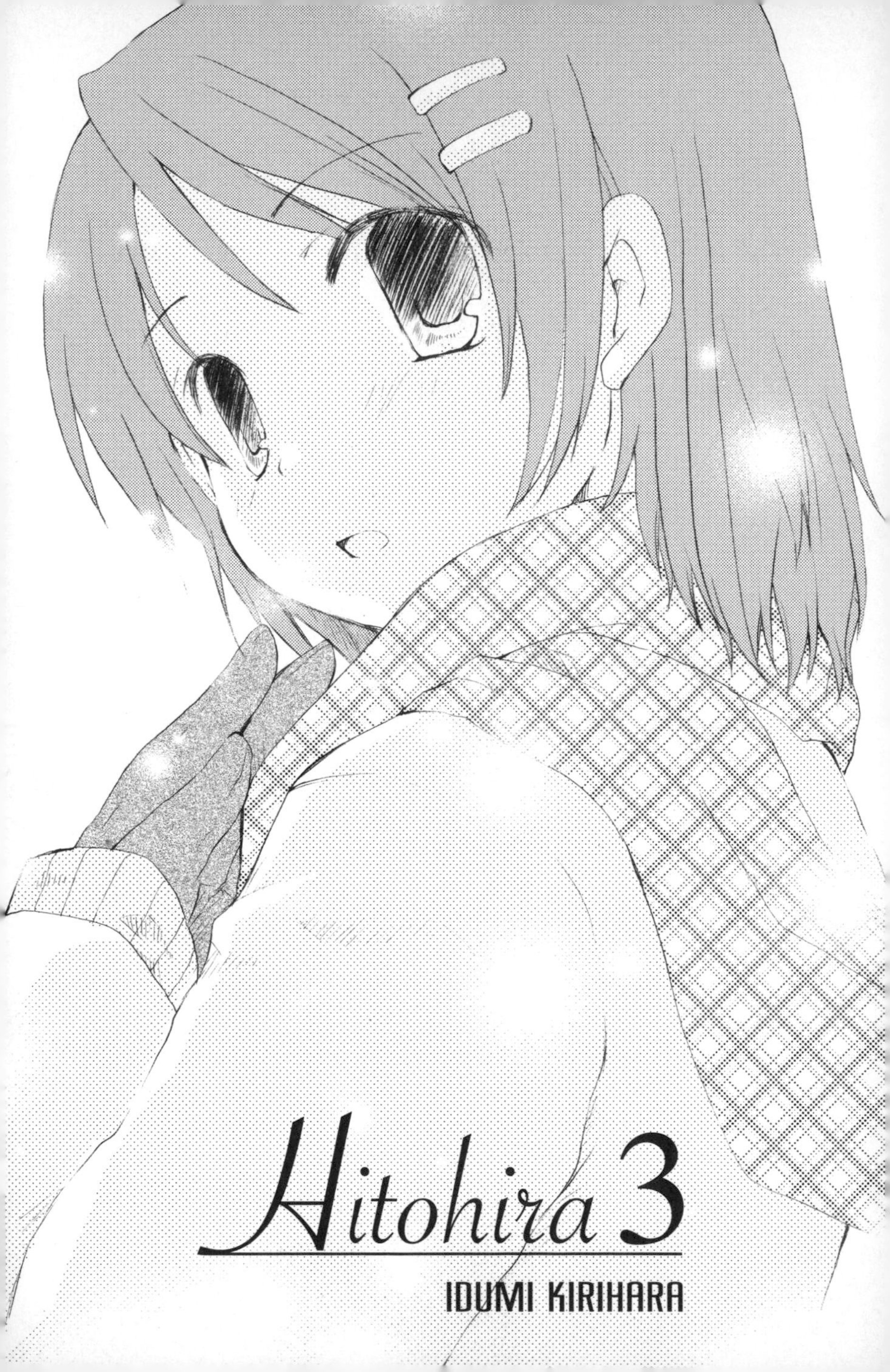
Hitohira 3
IDUMI KIRIHARA

Contents

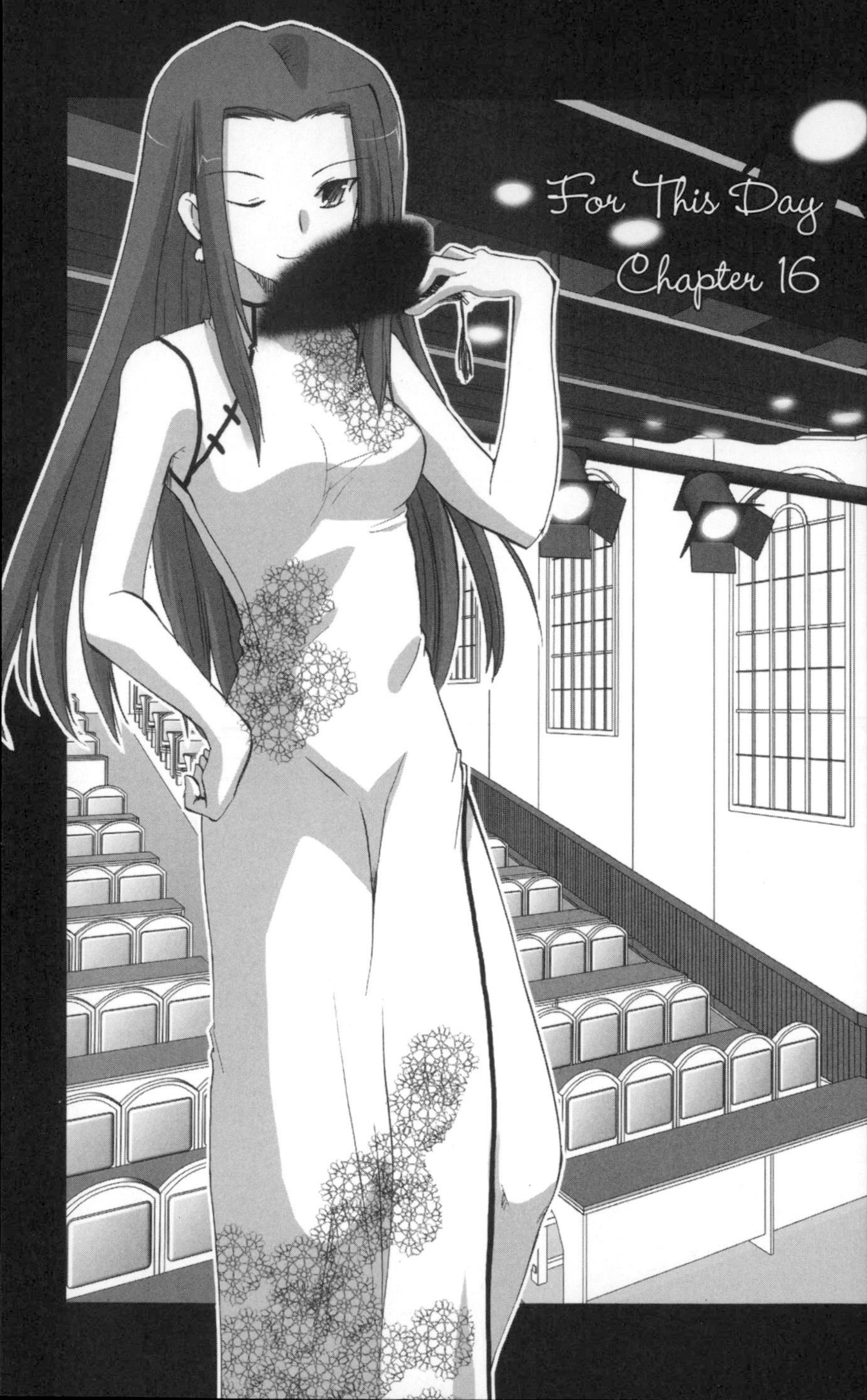
For This Day
Chapter 16

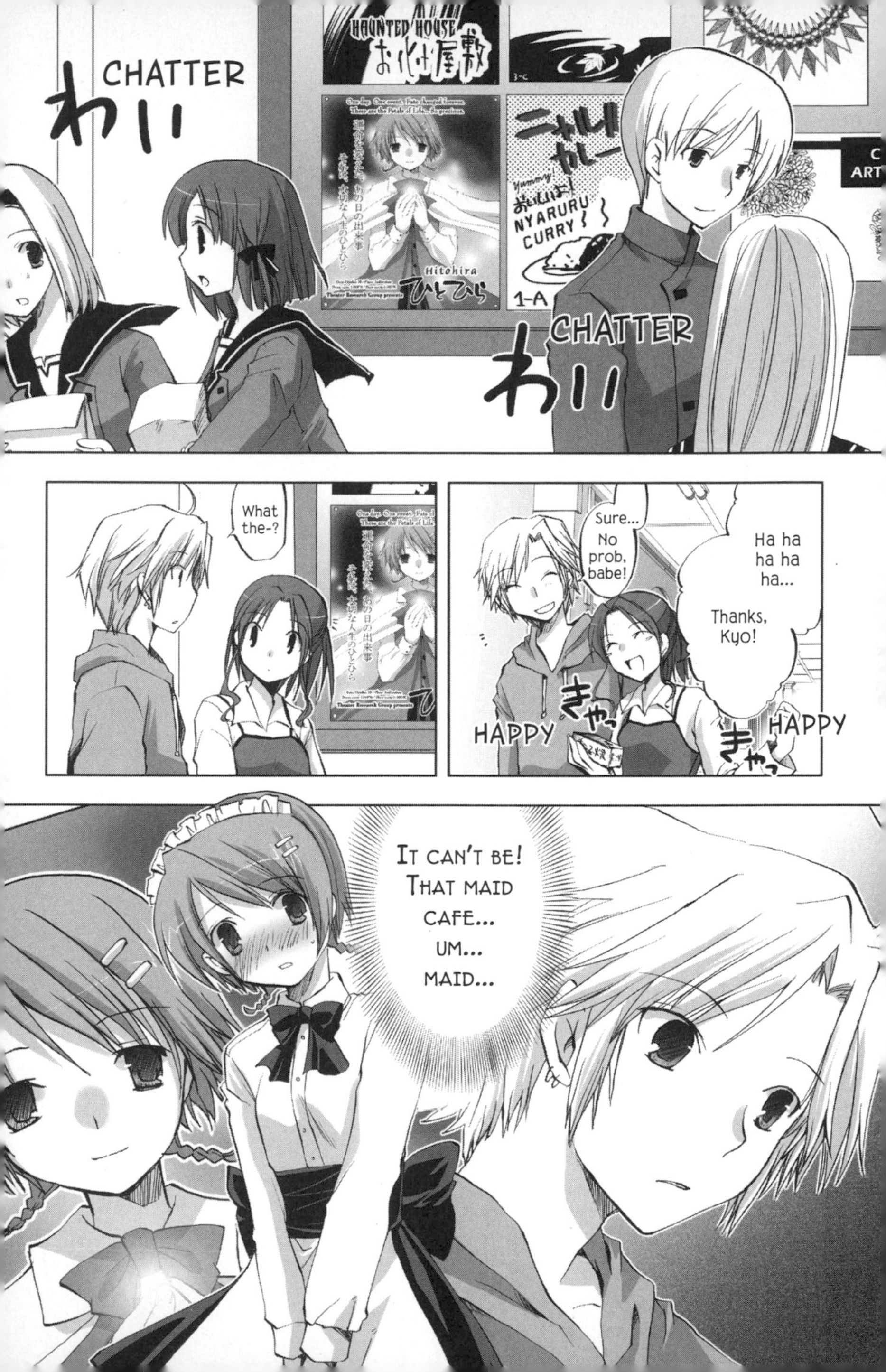
HAUNTED HOUSE
お化け屋敷
3-C
C
ART
ニャルルカレー
Yummy! おいしいよ!
NYARURU CURRY
1-A
CHATTER
わい
One day. One event. Fate changed forever. These are the Petals of Life. So precious.
Hitohira
ひとひら
Theater Research Group presents
CHATTER
わい
Sure... No prob, babe!
Ha ha ha ha ha...
Thanks, Kyo!
HAPPY
きゃっ
HAPPY
きゃっ
What the-?
It can't be! That maid cafe... um... maid...

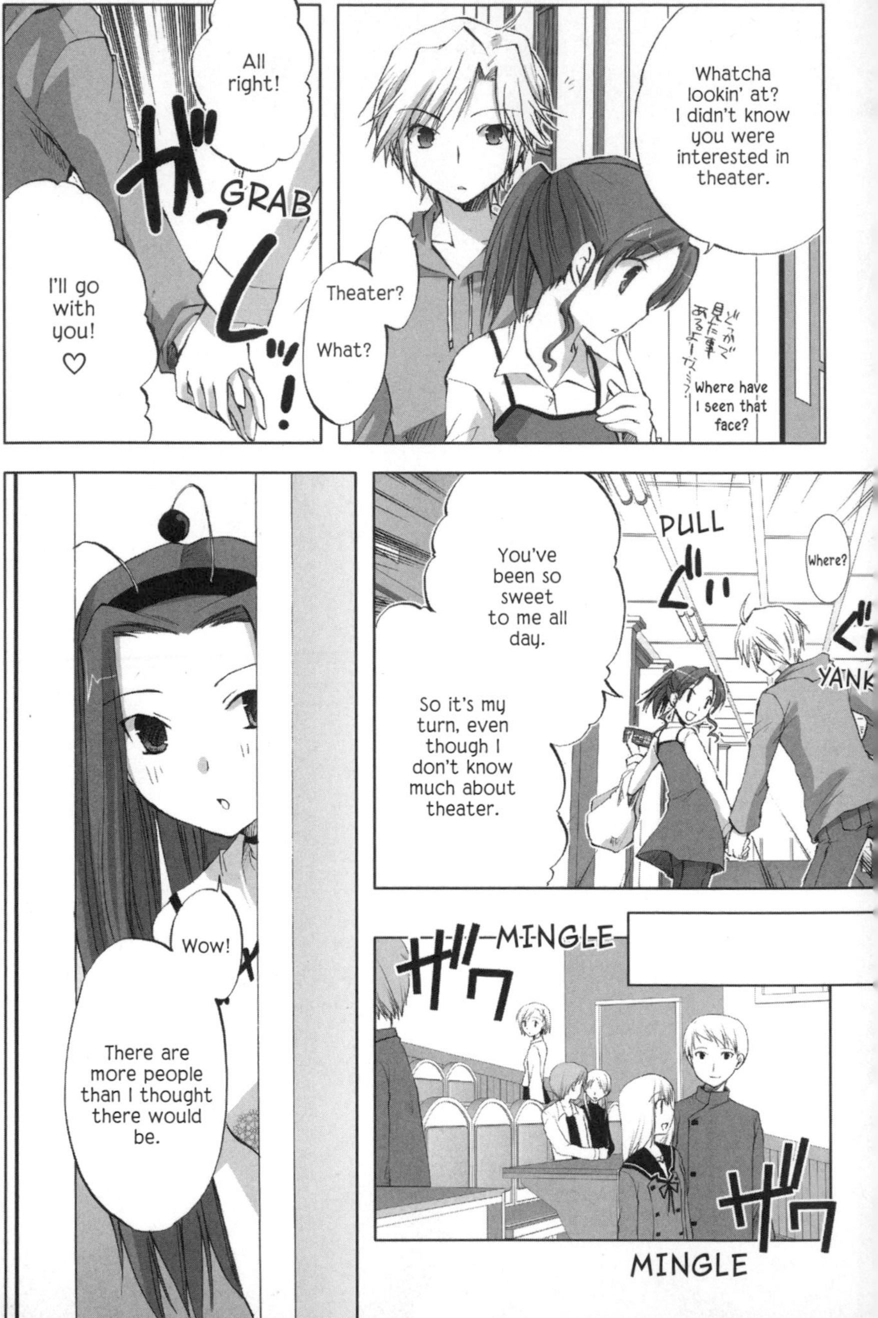

Whatcha lookin' at? I didn't know you were interested in theater.
Theater?
What?
Where have I seen that face?
All right!
GRAB
I'll go with you! ♡
You've been so sweet to me all day.
So it's my turn, even though I don't know much about theater.
PULL
Where?
YANK
MINGLE
MINGLE
Wow!
There are more people than I thought there would be.

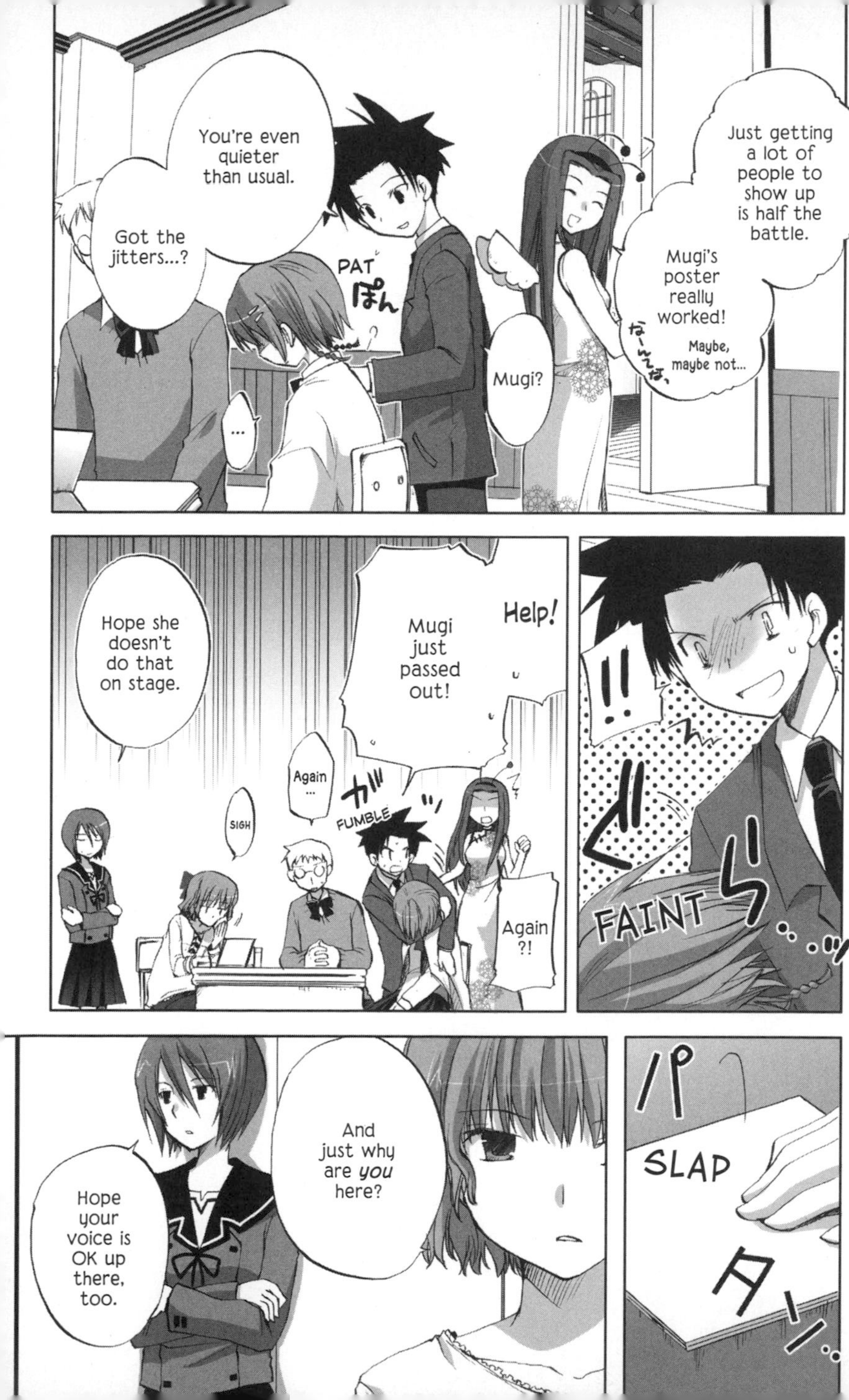
Just getting a lot of people to show up is half the battle.
Mugi's poster really worked!
なーんてな、
Maybe, maybe not...
You're even quieter than usual.
Got the jitters...?
PAT
ぽん
Mugi?
...
!!
FAINT
ら
Help!
Mugi just passed out!
Hope she doesn't do that on stage.
ガッ
FUMBLE
Again ?!
Again ...
SIGH
パ
SLAP
ター
And just why are *you* here?
Hope your voice is OK up there, too.

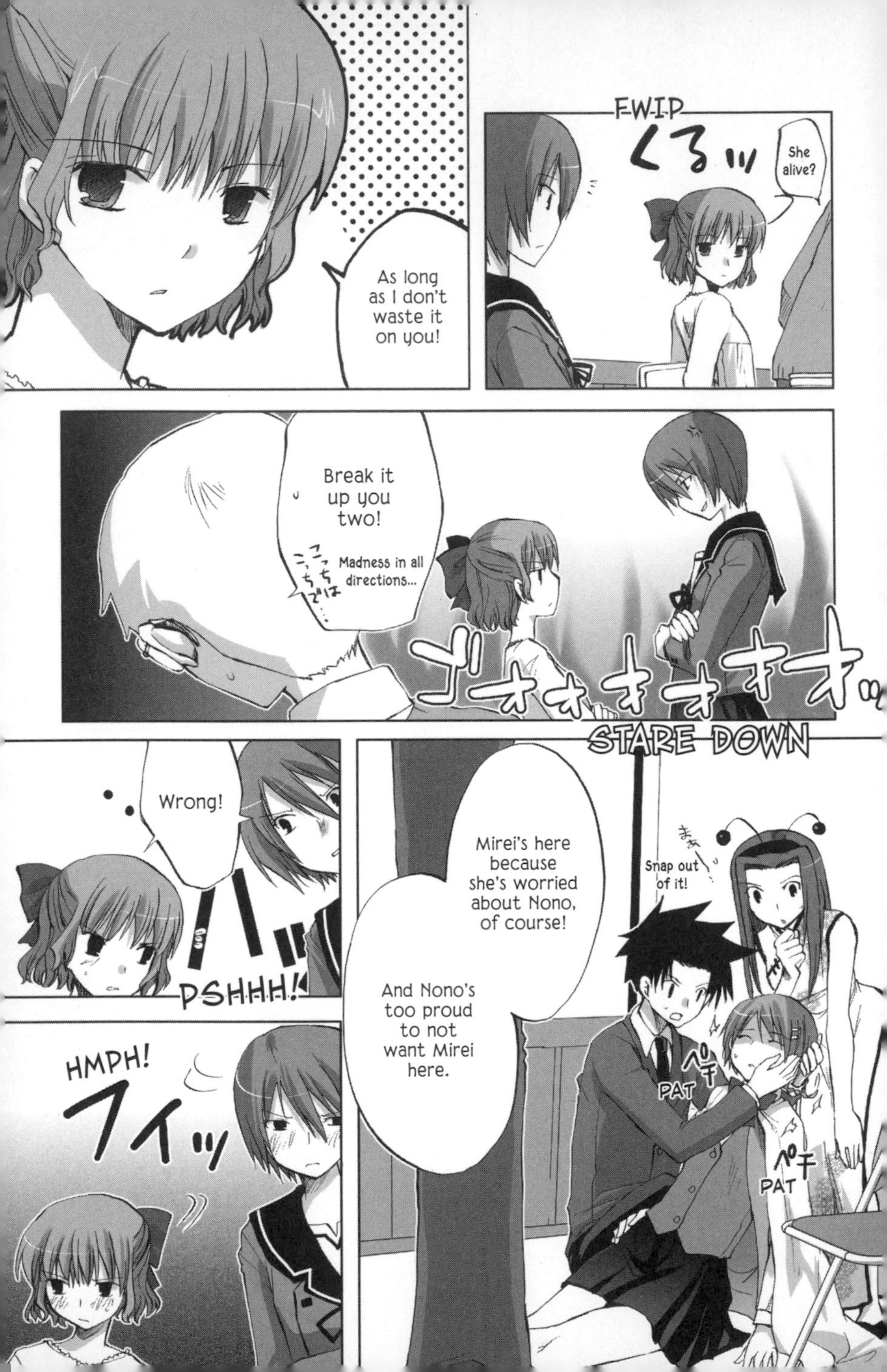
F-W-I-P
くるッ
She alive?
As long as I don't waste it on you!
Break it up you two!
Madness in all directions...
STARE DOWN
Mirei's here because she's worried about Nono, of course!
And Nono's too proud to not want Mirei here.
Snap out of it!
ペチ
PAT
ペチ
PAT
Wrong!
PSHHH!
HMPH!
フイッ

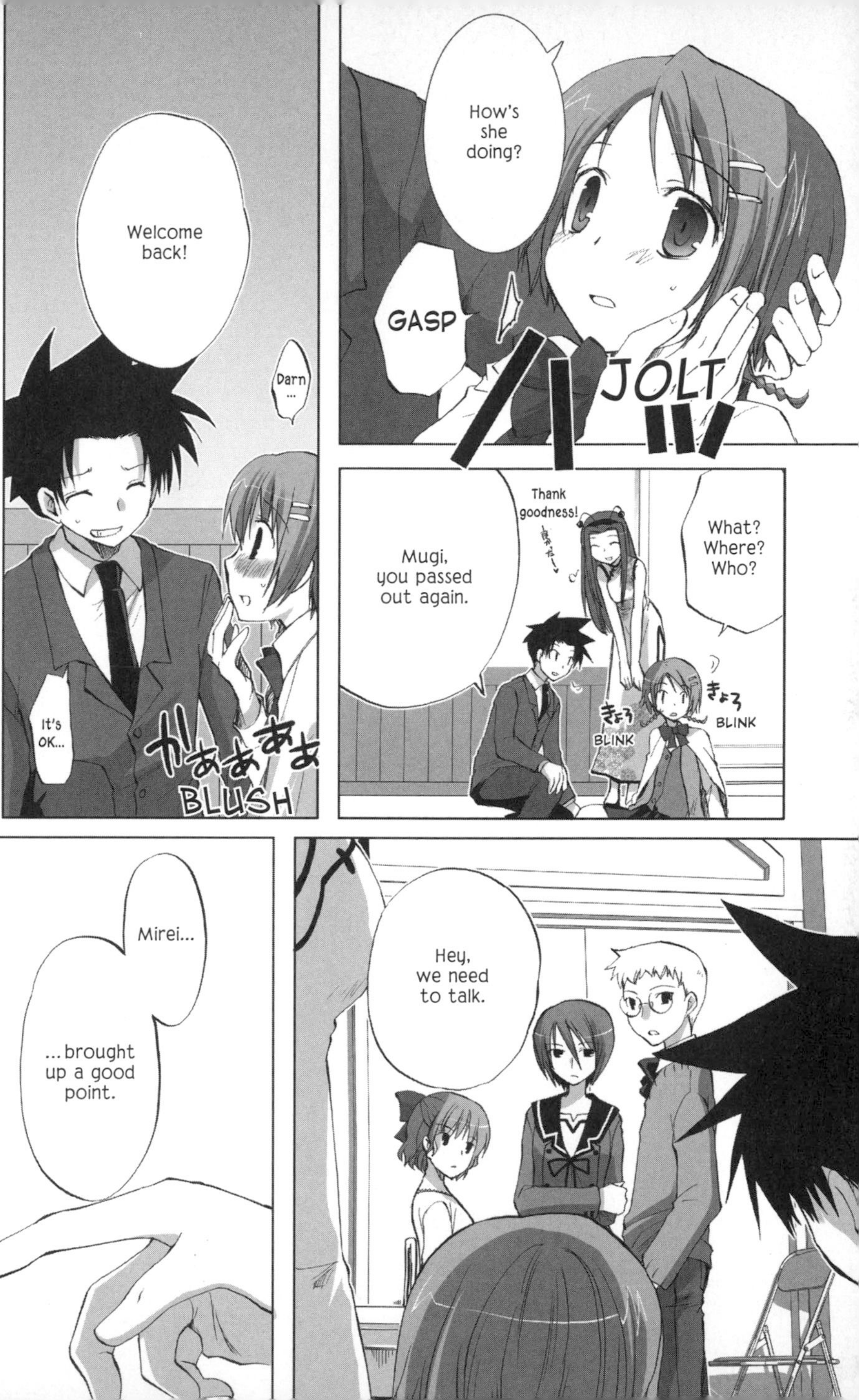
How's she doing?
GASP
JOLT
What? Where? Who?
Thank goodness!
Mugi, you passed out again.
きょろ
BLINK
きょろ
BLINK
Welcome back!
Darn...
It's OK...
BLUSH
Hey, we need to talk.
Mirei...
...brought up a good point.

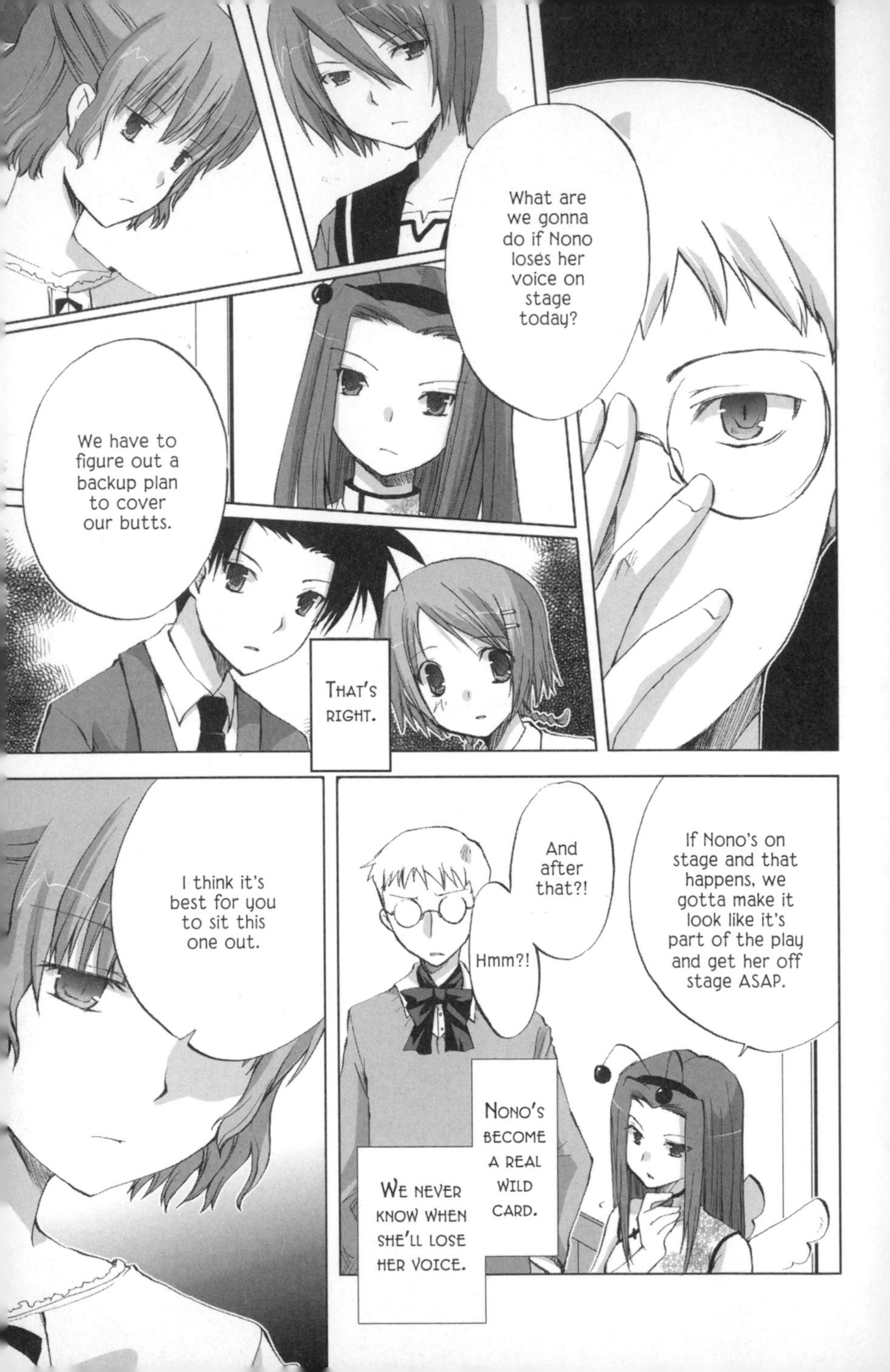
What are we gonna do if Nono loses her voice on stage today?
We have to figure out a backup plan to cover our butts.
THAT'S RIGHT.
If Nono's on stage and that happens, we gotta make it look like it's part of the play and get her off stage ASAP.
And after that?!
Hmm?!
NONO'S BECOME A REAL WILD CARD.
WE NEVER KNOW WHEN SHE'LL LOSE HER VOICE.
I think it's best for you to sit this one out.

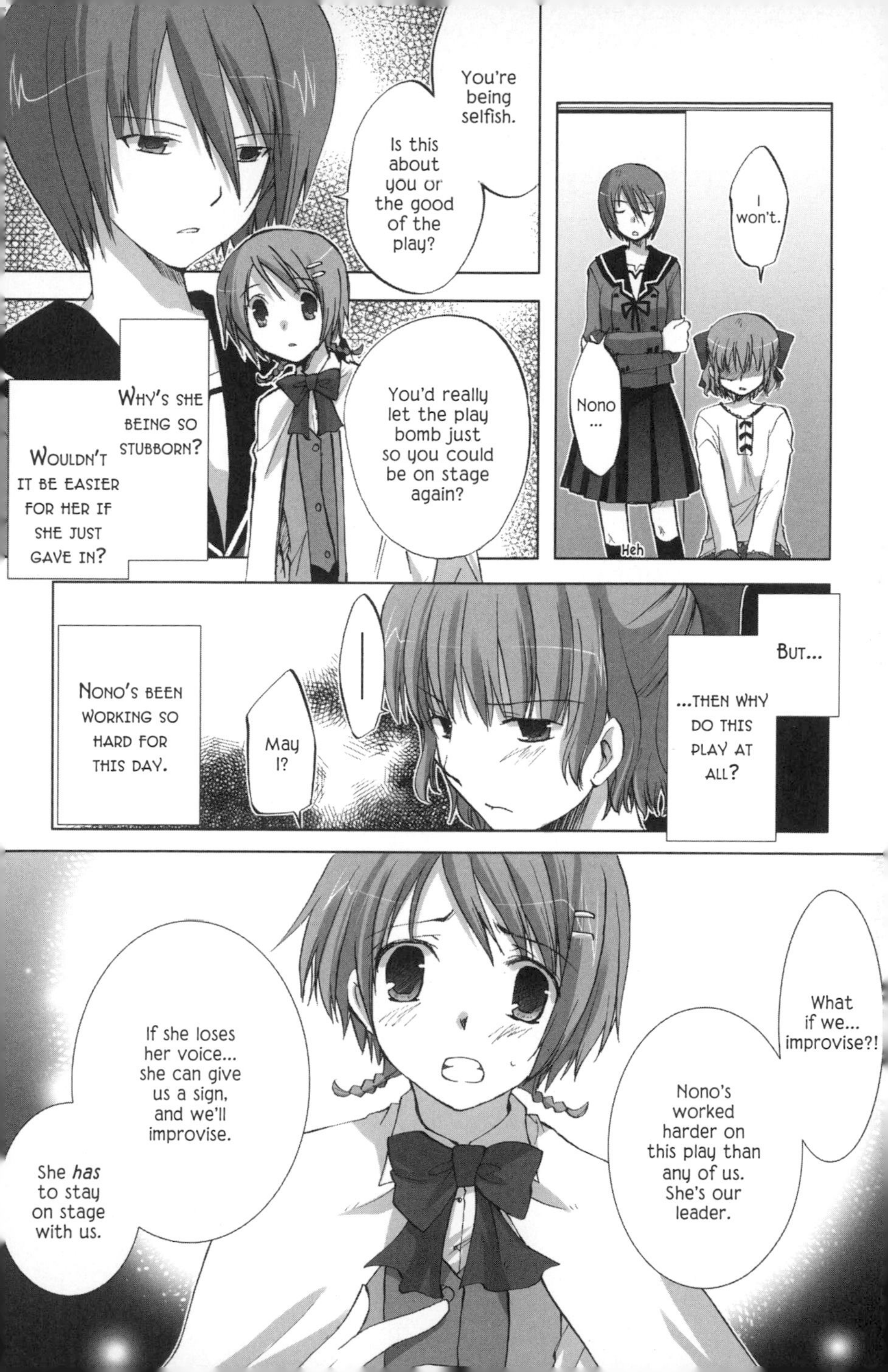
I won't.
Nono...
Heh
You're being selfish.
Is this about you or the good of the play?
You'd really let the play bomb just so you could be on stage again?
Why's she being so stubborn?
Wouldn't it be easier for her if she just gave in?
But...
...then why do this play at all?
May I?
Nono's been working so hard for this day.
What if we... improvise?!
Nono's worked harder on this play than any of us. She's our leader.
If she loses her voice... she can give us a sign, and we'll improvise.
She *has* to stay on stage with us.

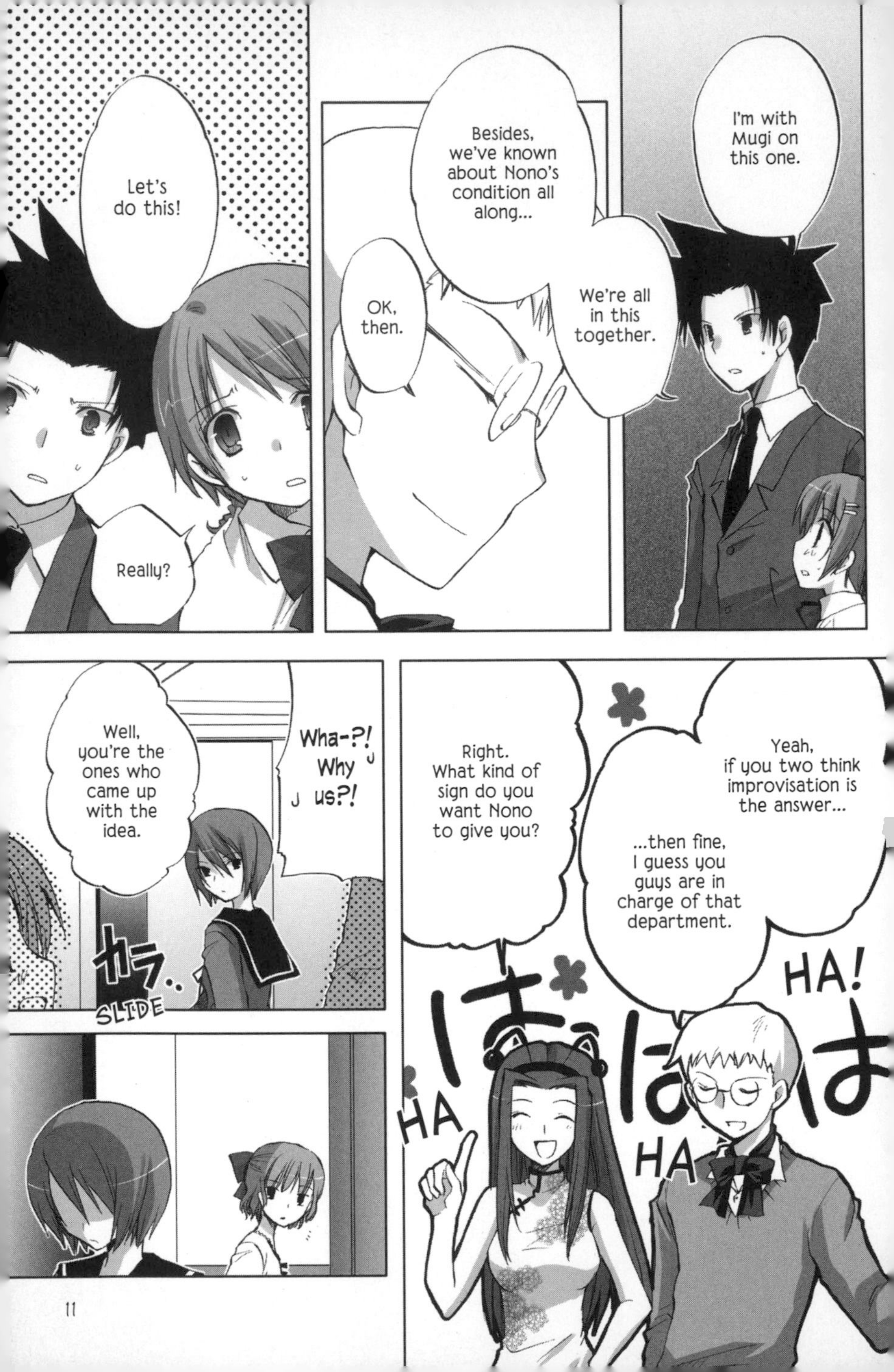

I'm with Mugi on this one.
Besides, we've known about Nono's condition all along...
We're all in this together.
OK, then.
Let's do this!
Really?
Yeah, if you two think improvisation is the answer...
...then fine, I guess you guys are in charge of that department.
Right. What kind of sign do you want Nono to give you?
HA!
HA
HA
Wha-?! Why us?!
Well, you're the ones who came up with the idea.
カラ..
SLIDE

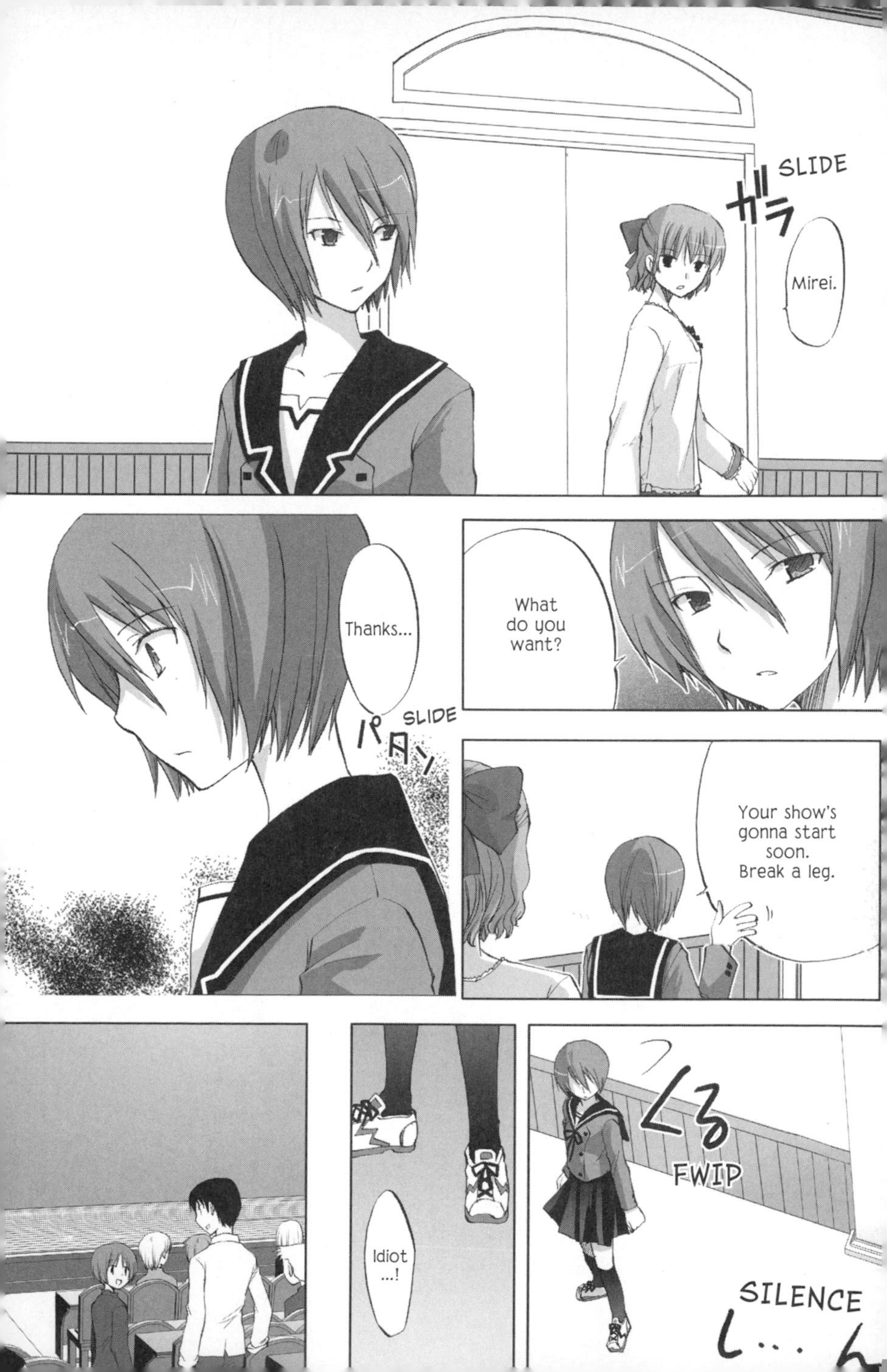
ガラ
SLIDE
Mirei.
What do you want?
Your show's gonna start soon. Break a leg.
Thanks...
パタン
SLIDE
くる
FWIP
し…ん
SILENCE
Idiot ...!

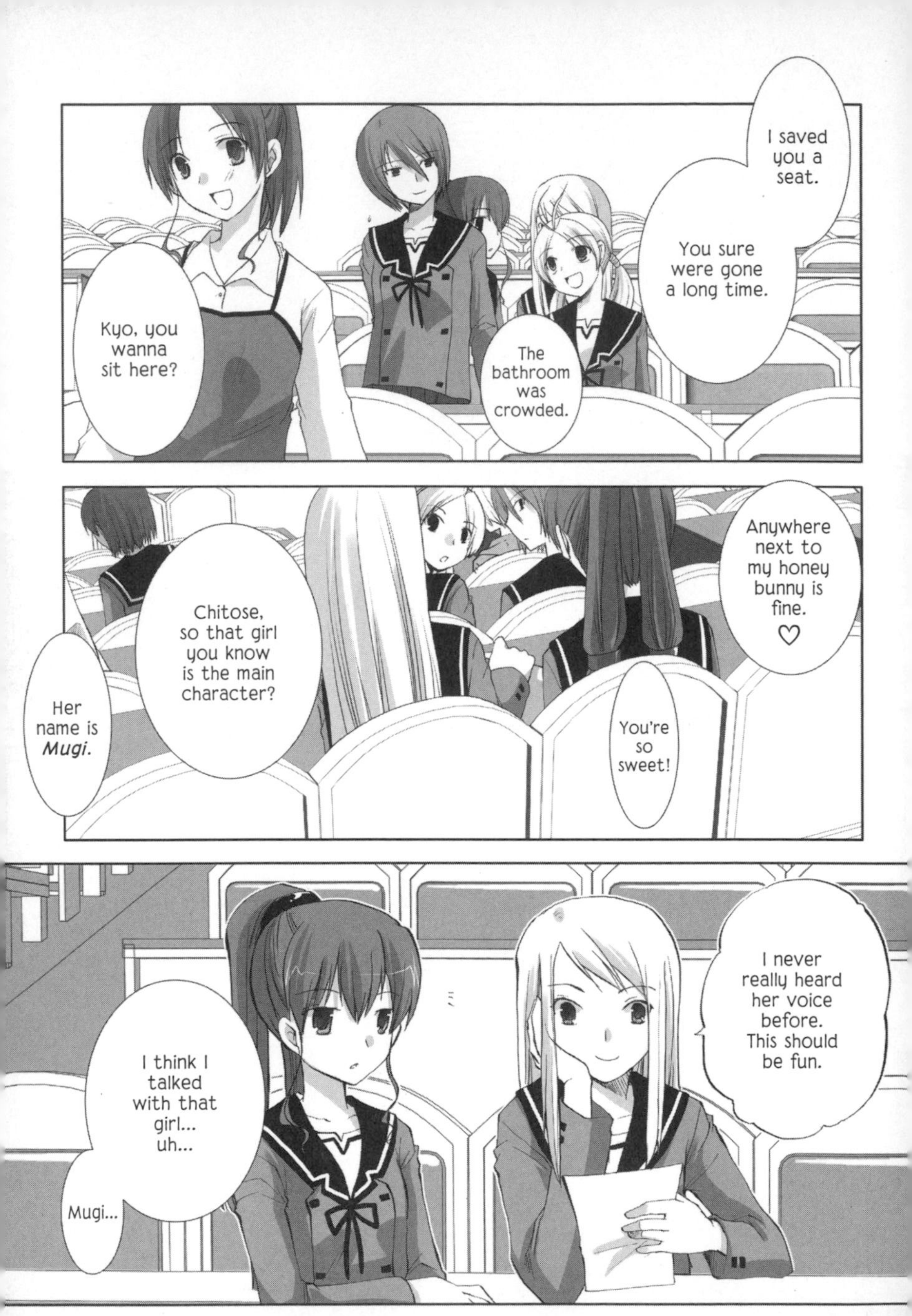
I saved you a seat.
You sure were gone a long time.
The bathroom was crowded.
Kyo, you wanna sit here?
Anywhere next to my honey bunny is fine. ♡
You're so sweet!
Chitose, so that girl you know is the main character?
Her name is *Mugi*.
I never really heard her voice before. This should be fun.
I think I talked with that girl... uh...
Mugi...

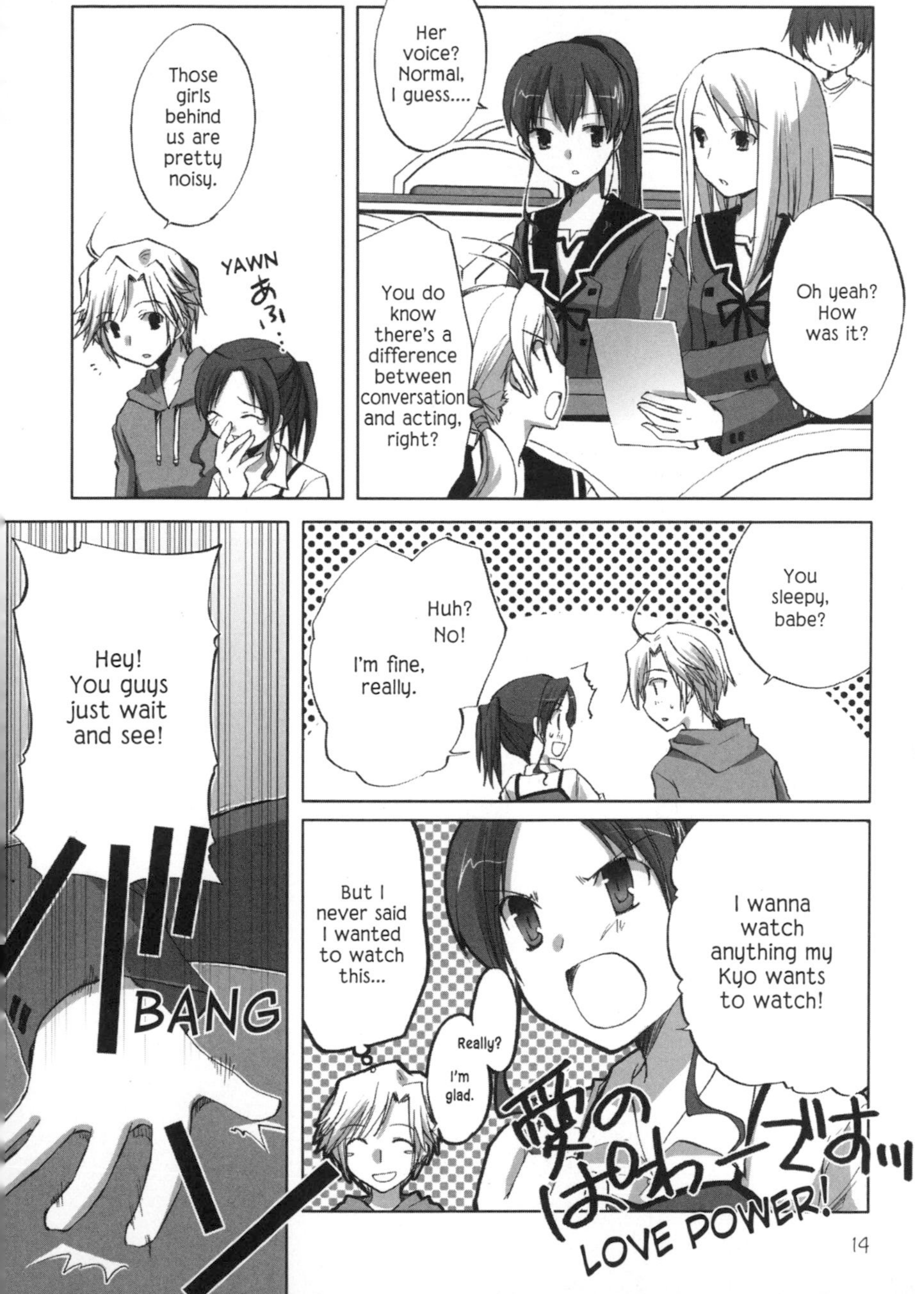
Oh yeah? How was it?
Her voice? Normal, I guess....
You do know there's a difference between conversation and acting, right?
Those girls behind us are pretty noisy.
YAWN
あふ…
You sleepy, babe?
Huh? No!
I'm fine, really.
I wanna watch anything my Kyo wants to watch!
But I never said I wanted to watch this...
Really?
I'm glad.
愛のぱわーですっ
LOVE POWER!
Hey! You guys just wait and see!
BANG

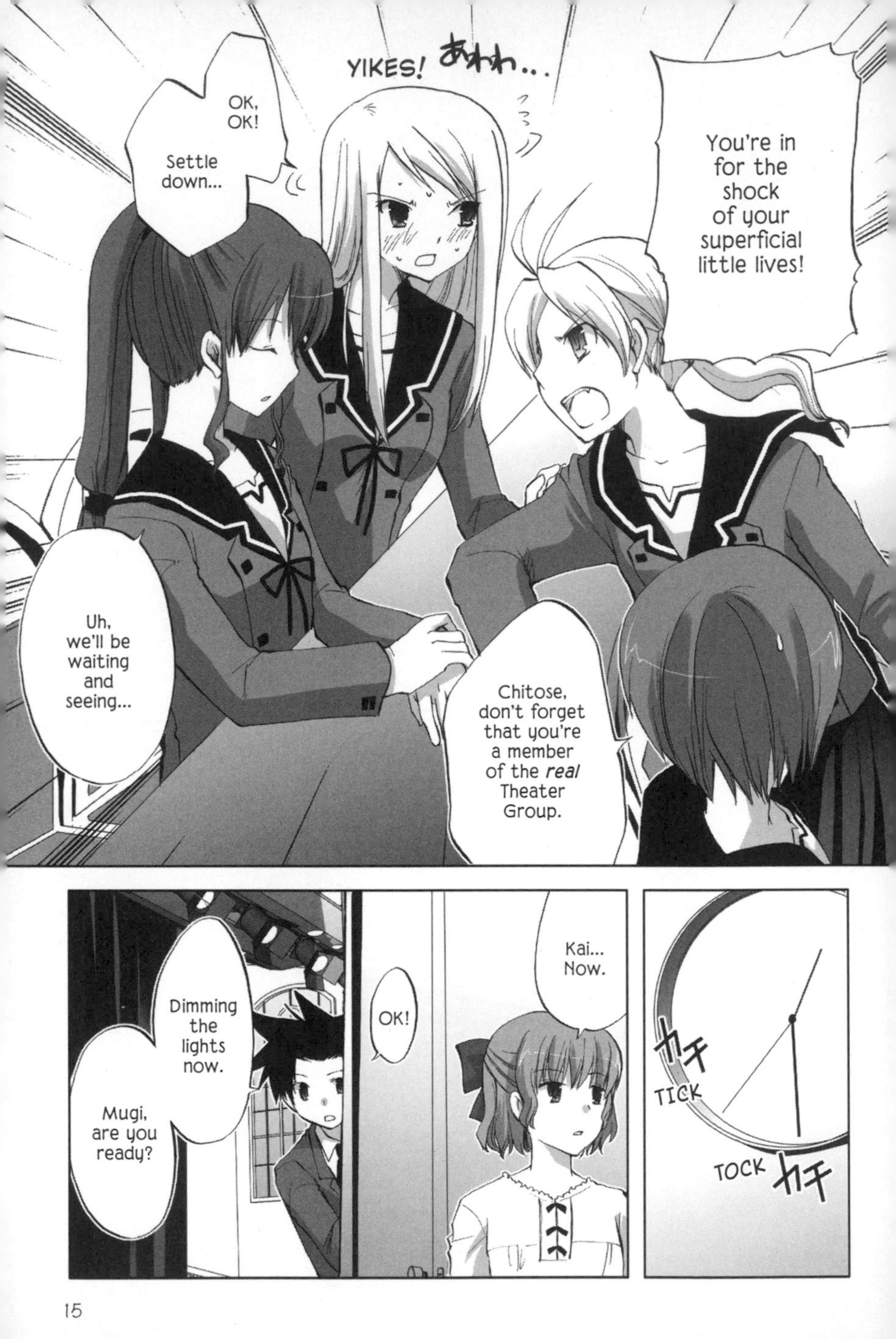
You're in for the shock of your superficial little lives!
YIKES! あわわ...
OK, OK!
Settle down...
Uh, we'll be waiting and seeing...
Chitose, don't forget that you're a member of the *real* Theater Group.
カチ
TICK
TOCK
カチ
Kai... Now.
OK!
Dimming the lights now.
Mugi, are you ready?

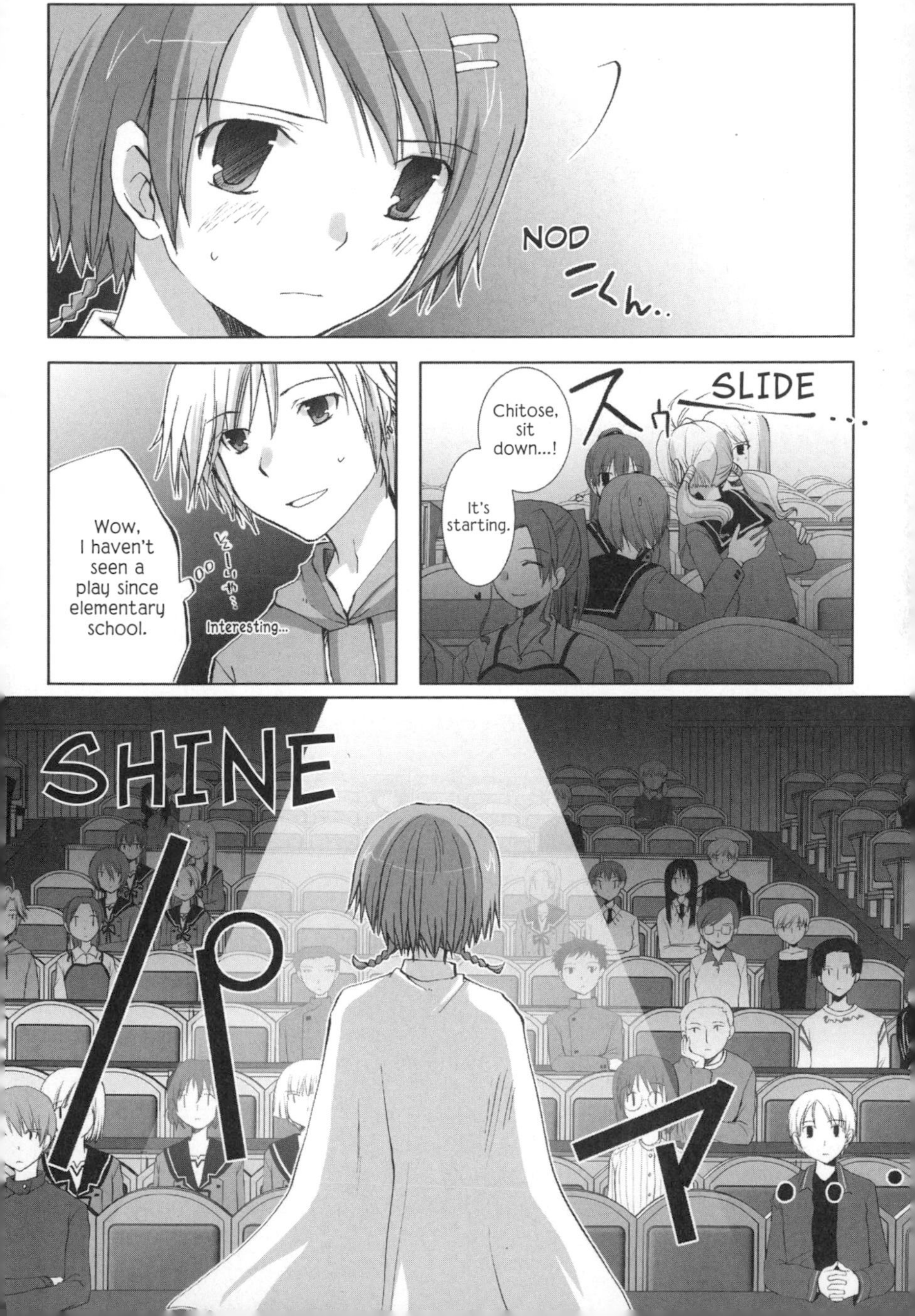
NOD
Chitose, sit down...!
It's starting.
SLIDE
Wow, I haven't seen a play since elementary school.
Interesting...
SHINE

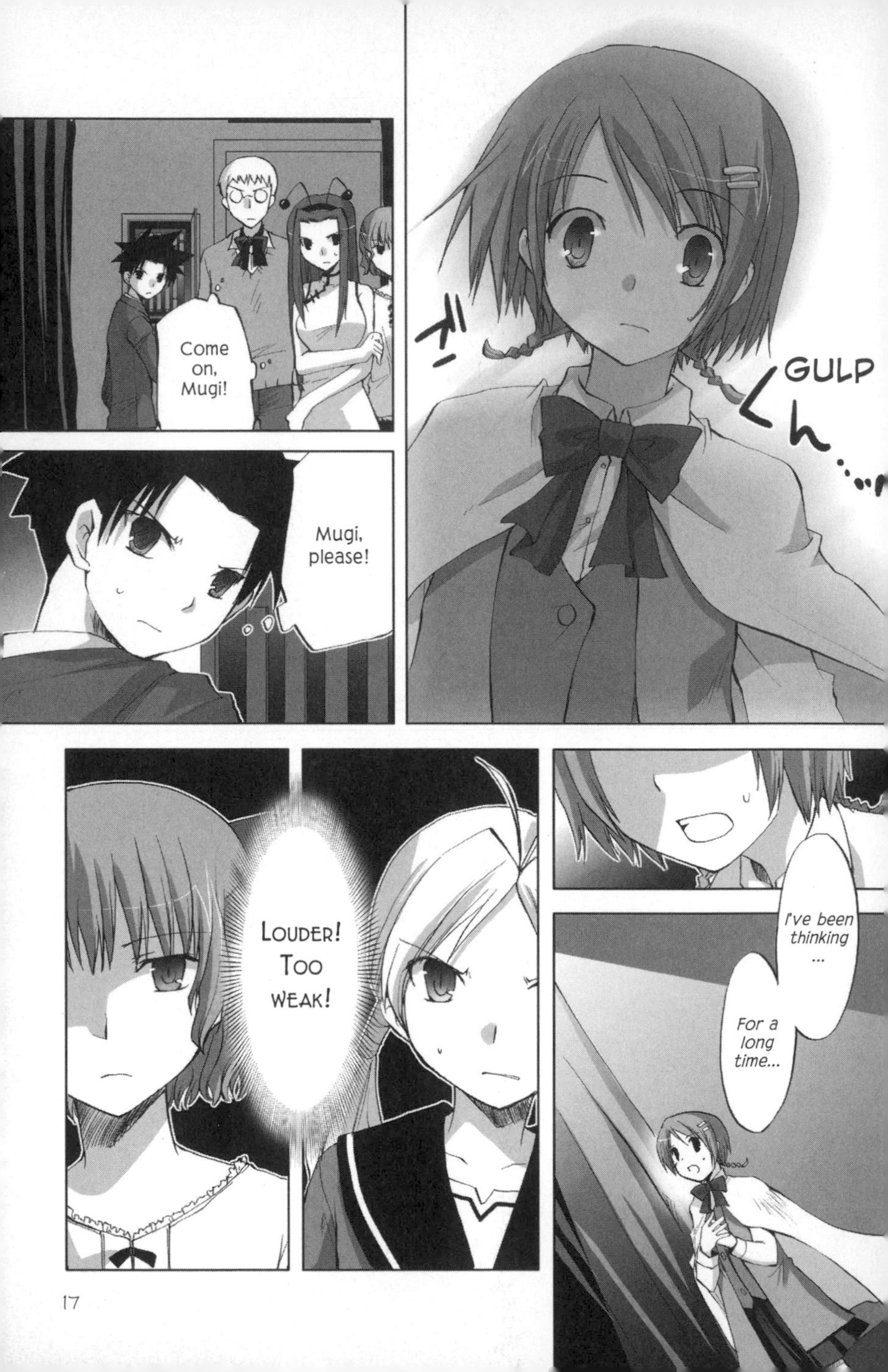
GULP
くん...
Come on, Mugi!
Mugi, please!
I've been thinking ...
For a long time...
Louder! Too weak!

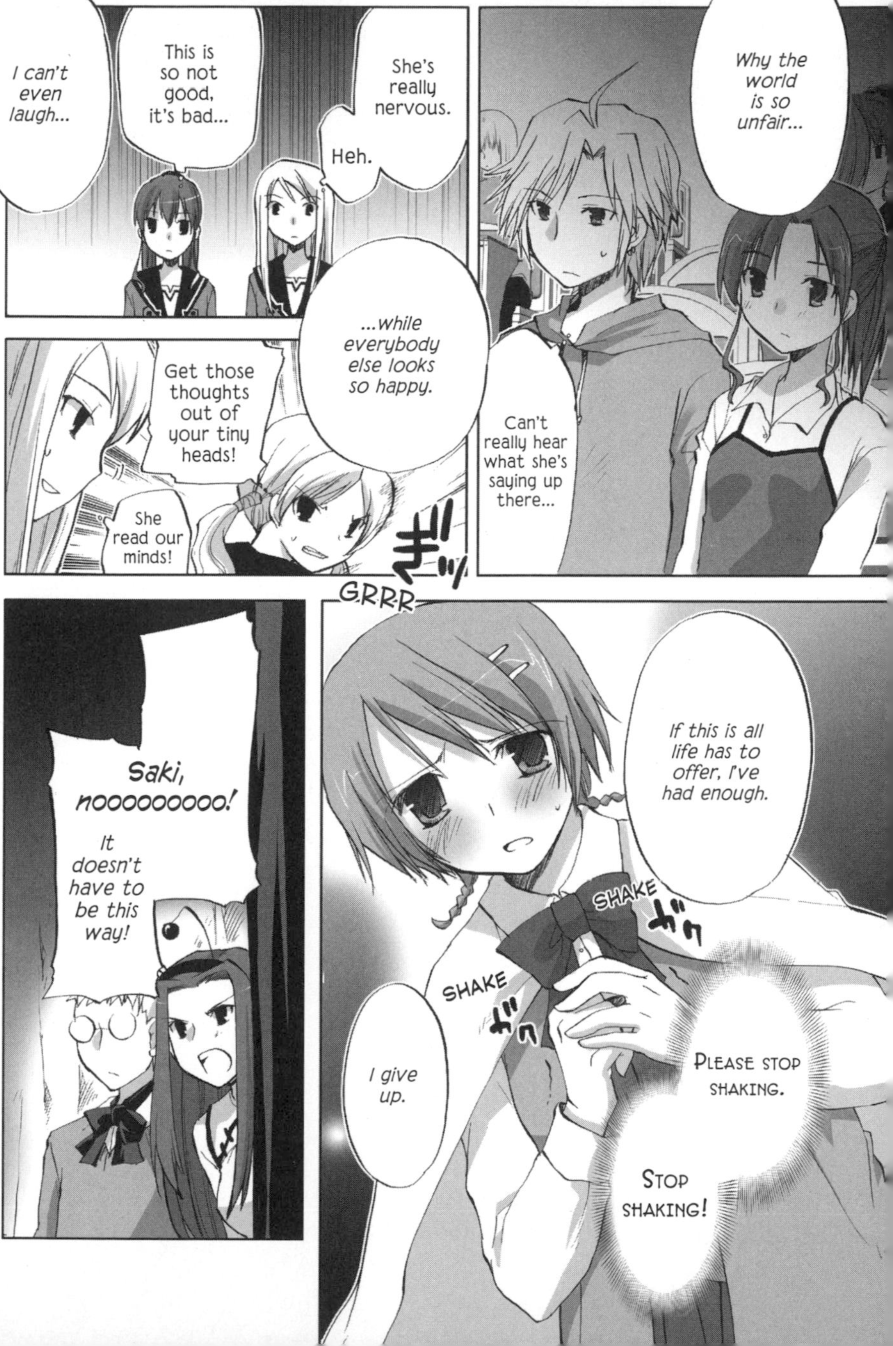
Why the world is so unfair...
...while everybody else looks so happy.
Can't really hear what she's saying up there...
She's really nervous.
Heh.
This is so not good, it's bad...
I can't even laugh...
Get those thoughts out of your tiny heads!
She read our minds!
ぎッ
GRRR
If this is all life has to offer, I've had enough.
SHAKE
SHAKE
I give up.
Please stop shaking.
Stop shaking!
Saki, nooooooooo!
It doesn't have to be this way!

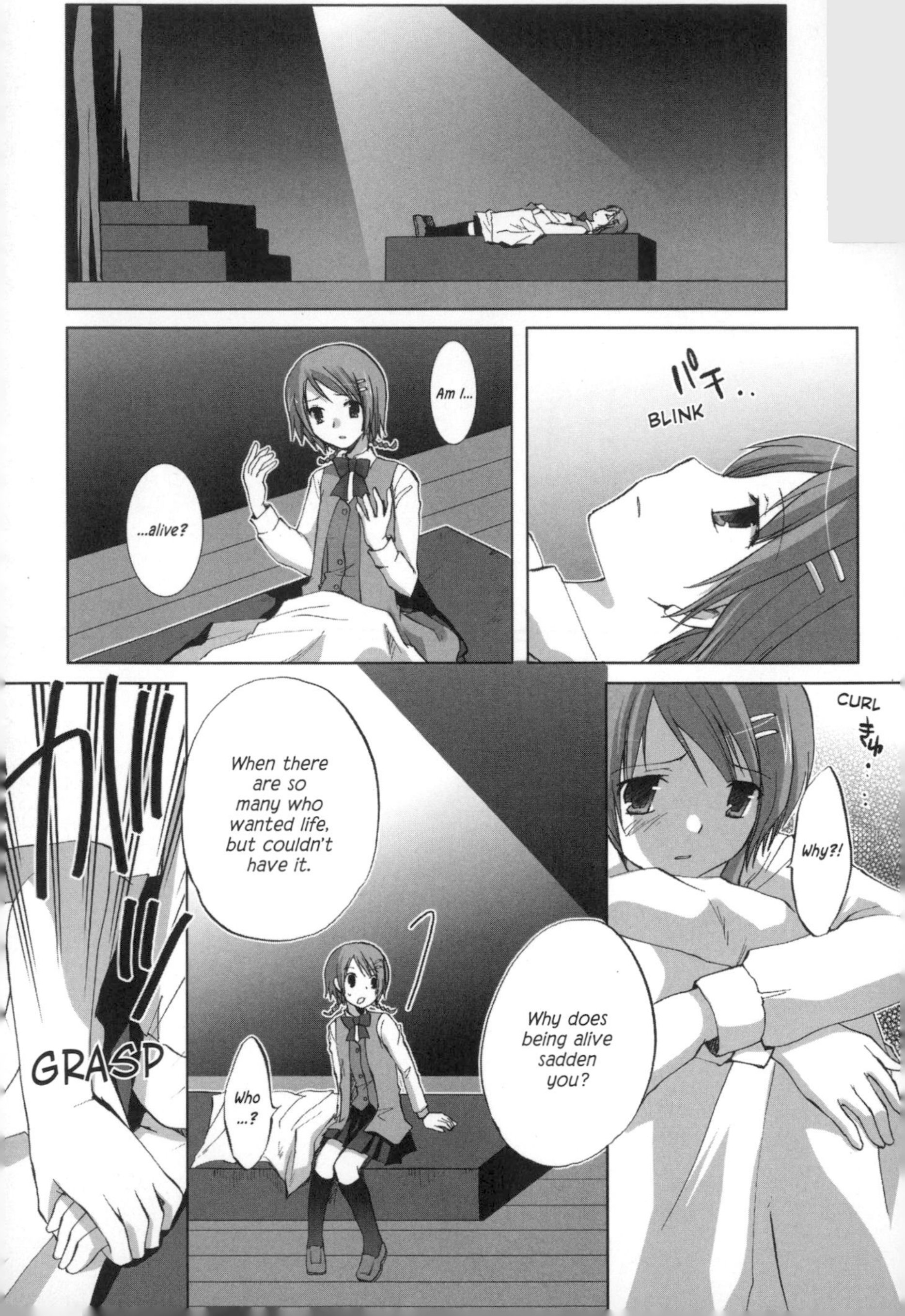
パチ..
BLINK
Am I...
...alive?
CURL
きゅ...
Why?!
Why does being alive sadden you?
When there are so many who wanted life, but couldn't have it.
Who ...?
GRASP

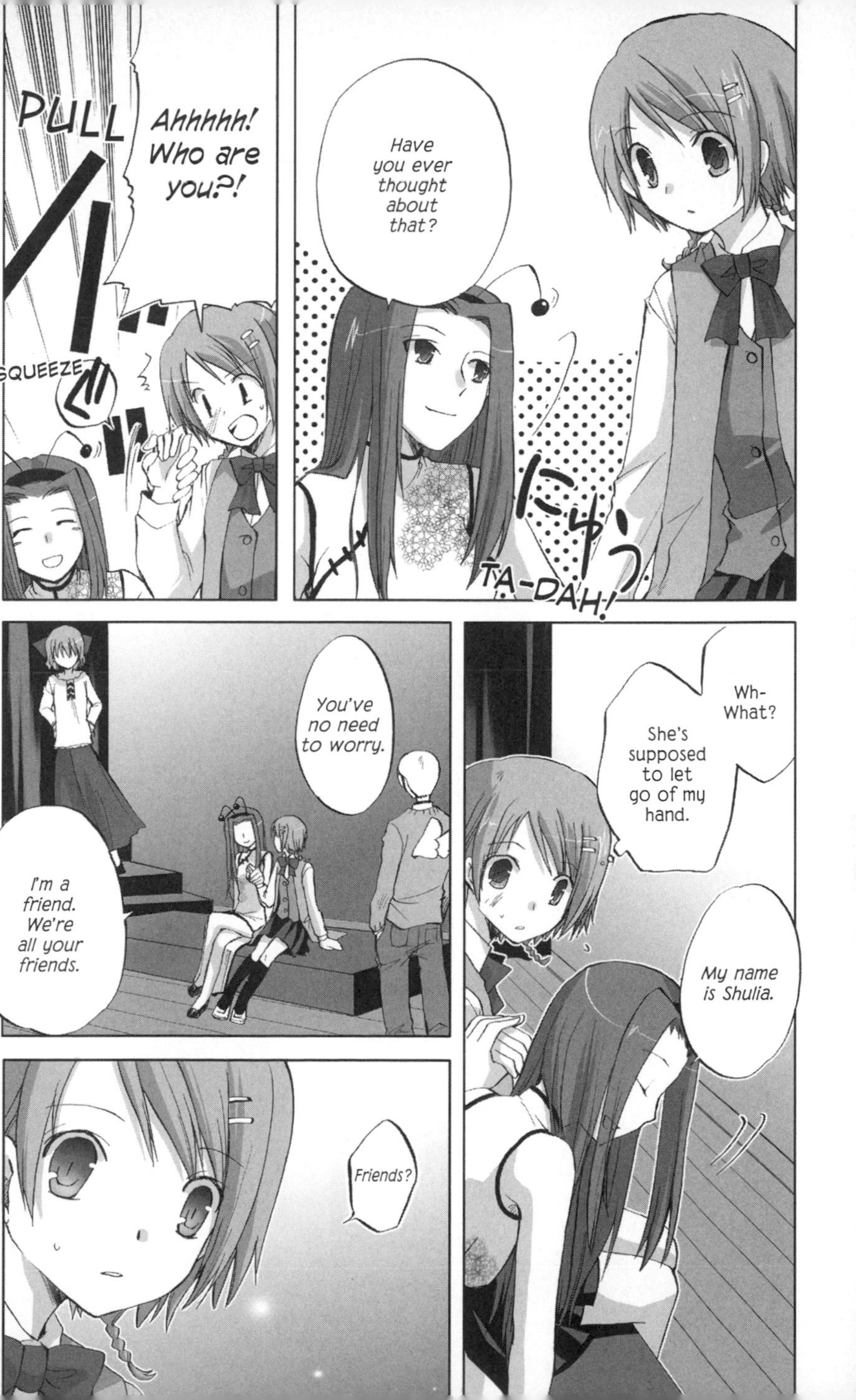

Have you ever thought about that?
にゅう
TA-DAH!
PULL
Ahhhhh! Who are you?!
SQUEEZE
Wh- What?
She's supposed to let go of my hand.
My name is Shulia.
You've no need to worry.
I'm a friend. We're all your friends.
Friends?

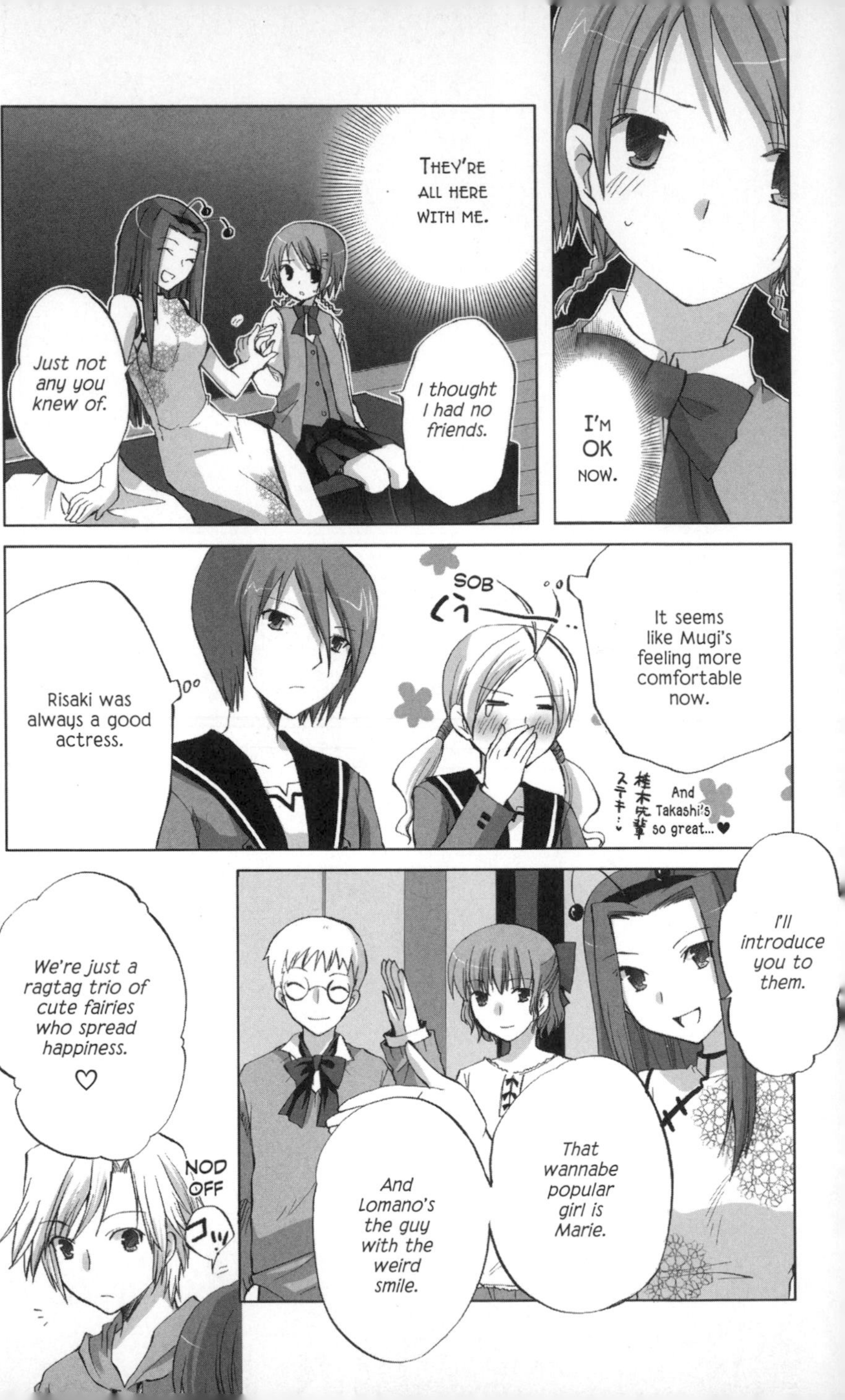
I'M OK NOW.
THEY'RE ALL HERE WITH ME.
I thought I had no friends.
Just not any you knew of.
SOB
くう
It seems like Mugi's feeling more comfortable now.
椎木先輩ステキ…
And Takashi's so great...♥
Risaki was always a good actress.
I'll introduce you to them.
That wannabe popular girl is Marie.
And Lomano's the guy with the weird smile.
We're just a ragtag trio of cute fairies who spread happiness. ♡
NOD OFF
コッ

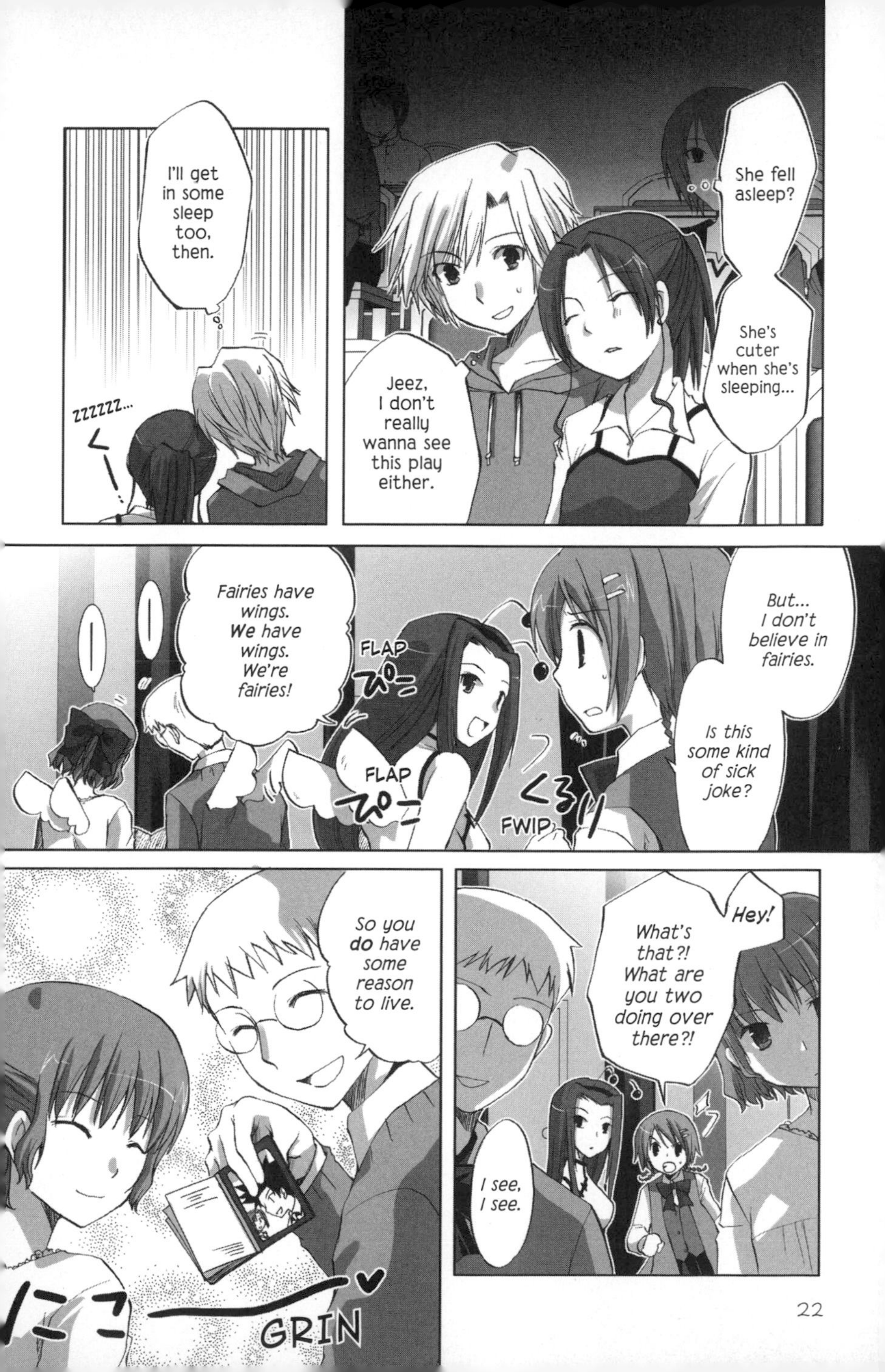
She fell asleep?
She's cuter when she's sleeping...
Jeez, I don't really wanna see this play either.
I'll get in some sleep too, then.
ZZZZZZ...
But... I don't believe in fairies.
Is this some kind of sick joke?
FWIP
FLAP
FLAP
Fairies have wings. We have wings. We're fairies!
Hey!
What's that?! What are you two doing over there?!
I see, I see.
So you do have some reason to live.
GRIN

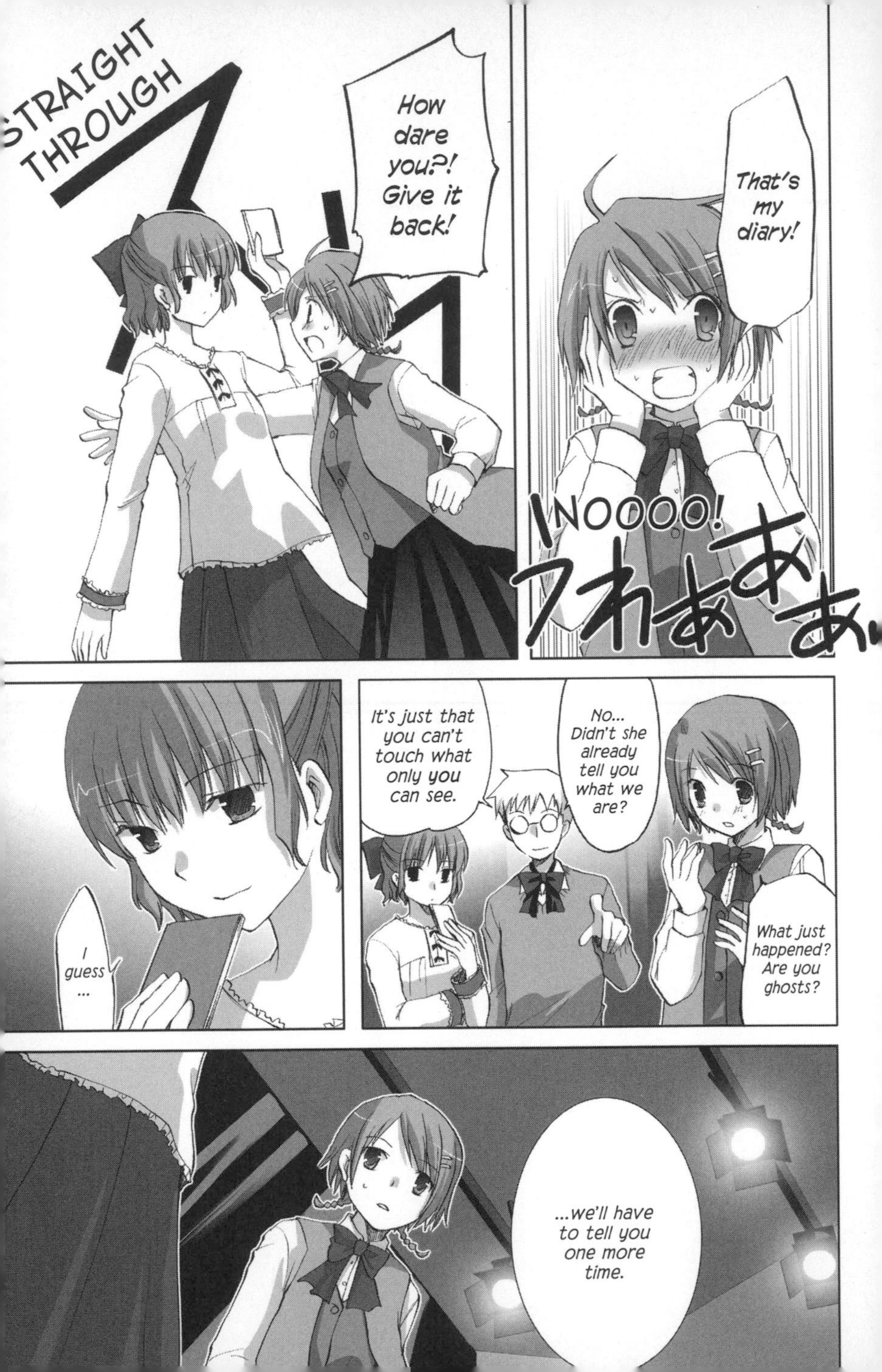
That's my diary!
NOOOO!
うわあああ
How dare you?! Give it back!
STRAIGHT THROUGH
What just happened? Are you ghosts?
No... Didn't she already tell you what we are?
It's just that you can't touch what only **you** can see.
I guess ...
...we'll have to tell you one more time.

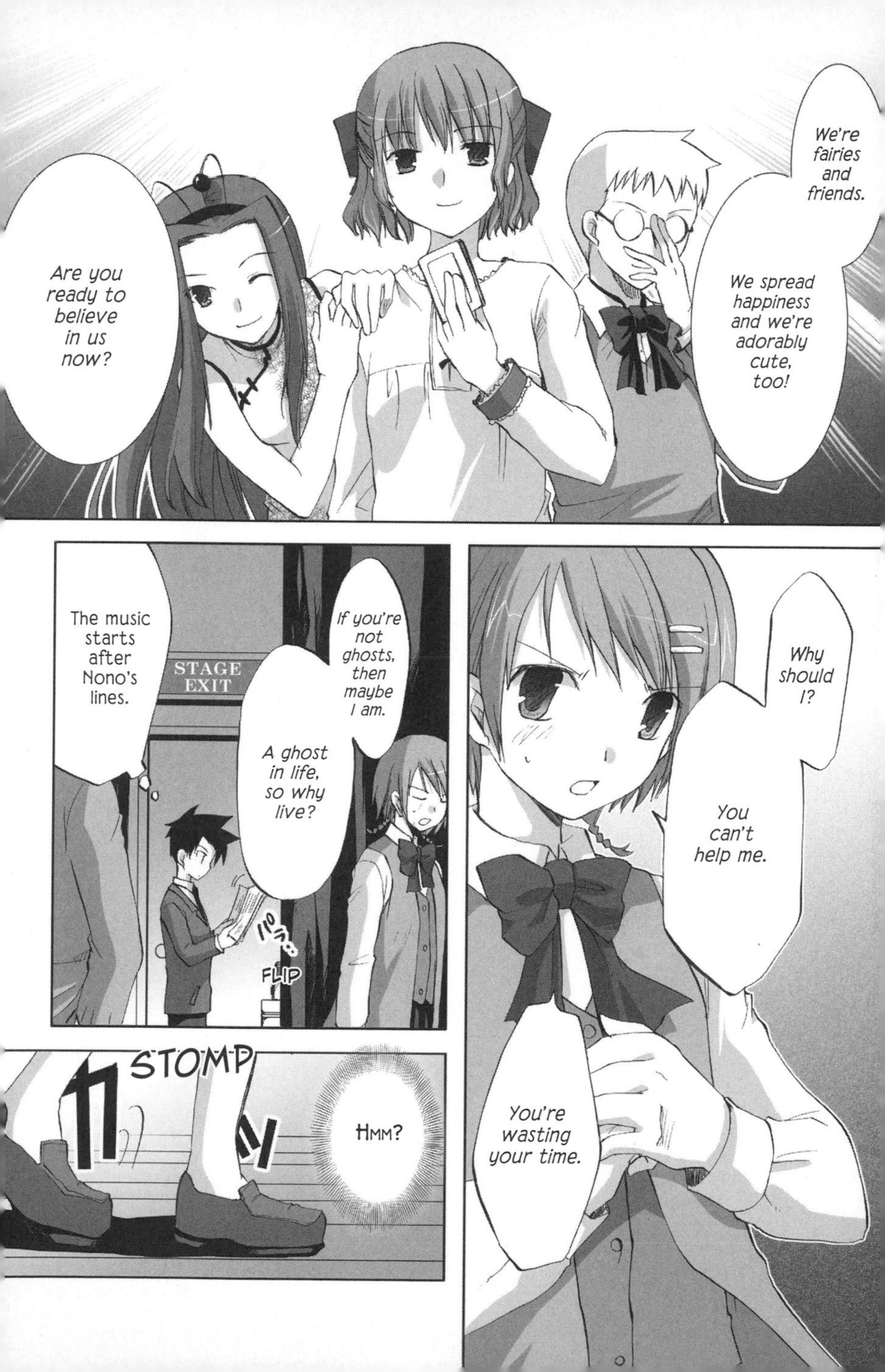
We're fairies and friends.
We spread happiness and we're adorably cute, too!
Are you ready to believe in us now?
Why should I?
You can't help me.
You're wasting your time.
If you're not ghosts, then maybe I am.
A ghost in life, so why live?
The music starts after Nono's lines.
STAGE EXIT
FLIP
STOMP
Hmm?

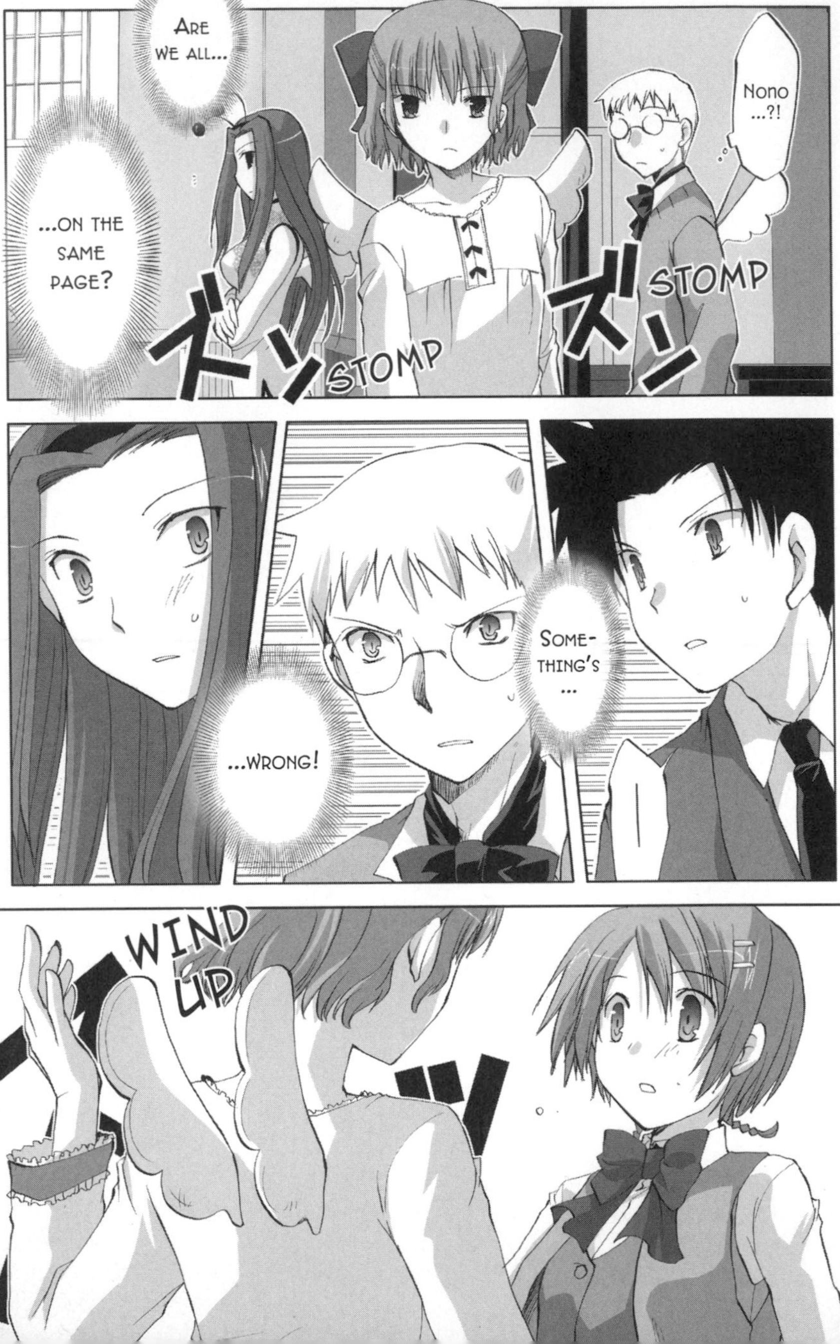

Nono ...?!
STOMP
Are we all...
...on the same page?
STOMP
Something's ...
...wrong!
WIND UP

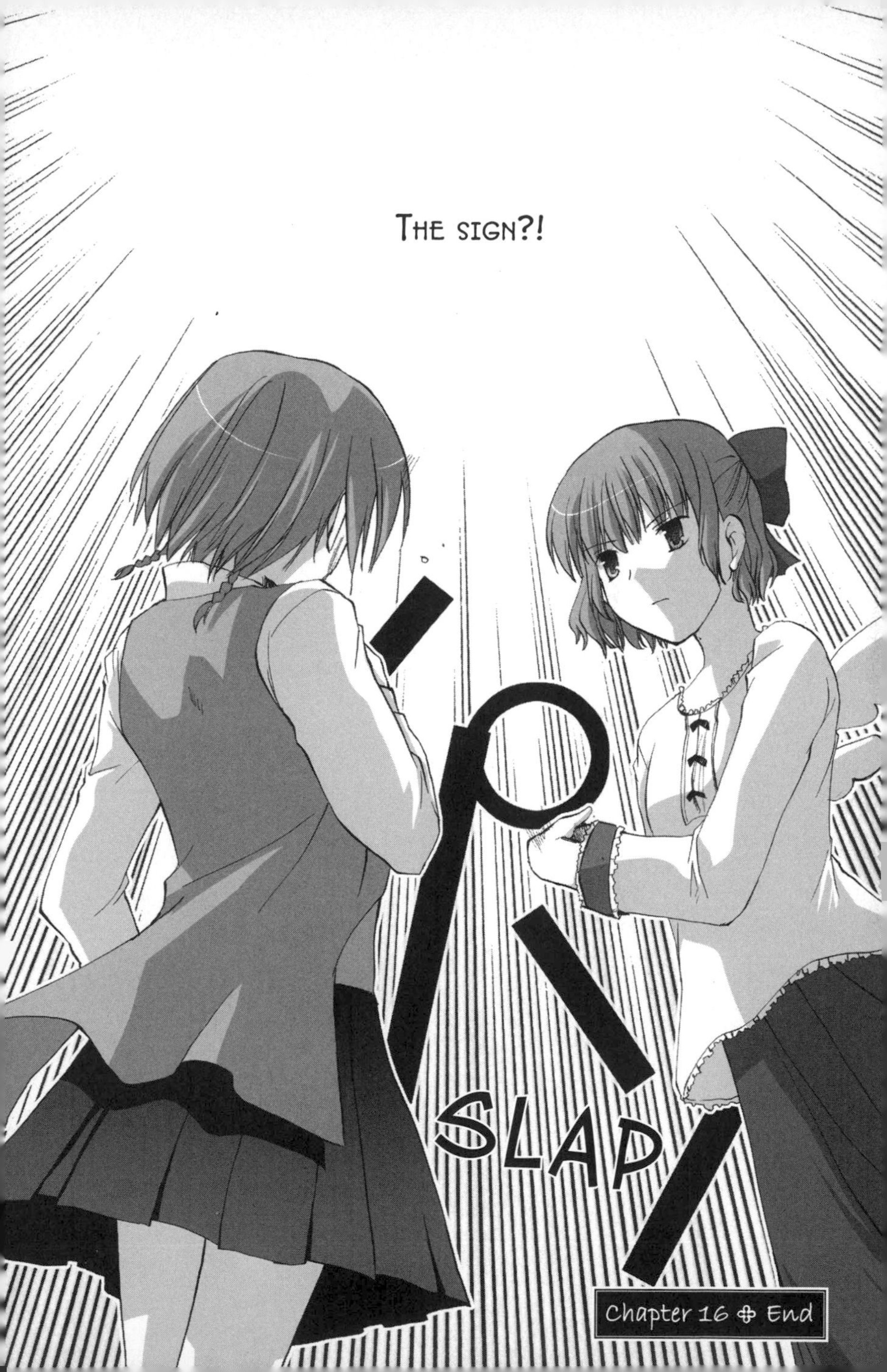
THE SIGN?!
SLAP
Chapter 16 ✤ End

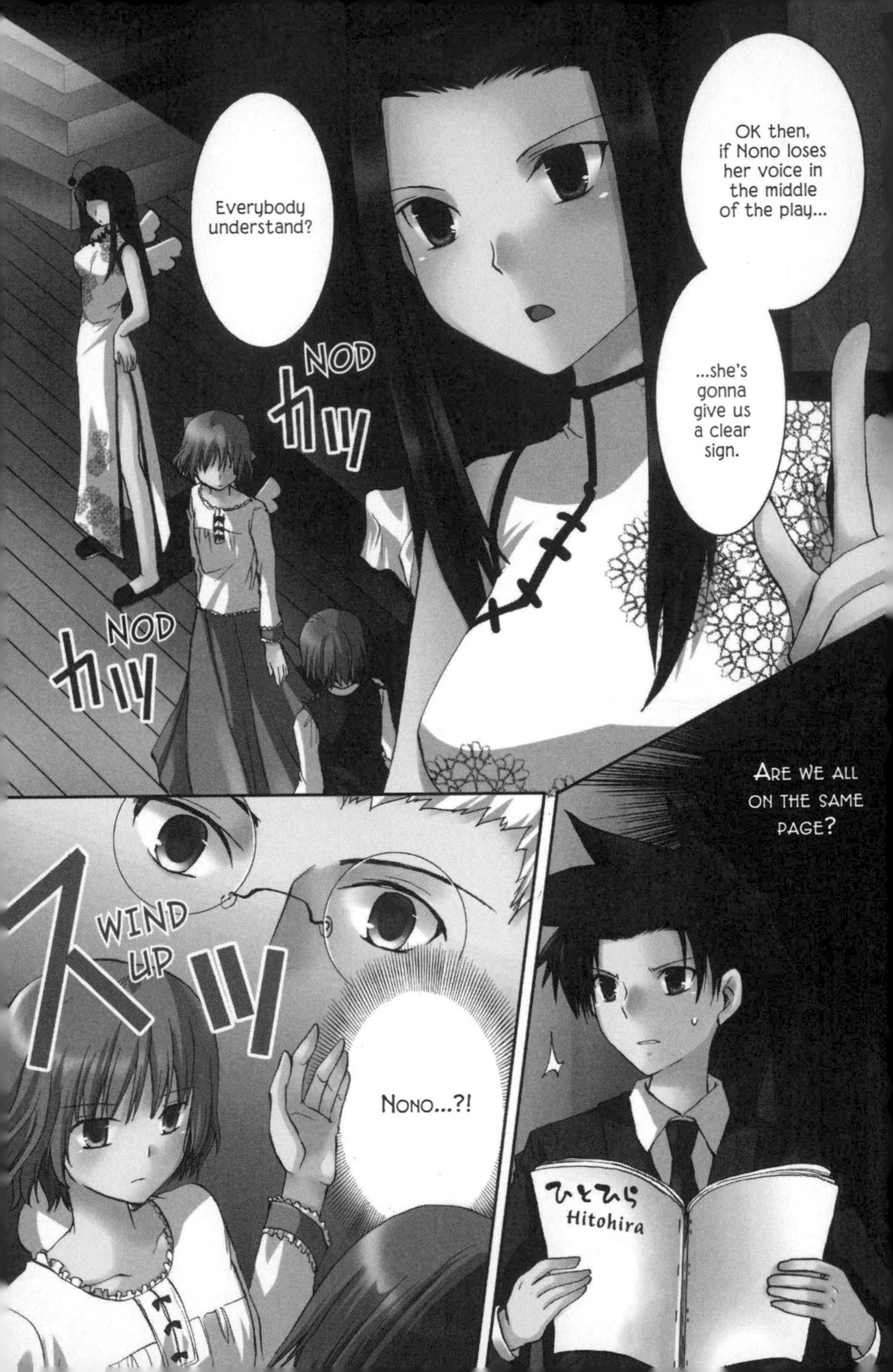
OK then, if Nono loses her voice in the middle of the play...
...she's gonna give us a clear sign.
Everybody understand?
NOD
NOD
Are we all on the same page?
WIND UP
Nono...?!
ひとひら
Hitohira

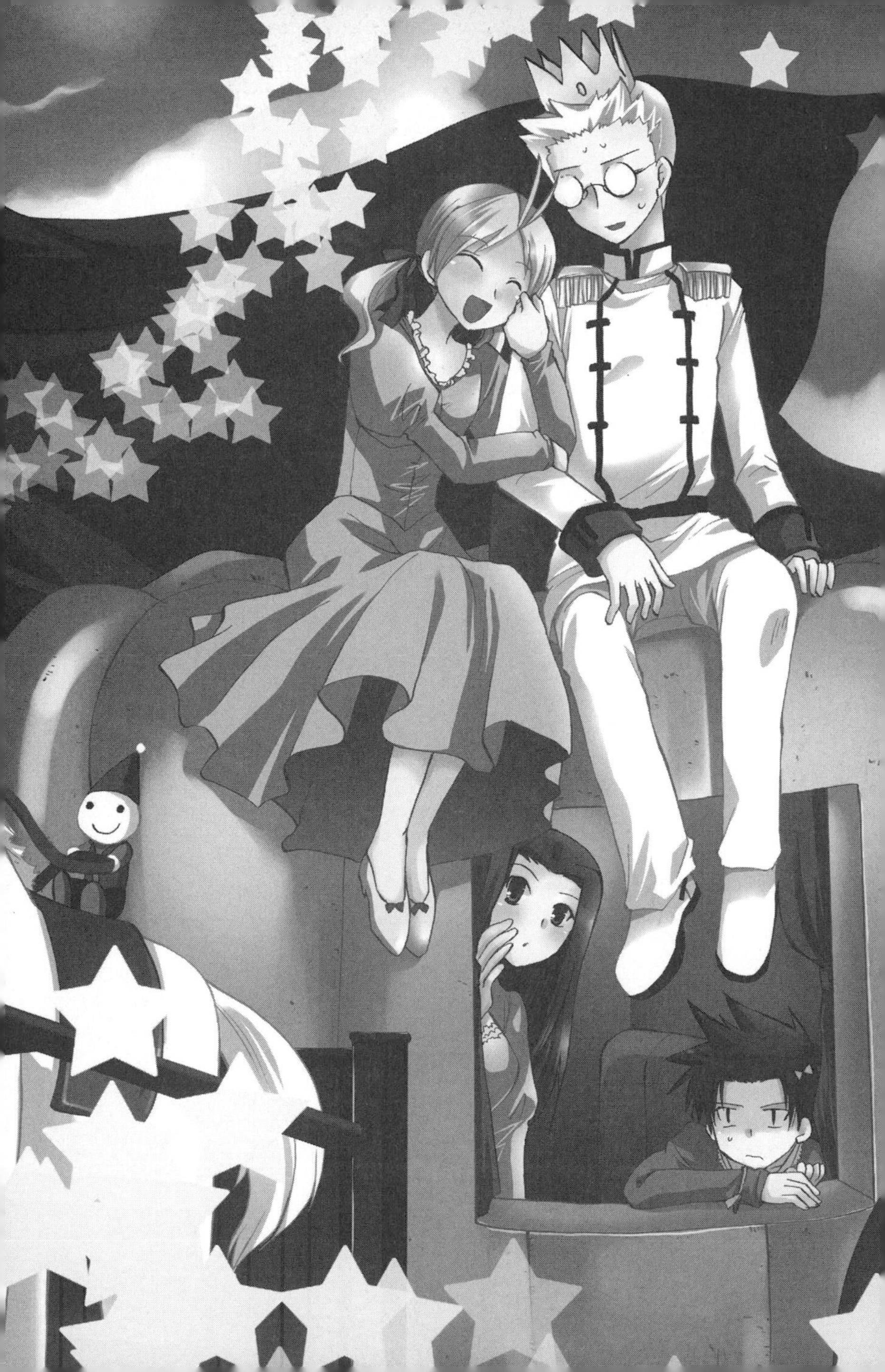

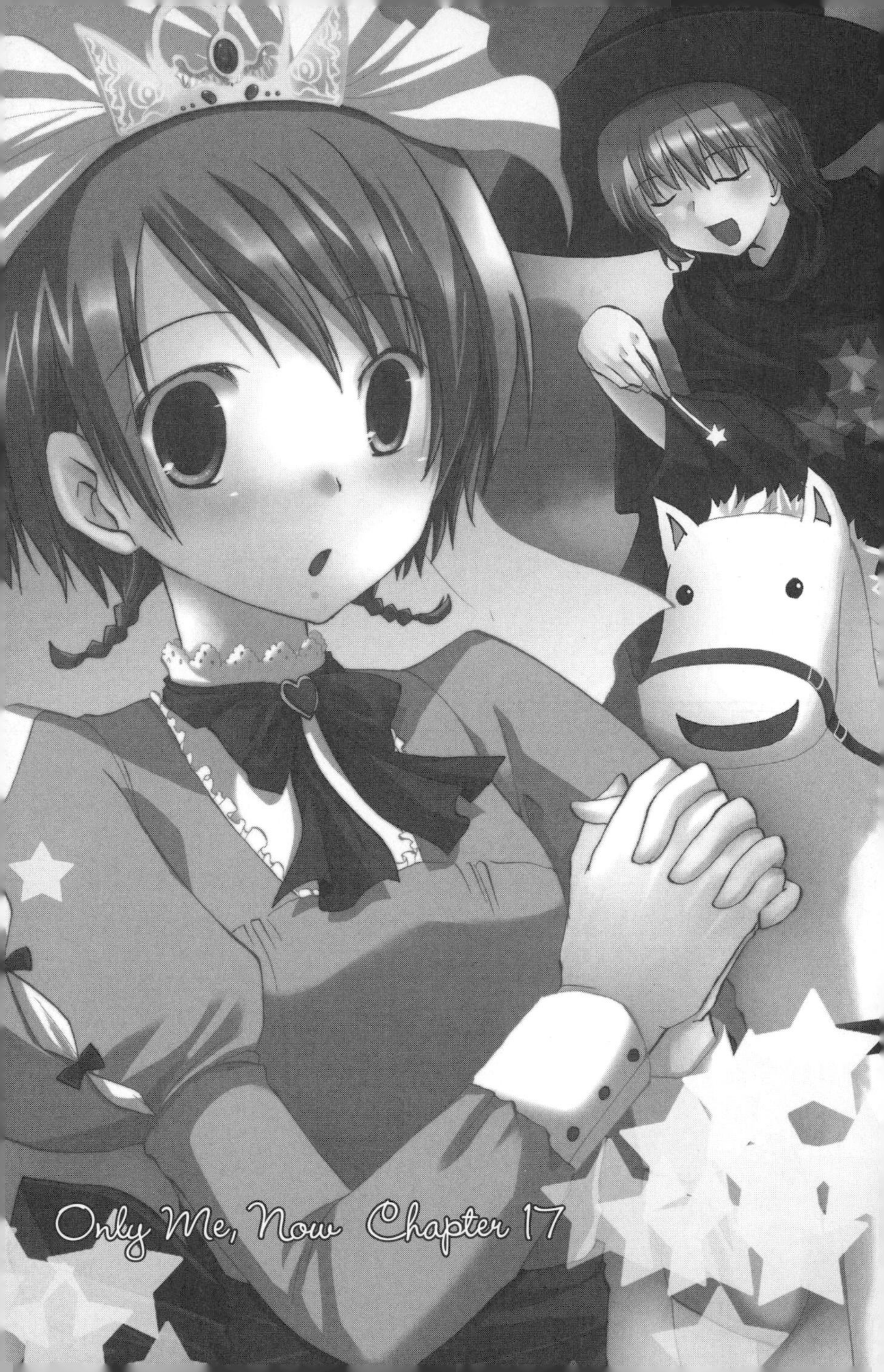
Only Me, Now Chapter 17

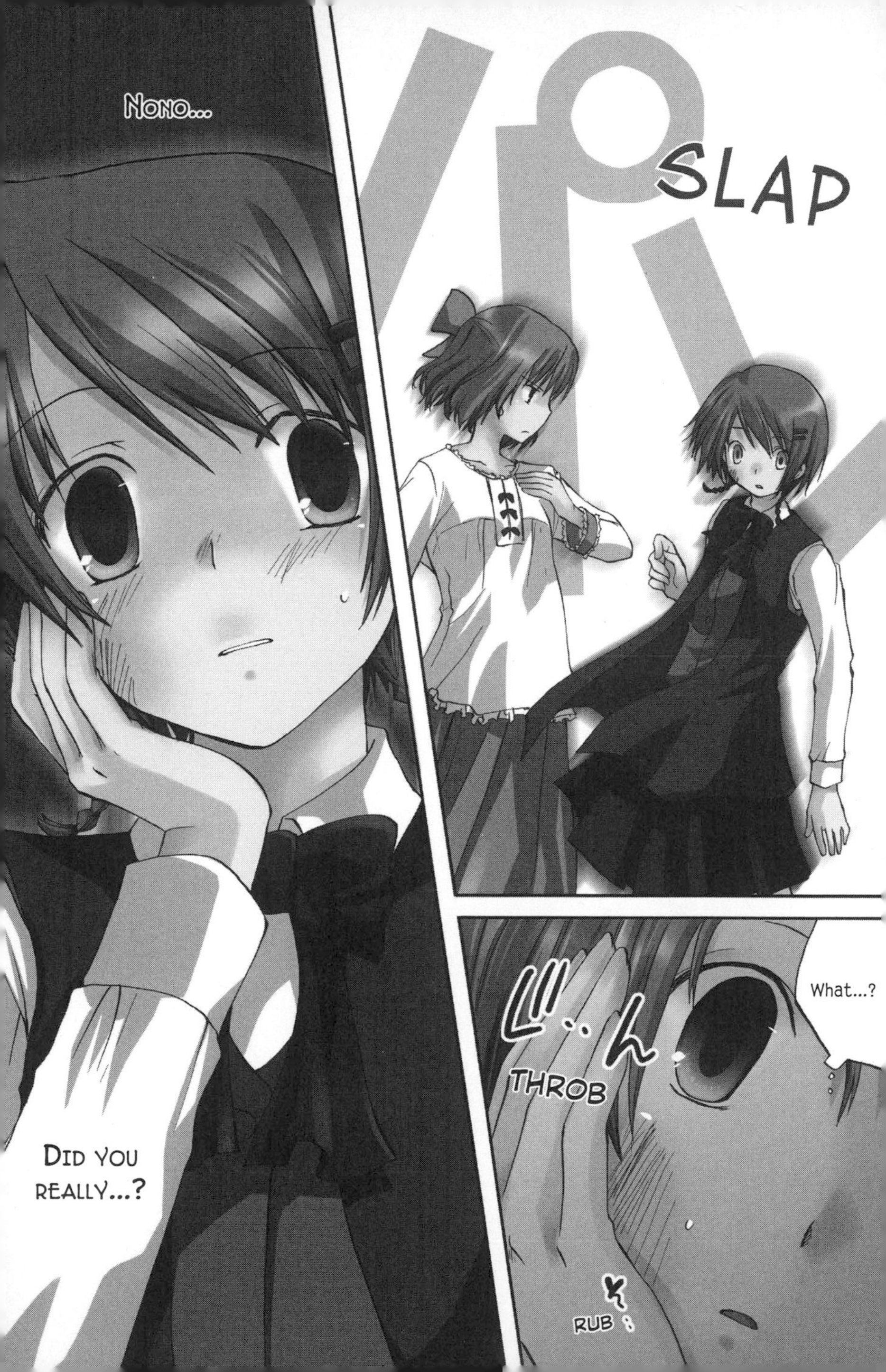
SLAP
What...?
じ..ん
THROB
RUB
Nono...
Did you really...?

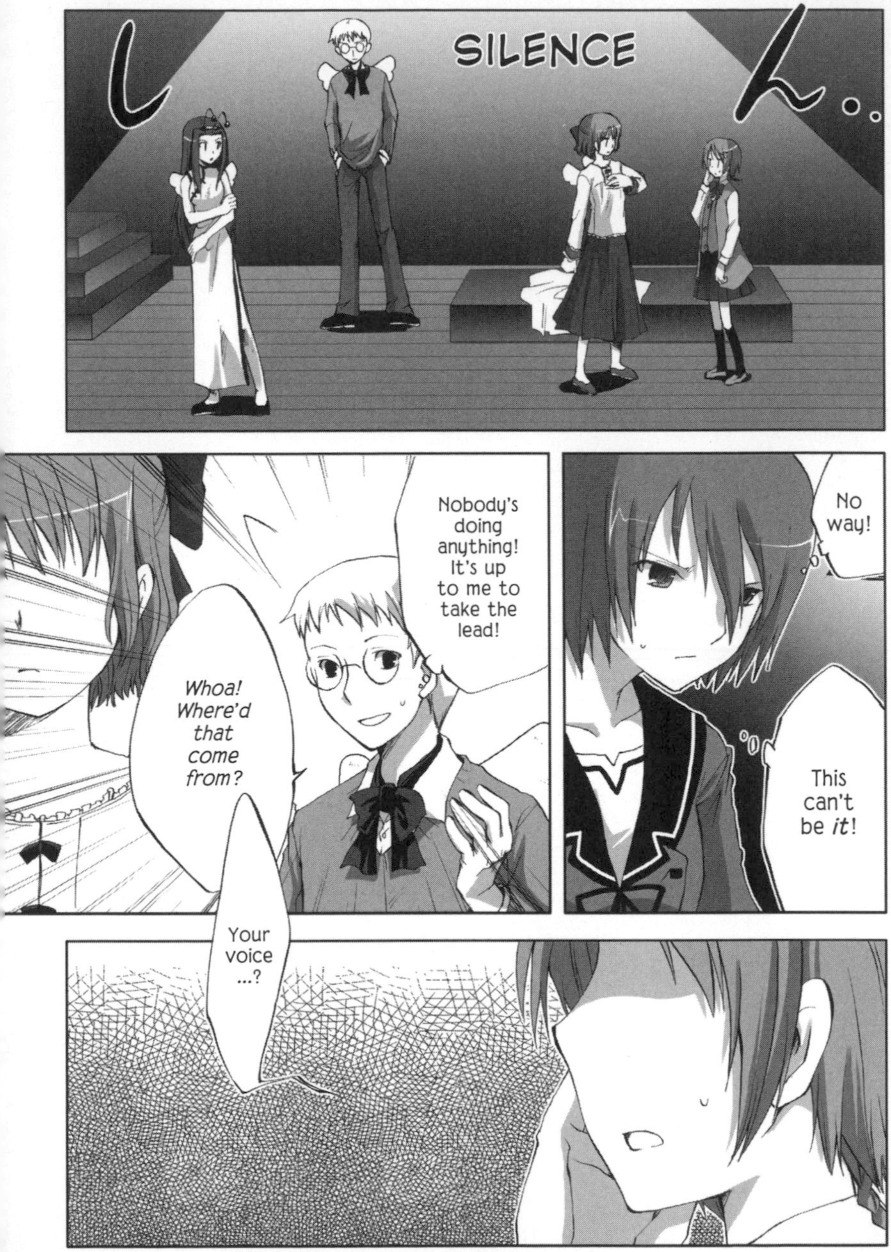
し
SILENCE
ん..
No way!
This can't be *it*!
Nobody's doing anything! It's up to me to take the lead!
Whoa! Where'd that come from?
Your voice ...?

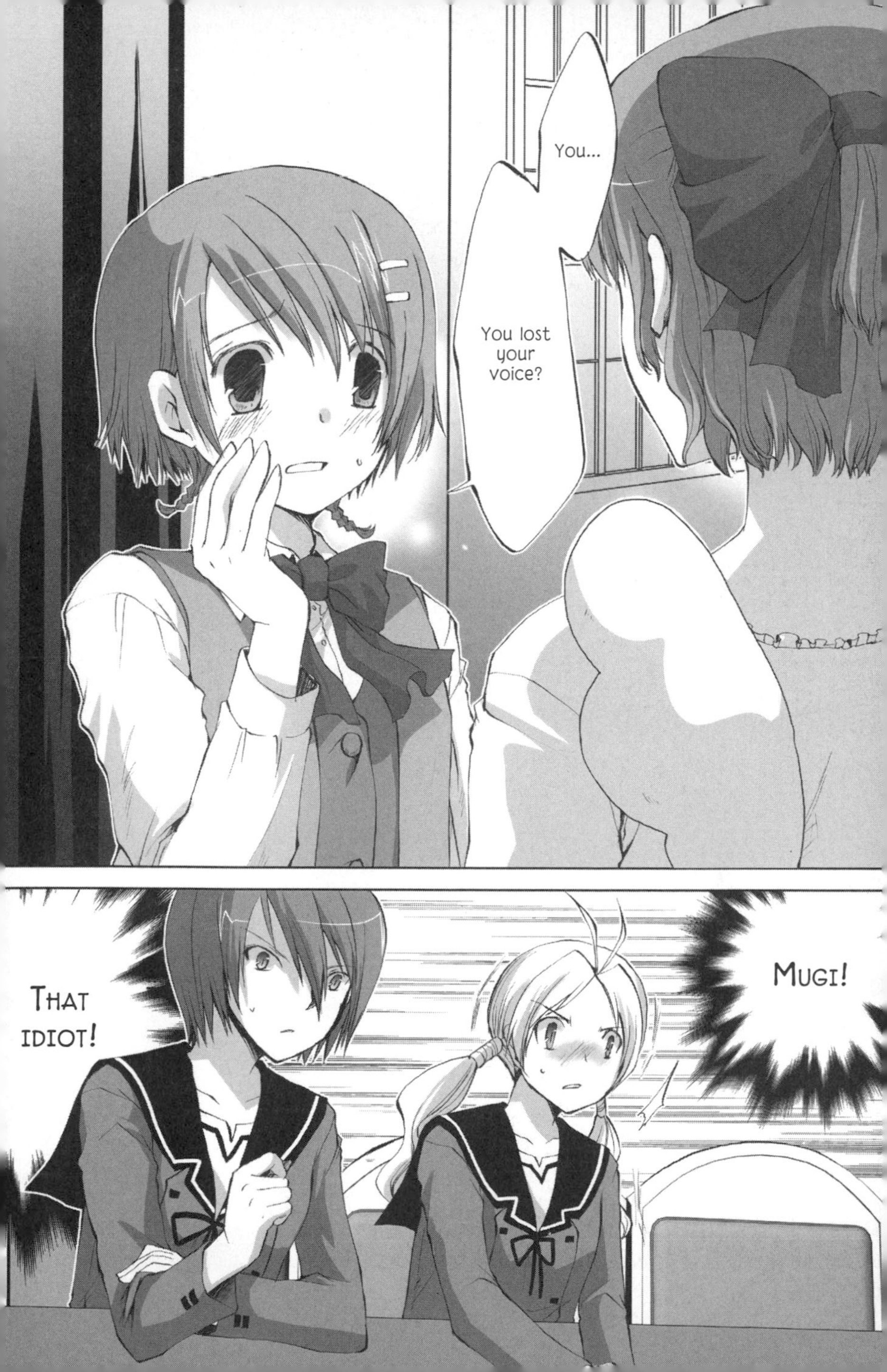
You...
You lost your voice?
Mugi!
That idiot!

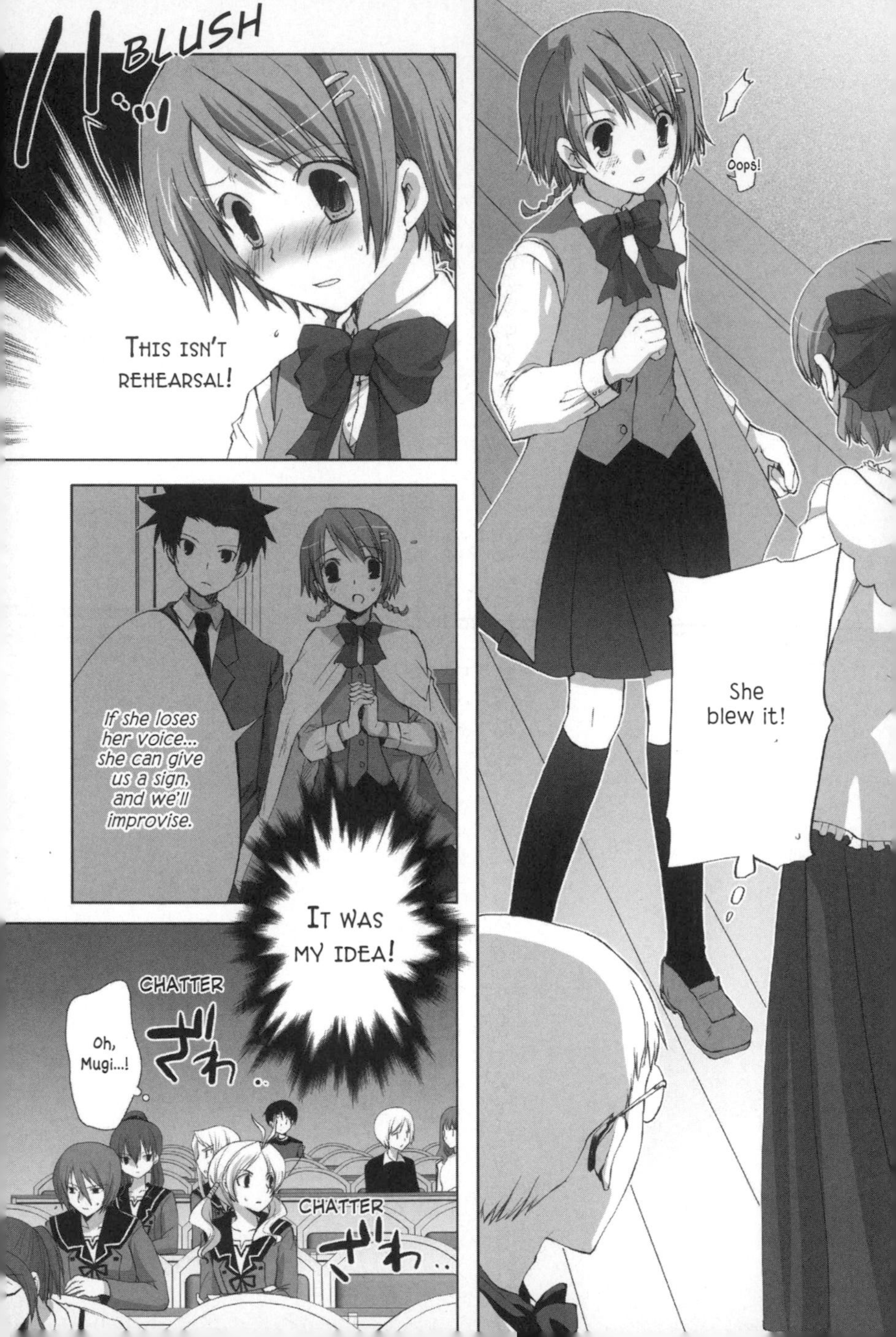
Oops!
She blew it!
BLUSH
This isn't rehearsal!
If she loses her voice... she can give us a sign, and we'll improvise.
It was my idea!
CHATTER
ざわ
Oh, Mugi...!
CHATTER
ざわ

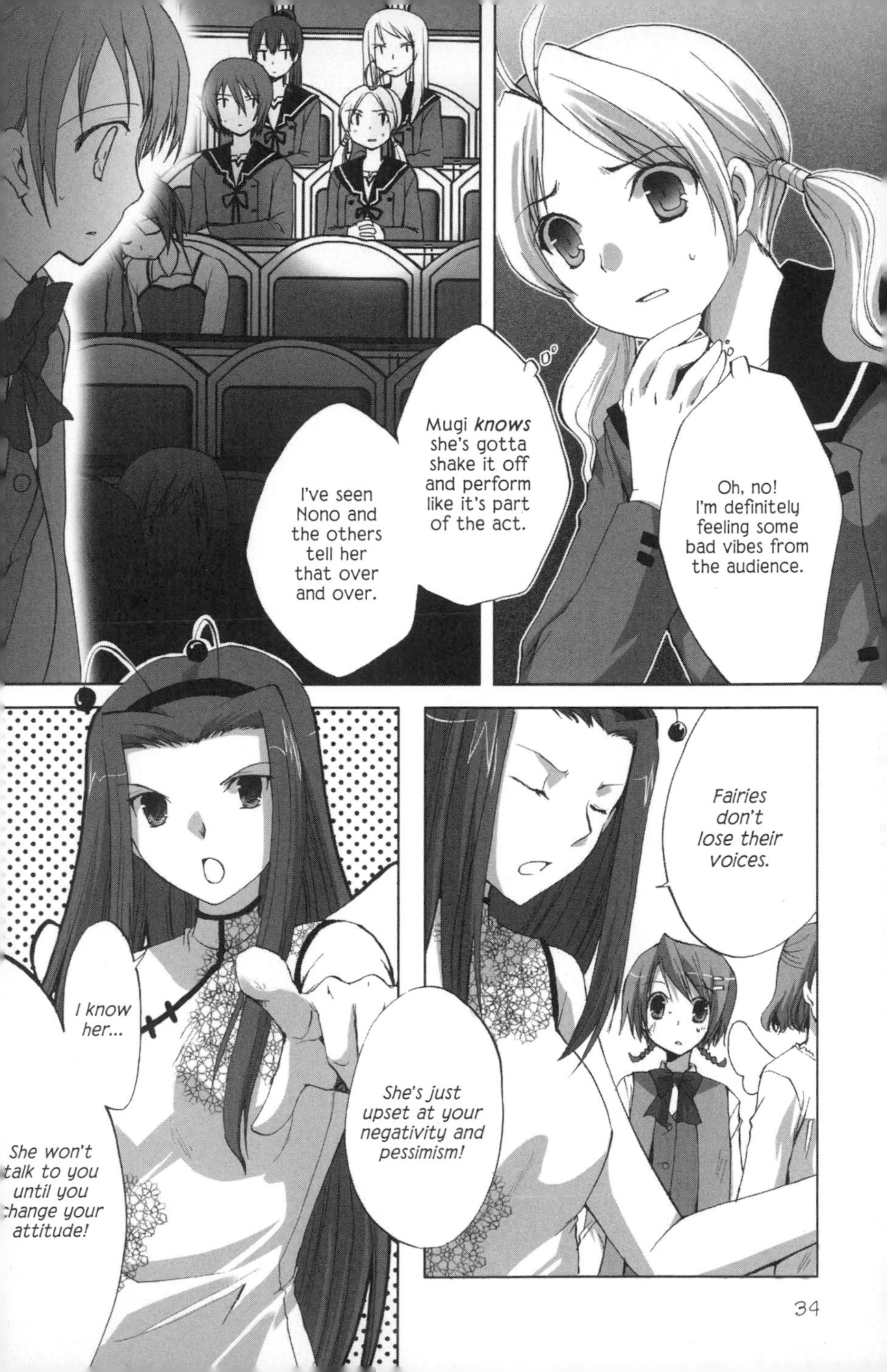

Oh, no! I'm definitely feeling some bad vibes from the audience.
Mugi *knows* she's gotta shake it off and perform like it's part of the act.
I've seen Nono and the others tell her that over and over.
Fairies don't lose their voices.
I know her...
She's just upset at your negativity and pessimism!
She won't talk to you until you change your attitude!

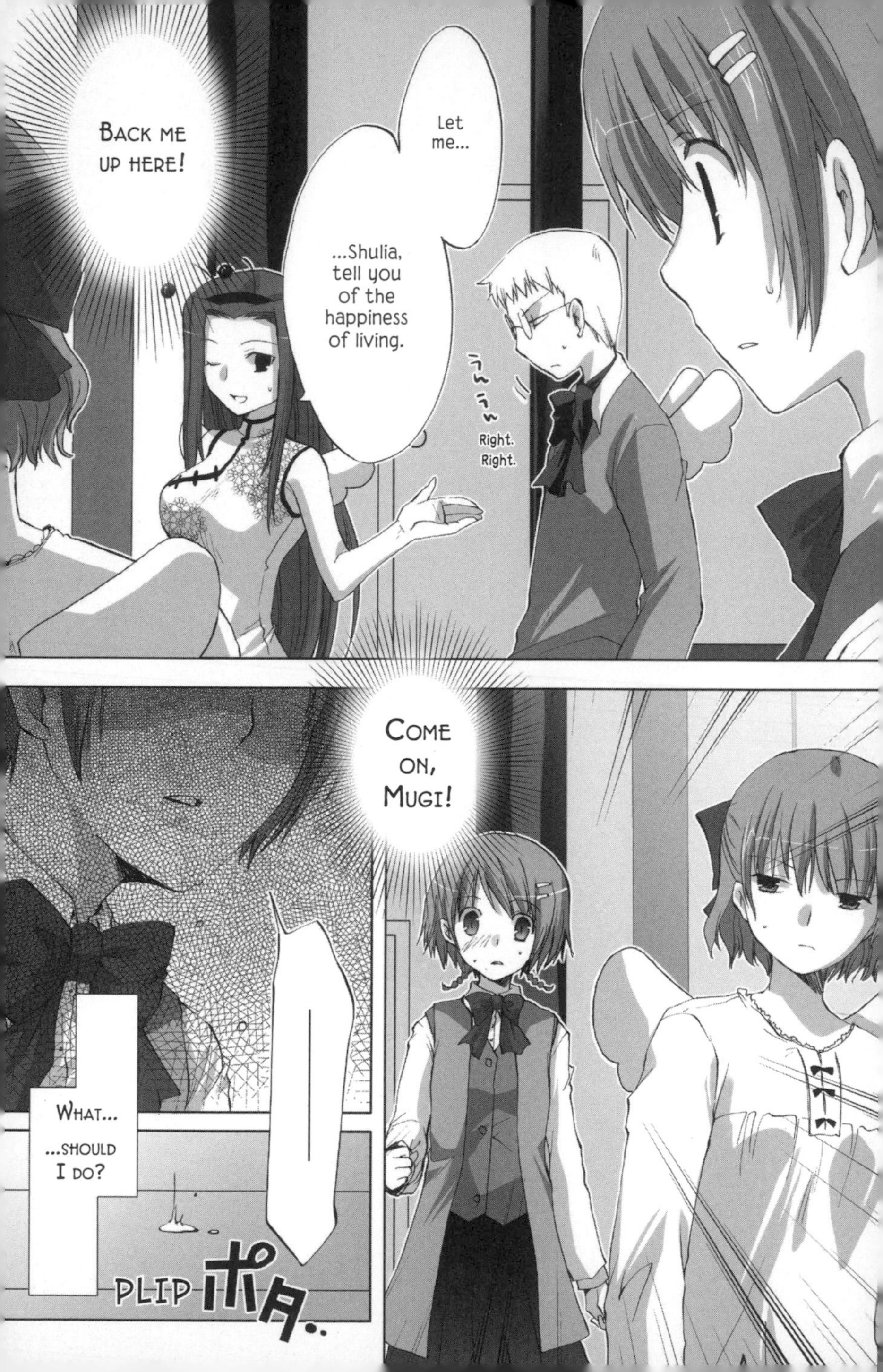
Let me...
...Shulia, tell you of the happiness of living.
うんうん
Right. Right.
Back me up here!
Come on, Mugi!
What...
...should I do?
PLIP ポタ..

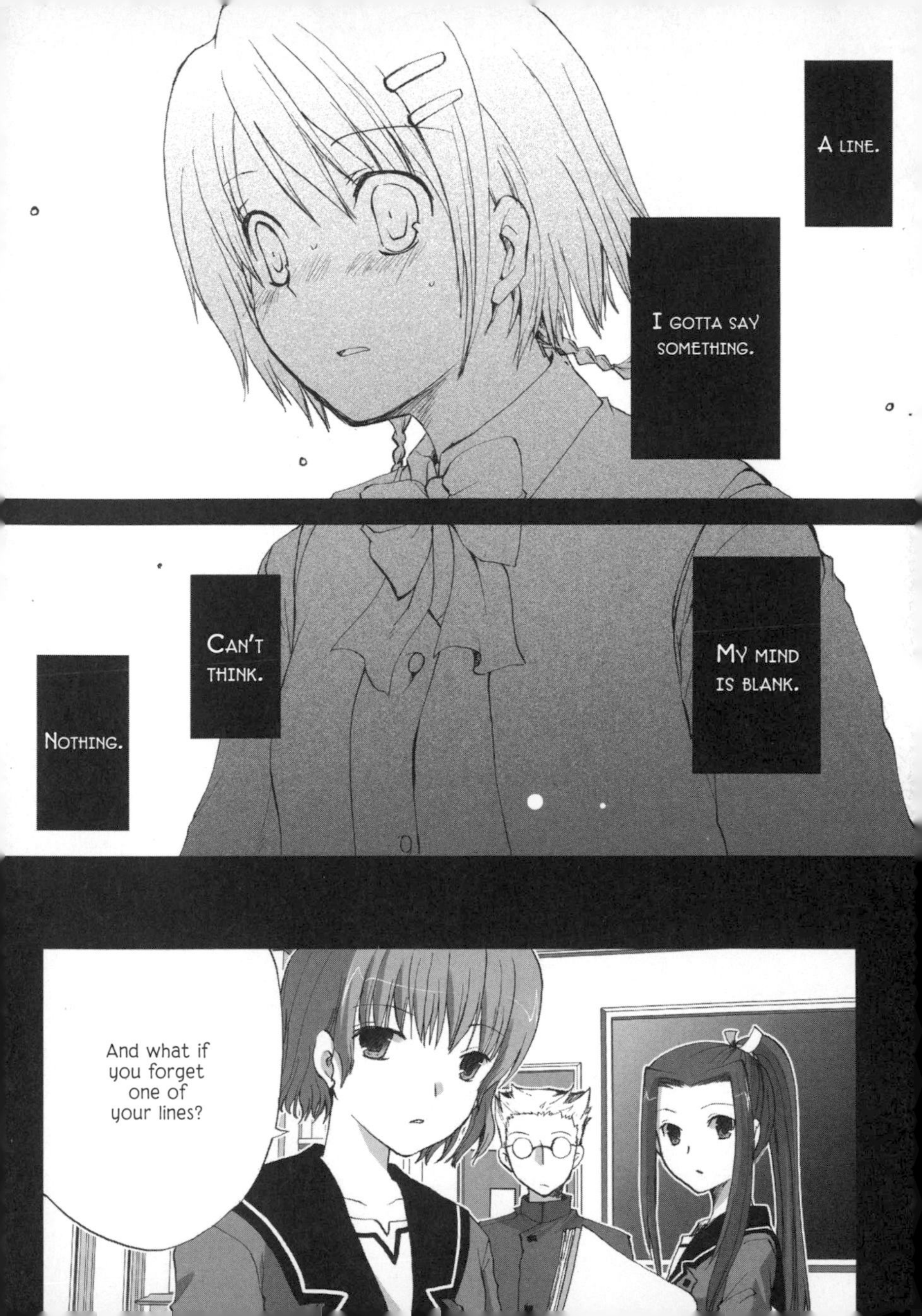

A line.
I gotta say something.
My mind is blank.
Can't think.
Nothing.
And what if you forget one of your lines?

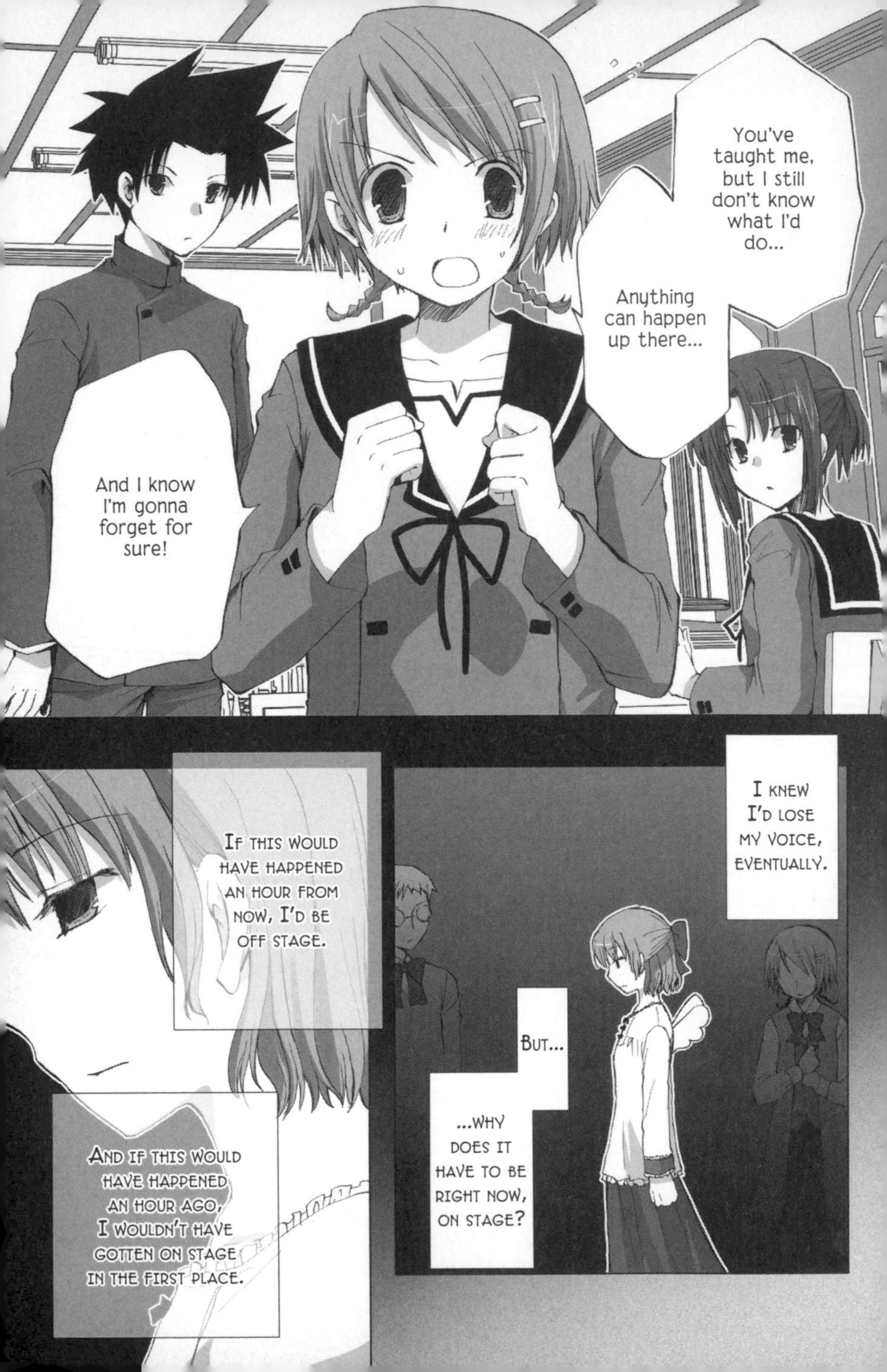
You've taught me, but I still don't know what I'd do...
Anything can happen up there...
And I know I'm gonna forget for sure!
I knew I'd lose my voice, eventually.
But...
...why does it have to be right now, on stage?
If this would have happened an hour from now, I'd be off stage.
And if this would have happened an hour ago, I wouldn't have gotten on stage in the first place.

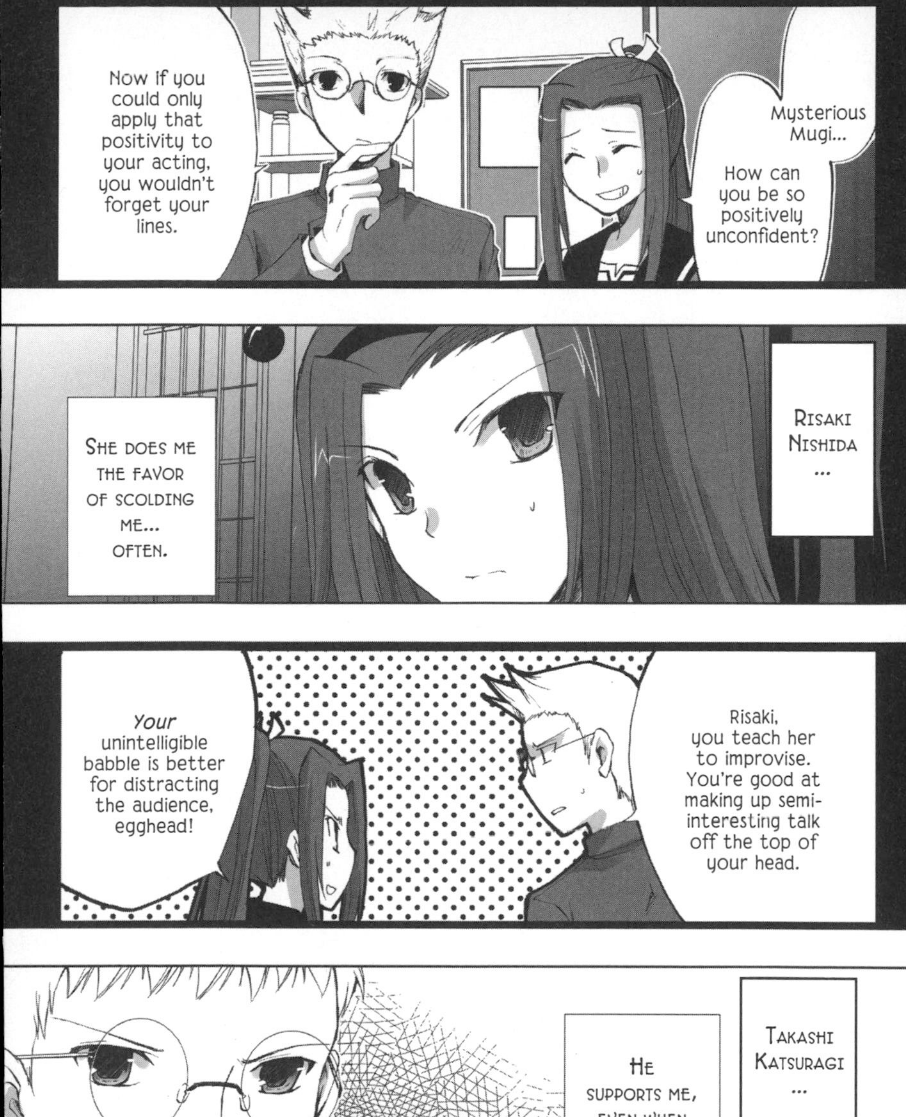
Mysterious Mugi...
How can you be so positively unconfident?
Now if you could only apply that positivity to your acting, you wouldn't forget your lines.
Risaki Nishida ...
She does me the favor of scolding me... often.
Risaki, you teach her to improvise. You're good at making up semi-interesting talk off the top of your head.
Your unintelligible babble is better for distracting the audience, egghead!
Takashi Katsuragi ...
He supports me, even when I don't realize it.

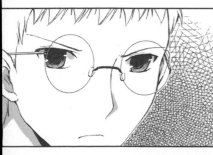

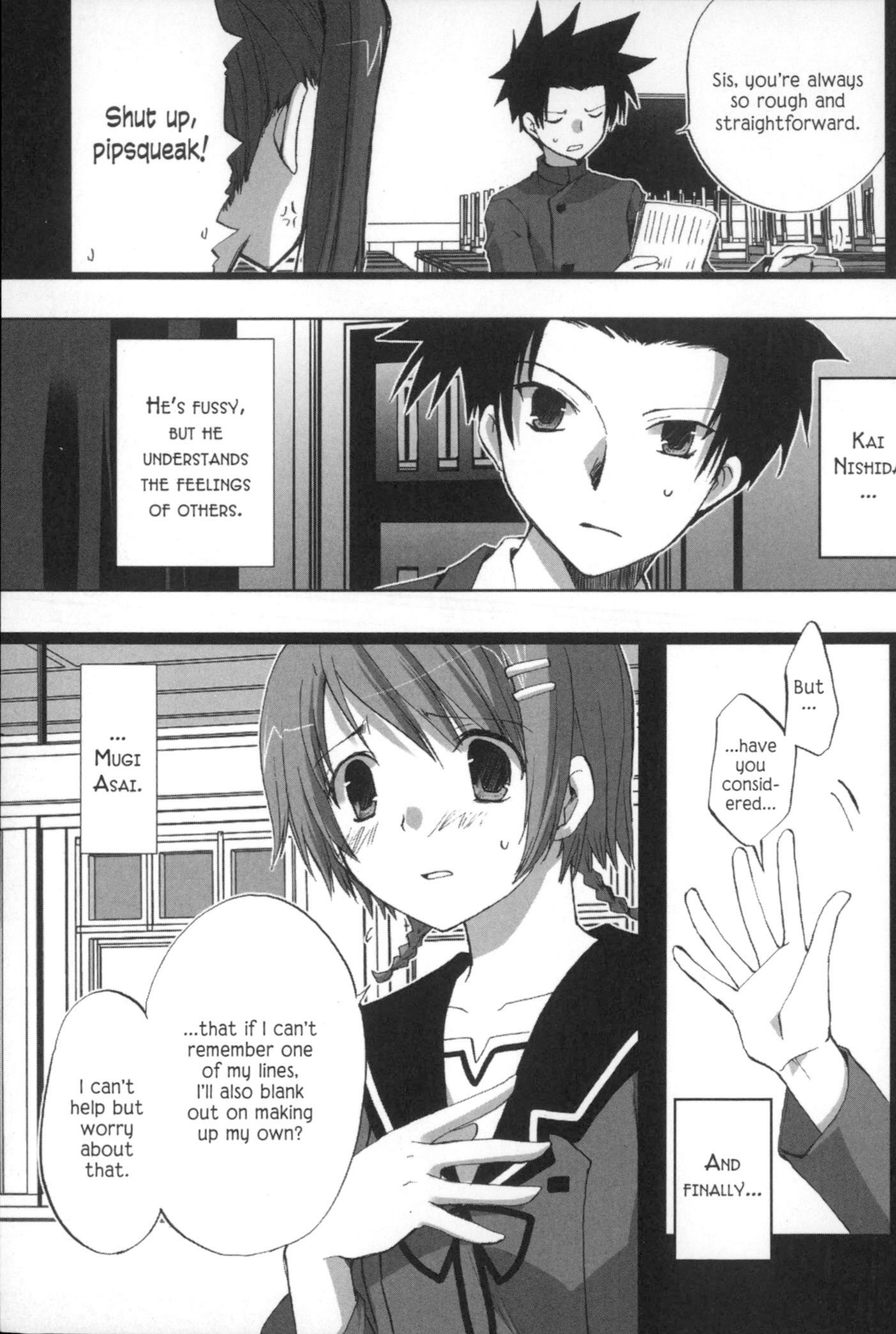

Sis, you're always so rough and straightforward.
Shut up, pipsqueak!
Kai Nishida ...
He's fussy, but he understands the feelings of others.
But ...
...have you consid-ered...
And finally...
... Mugi Asai.
...that if I can't remember one of my lines, I'll also blank out on making up my own?
I can't help but worry about that.

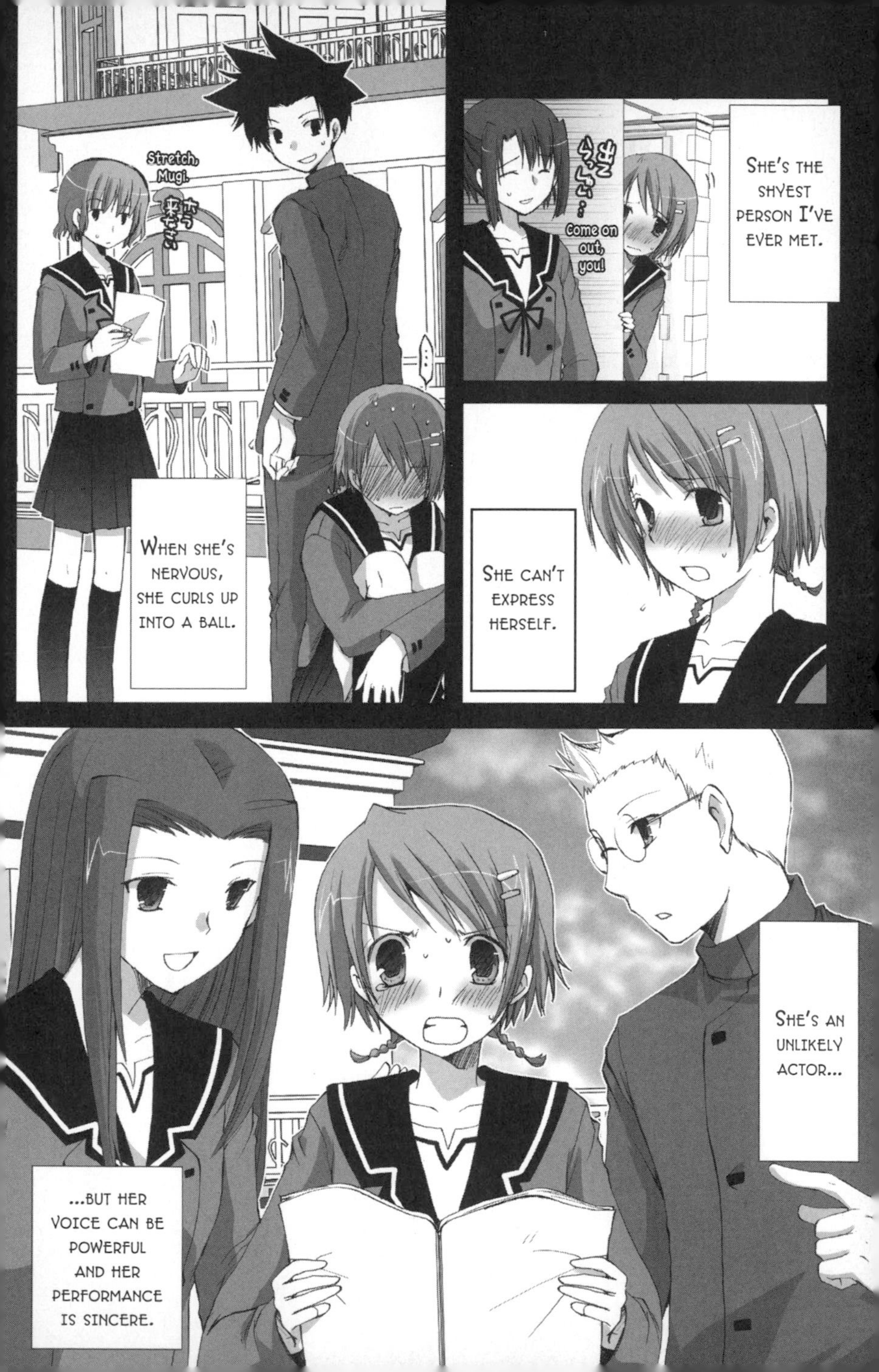
She's the shyest person I've ever met.
Come on out, you!
She can't express herself.
Stretch, Mugi.
...
When she's nervous, she curls up into a ball.
She's an unlikely actor...
...but her voice can be powerful and her performance is sincere.

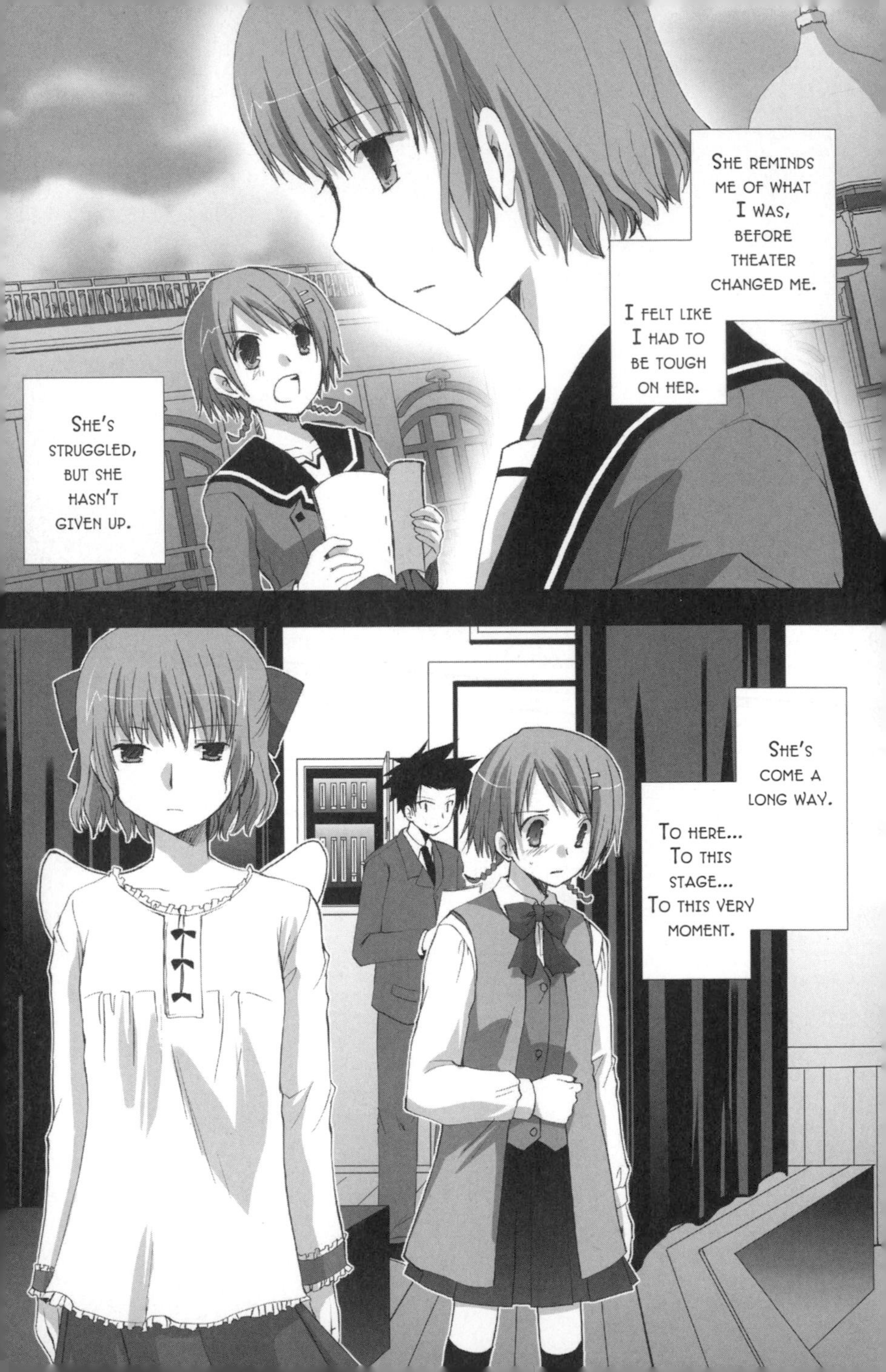
She reminds me of what I was, before theater changed me.
I felt like I had to be tough on her.
She's struggled, but she hasn't given up.
She's come a long way.
To here... To this stage... To this very moment.

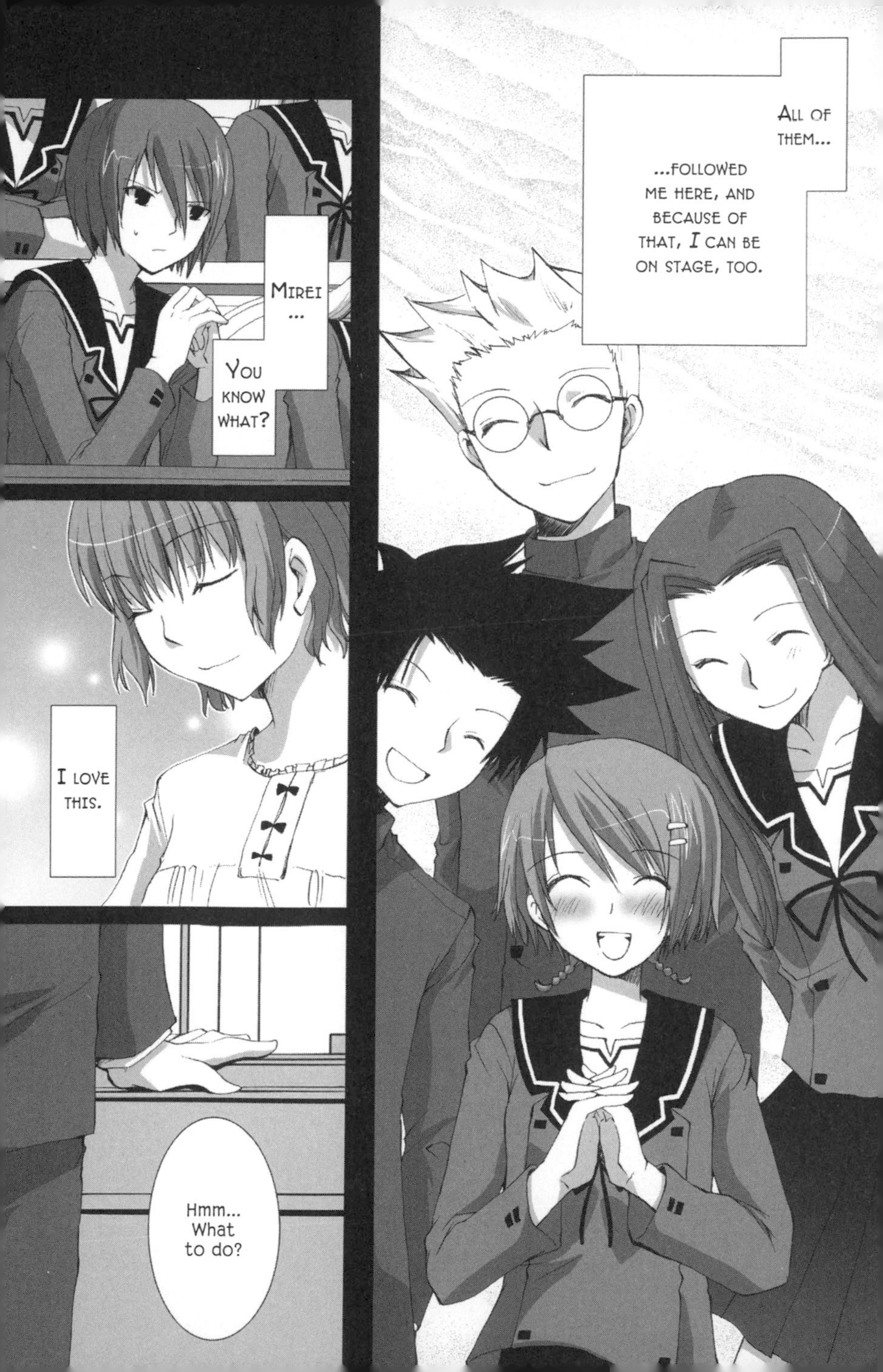
All of them...
...followed me here, and because of that, I can be on stage, too.
Mirei ...
You know what?
I love this.
Hmm... What to do?

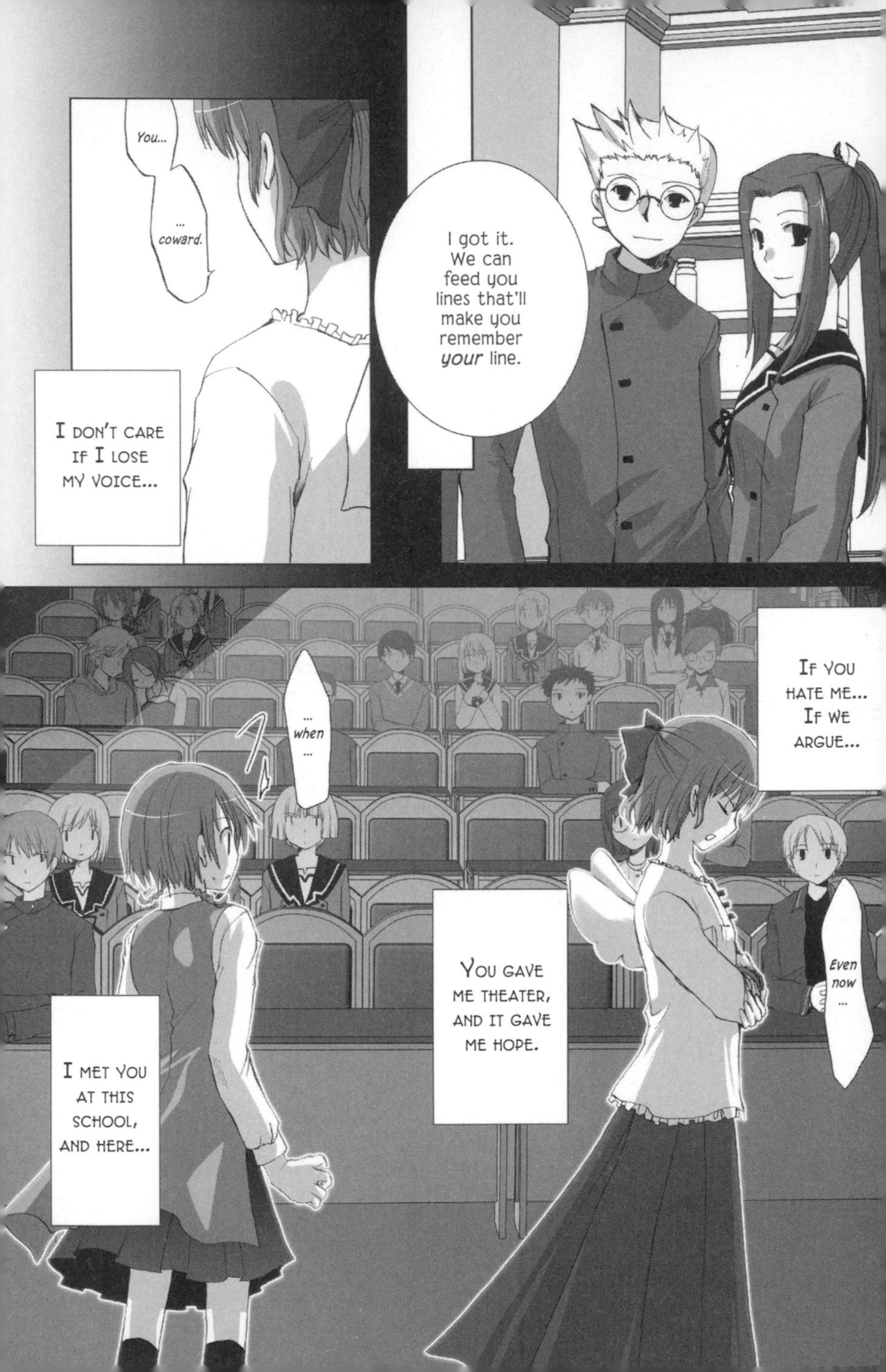
I got it. We can feed you lines that'll make you remember *your* line.
You...
... coward.
I DON'T CARE IF I LOSE MY VOICE...
IF YOU HATE ME... IF WE ARGUE...
Even now ...
YOU GAVE ME THEATER, AND IT GAVE ME HOPE.
... when ...
I MET YOU AT THIS SCHOOL, AND HERE...

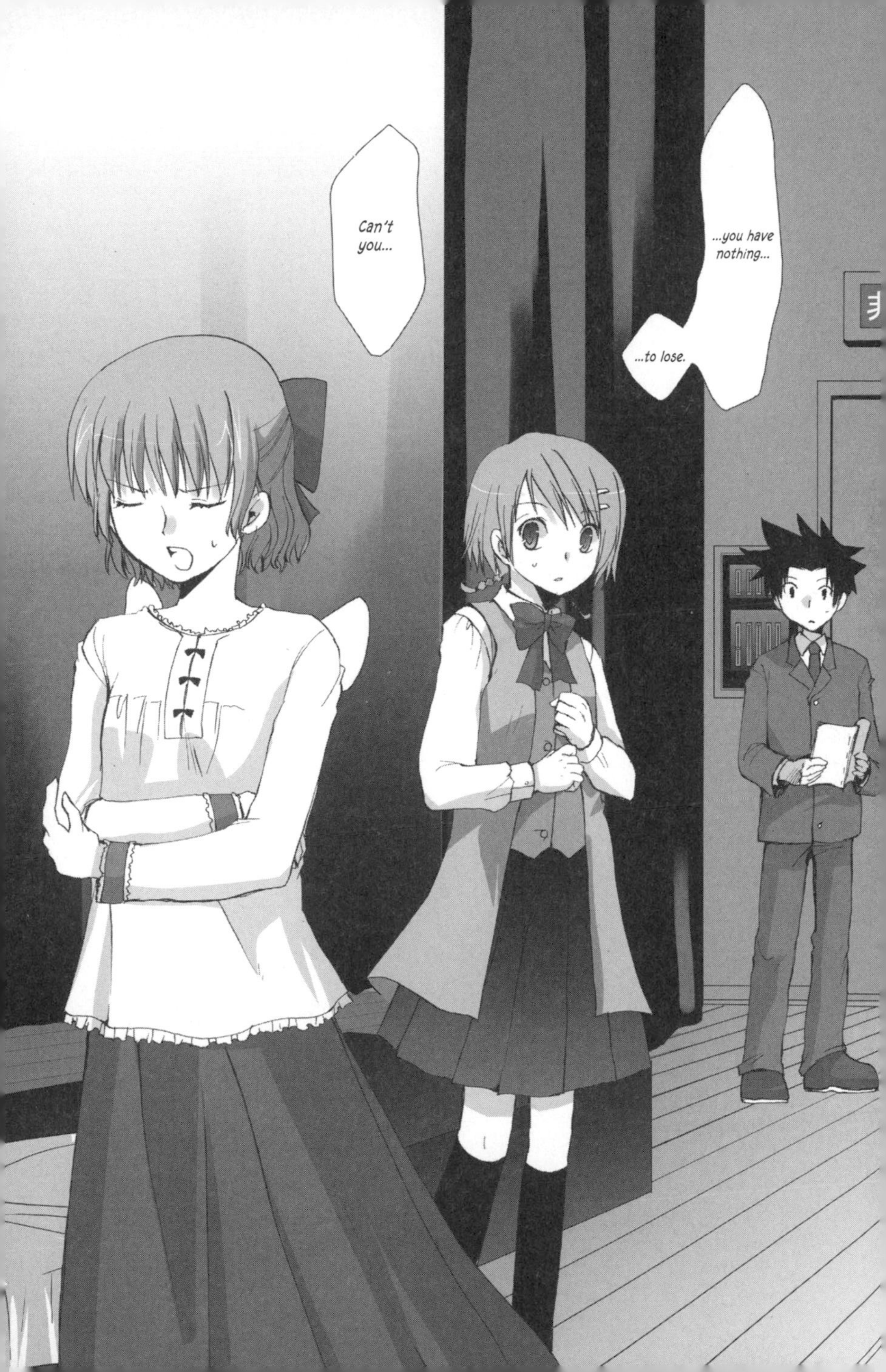
...you have nothing...
...to lose.
Can't you...

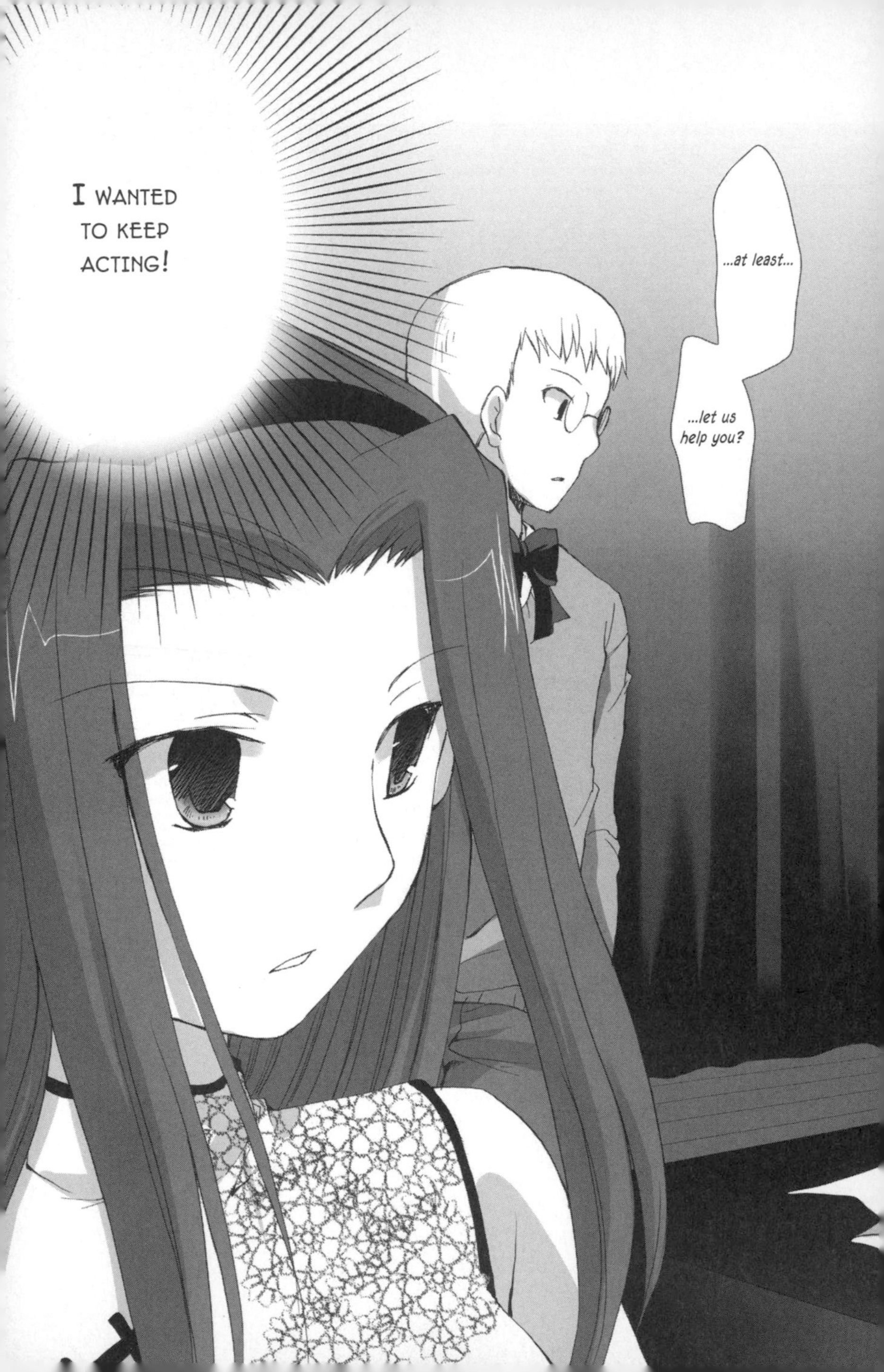
...at least...
...let us help you?
I WANTED TO KEEP ACTING!

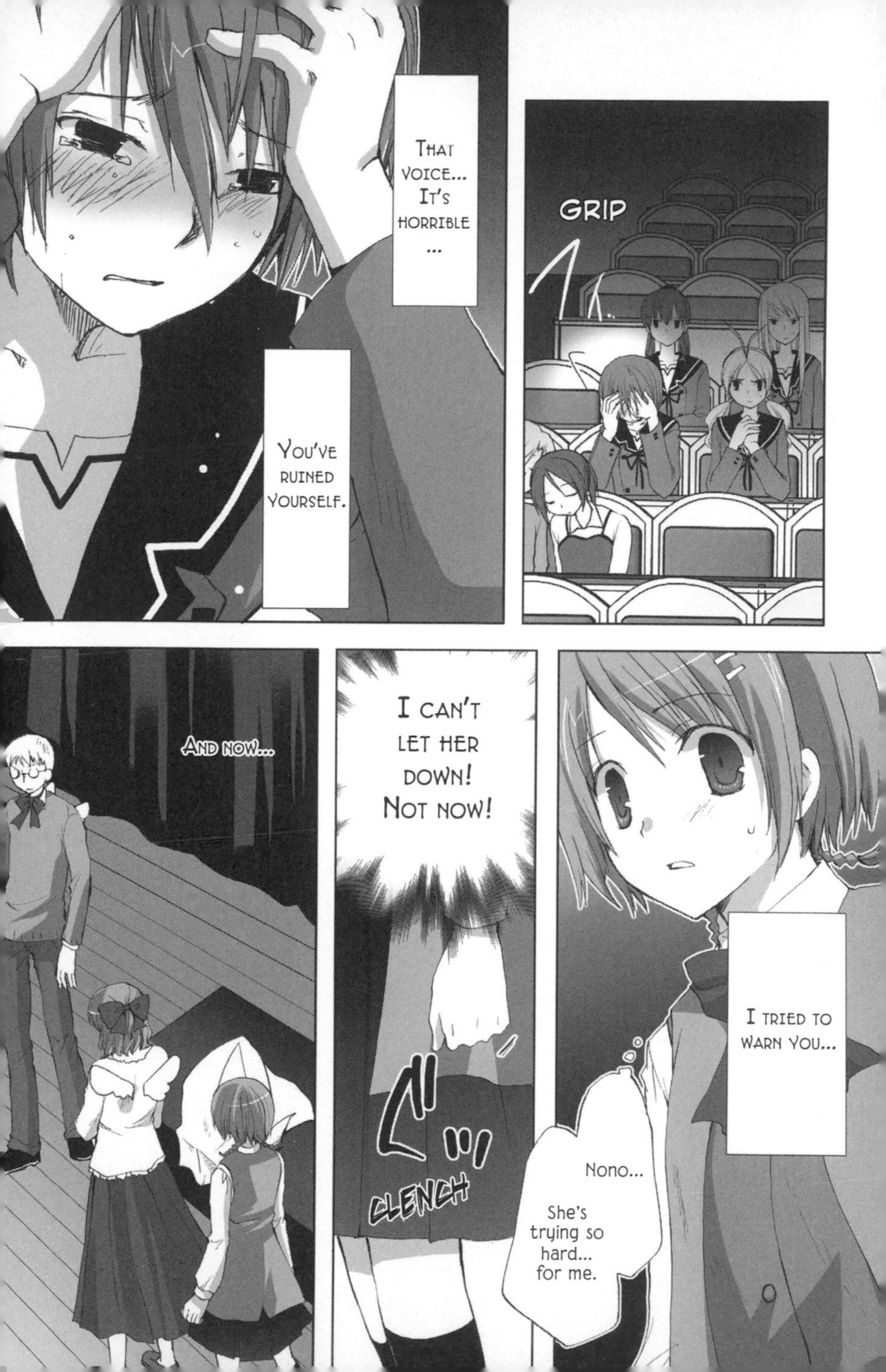
GRIP
That voice... It's horrible ...
You've ruined yourself.
I tried to warn you...
Nono...
She's trying so hard... for me.
I can't let her down! Not now!
CLENCH
And now...

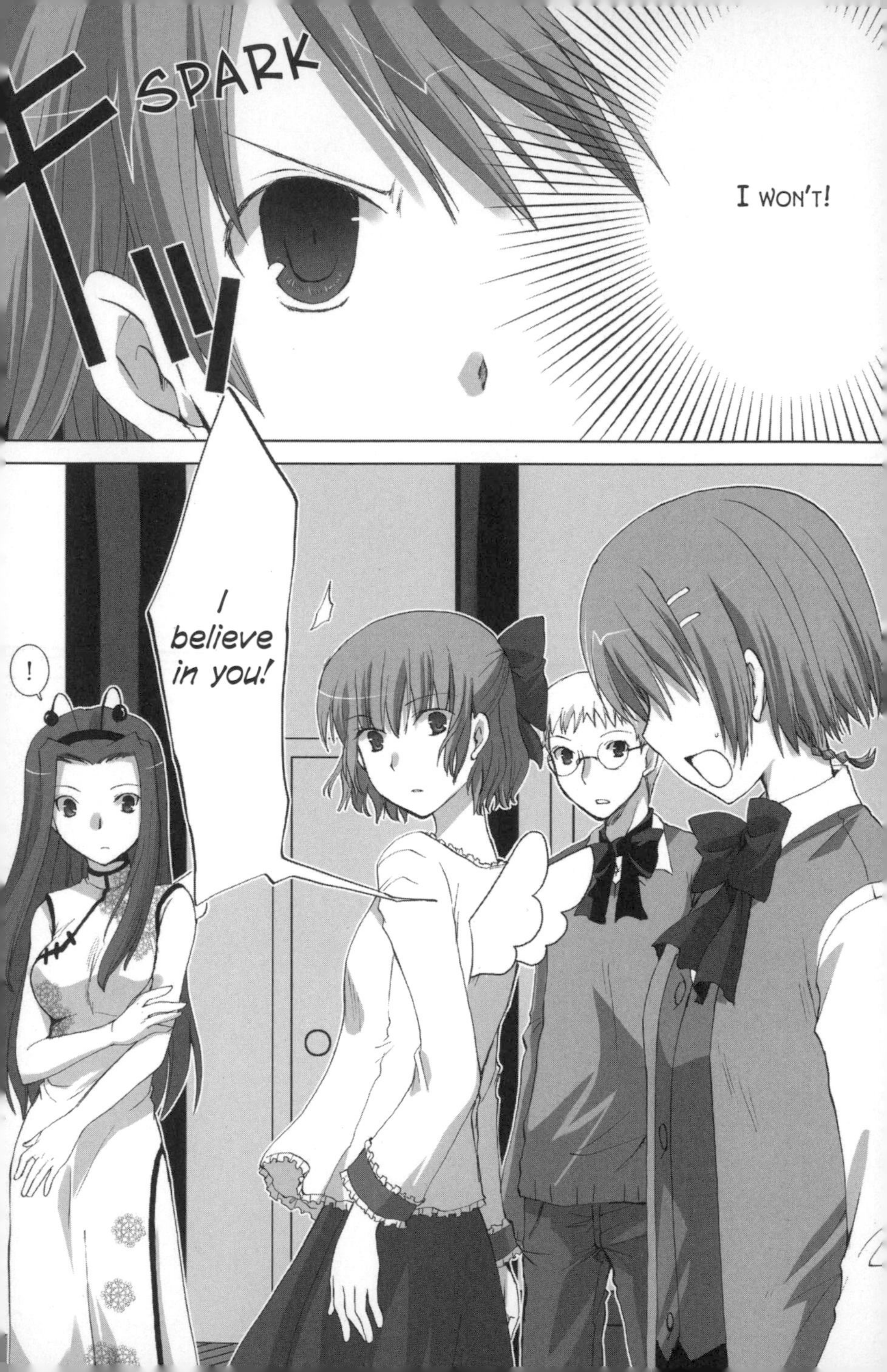
I WON'T!
SPARK
I believe in you!
!

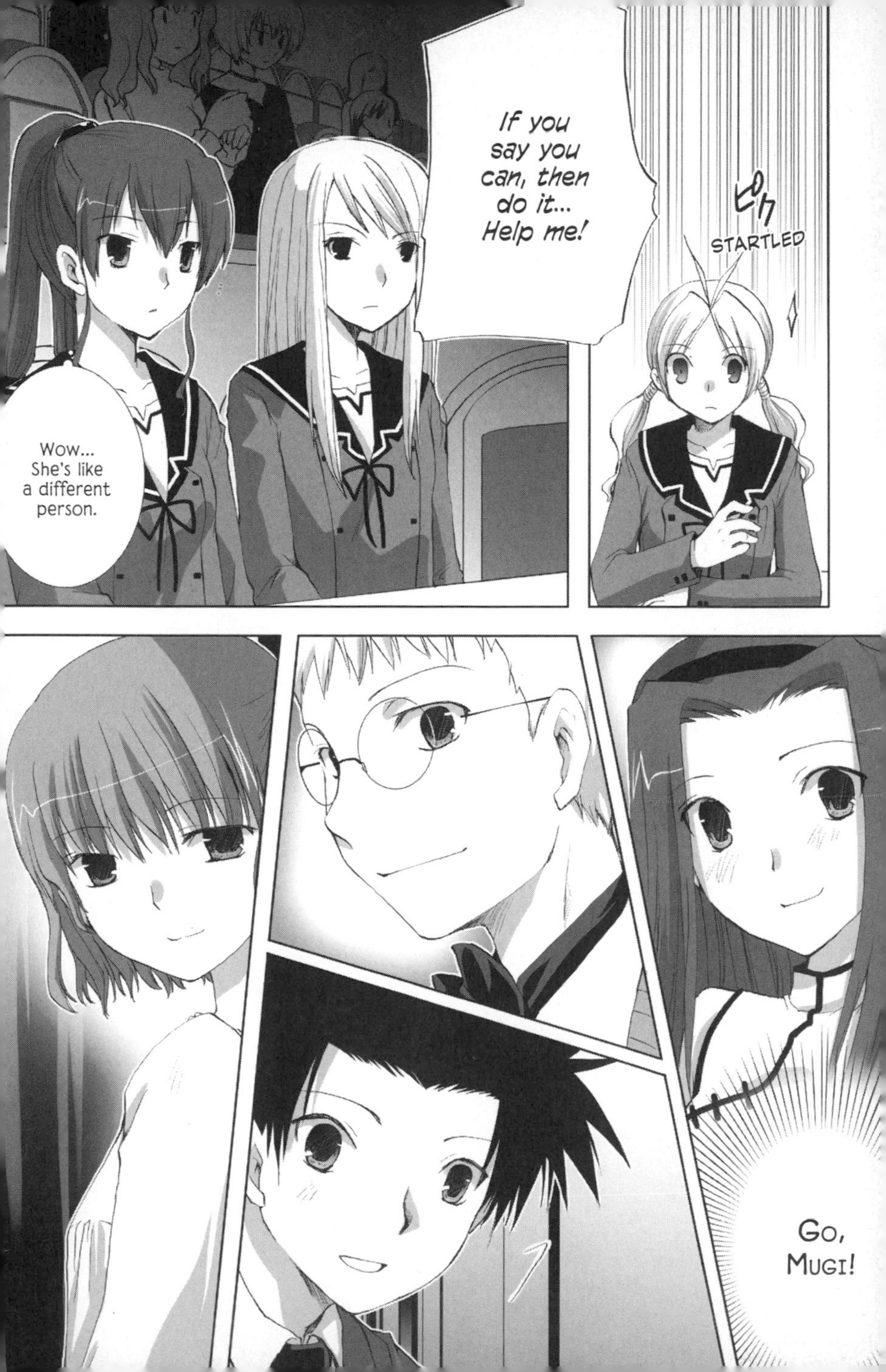
ピク
STARTLED
If you say you can, then do it... Help me!
Wow... She's like a different person.
Go, Mugi!

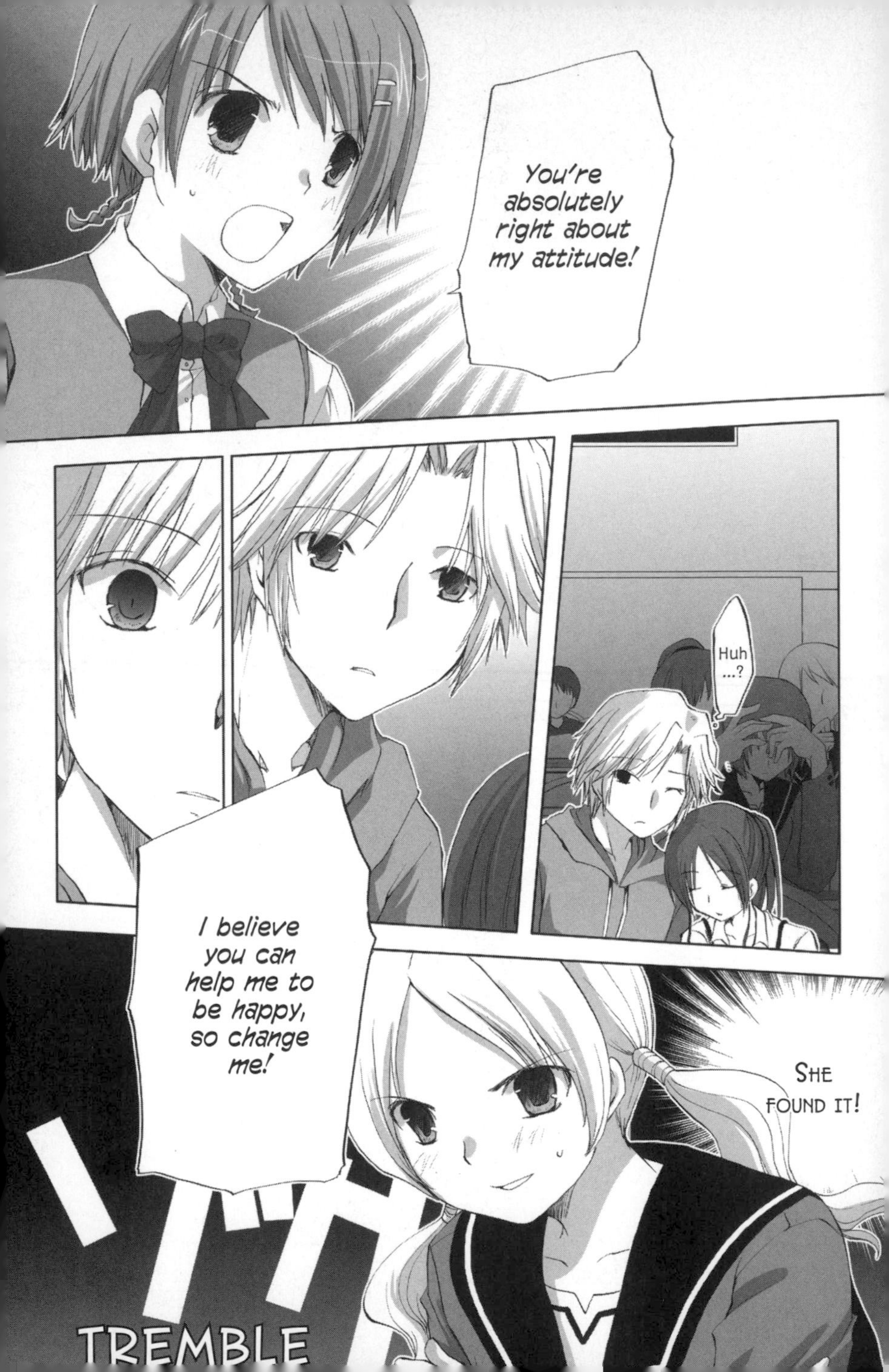
You're absolutely right about my attitude!
Huh ...?
I believe you can help me to be happy, so change me!
She found it!
TREMBLE

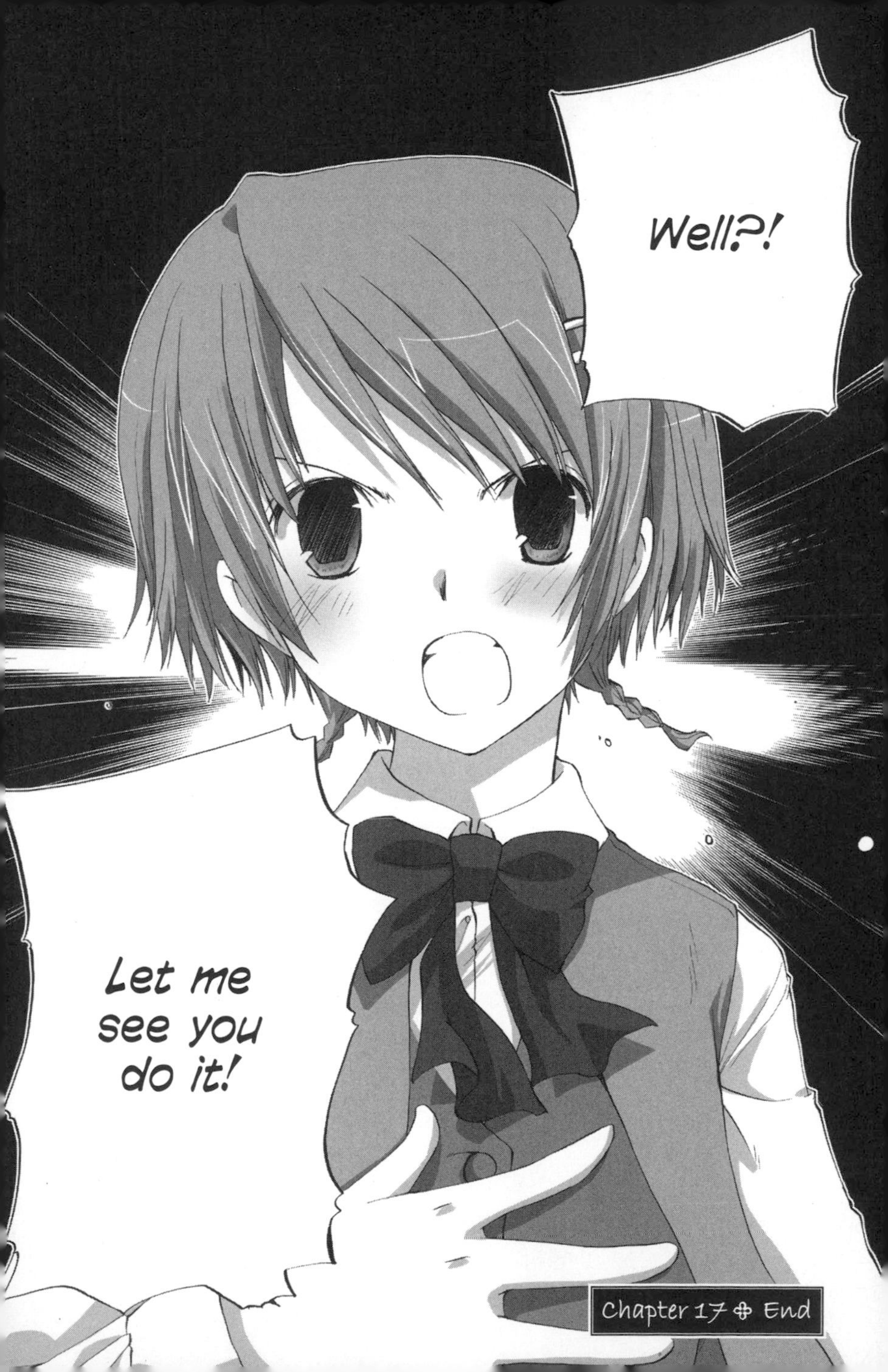
Well?!
Let me see you do it!
Chapter 17 ✣ End

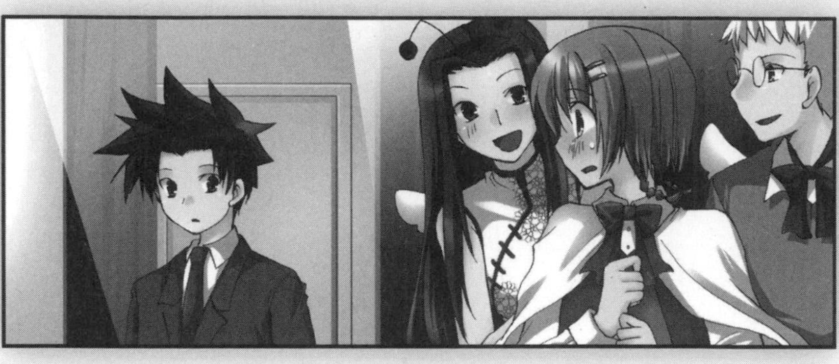

She was a normal girl who hated being
the center of attention.

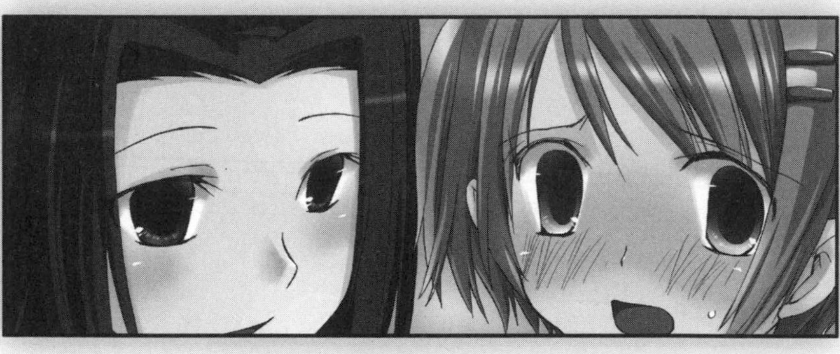

But with lots of effort and support
on the part of her friends...

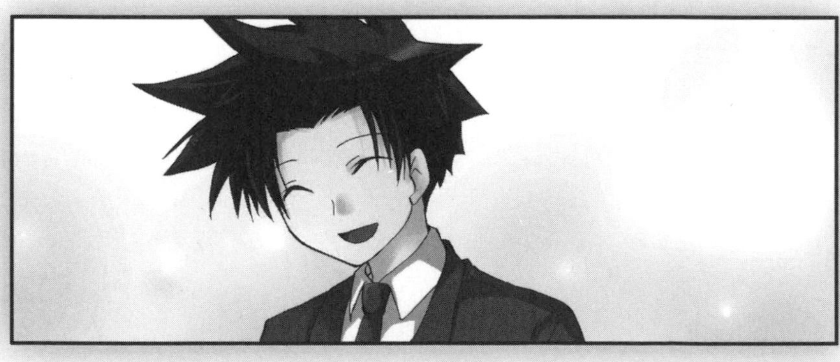

Here she is, right now...

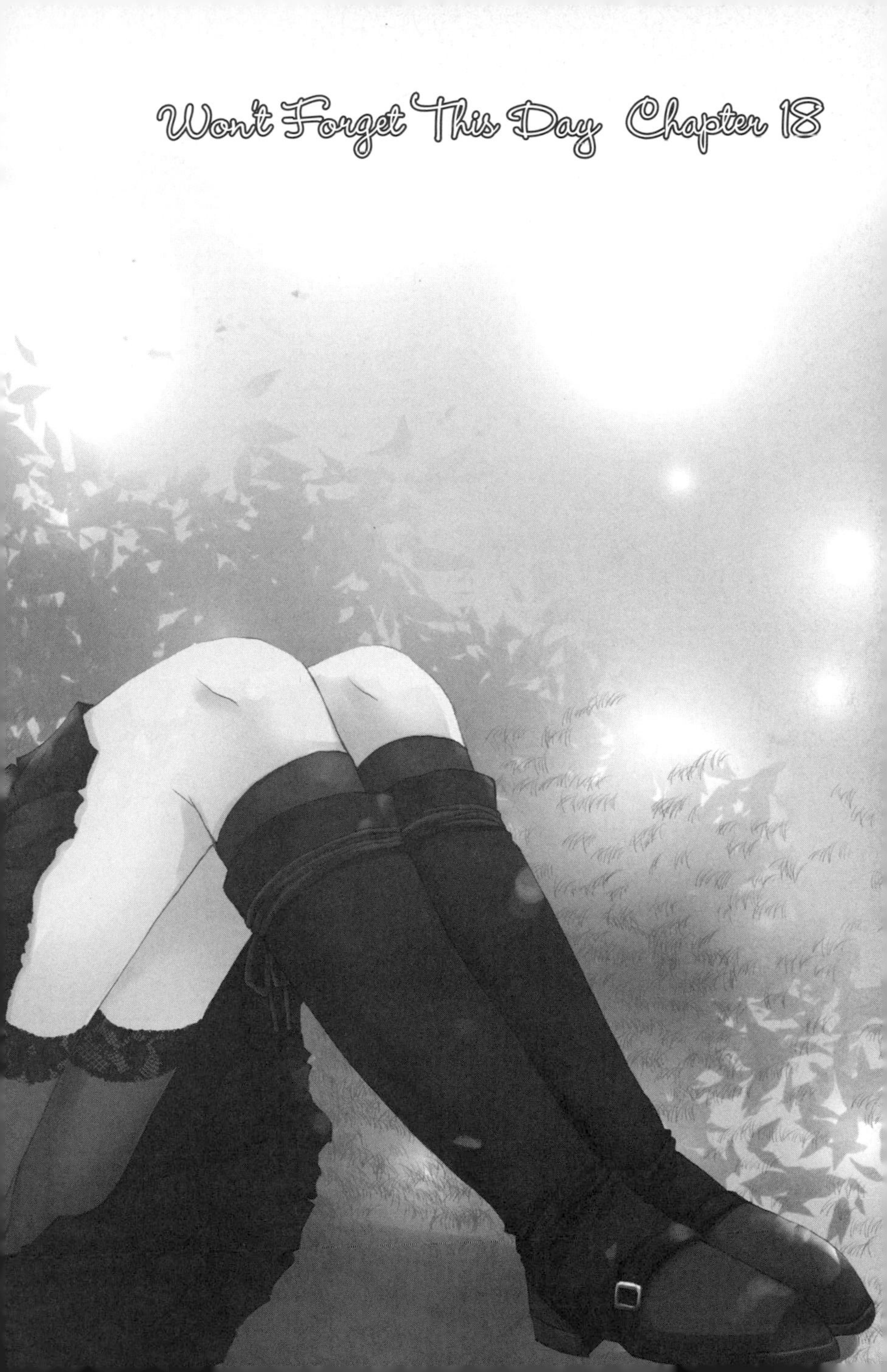
Won't Forget This Day Chapter 18

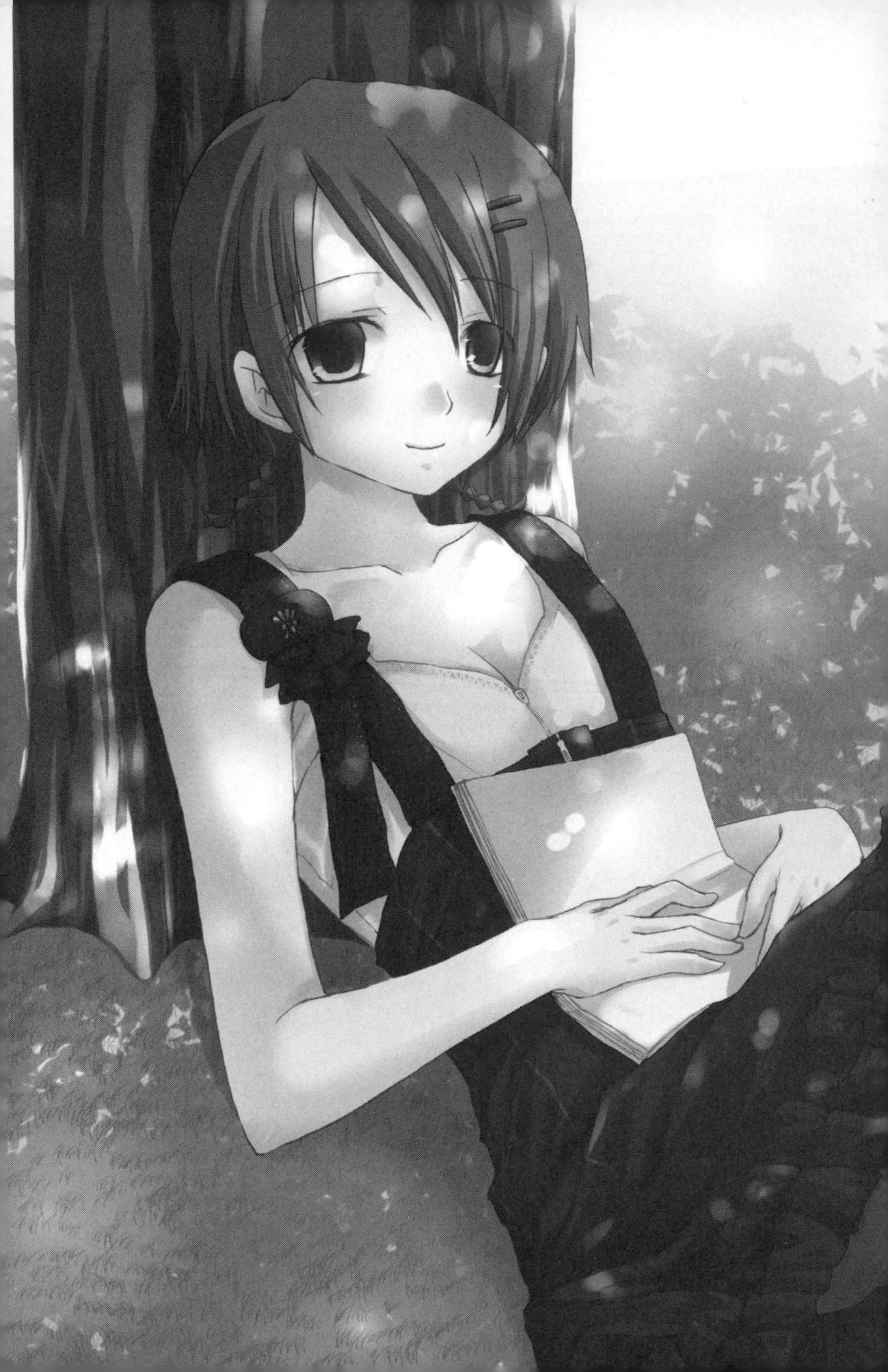

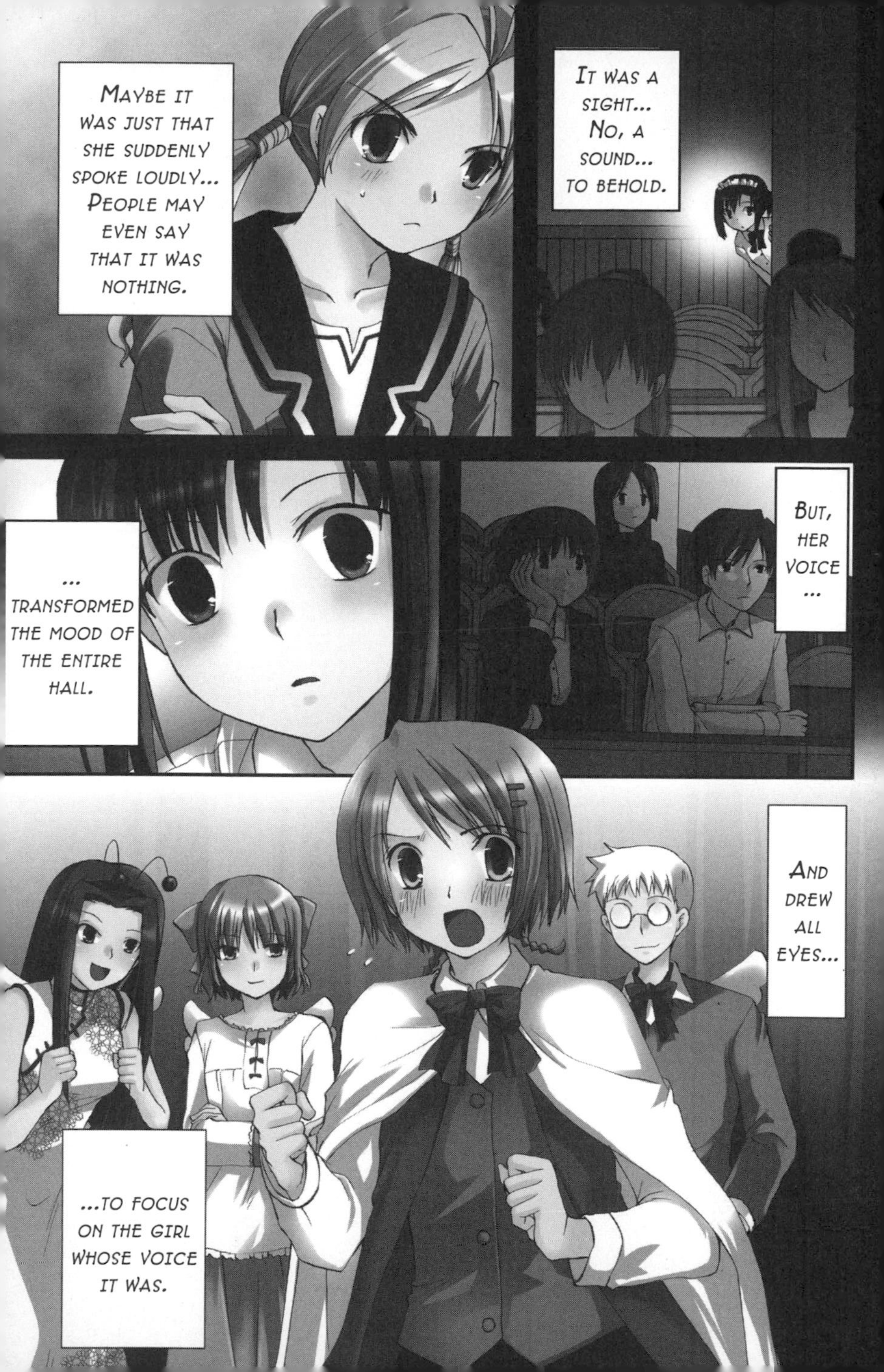
It was a sight... No, a sound... to behold.
Maybe it was just that she suddenly spoke loudly... People may even say that it was nothing.
But, her voice...
...transformed the mood of the entire hall.
And drew all eyes...
...to focus on the girl whose voice it was.

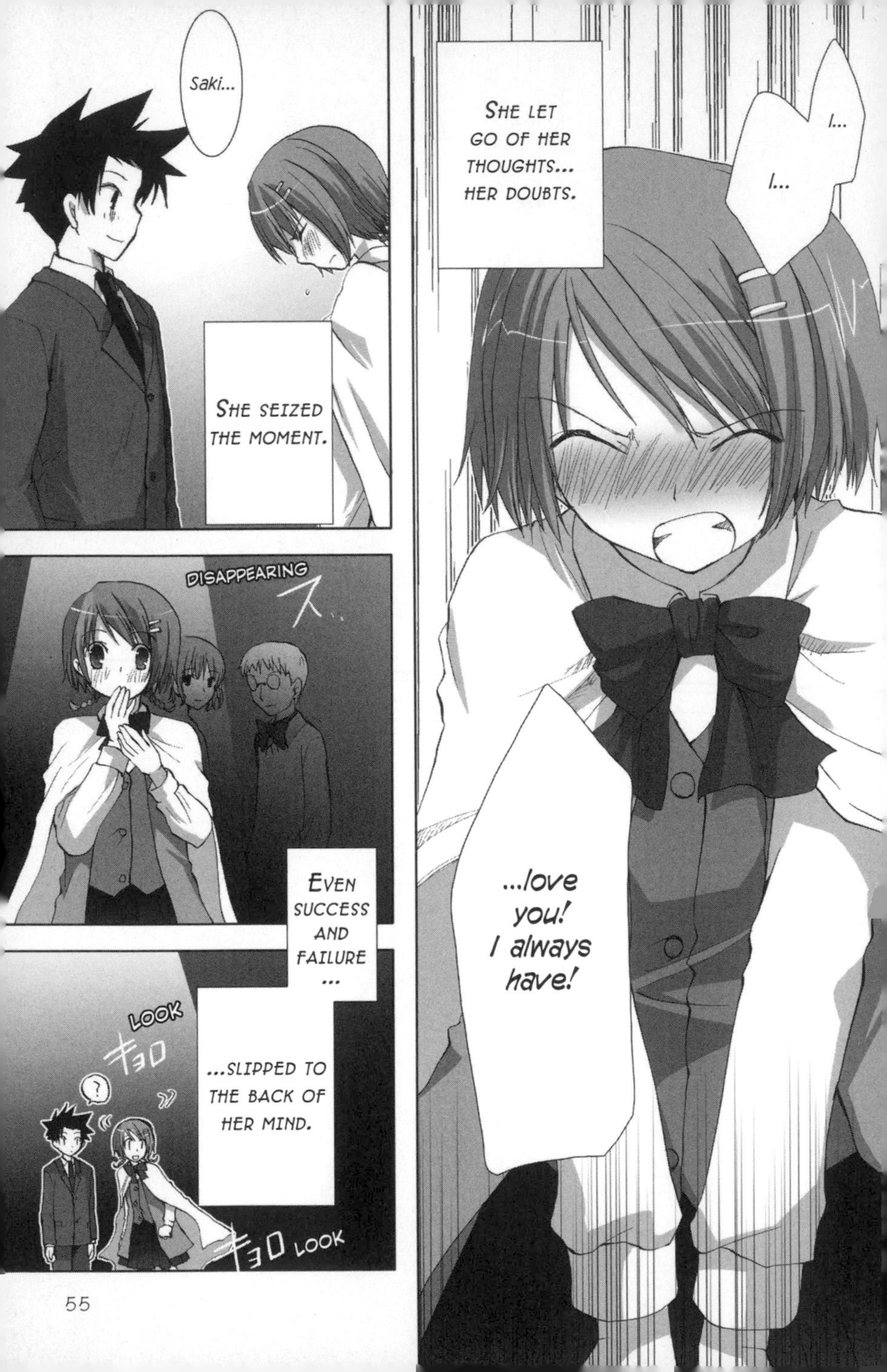
She let go of her thoughts... her doubts.
I...
I...
...love you! I always have!
Saki...
She seized the moment.
DISAPPEARING
Even success and failure ...
...slipped to the back of her mind.
LOOK
?
LOOK

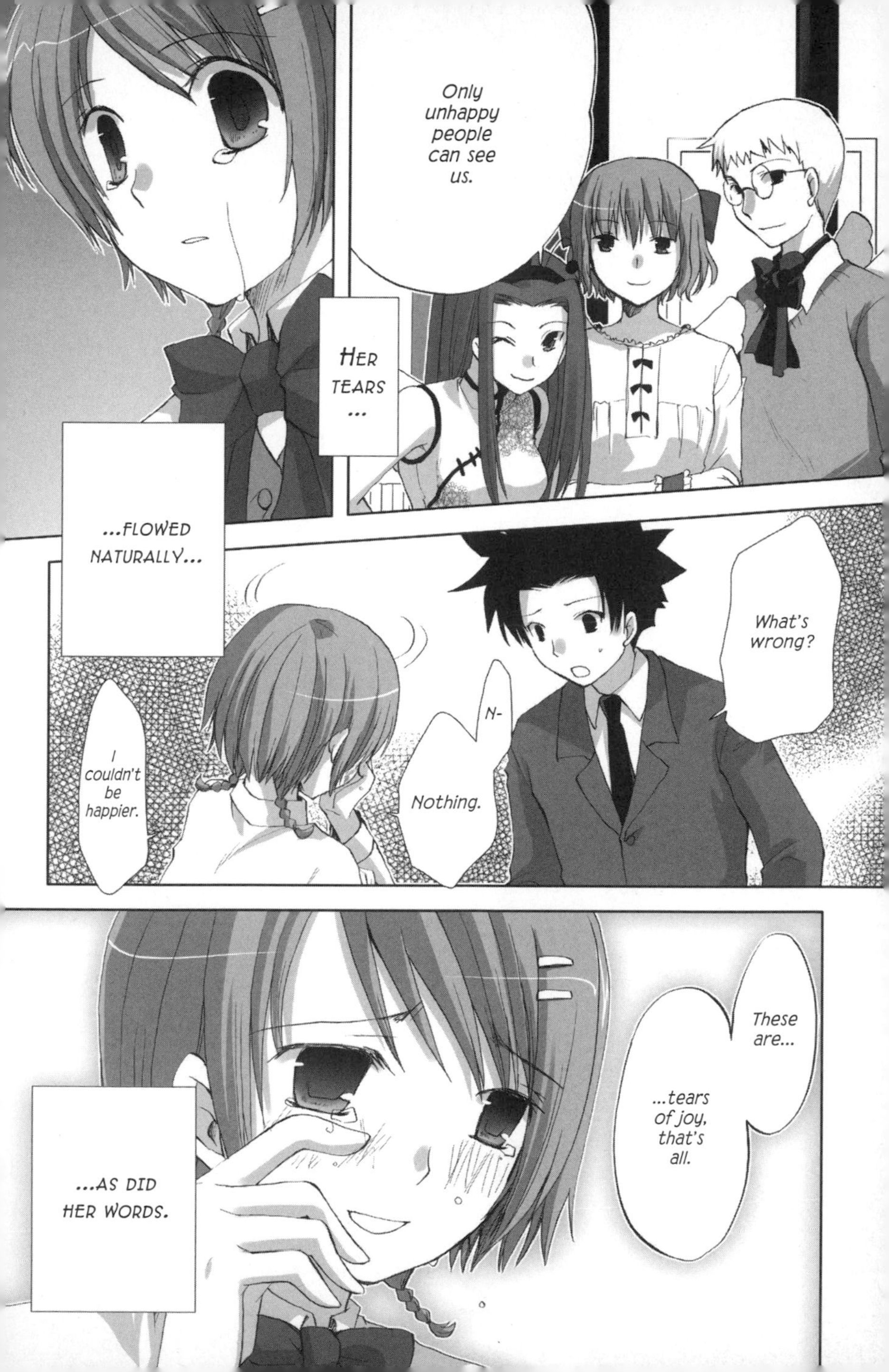
Only unhappy people can see us.
HER TEARS ...
...FLOWED NATURALLY...
What's wrong?
N-
Nothing.
I couldn't be happier.
These are...
...tears of joy, that's all.
...AS DID HER WORDS.

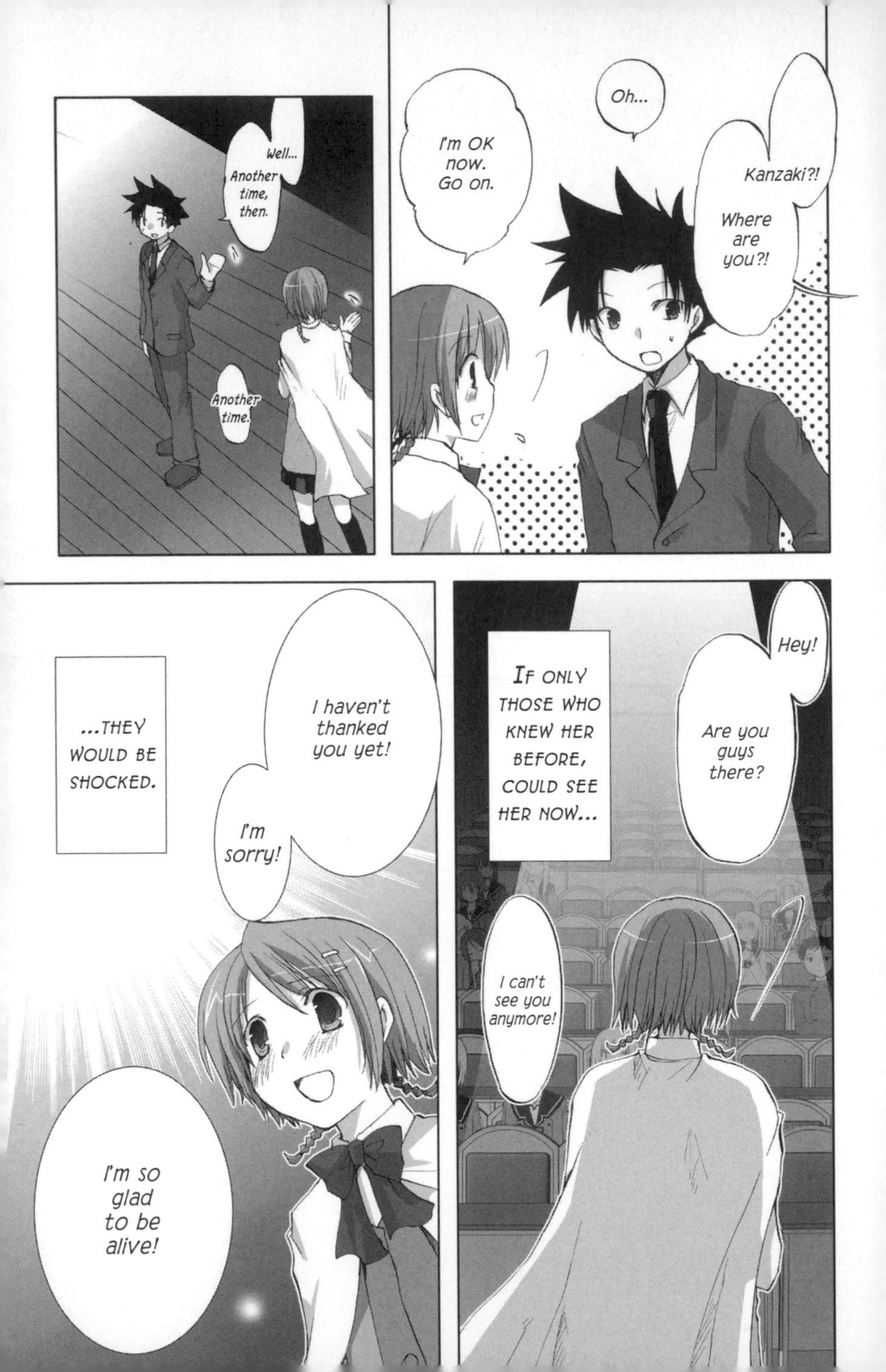
Kanzaki?!
Where are you?!
Oh...
I'm OK now. Go on.
Well... Another time, then.
Another time.
Hey!
Are you guys there?
IF ONLY THOSE WHO KNEW HER BEFORE, COULD SEE HER NOW...
I can't see you anymore!
I haven't thanked you yet!
I'm sorry!
...THEY WOULD BE SHOCKED.
I'm so glad to be alive!

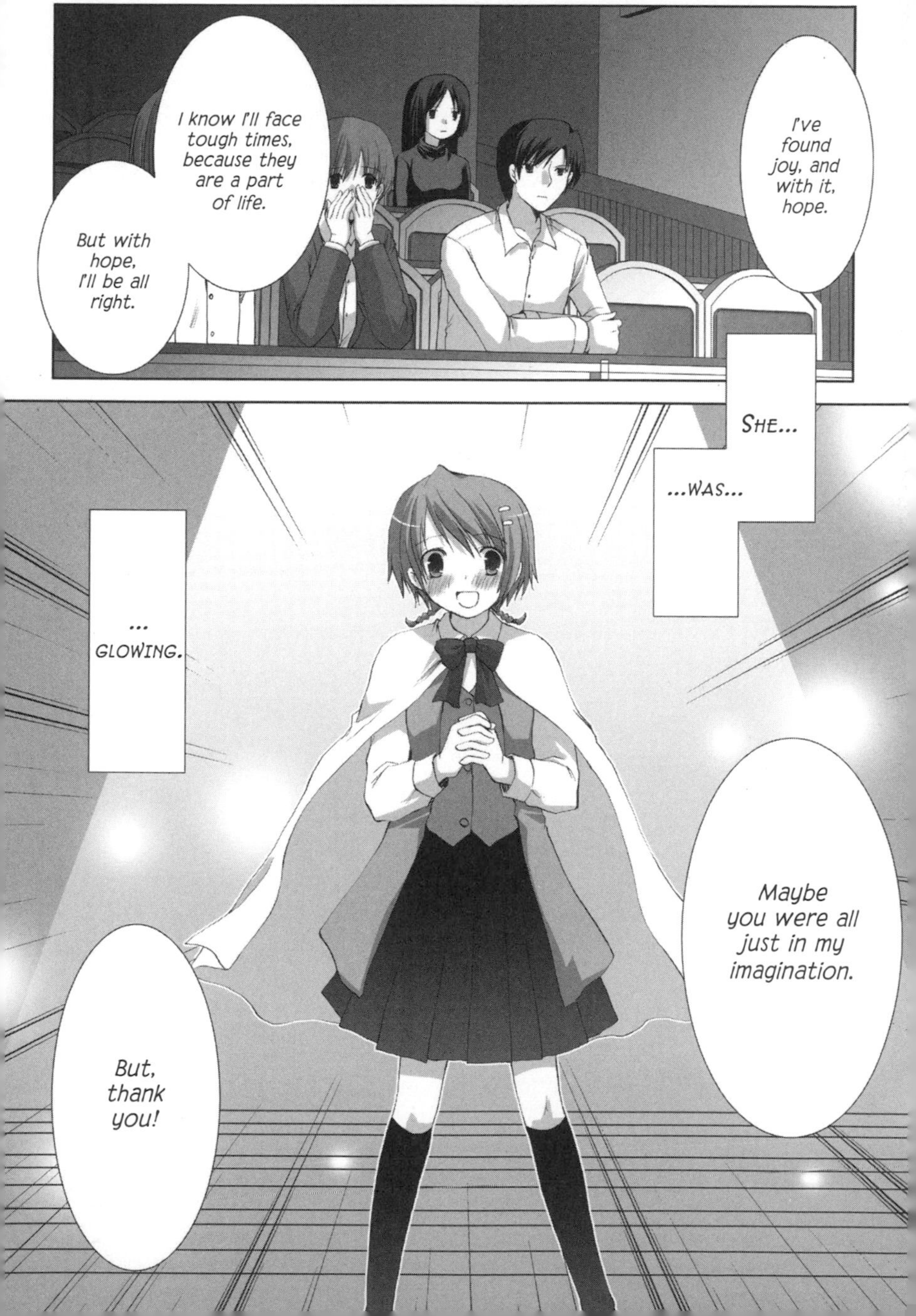
I've found joy, and with it, hope.
I know I'll face tough times, because they are a part of life.
But with hope, I'll be all right.
SHE...
...WAS...
...GLOWING.
Maybe you were all just in my imagination.
But, thank you!

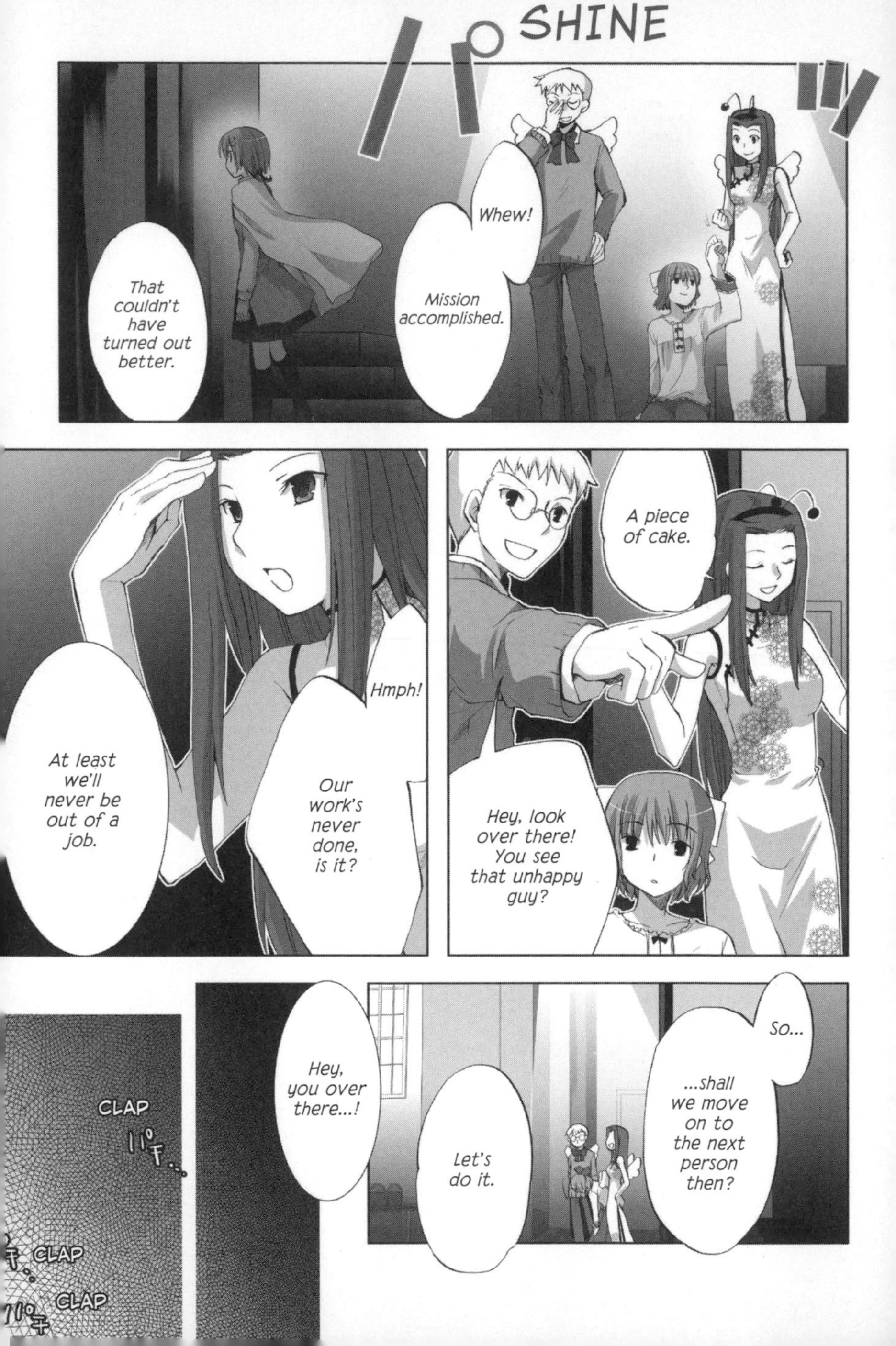
SHINE
Whew!
Mission accomplished.
That couldn't have turned out better.
A piece of cake.
Hey, look over there! You see that unhappy guy?
Hmph!
Our work's never done, is it?
At least we'll never be out of a job.
So...
...shall we move on to the next person then?
Let's do it.
Hey, you over there...!
CLAP
CLAP
CLAP

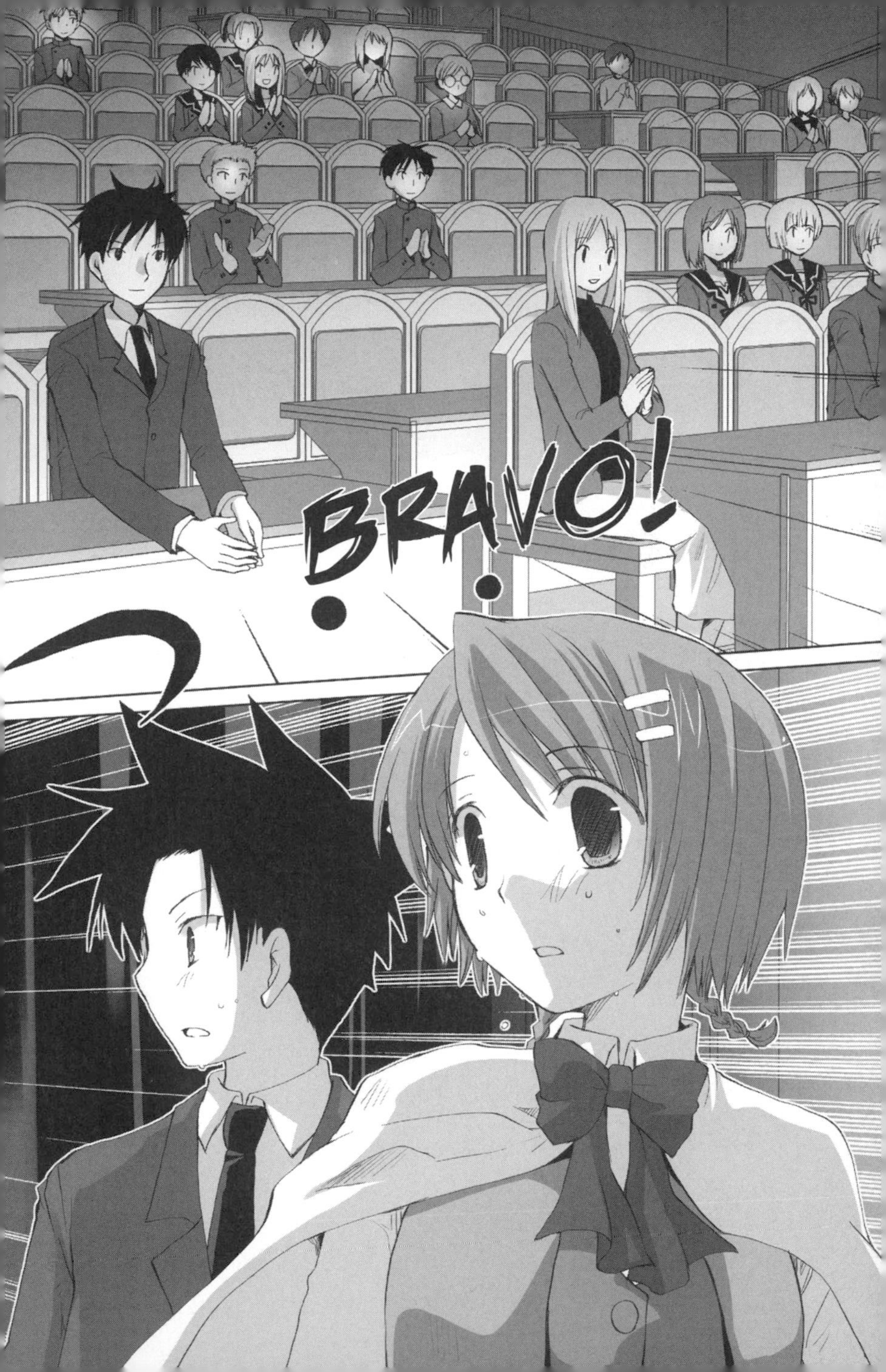
BRAVO!

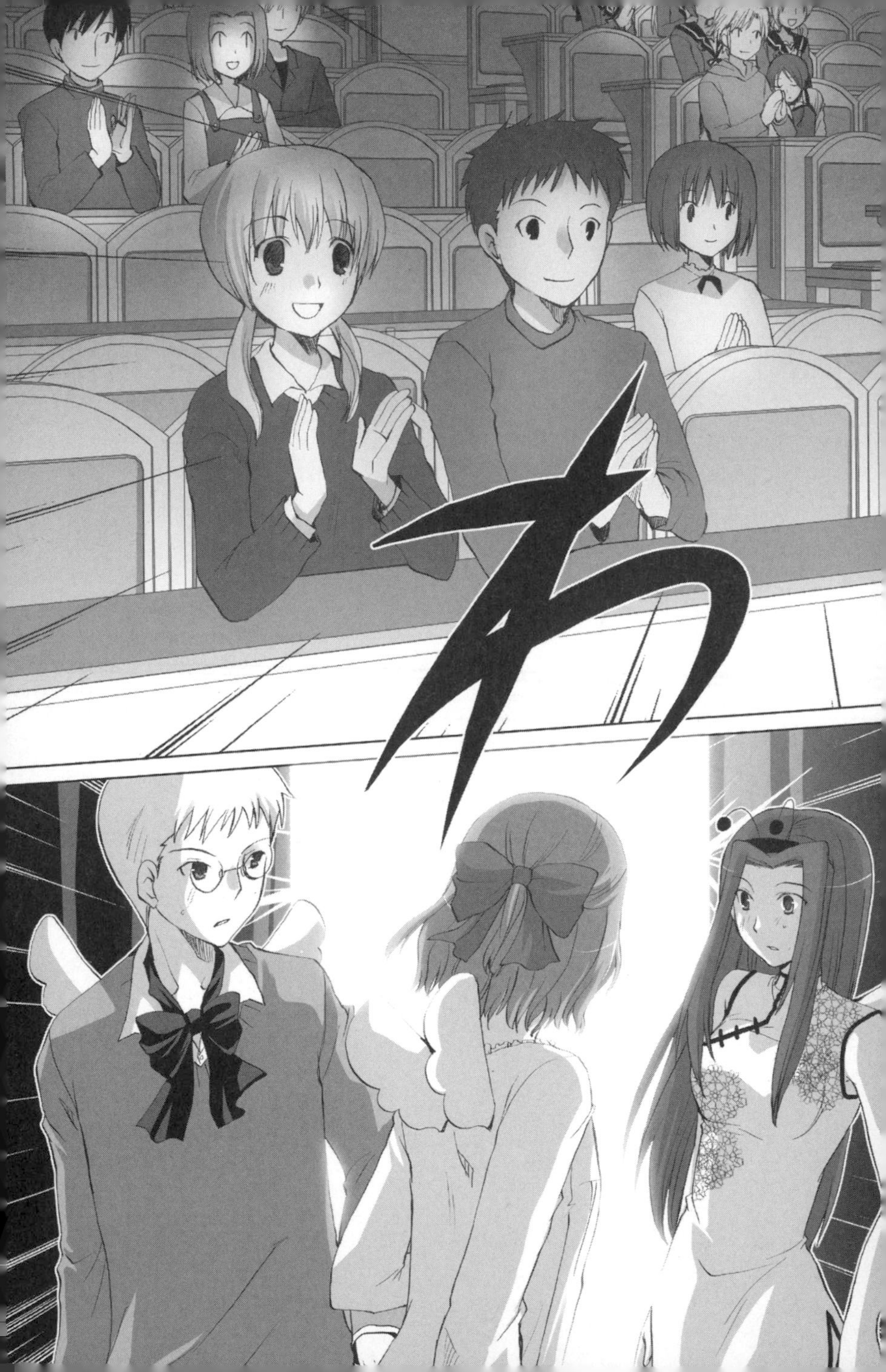

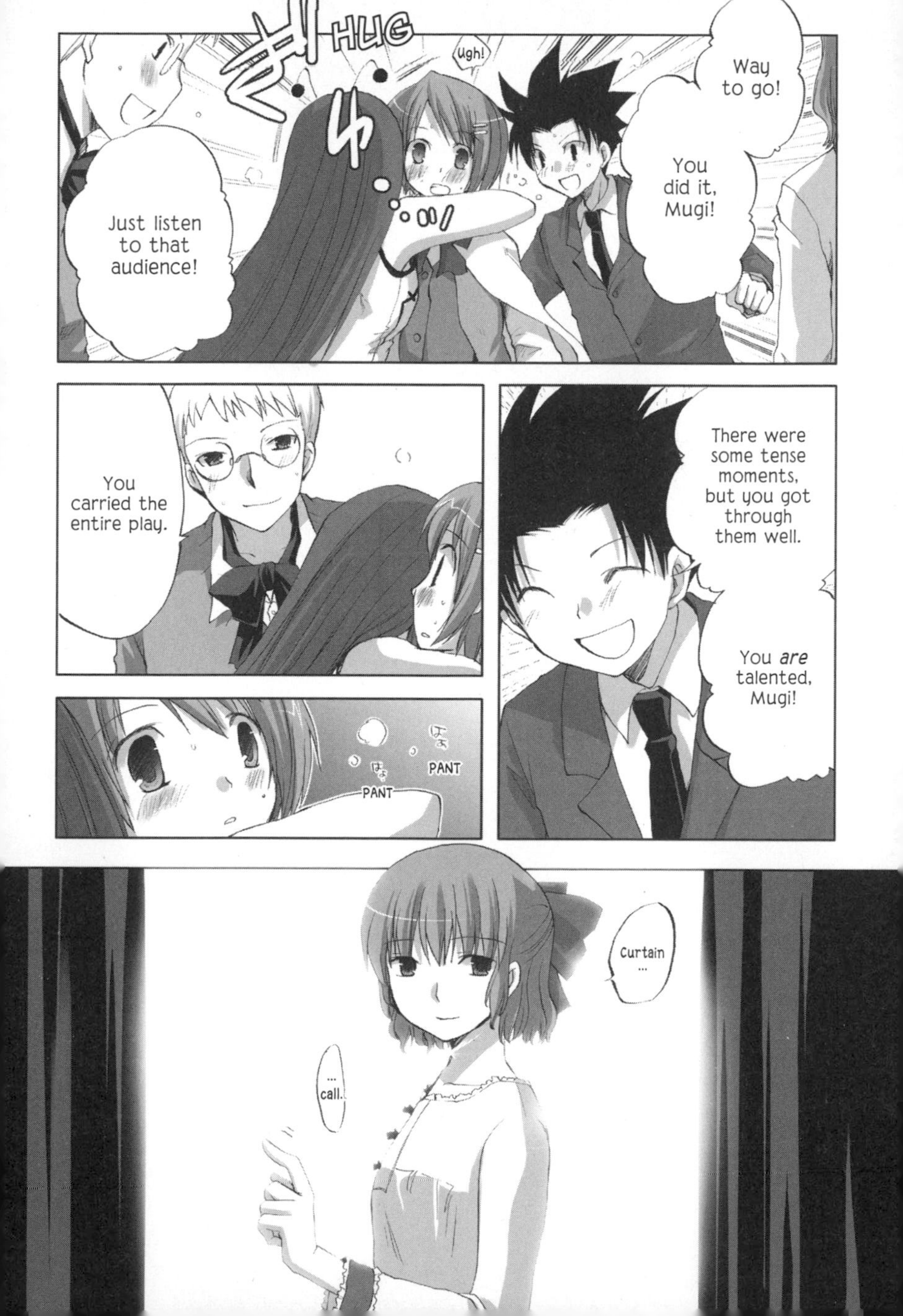
Way to go!
You did it, Mugi!
Ugh!
HUG
Just listen to that audience!
There were some tense moments, but you got through them well.
You *are* talented, Mugi!
You carried the entire play.
PANT
PANT
Curtain ...
... call.

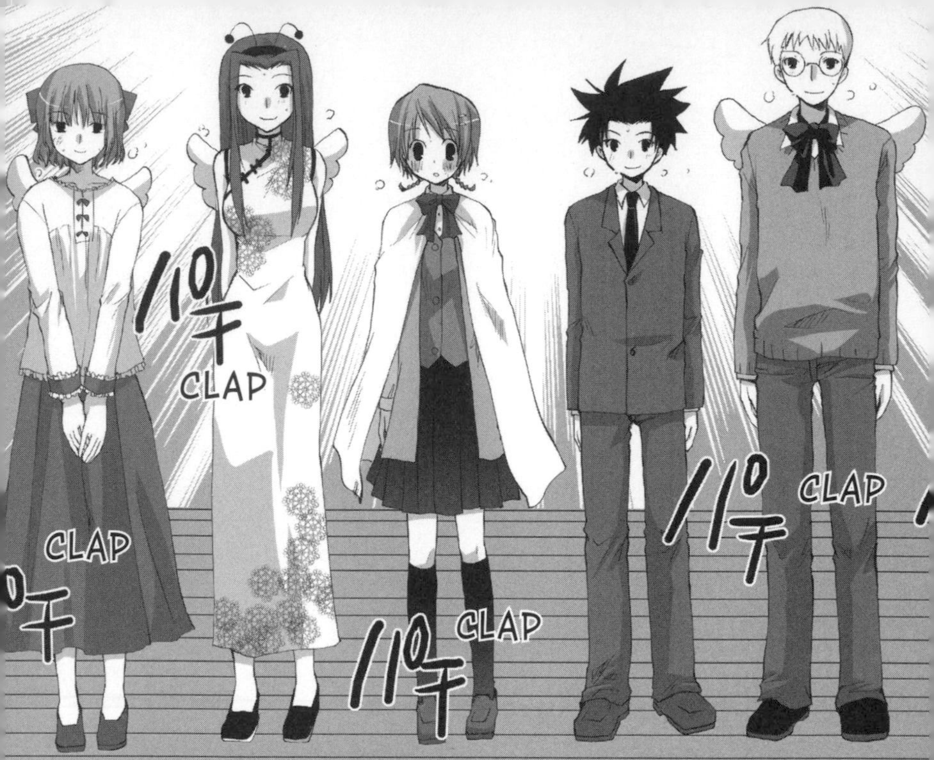
パチ
CLAP
パチ
CLAP
CLAP
パチ
CLAP
パチ
CLAP

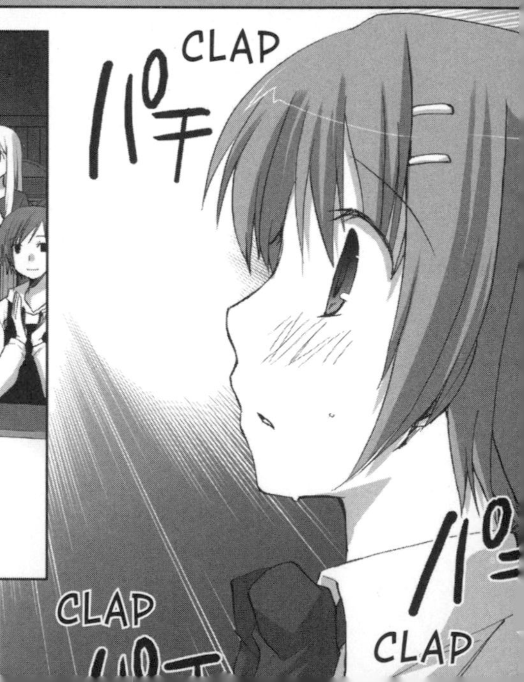
パチ
CLAP
CLAP
CLAP

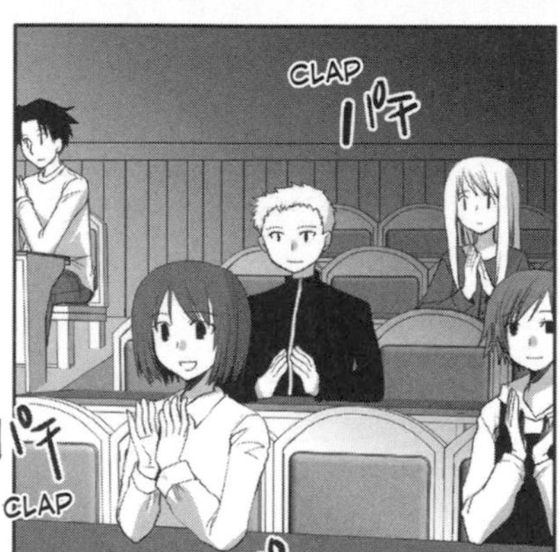
CLAP
パチ
パチ
CLAP
パチ
CLAP

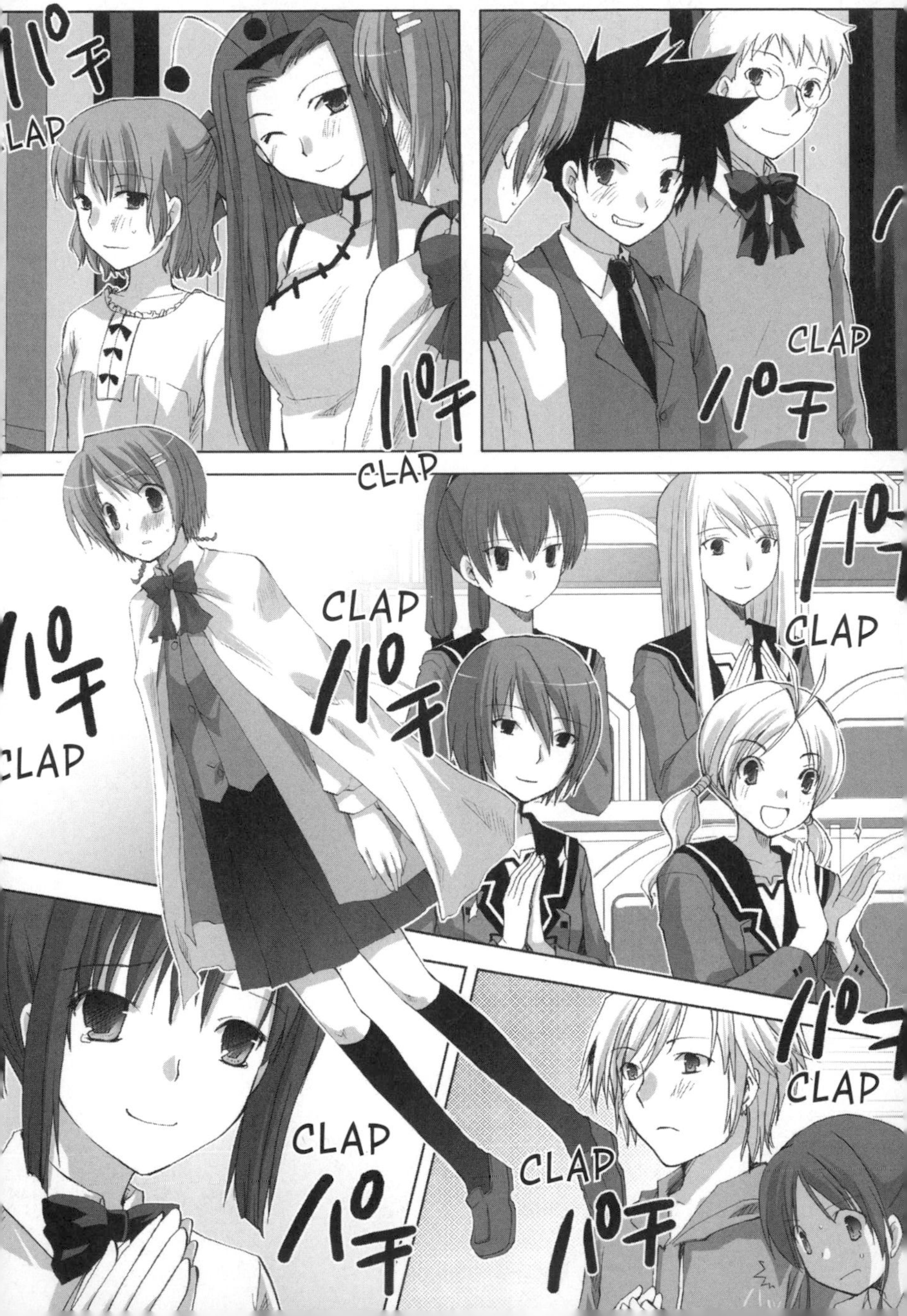

パチ
CLAP
パチ
CLAP
パチ
CLAP
パチ
CLAP
パチ
CLAP
パチ
CLAP
パチ
CLAP
CLAP
パチ
CLAP
パチ

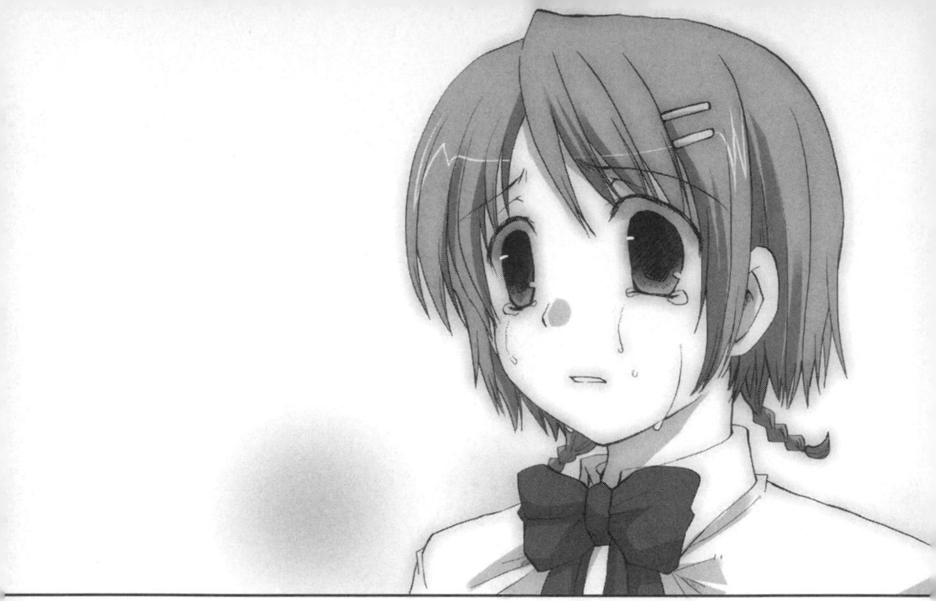

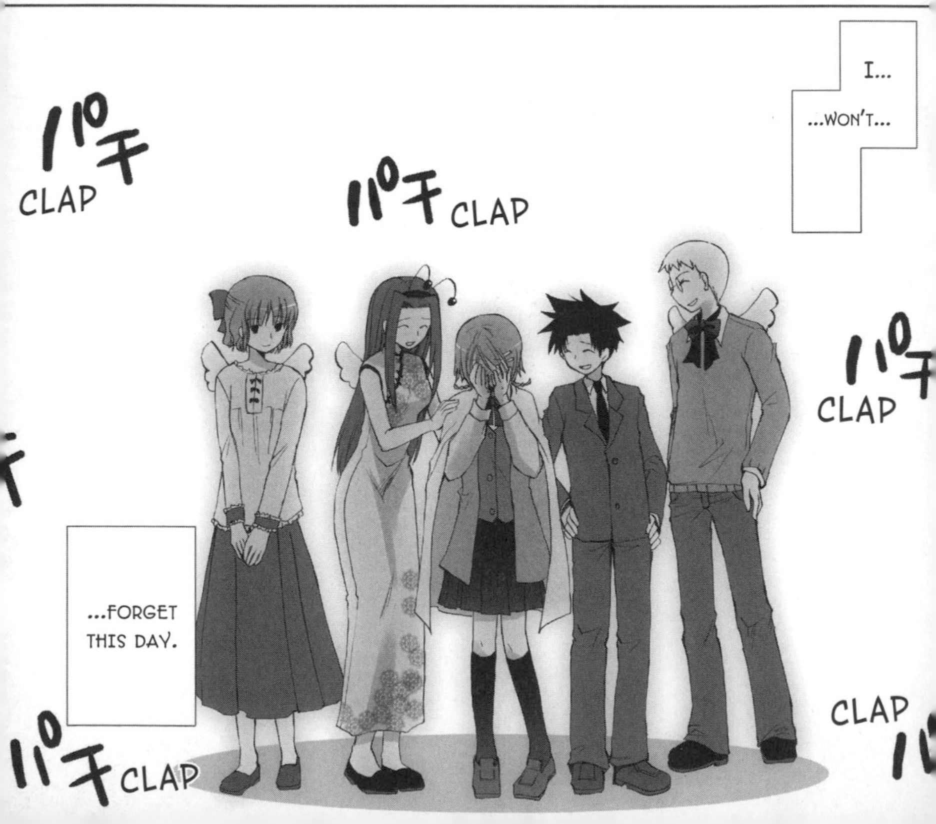
I...
...WON'T...
パチ CLAP
パチ CLAP
パチ CLAP
...FORGET THIS DAY.
CLAP
パチ CLAP

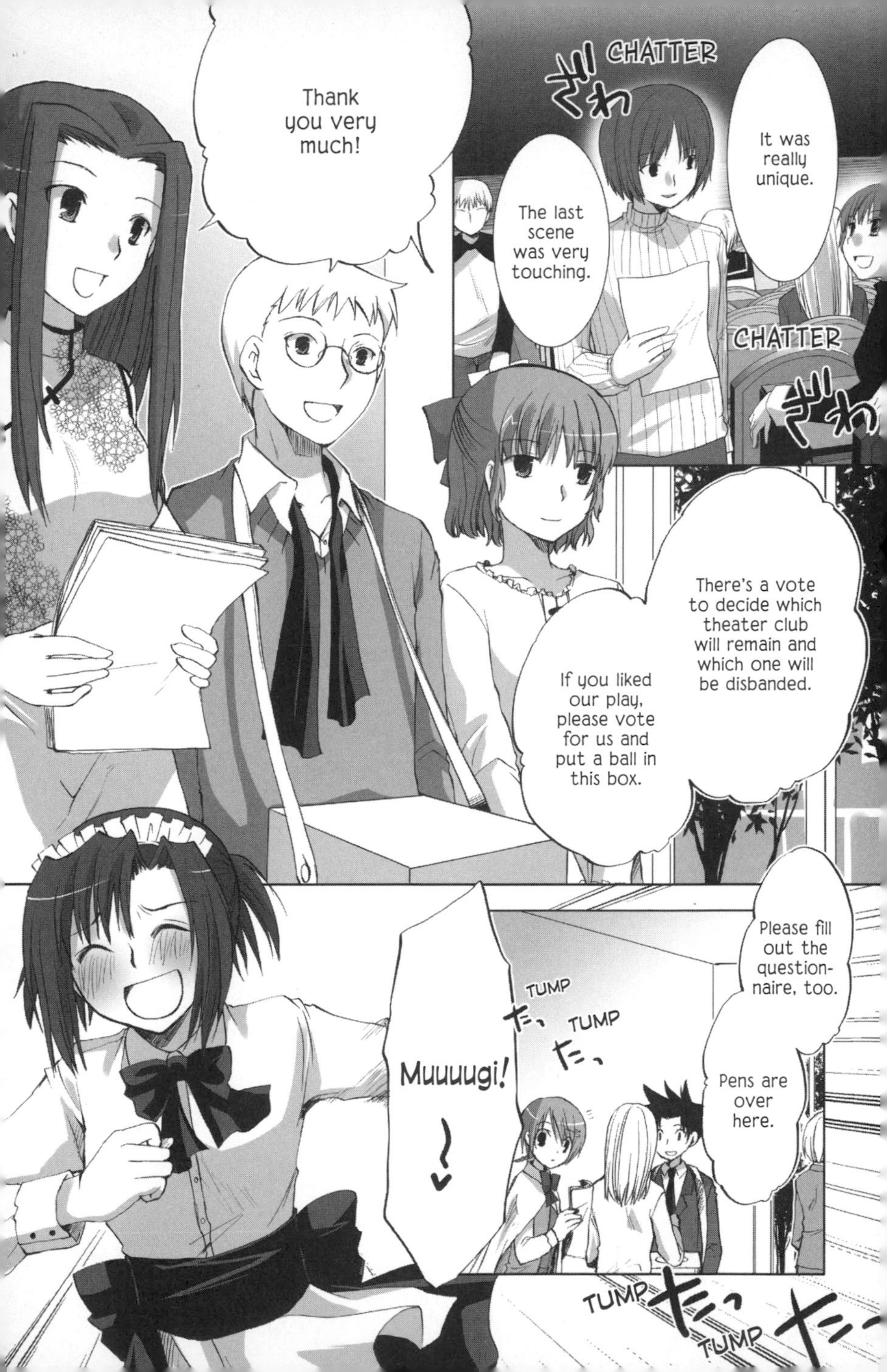
ざわ CHATTER
It was really unique.
The last scene was very touching.
CHATTER ざわ
There's a vote to decide which theater club will remain and which one will be disbanded.
If you liked our play, please vote for us and put a ball in this box.
Thank you very much!
Please fill out the questionnaire, too.
Pens are over here.
TUMP た、
TUMP た、
TUMP たっ
TUMP たっ
Muuuugi!

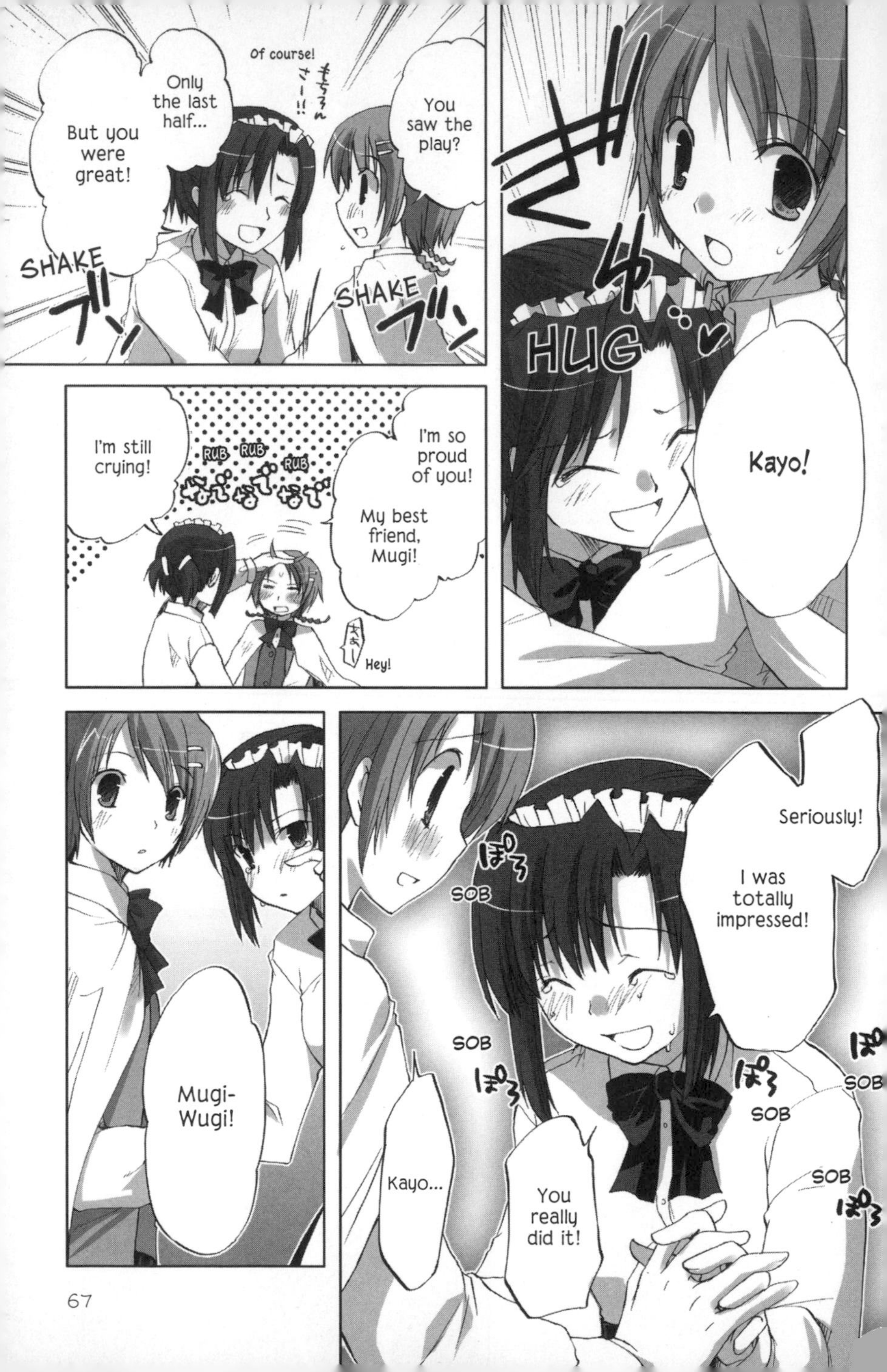
ぎゅ
HUG
Kayo!
You saw the play?
もちろんさー!!
Of course!
Only the last half...
But you were great!
SHAKE
ブン
SHAKE
ブン
I'm so proud of you!
My best friend, Mugi!
なでなでなで
RUB RUB RUB
I'm still crying!
Hey!
Seriously!
I was totally impressed!
ぽろ
SOB
ぽろ
SOB
ぽろ
SOB
ぽろ
SOB
ぽろ
SOB
ぽろ
SOB
You really did it!
Kayo...
Mugi-Wugi!

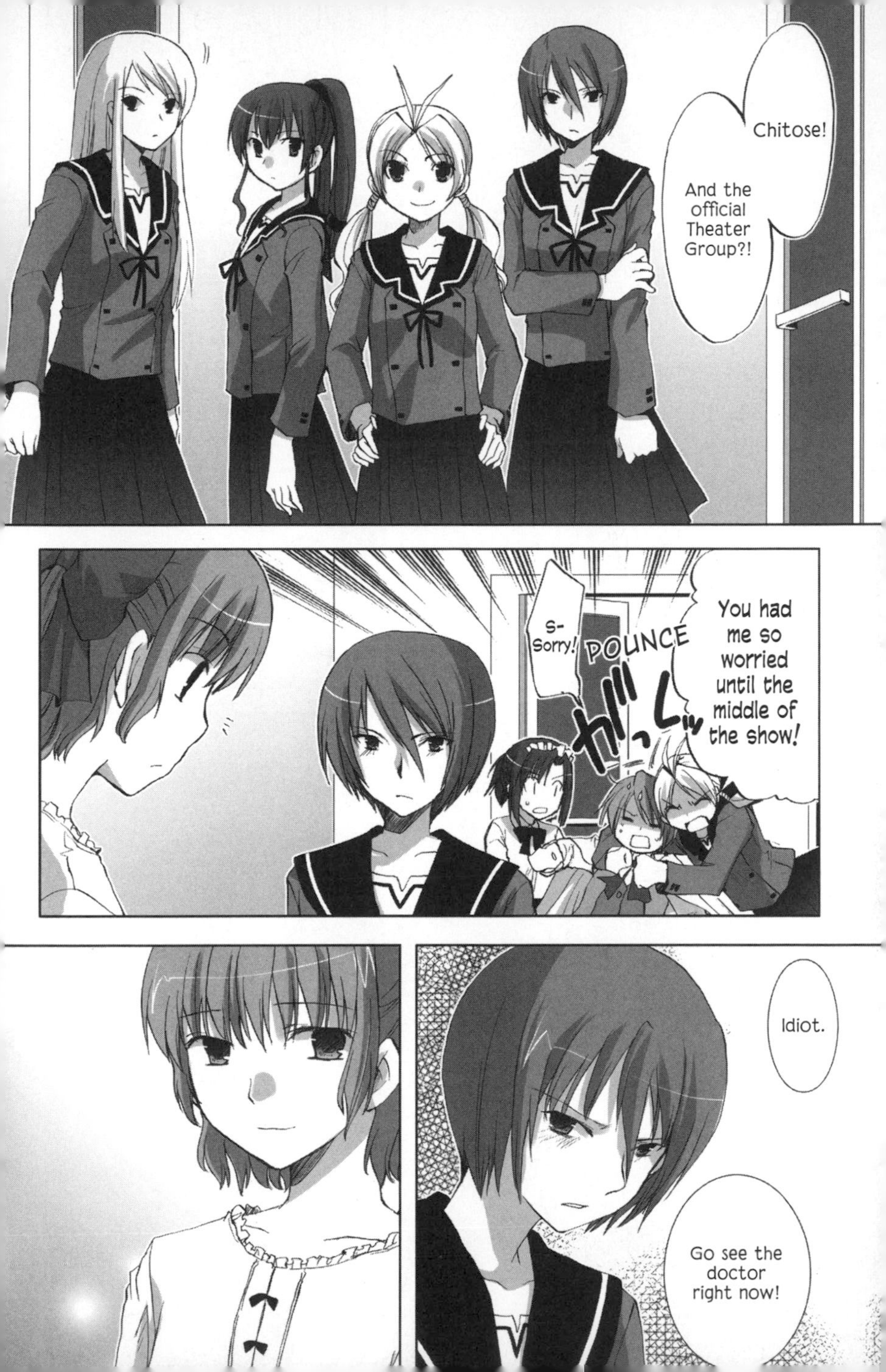
Chitose!
And the official Theater Group?!
You had me so worried until the middle of the show!
POUNCE
S-Sorry!
Idiot.
Go see the doctor right now!

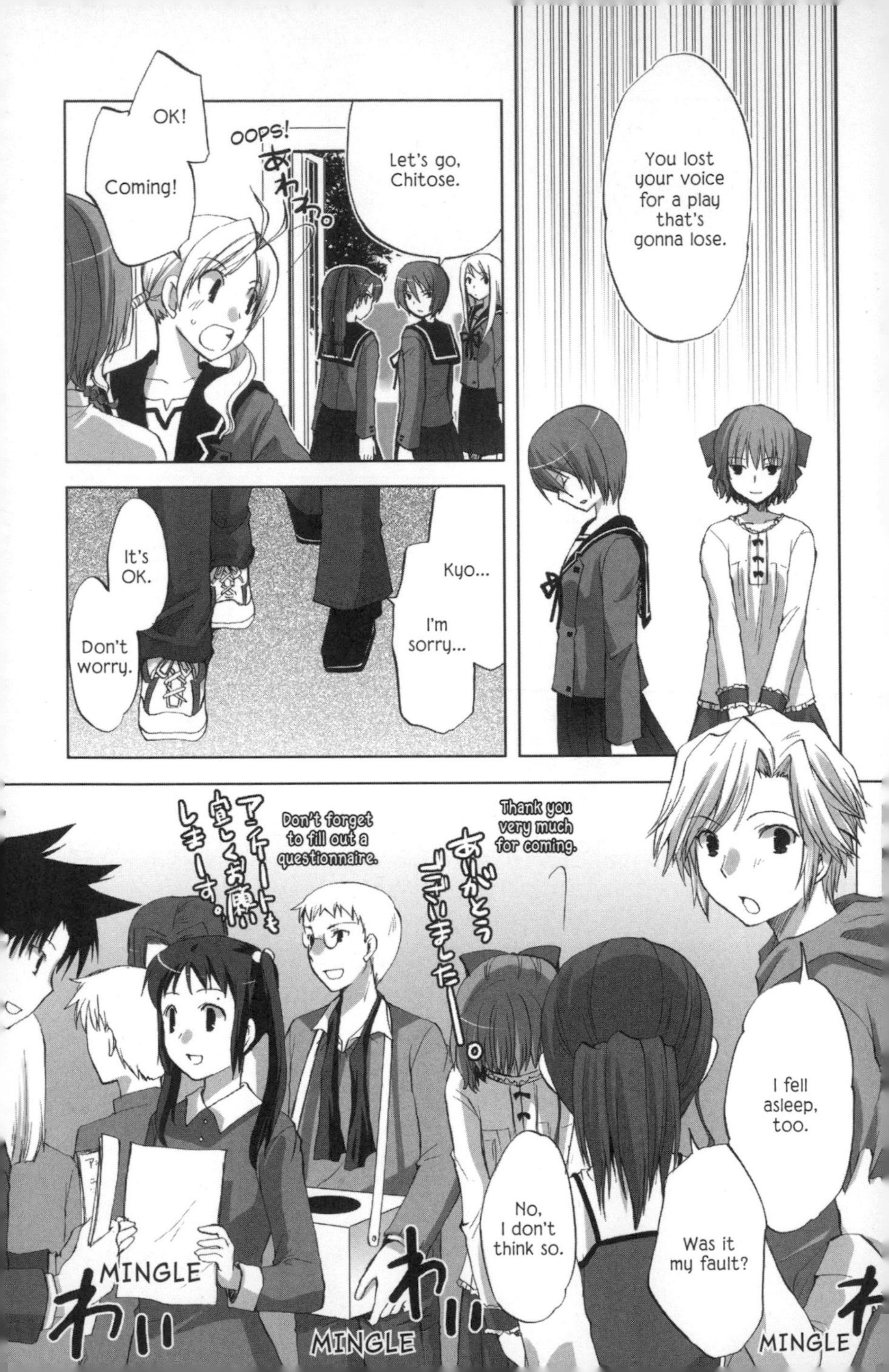
You lost your voice for a play that's gonna lose.
Let's go, Chitose.
OOPS!
あわわ。
OK!
Coming!
Kyo...
I'm sorry...
It's OK.
Don't worry.
Thank you very much for coming.
ありがとうございましたー。
Don't forget to fill out a questionnaire.
アンケートも宜しくお願いしまーす。
I fell asleep, too.
Was it my fault?
No, I don't think so.
MINGLE
MINGLE
MINGLE

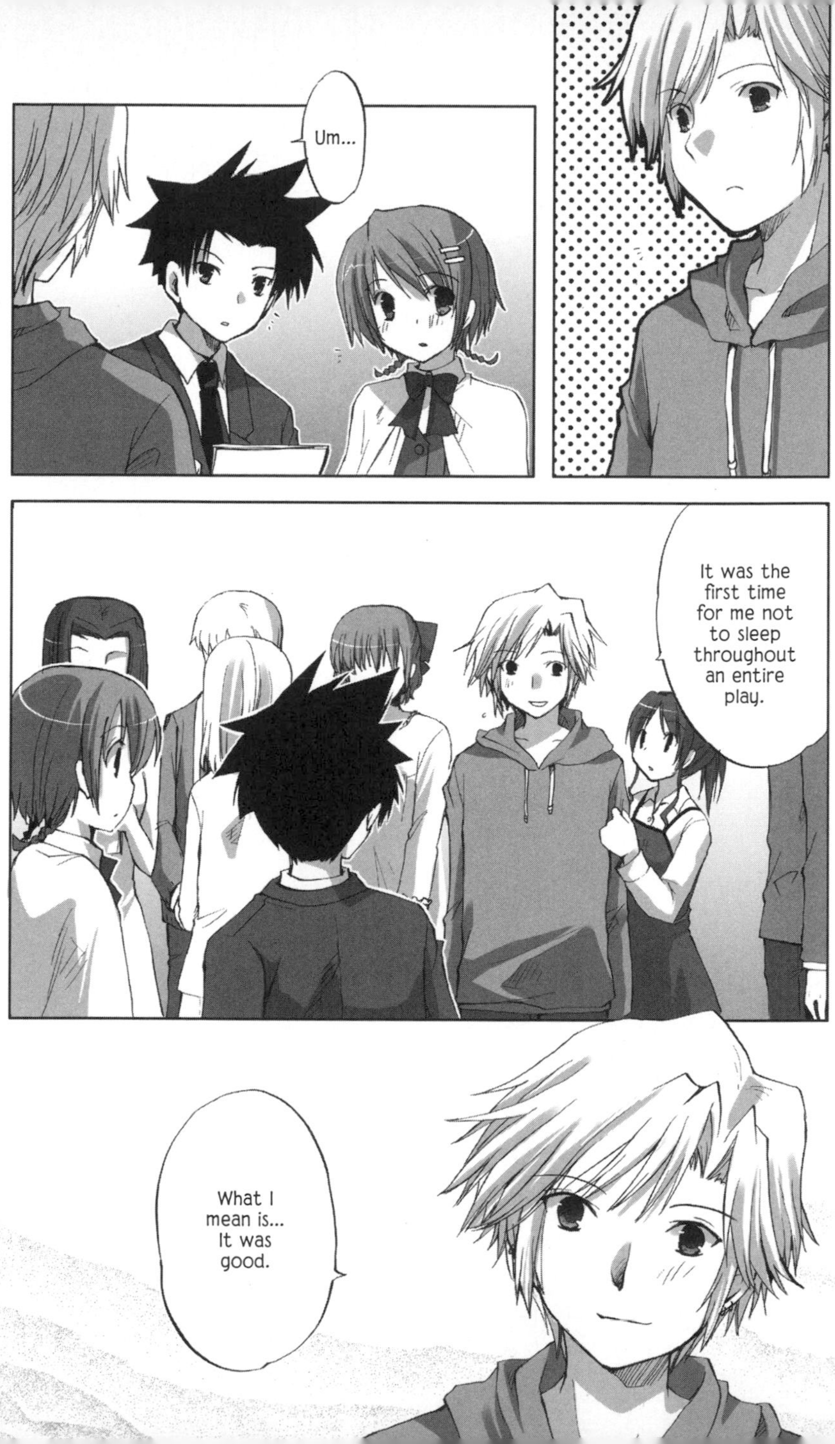
Um...
It was the first time for me not to sleep throughout an entire play.
What I mean is... It was good.

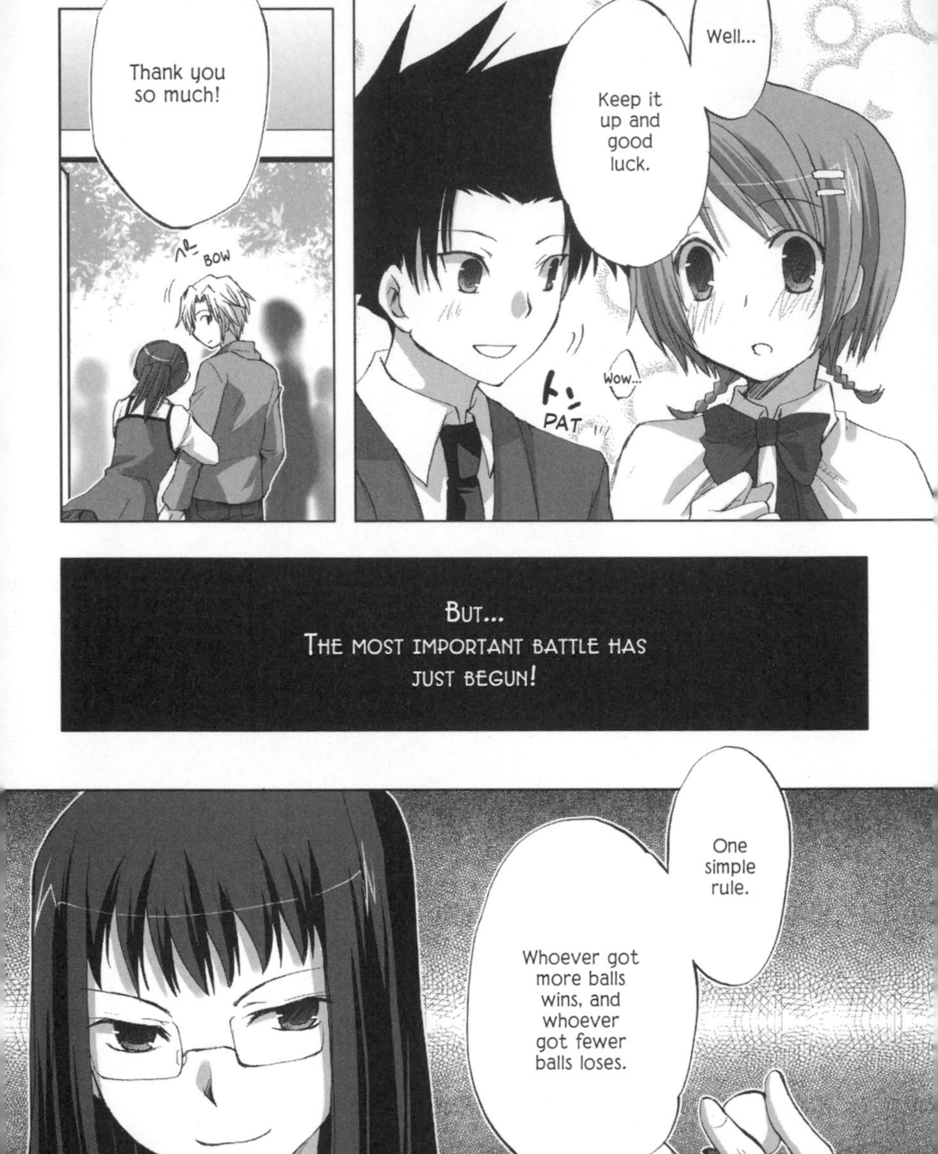
Well...
Keep it up and good luck.
Wow...
PAT
Thank you so much!
BOW
But...
The most important battle has just begun!
One simple rule.
Whoever got more balls wins, and whoever got fewer balls loses.

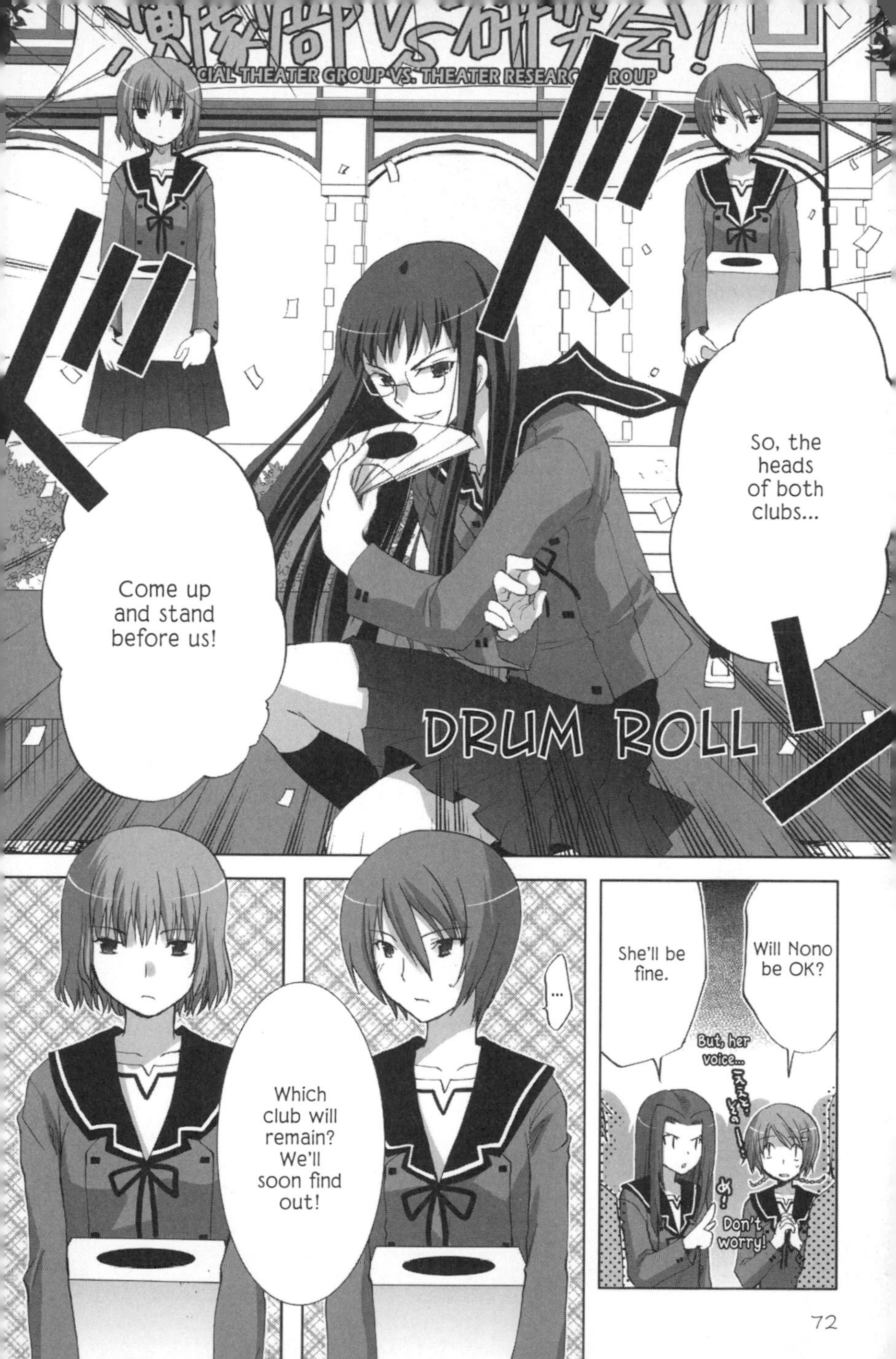
CIAL THEATER GROUP VS. THEATER RESEARC ROUP
So, the heads of both clubs...
Come up and stand before us!
DRUM ROLL
Will Nono be OK?
She'll be fine.
But, her voice...
Don't worry!
...
Which club will remain? We'll soon find out!

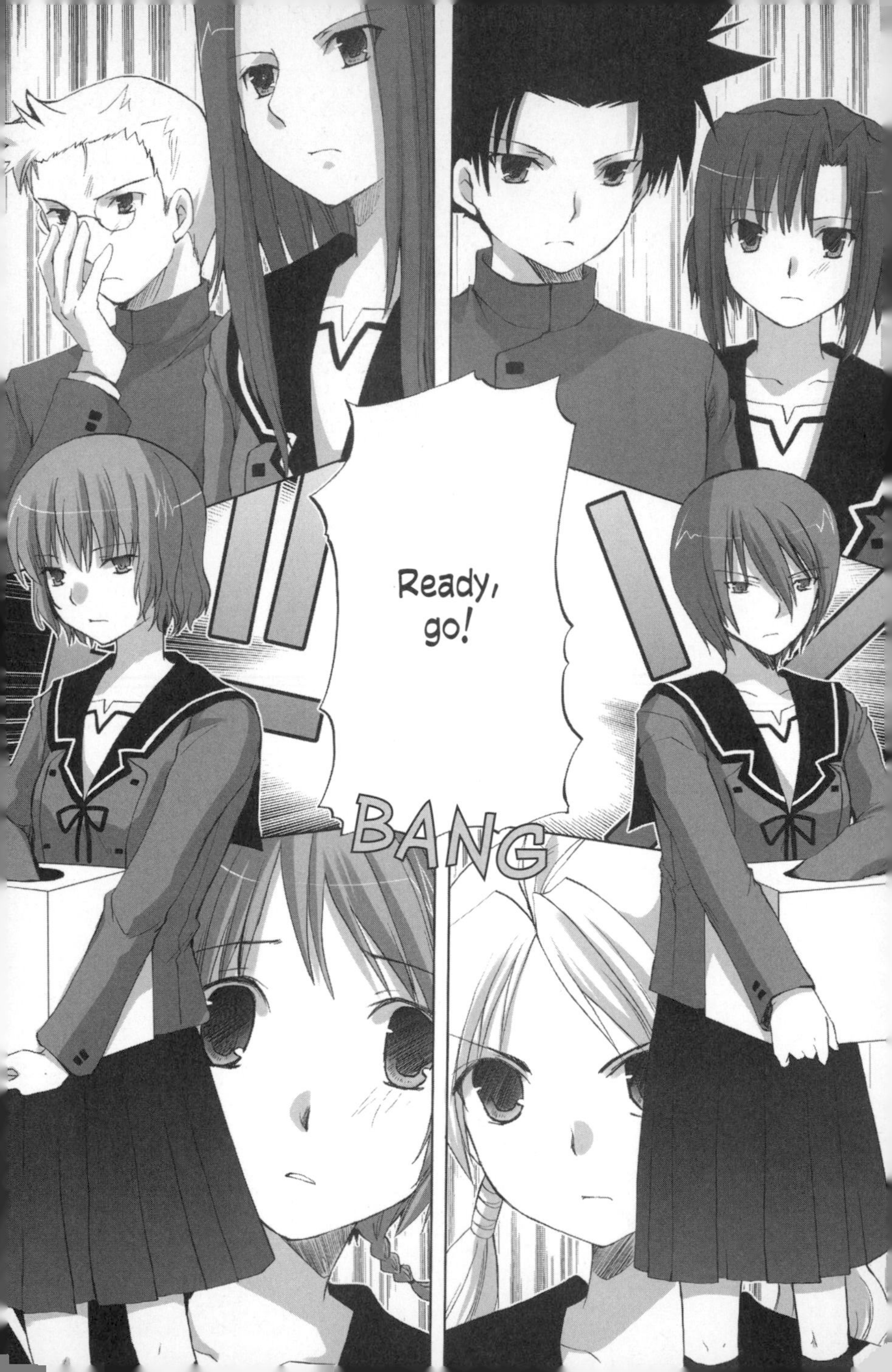
Ready, go!
BANG

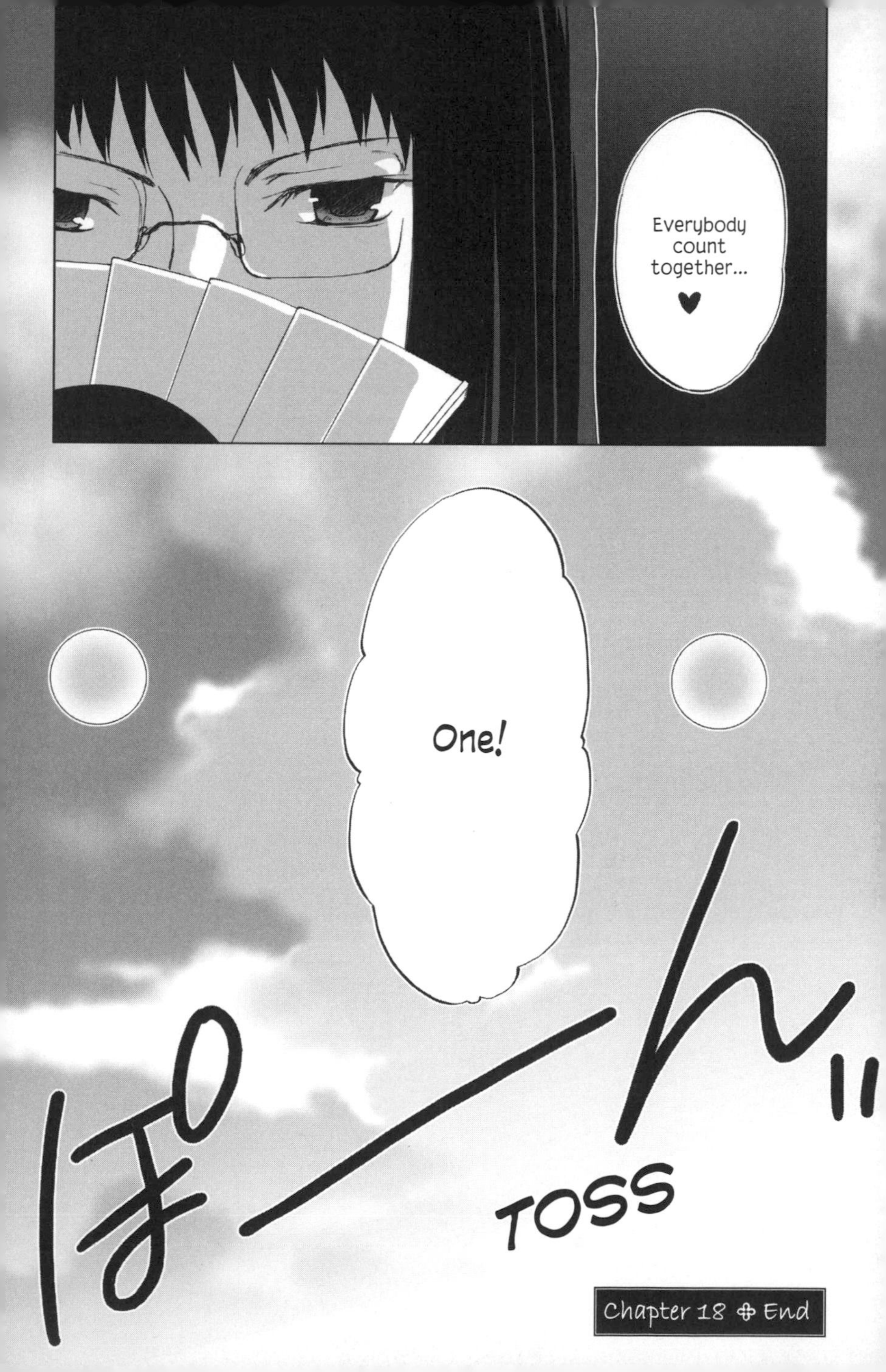
Everybody count together... ♥
One!
ぽーん"
TOSS
Chapter 18 ✤ End

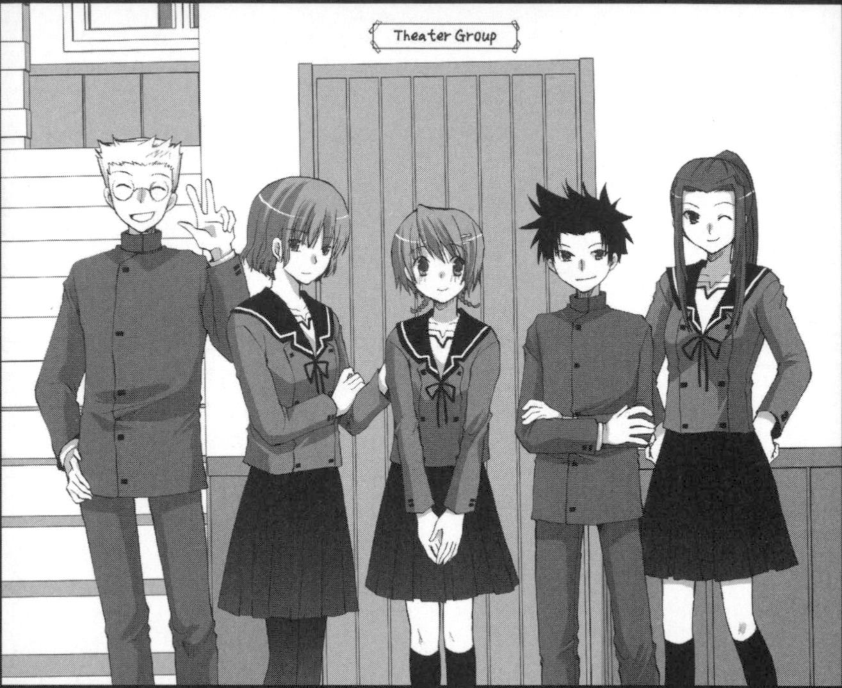
Theater Group

Showdown Chapter 19

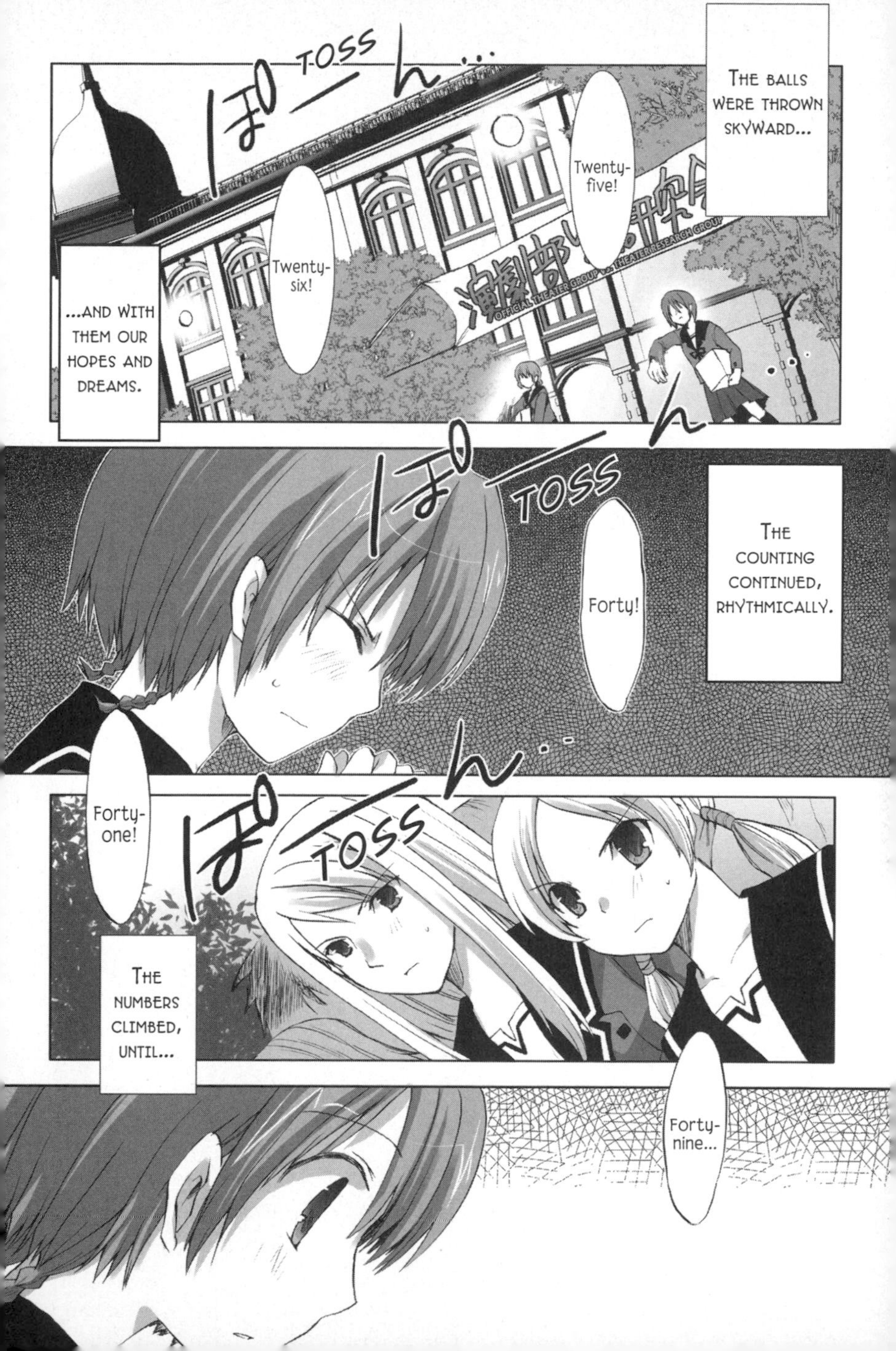

The balls were thrown skyward...
ぽーん…
TOSS
Twenty-five!
OFFICIAL THEATER GROUP
THEATER RESEARCH GROUP
Twenty-six!
...and with them our hopes and dreams.
The counting continued, rhythmically.
ぽーん
TOSS
Forty!
ぽーん…
TOSS
Forty-one!
The numbers climbed, until...
Forty-nine...

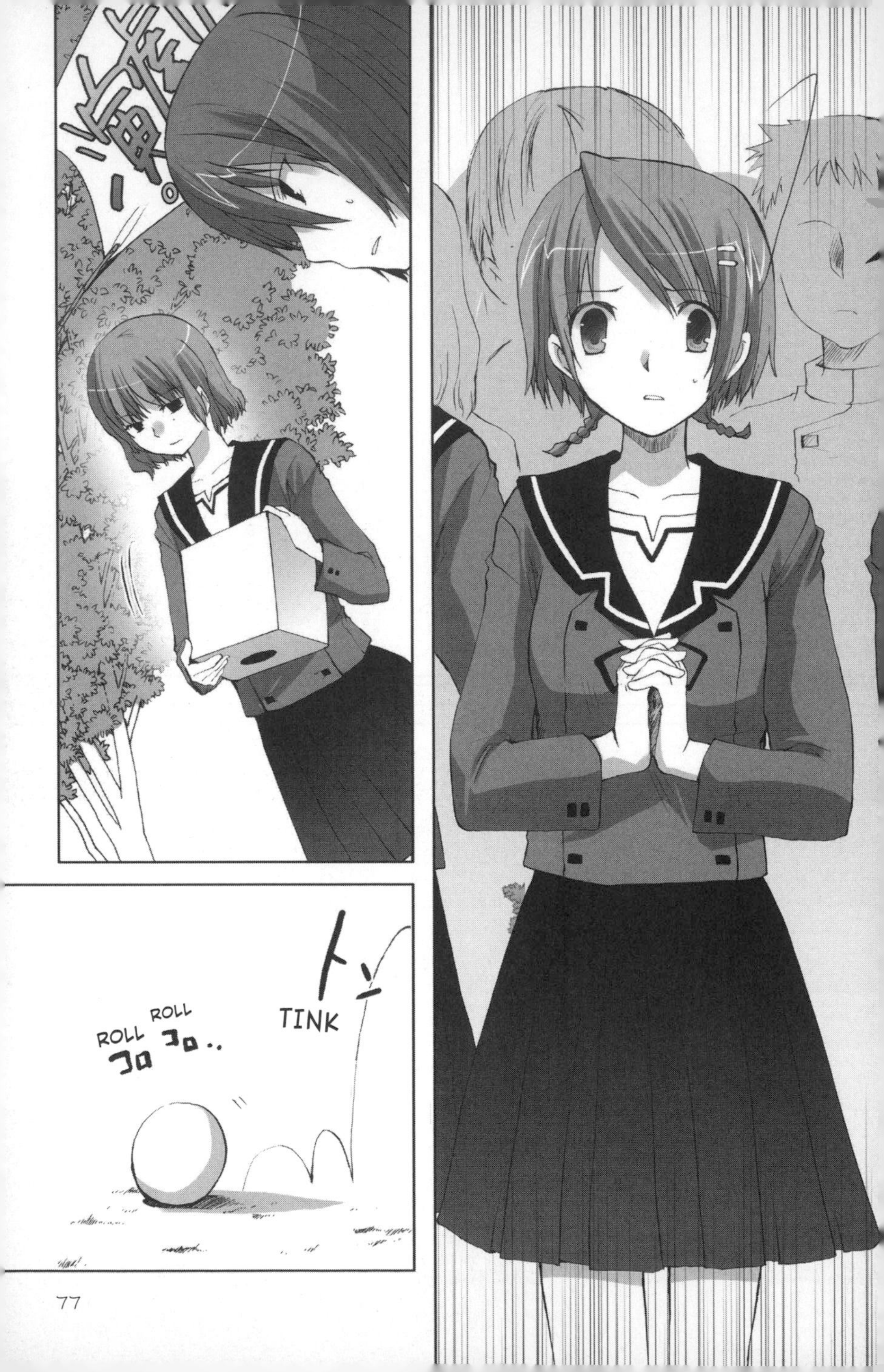
トン
TINK
ROLL ROLL
コロ コロ..

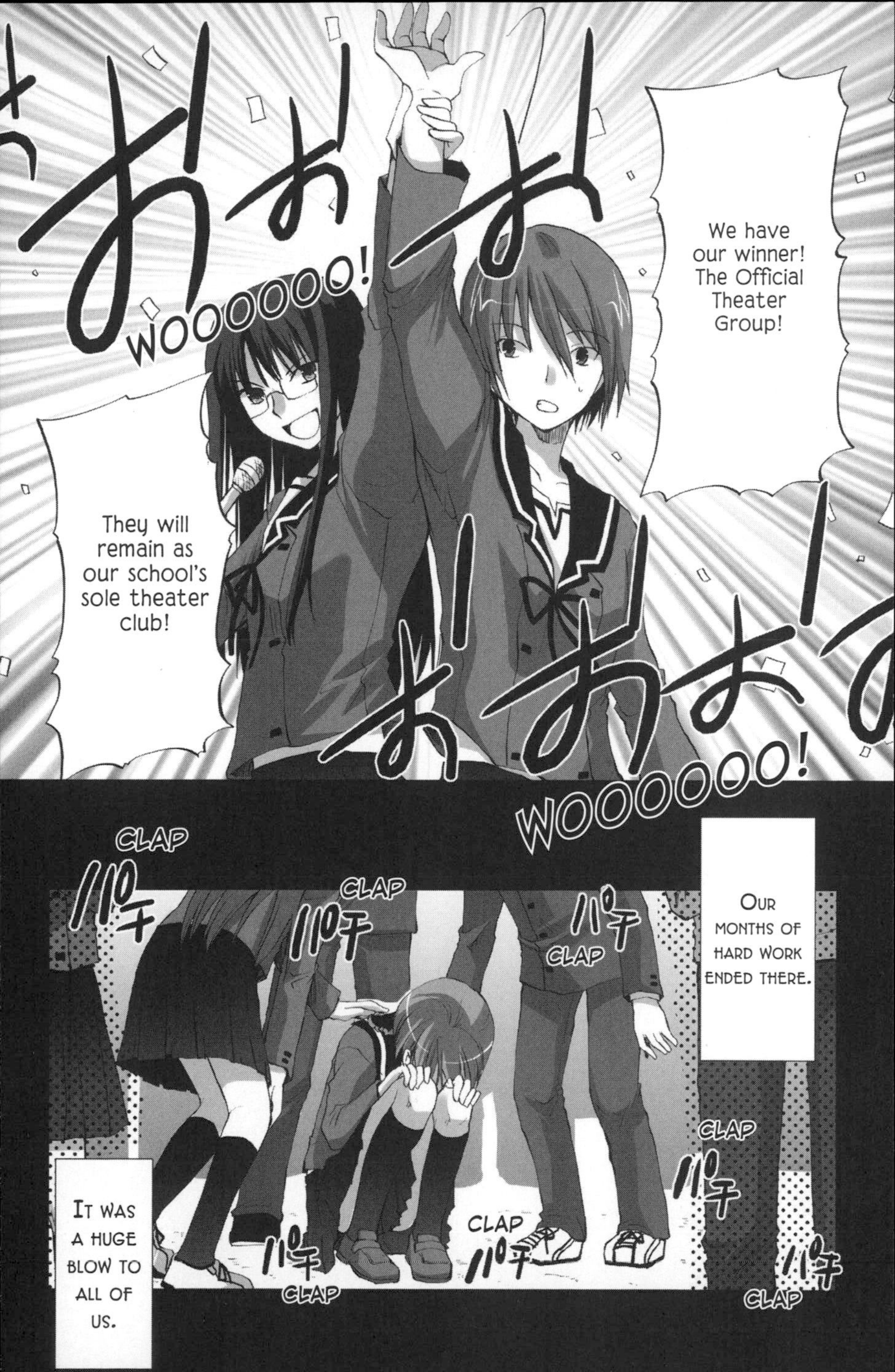
We have our winner! The Official Theater Group!
WOOOOOO!
They will remain as our school's sole theater club!
WOOOOOO!
Our months of hard work ended there.
CLAP
CLAP
CLAP
CLAP
CLAP
CLAP
CLAP
It was a huge blow to all of us.

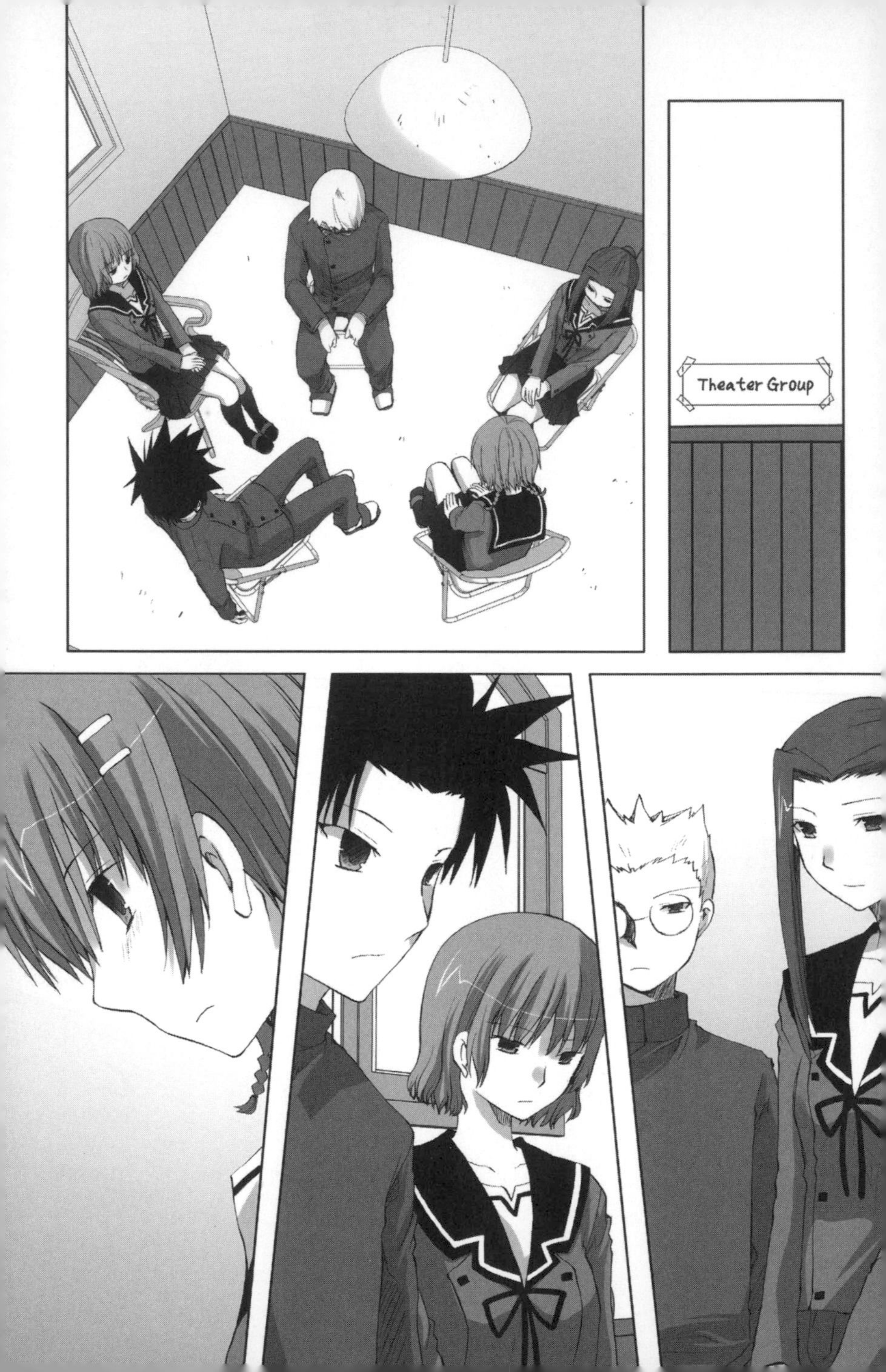
Theater Group

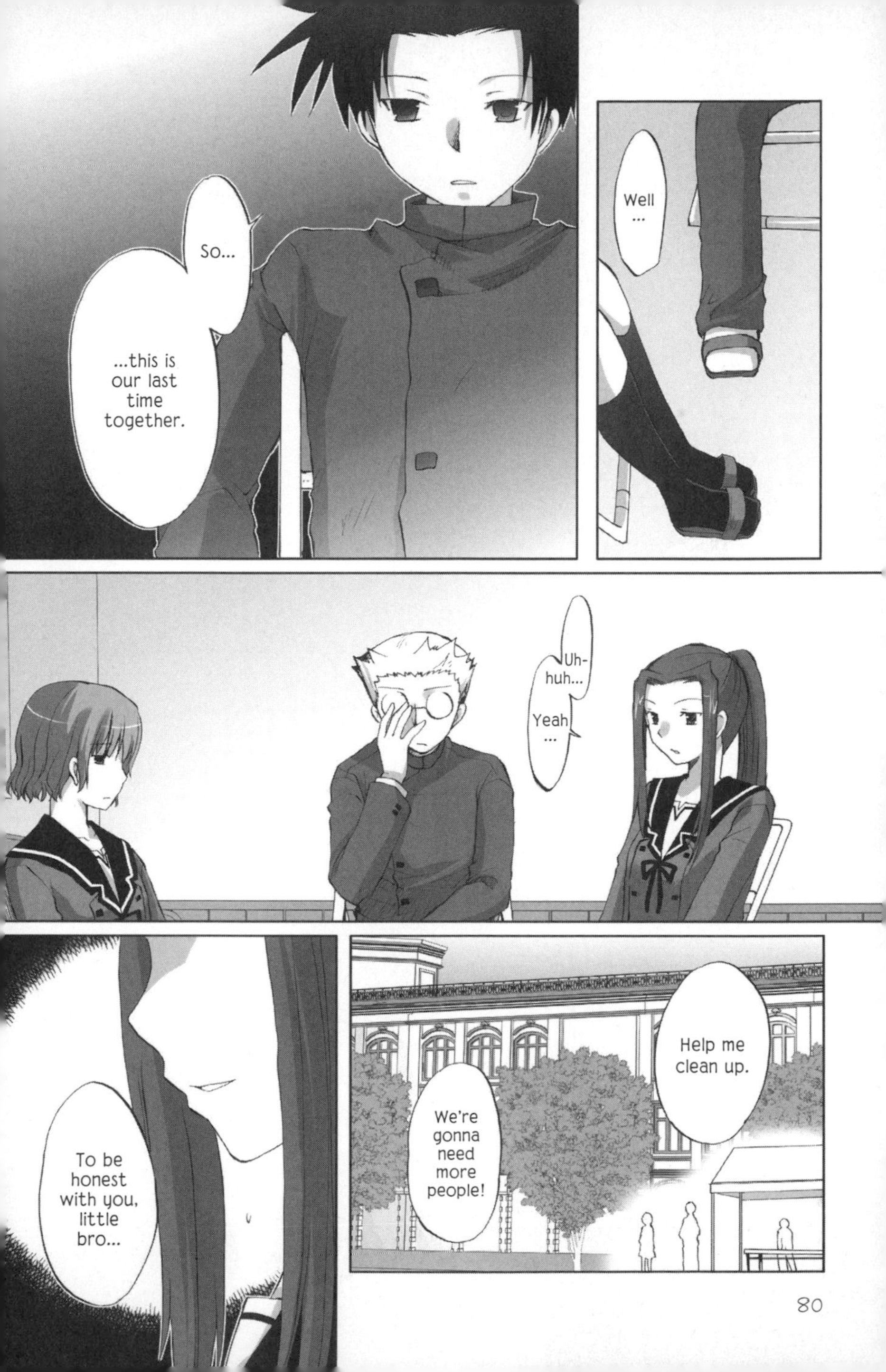
Well ...
So...
...this is our last time together.
Uh-huh...
Yeah ...
Help me clean up.
We're gonna need more people!
To be honest with you, little bro...

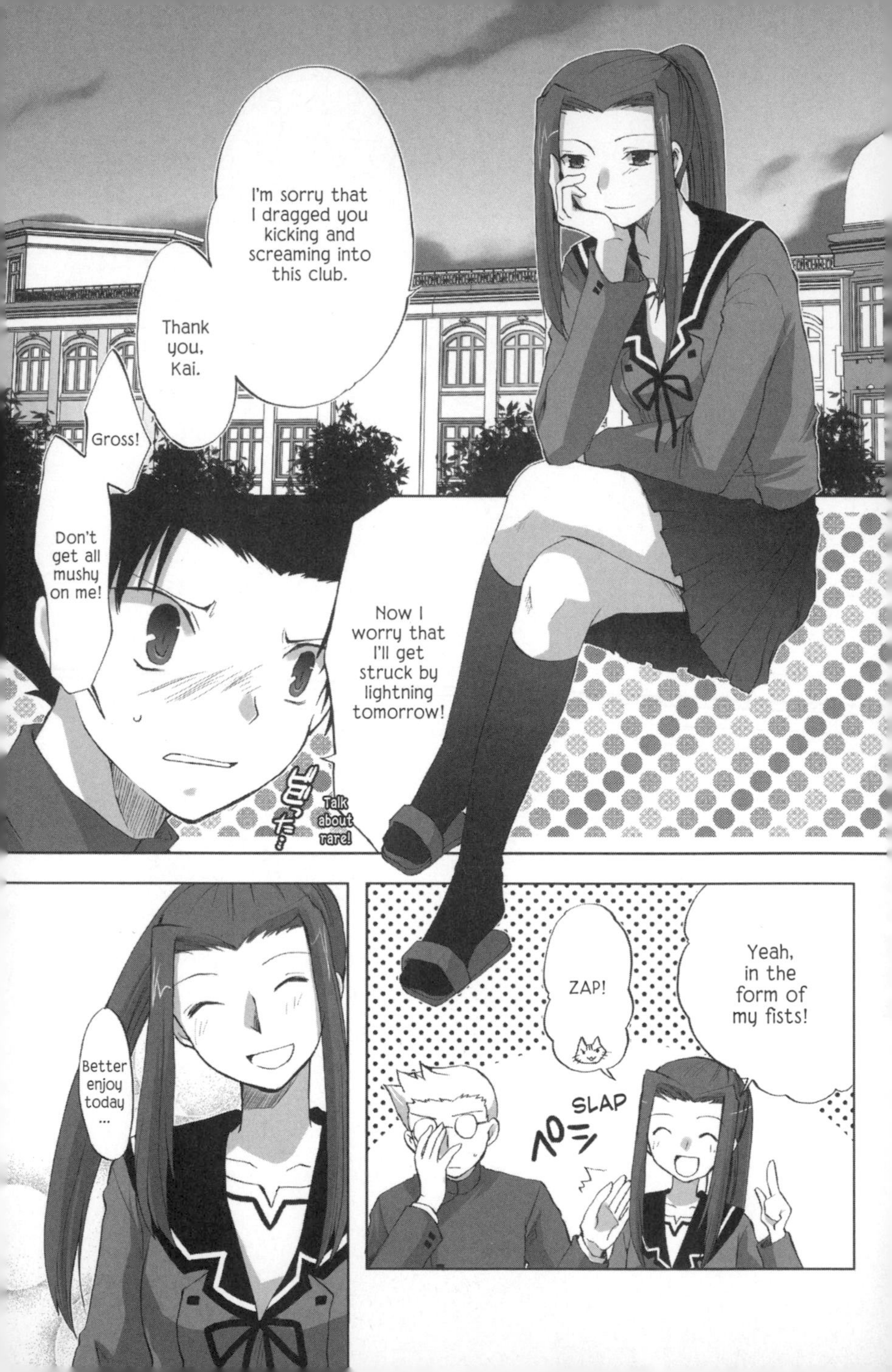
I'm sorry that I dragged you kicking and screaming into this club.
Thank you, Kai.
Gross!
Don't get all mushy on me!
Now I worry that I'll get struck by lightning tomorrow!
Talk about rare!
Yeah, in the form of my fists!
ZAP!
SLAP
Better enjoy today ...

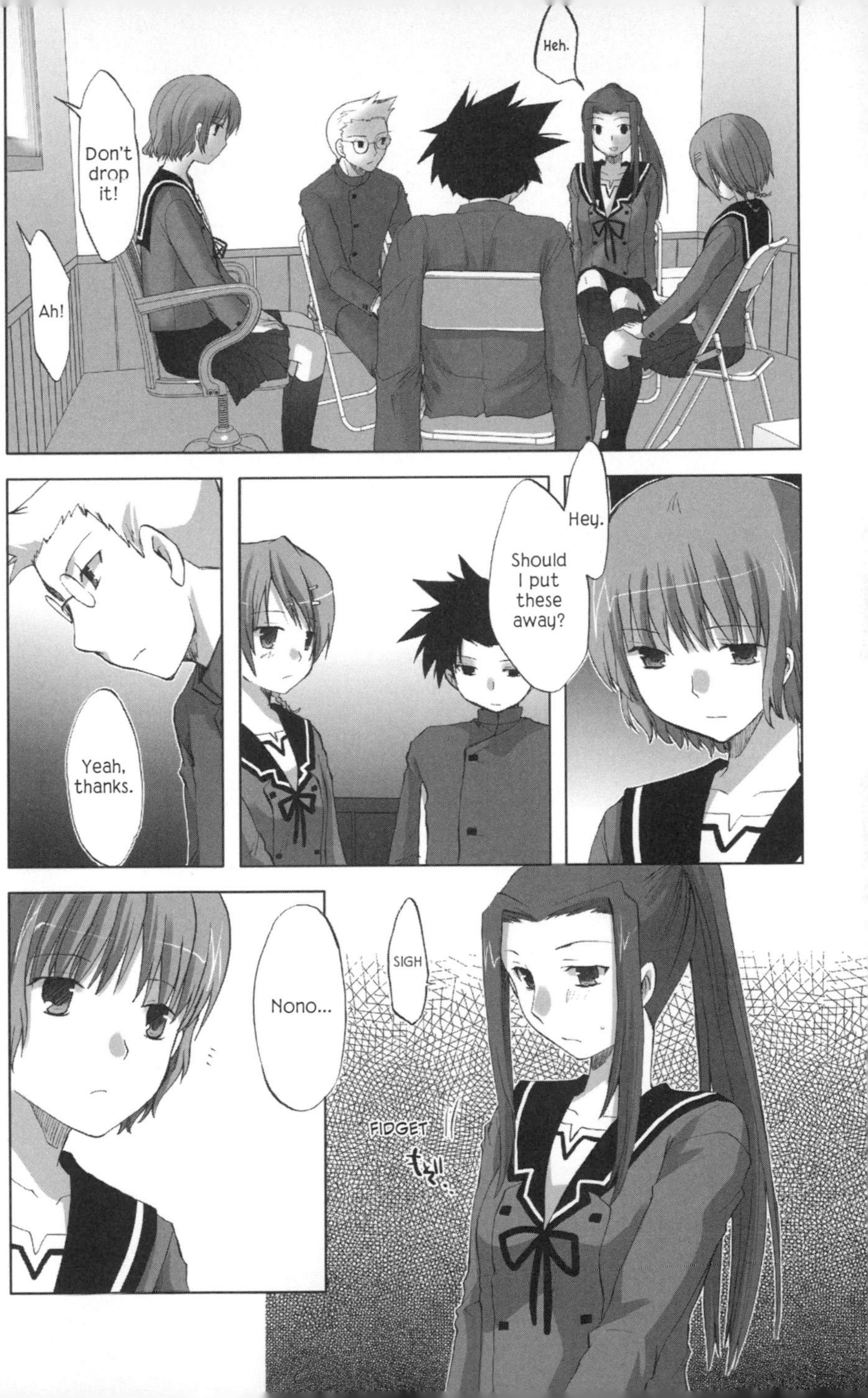
Heh.
Don't drop it!
Ah!
Hey.
Should I put these away?
Yeah, thanks.
SIGH
FIDGET
Nono...

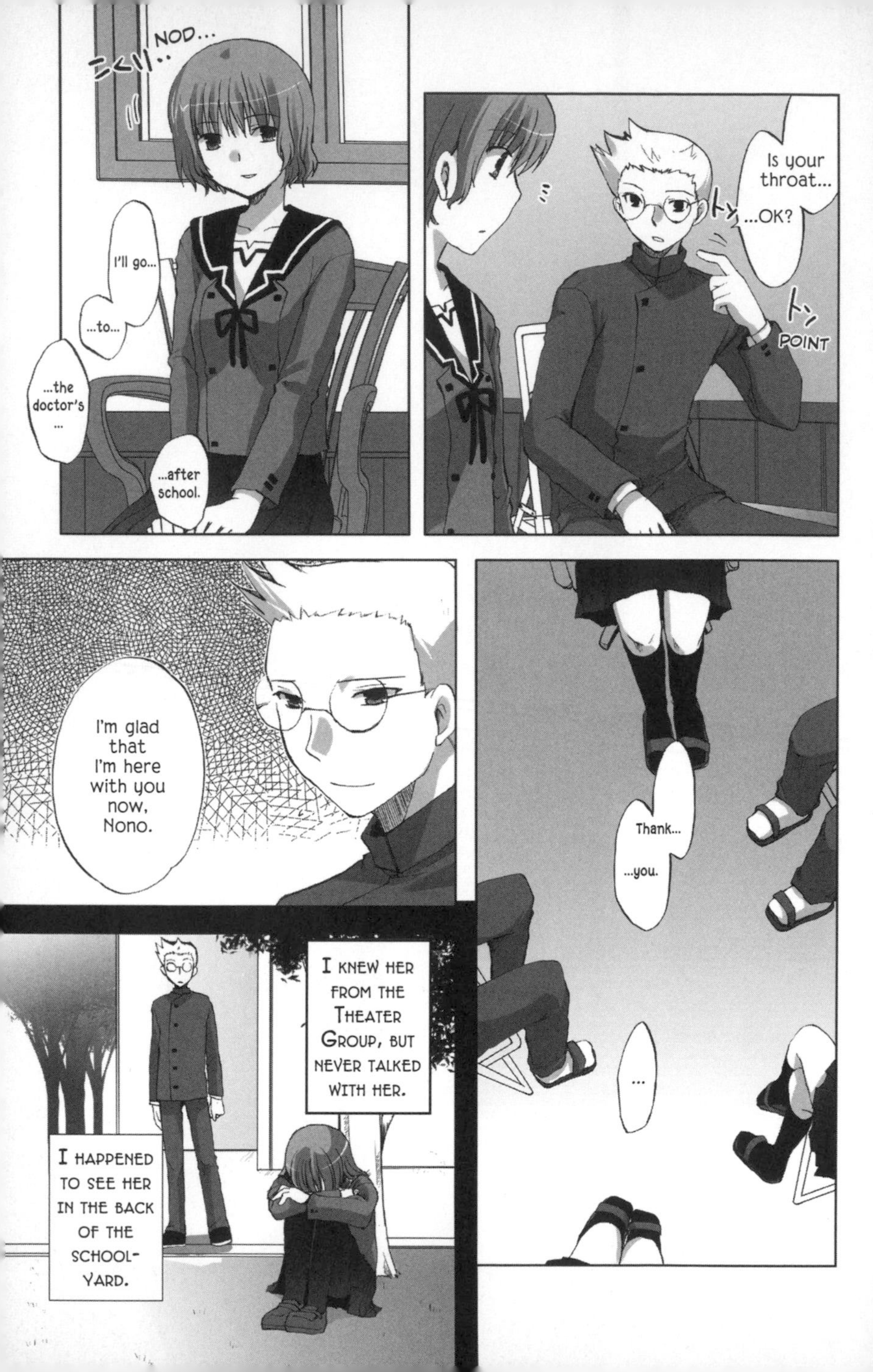
Is your throat...
トン
...OK?
トン
POINT
NOD...
こくり...
I'll go...
...to...
...the doctor's...
...after school.
Thank...
...you.
...
I'm glad that I'm here with you now, Nono.
I knew her from the Theater Group, but never talked with her.
I happened to see her in the back of the school-yard.

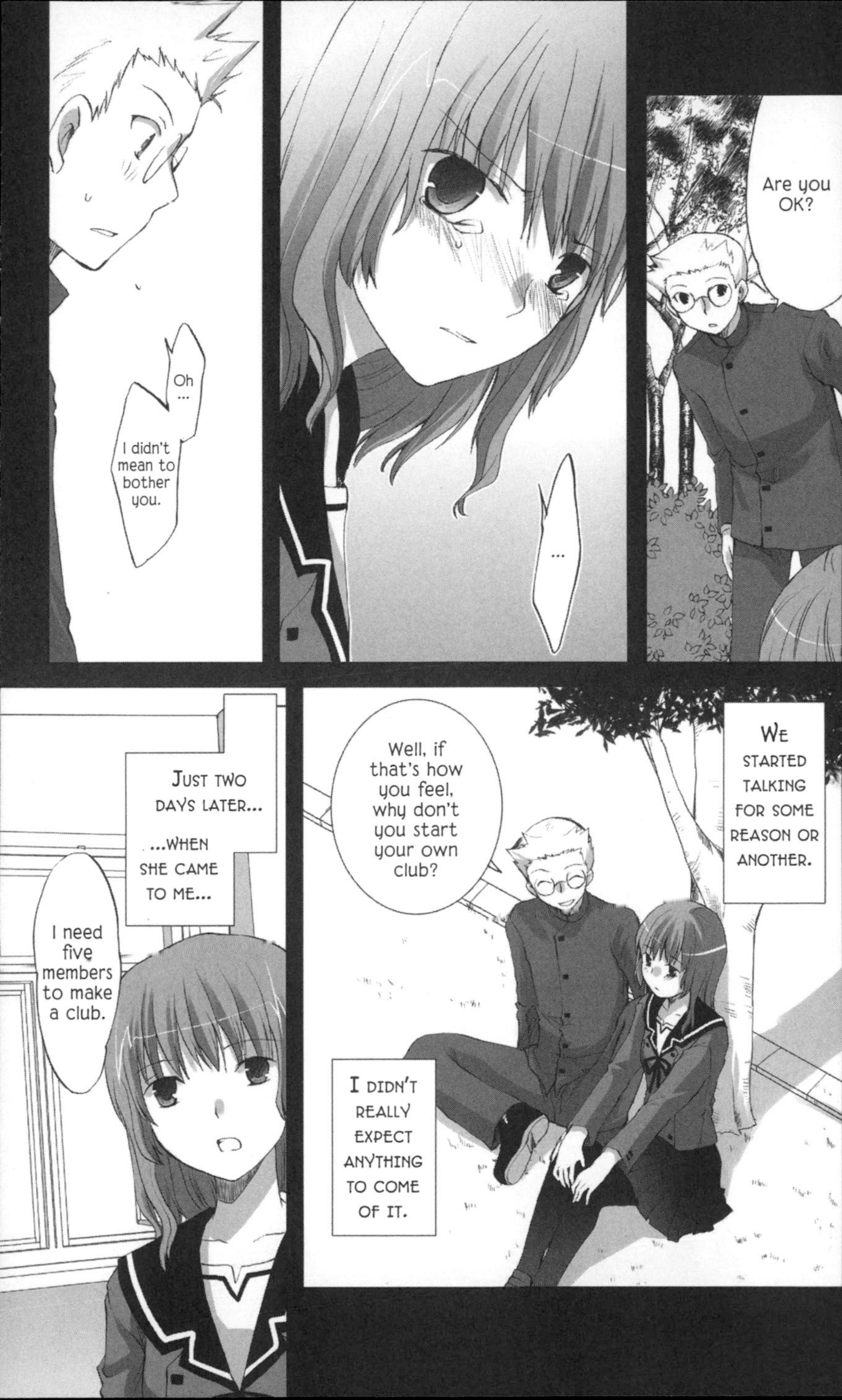
Are you OK?
...
Oh ...
I didn't mean to bother you.
We started talking for some reason or another.
Well, if that's how you feel, why don't you start your own club?
I didn't really expect anything to come of it.
Just two days later...
...when she came to me...
I need five members to make a club.

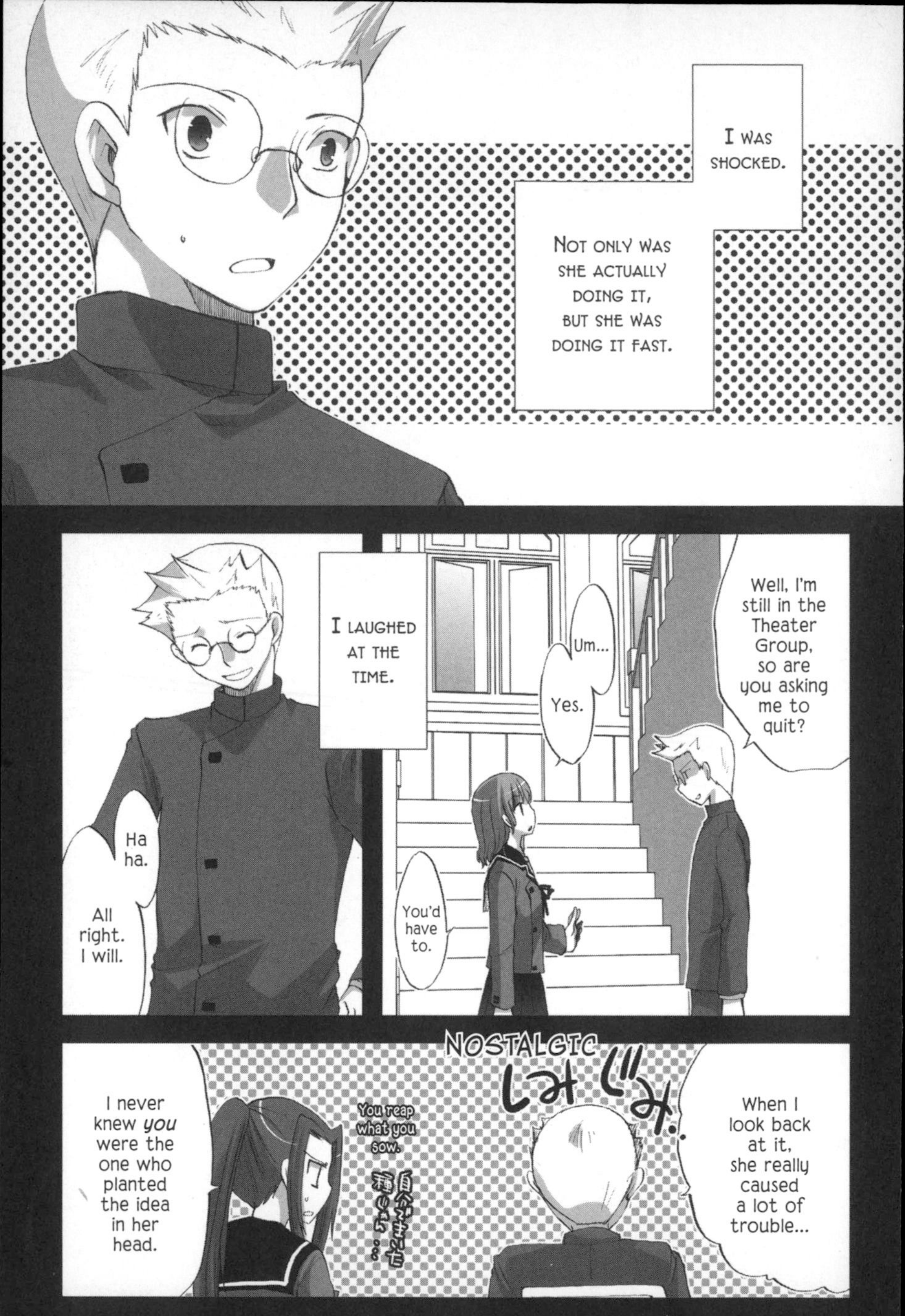

I was shocked.
Not only was she actually doing it, but she was doing it fast.
Well, I'm still in the Theater Group, so are you asking me to quit?
Um...
Yes.
You'd have to.
I laughed at the time.
Ha ha.
All right. I will.
When I look back at it, she really caused a lot of trouble...
NOSTALGIC
しみじみ。
You reap what you sow.
自分がまいた種から・・
I never knew *you* were the one who planted the idea in her head.

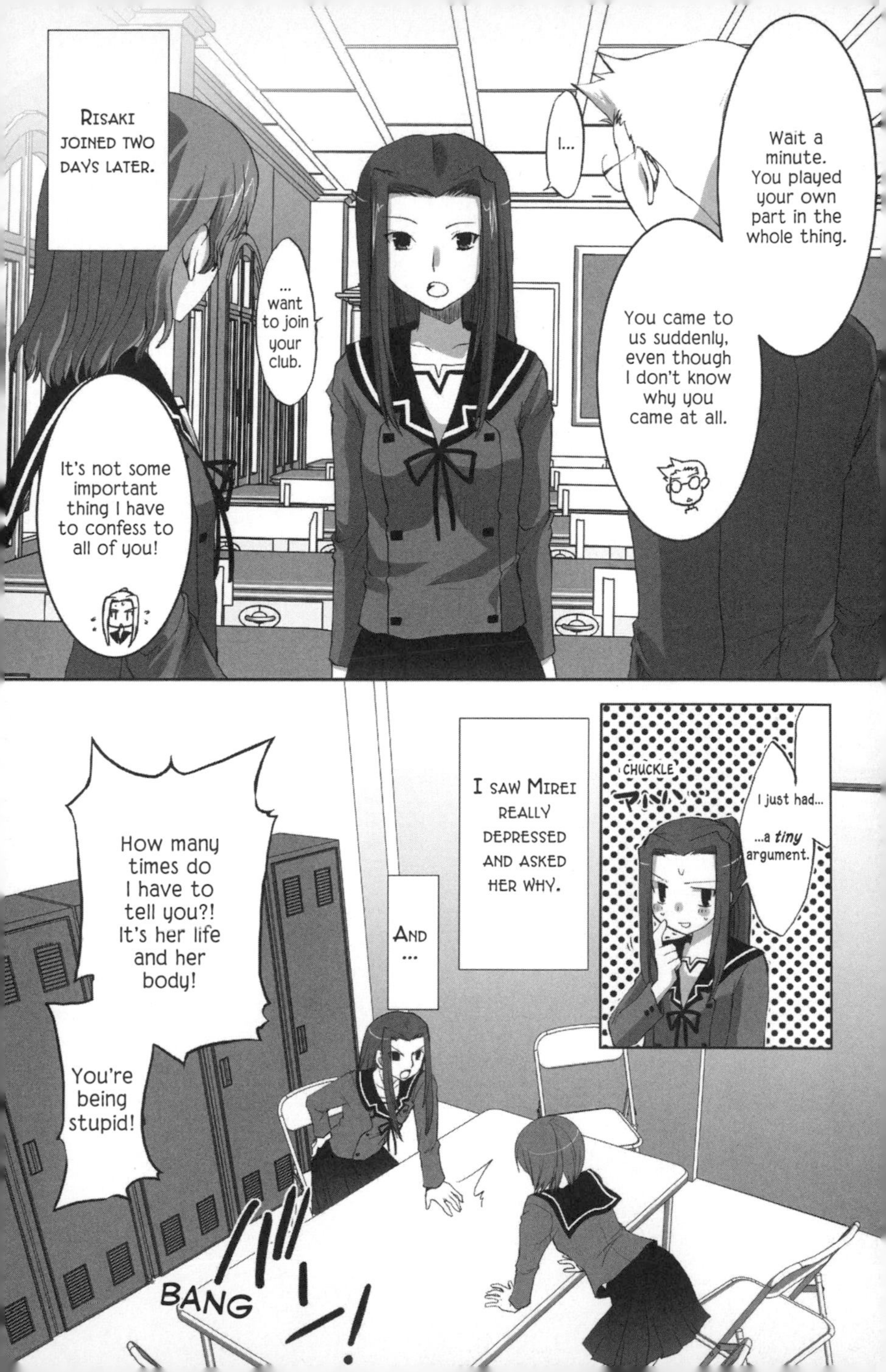
Wait a minute. You played your own part in the whole thing.
I...
You came to us suddenly, even though I don't know why you came at all.
... want to join your club.
Risaki joined two days later.
It's not some important thing I have to confess to all of you!
CHUCKLE
I just had... ...a *tiny* argument.
I saw Mirei really depressed and asked her why.
And ...
How many times do I have to tell you?! It's her life and her body!
You're being stupid!
BANG

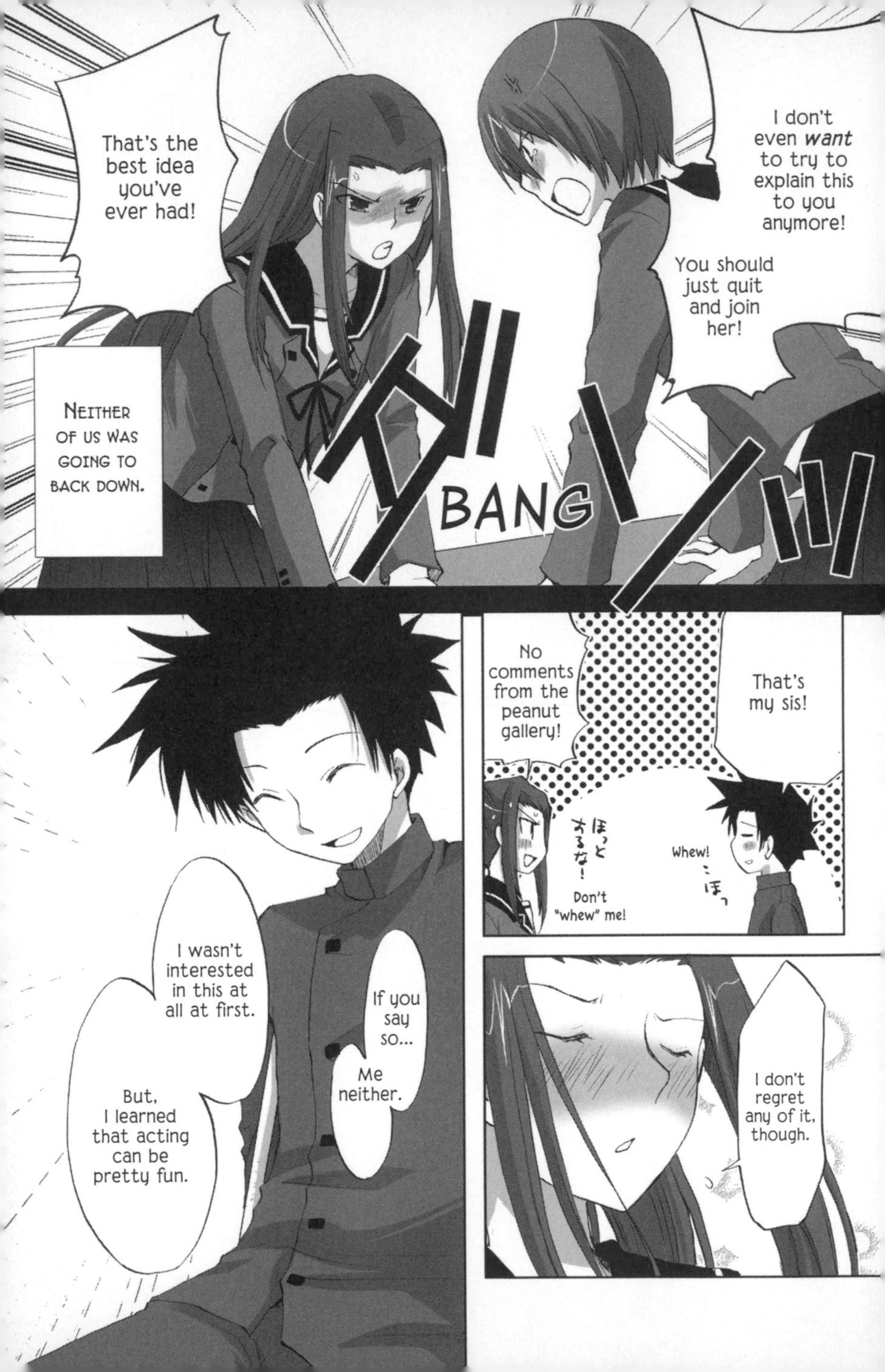
I don't even *want* to try to explain this to you anymore!
You should just quit and join her!
That's the best idea you've ever had!
NEITHER OF US WAS GOING TO BACK DOWN.
BANG
That's my sis!
No comments from the peanut gallery!
Whew!
こほっ
ほっとするな!
Don't "whew" me!
I don't regret any of it, though.
I wasn't interested in this at all at first.
If you say so...
But, I learned that acting can be pretty fun.
Me neither.

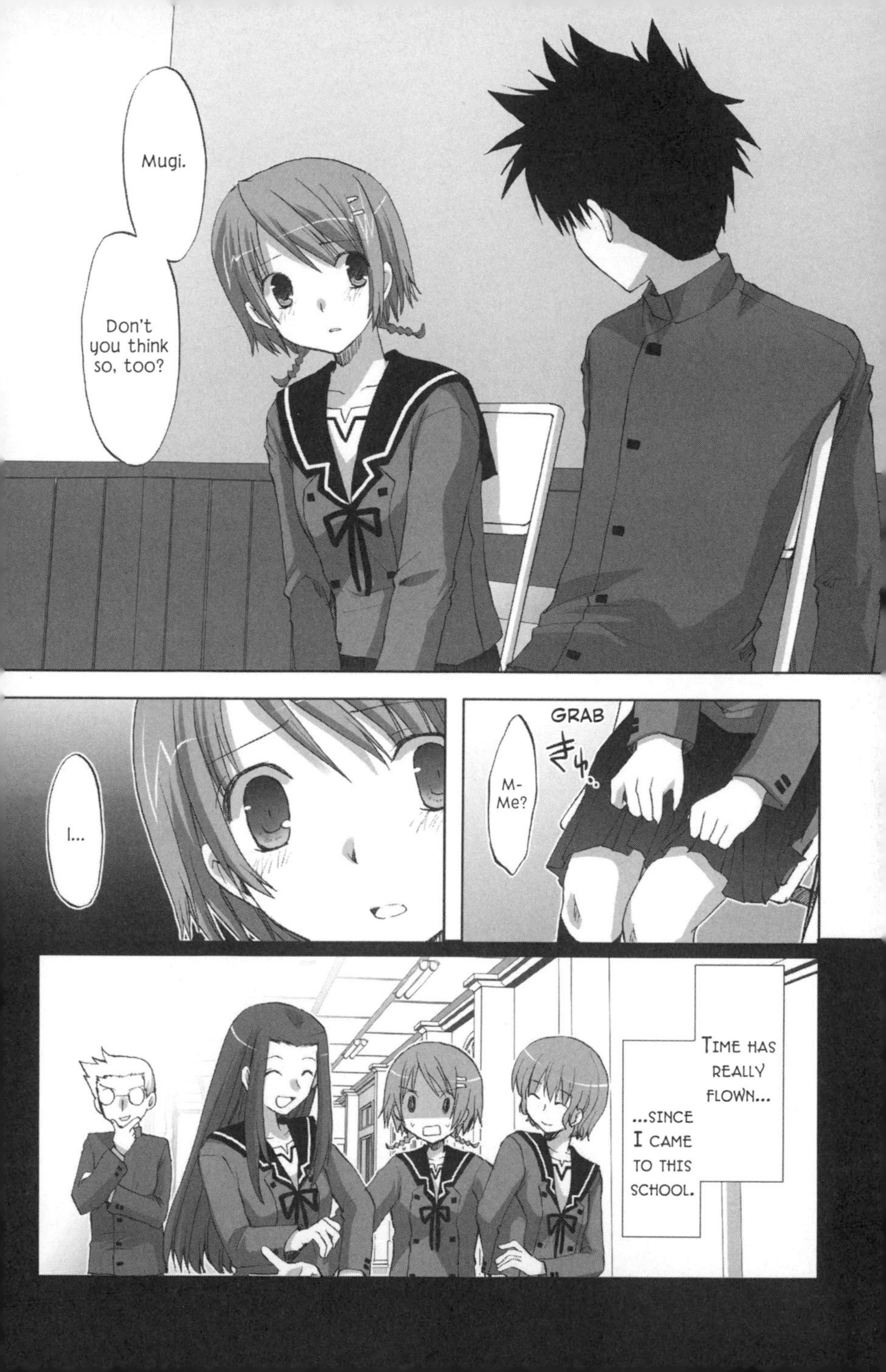
Mugi.
Don't you think so, too?
GRAB
きゅ
M-Me?
I...
Time has really flown...
...since I came to this school.

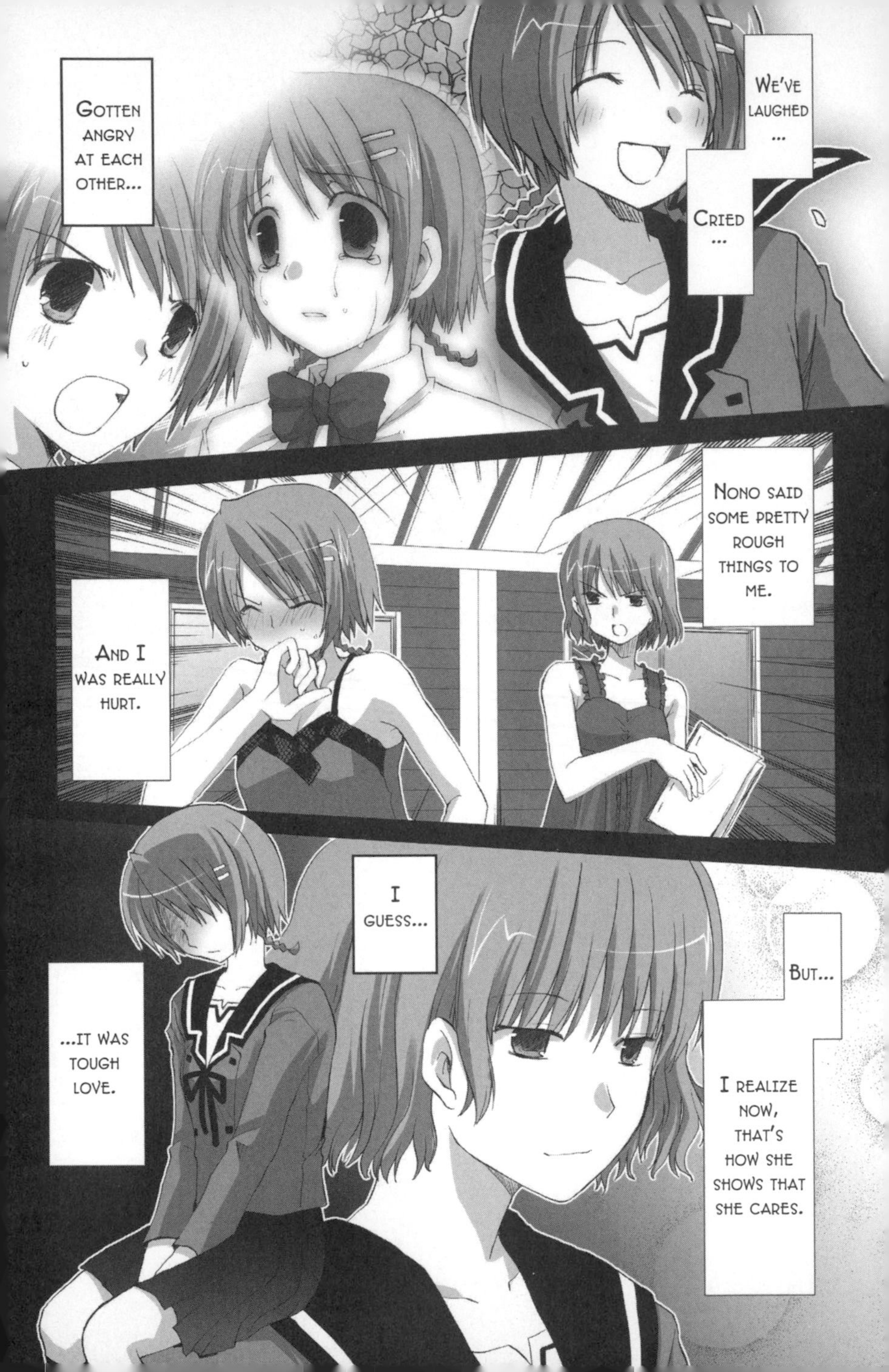
We've laughed...
Cried...
Gotten angry at each other...
Nono said some pretty rough things to me.
And I was really hurt.
But...
I realize now, that's how she shows that she cares.
I guess...
...it was tough love.

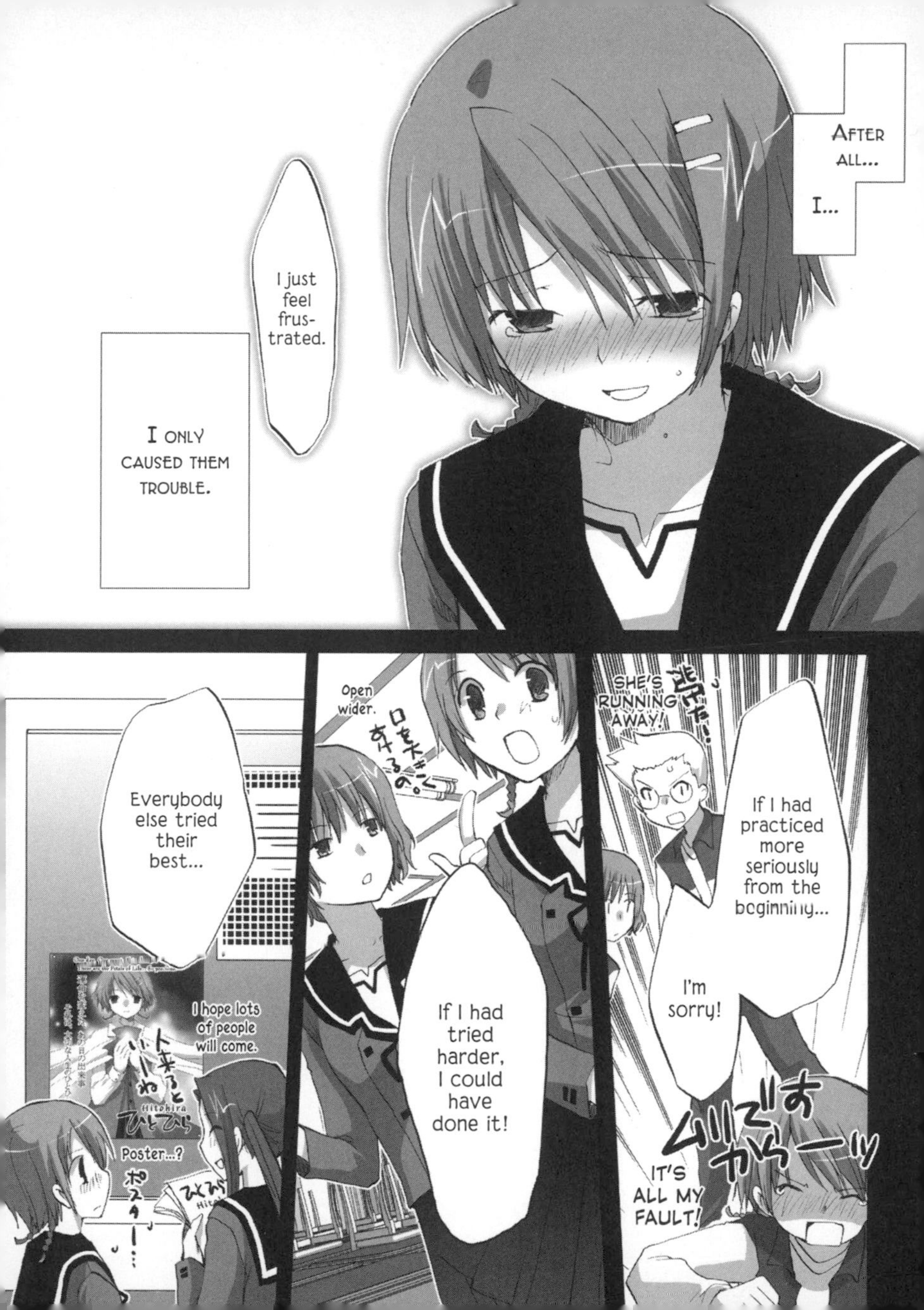

After all...
I...
I just feel frustrated.
I only caused them trouble.
SHE'S RUNNING AWAY!
逃げた!
If I had practiced more seriously from the beginning...
I'm sorry!
ムリですから—ッ
IT'S ALL MY FAULT!
Open wider.
口を大きくあけるの。
If I had tried harder, I could have done it!
Everybody else tried their best...
Hitohira
ひとひら
I hope lots of people will come.
来るといいーね
Poster...?
ポスター…

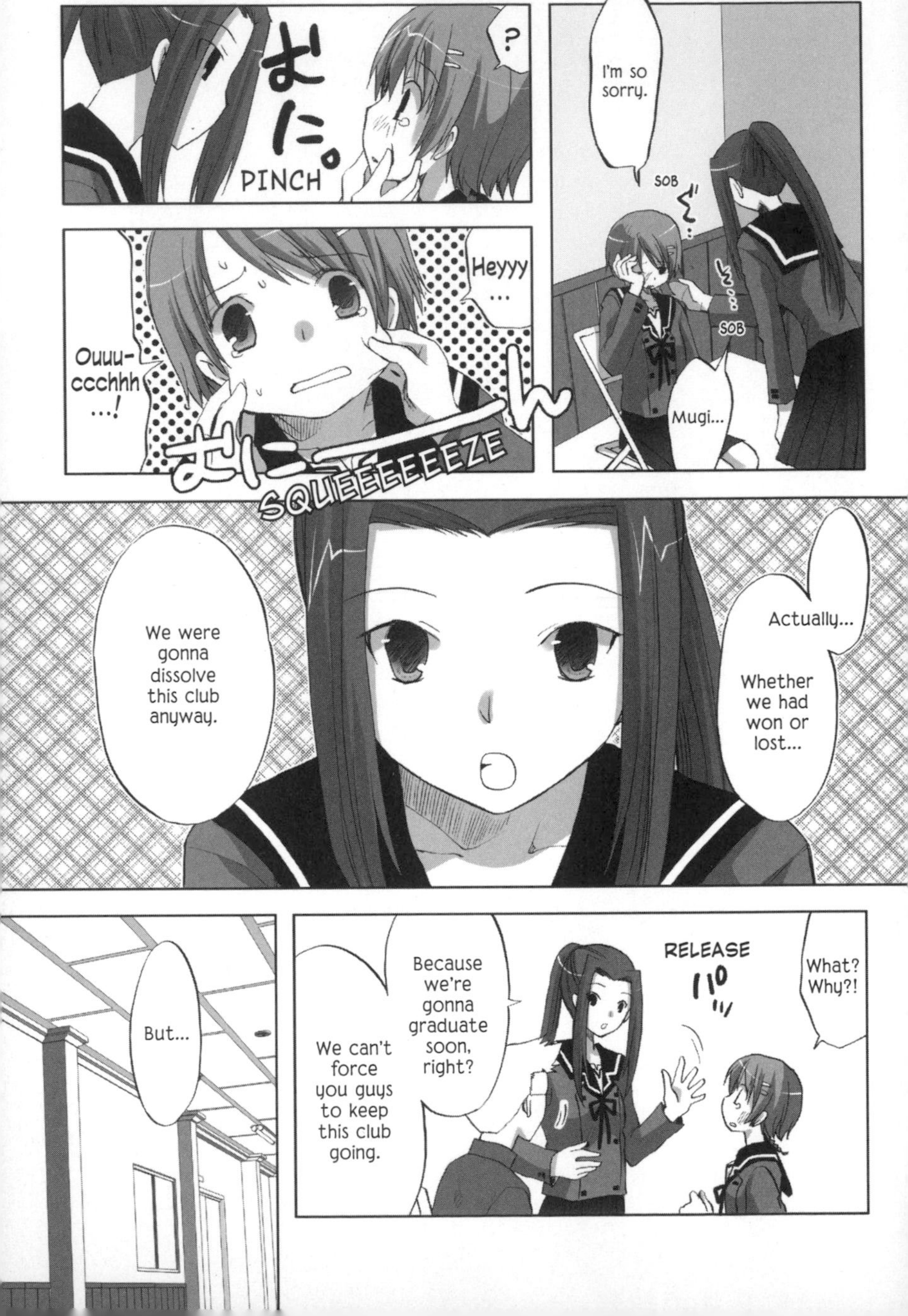

I'm so sorry.
SOB
SOB
Mugi...
?
PINCH
Heyyy ...
Ouuu-ccchhh ...!
SQUEEEEEEEZE
Actually...
Whether we had won or lost...
We were gonna dissolve this club anyway.
What? Why?!
RELEASE
Because we're gonna graduate soon, right?
We can't force you guys to keep this club going.
But...

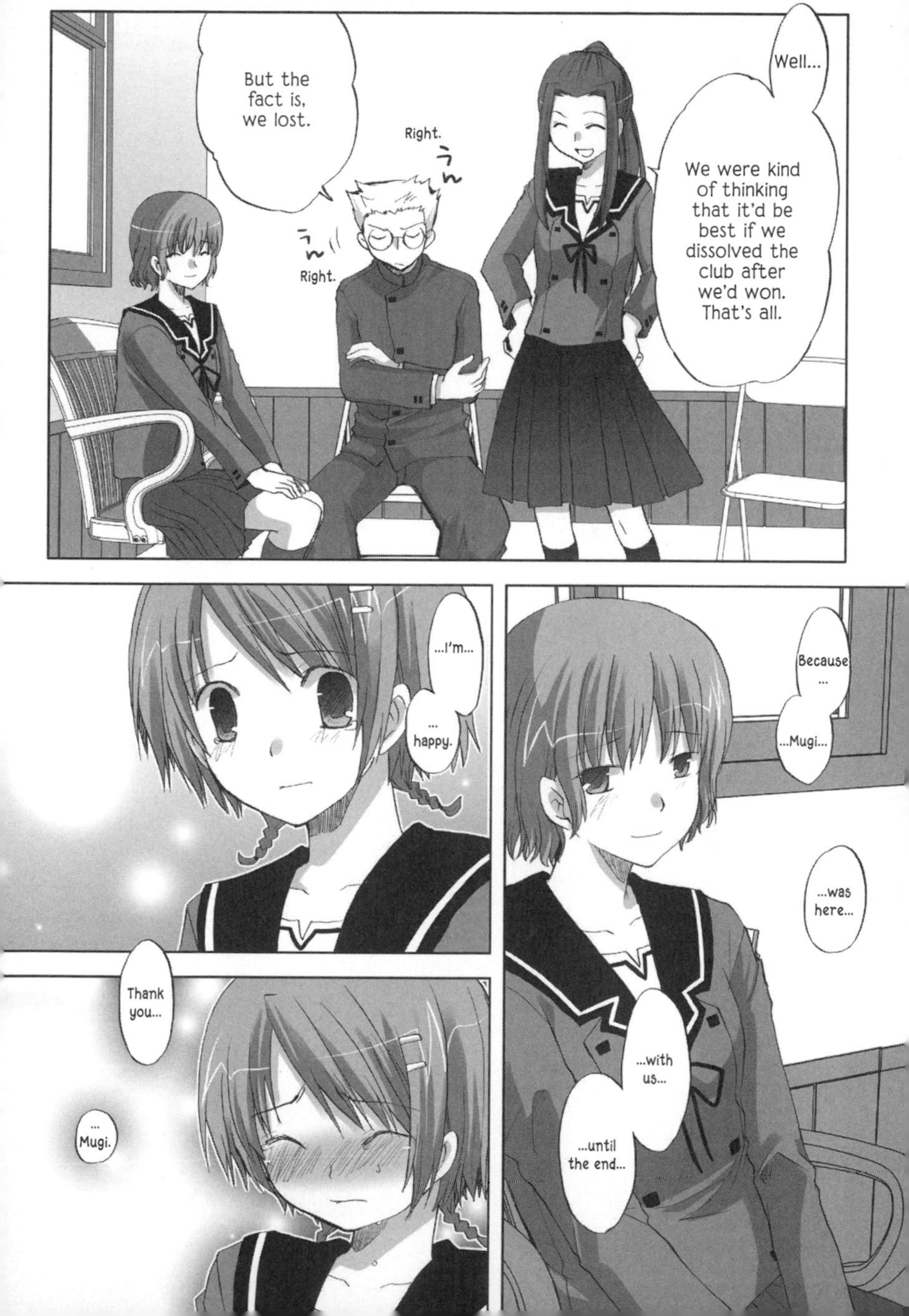
Well...
We were kind of thinking that it'd be best if we dissolved the club after we'd won. That's all.
Right.
うん
うん
Right.
But the fact is, we lost.
Because...
...Mugi...
...was here...
...with us...
...until the end...
...I'm...
... happy.
Thank you...
... Mugi.

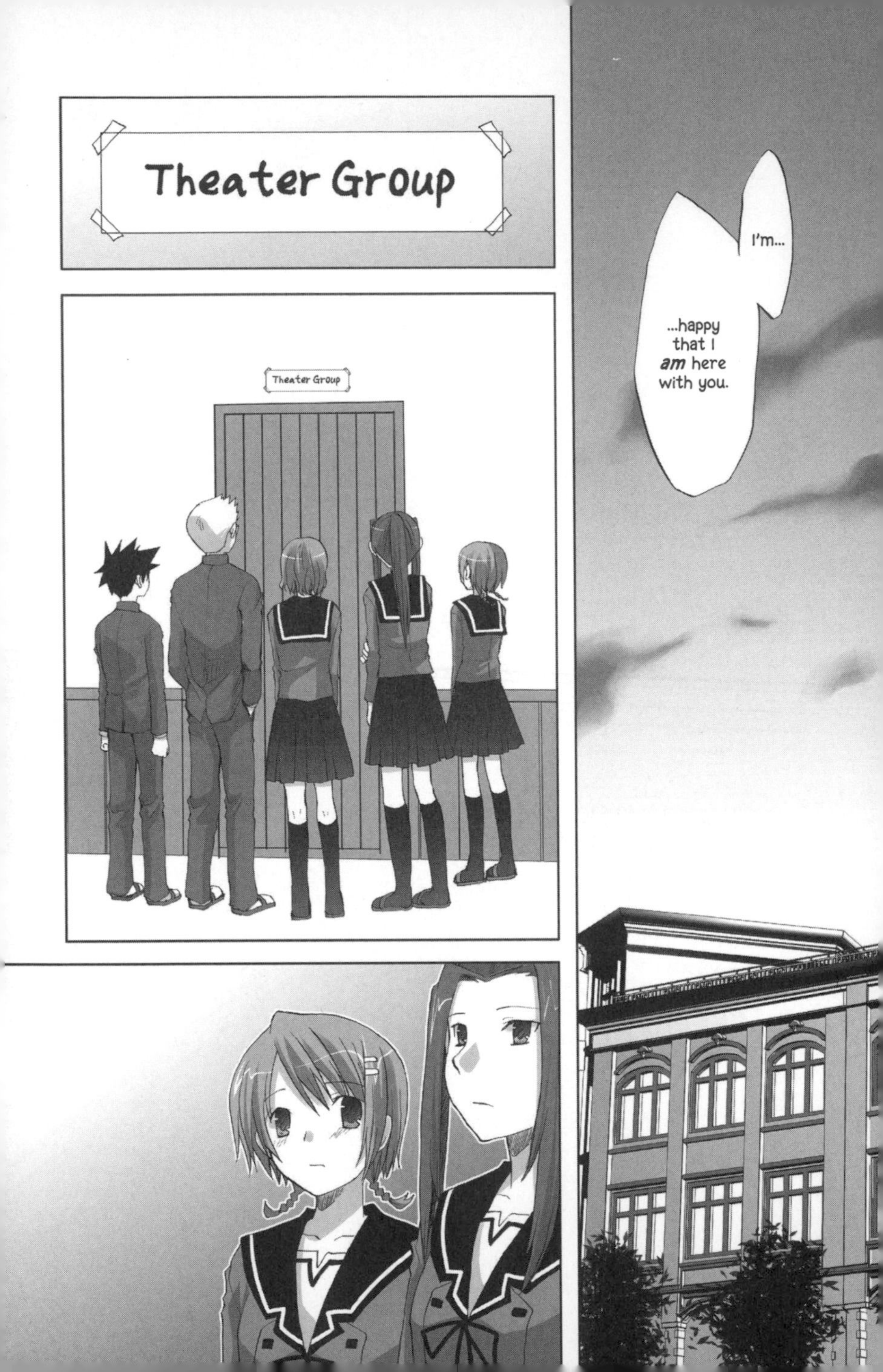
I'm...
...happy that I *am* here with you.
Theater Group
Theater Group

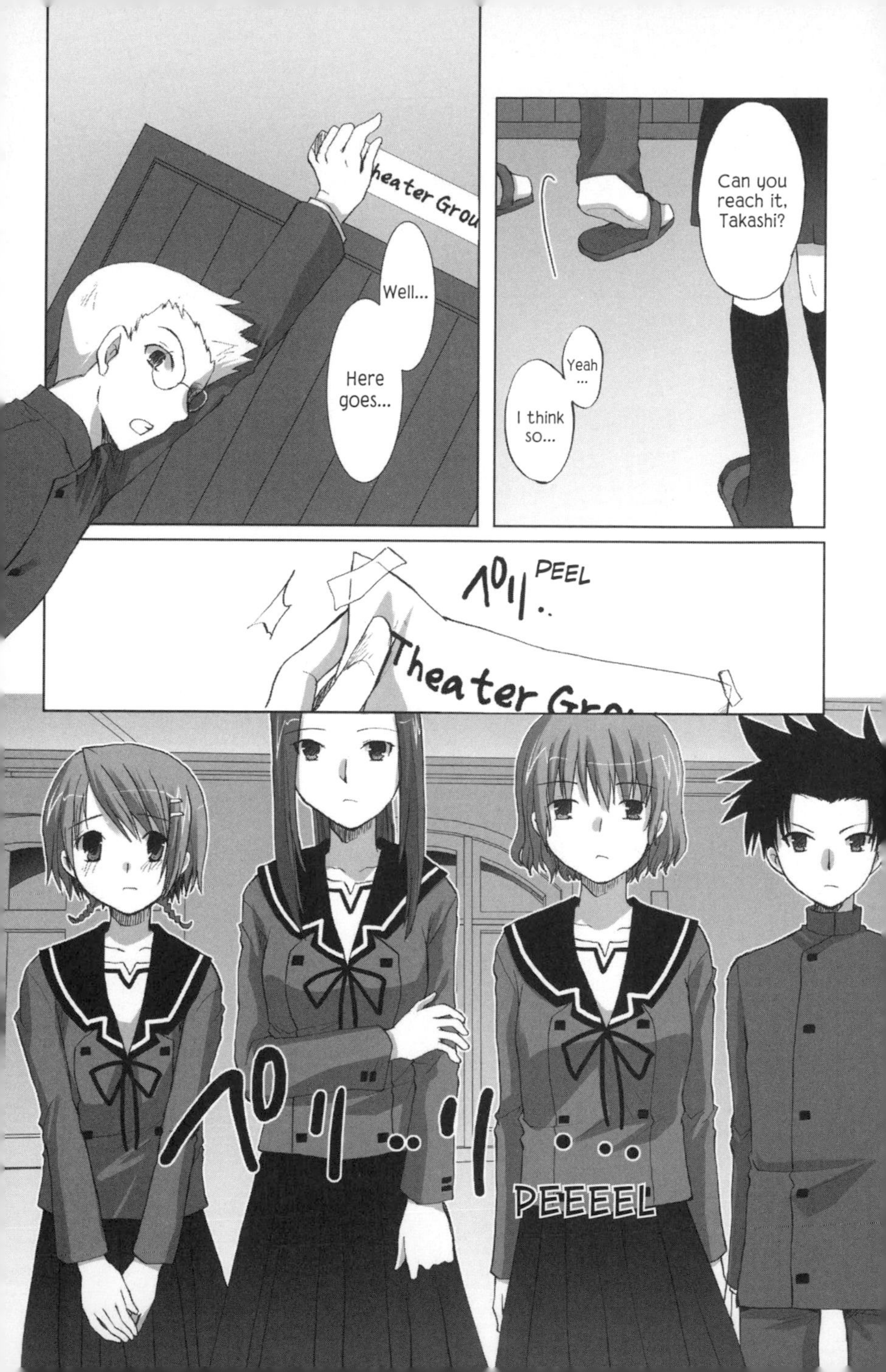

Can you reach it, Takashi?
Yeah...
I think so...
Well...
Here goes...
PEEL
PEEEEL

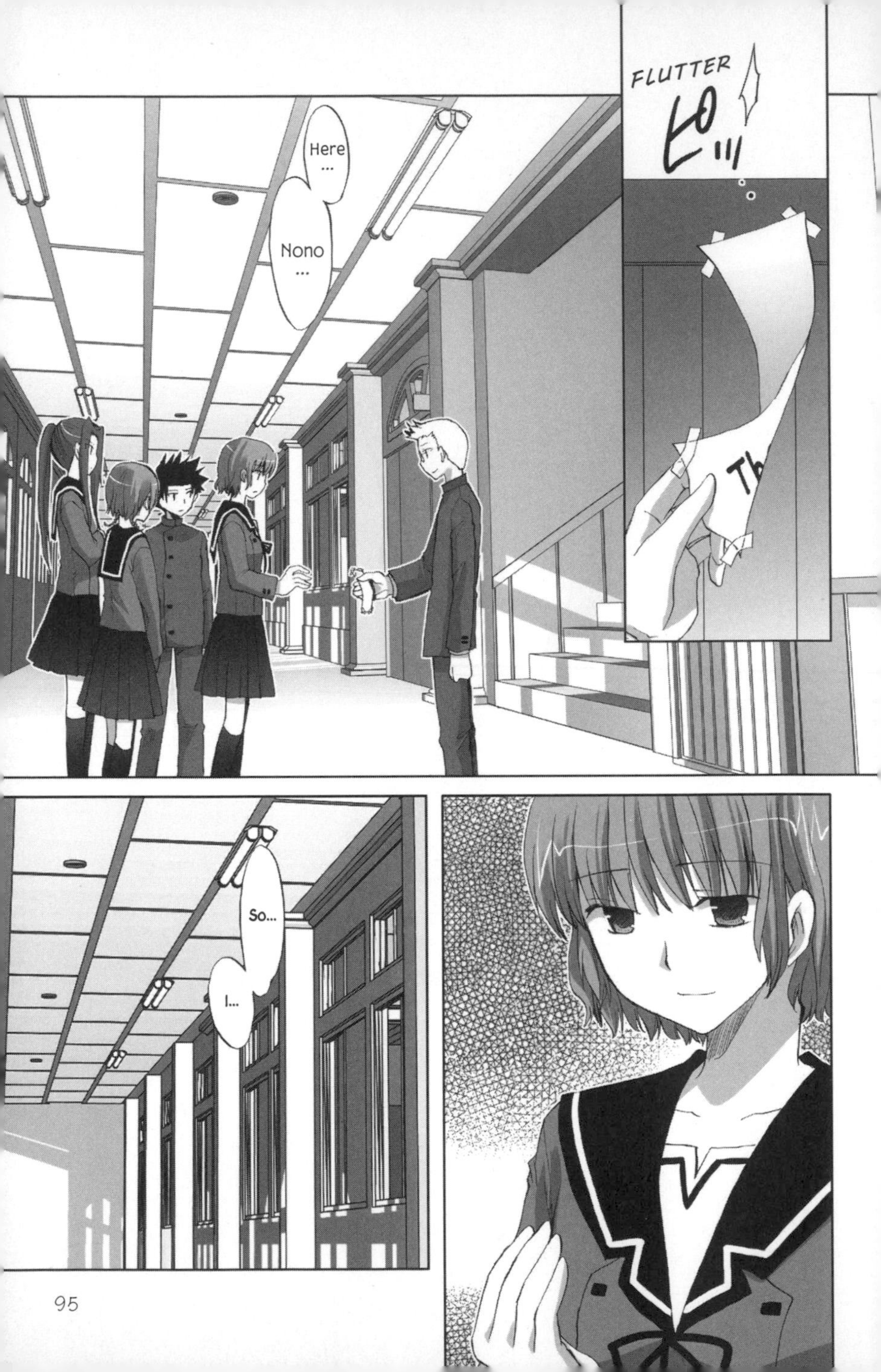
FLUTTER
Th
Here...
Nono...
So...
I...

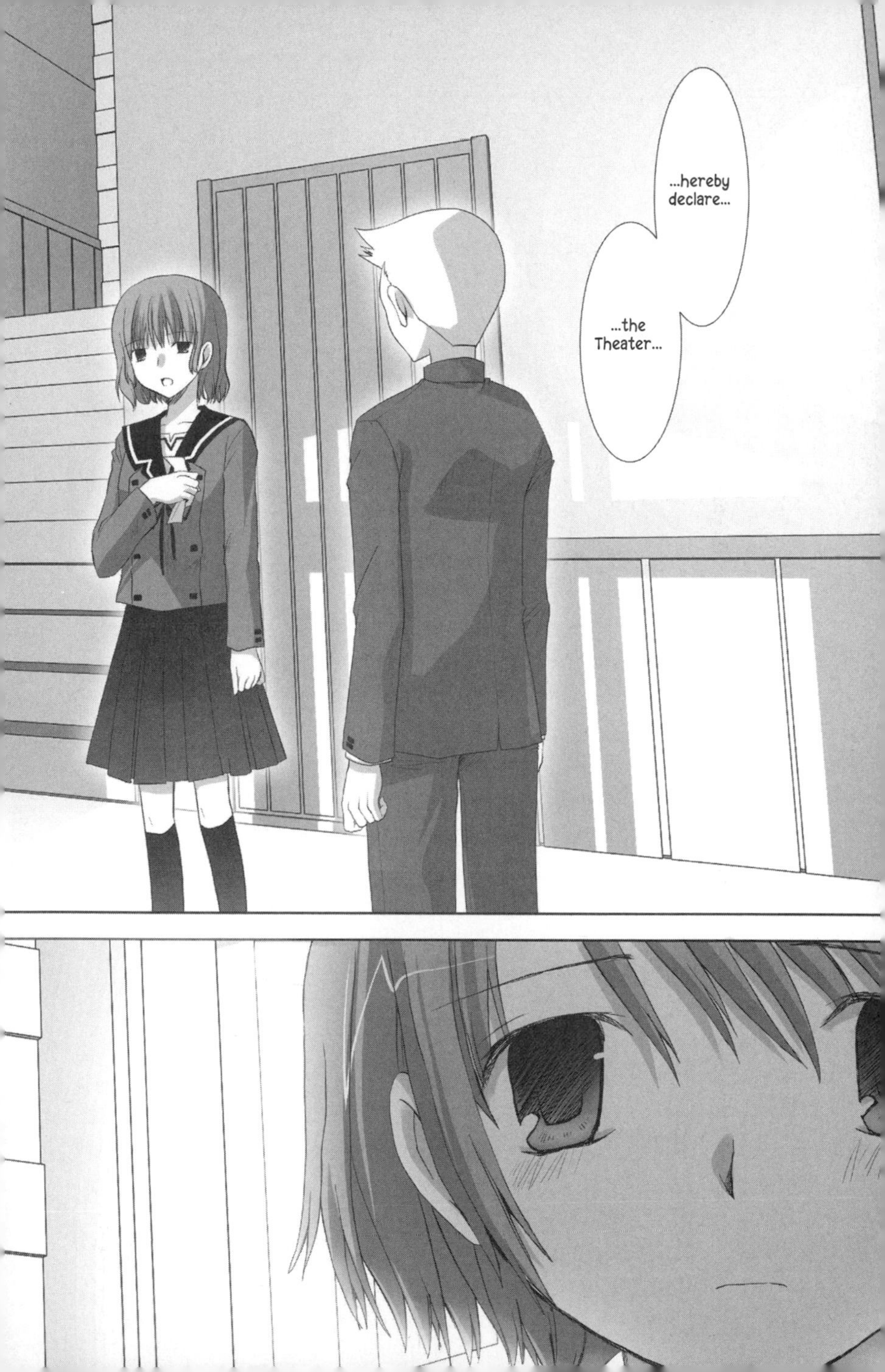
...hereby declare...
...the Theater...

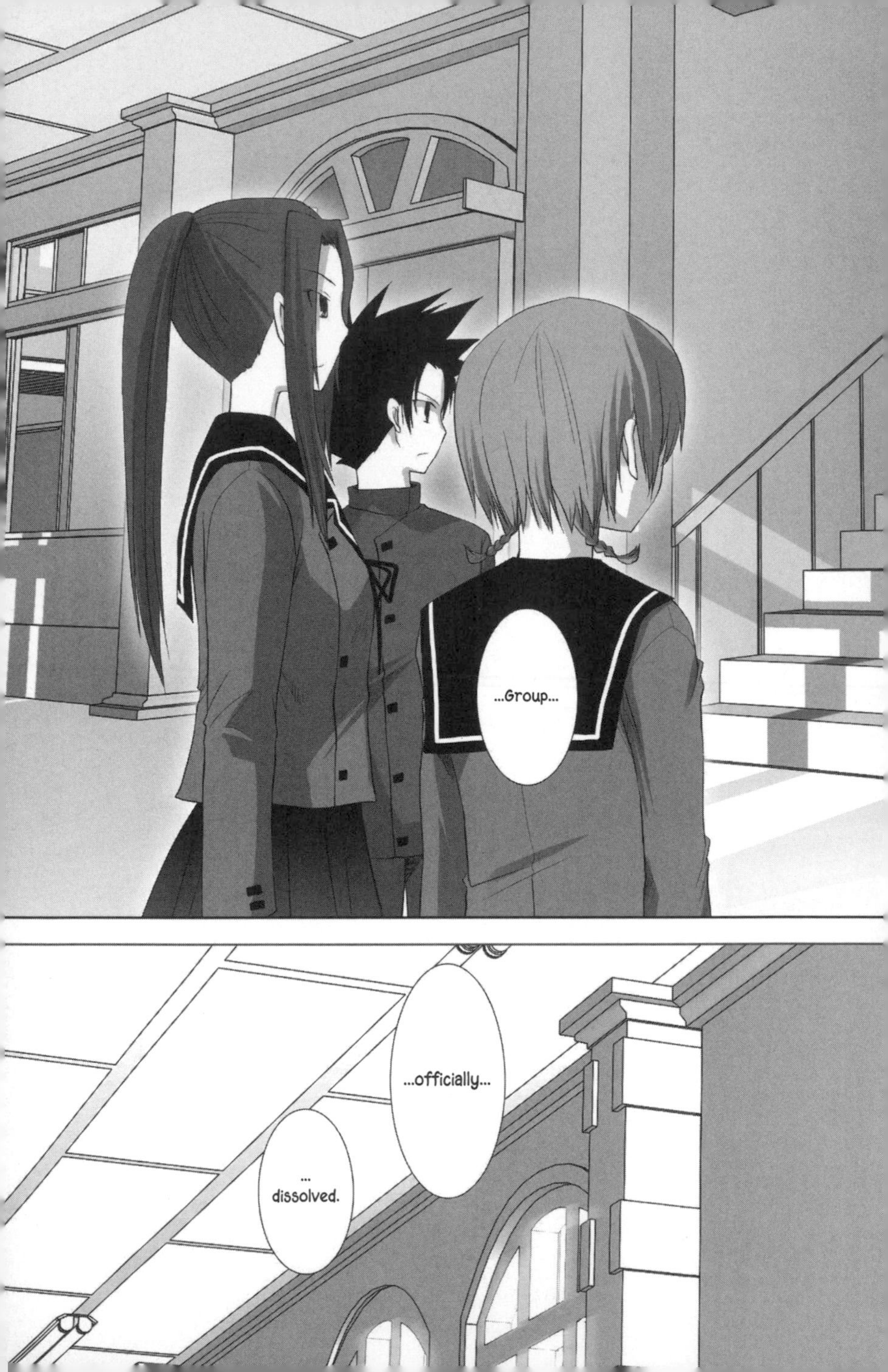
...Group...
...officially...
...
dissolved.

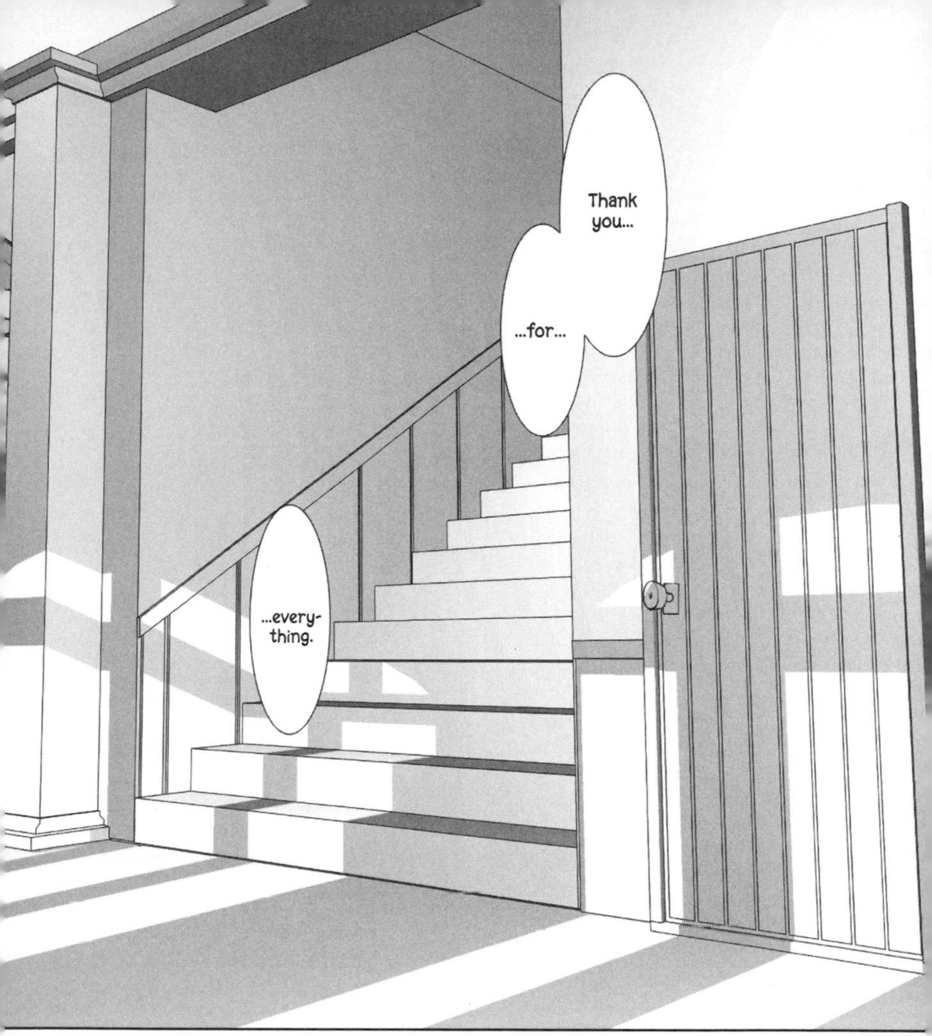
Thank you...
...for...
...every-thing.

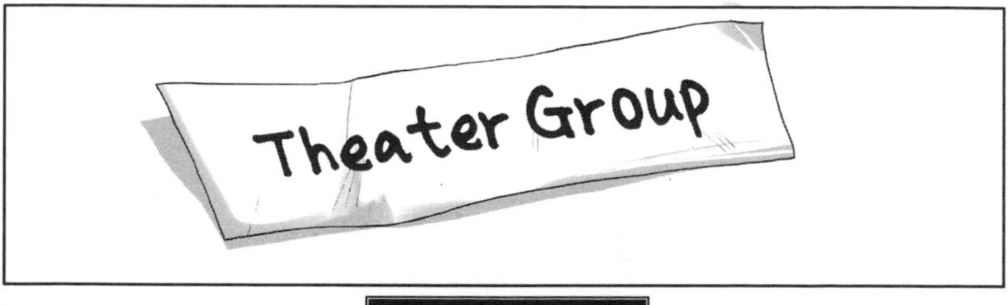
Theater Group

Chapter 19 ✤ End

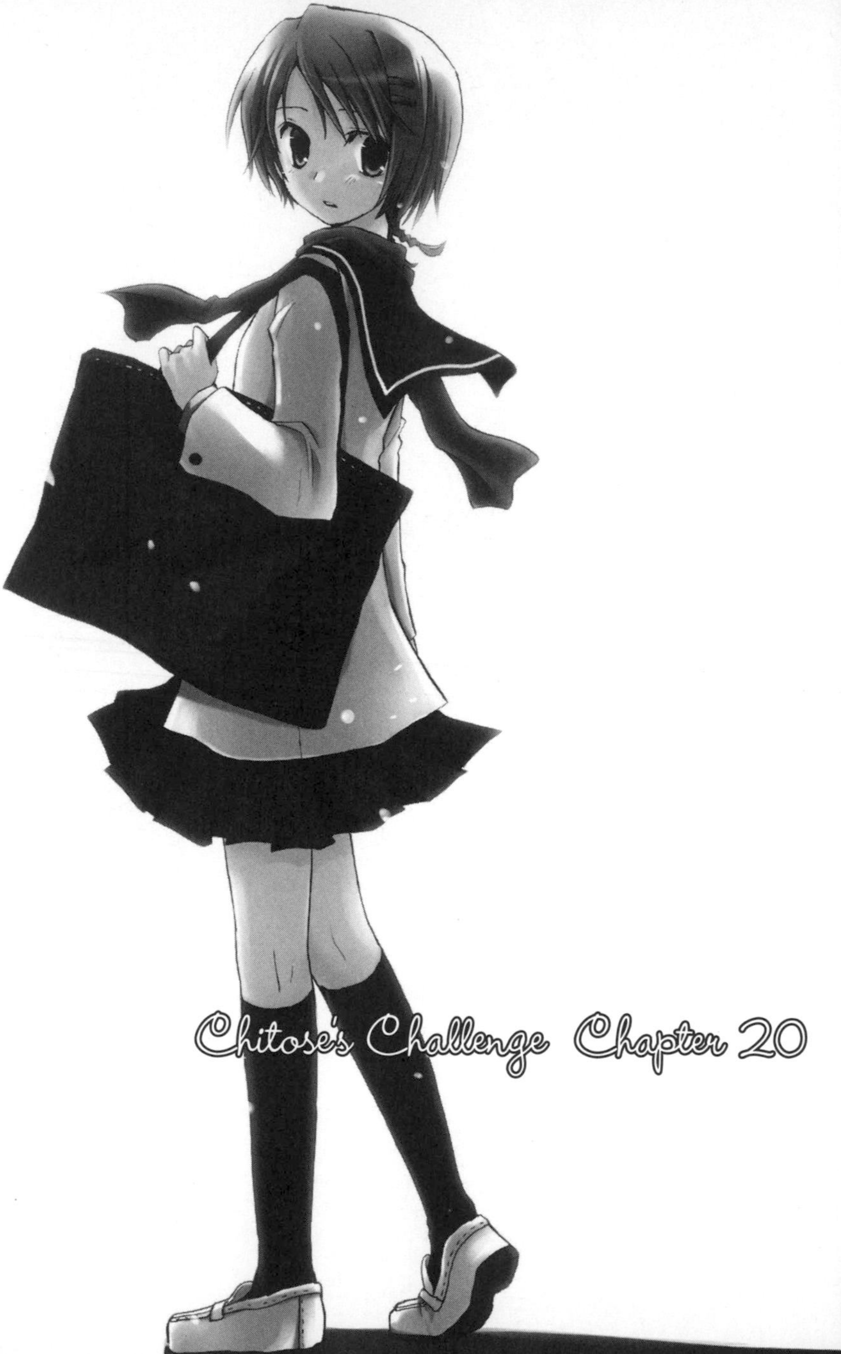
Chitose's Challenge Chapter 20

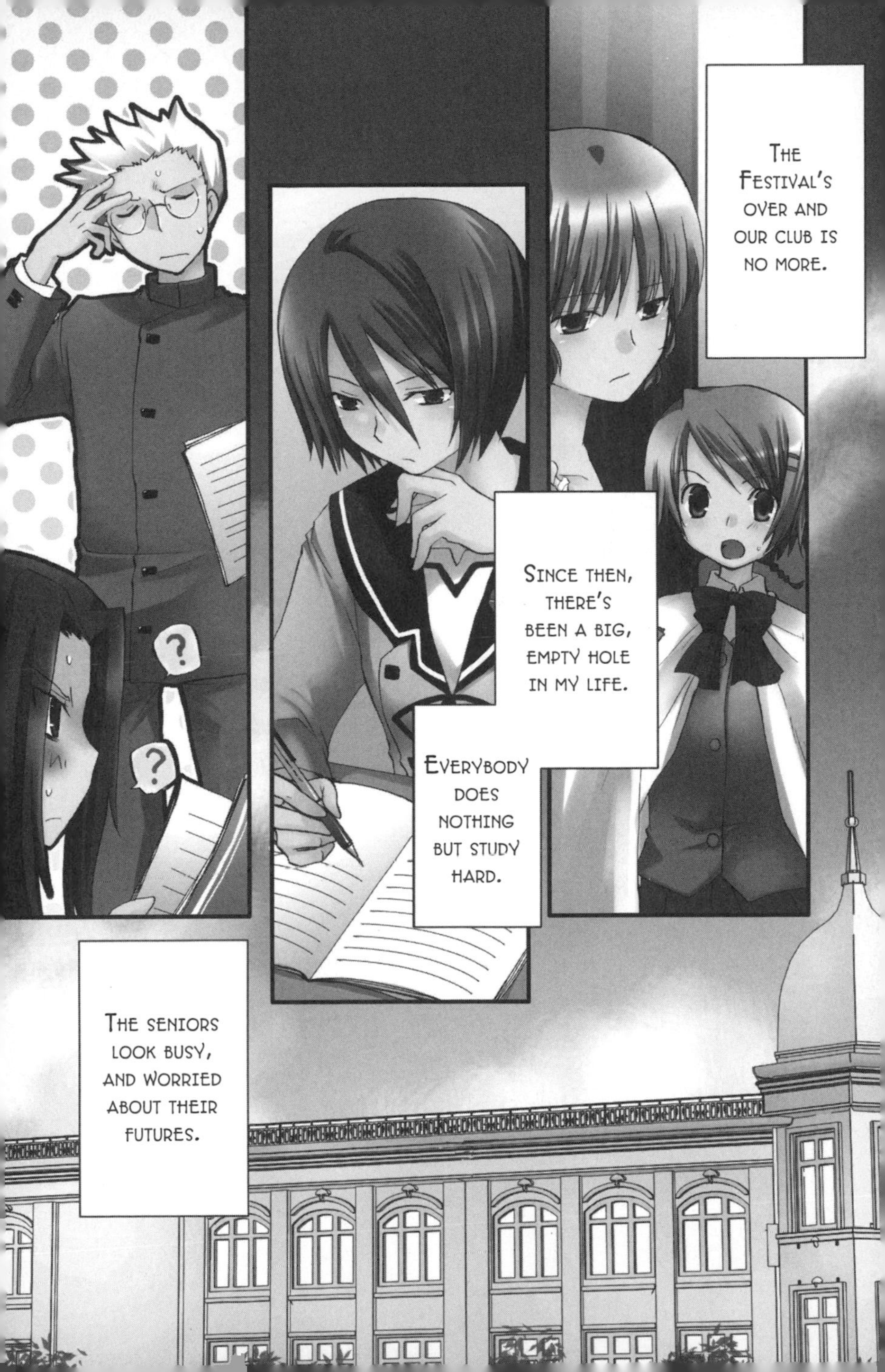
The Festival's over and our club is no more.
Since then, there's been a big, empty hole in my life.
Everybody does nothing but study hard.
?
?
The seniors look busy, and worried about their futures.

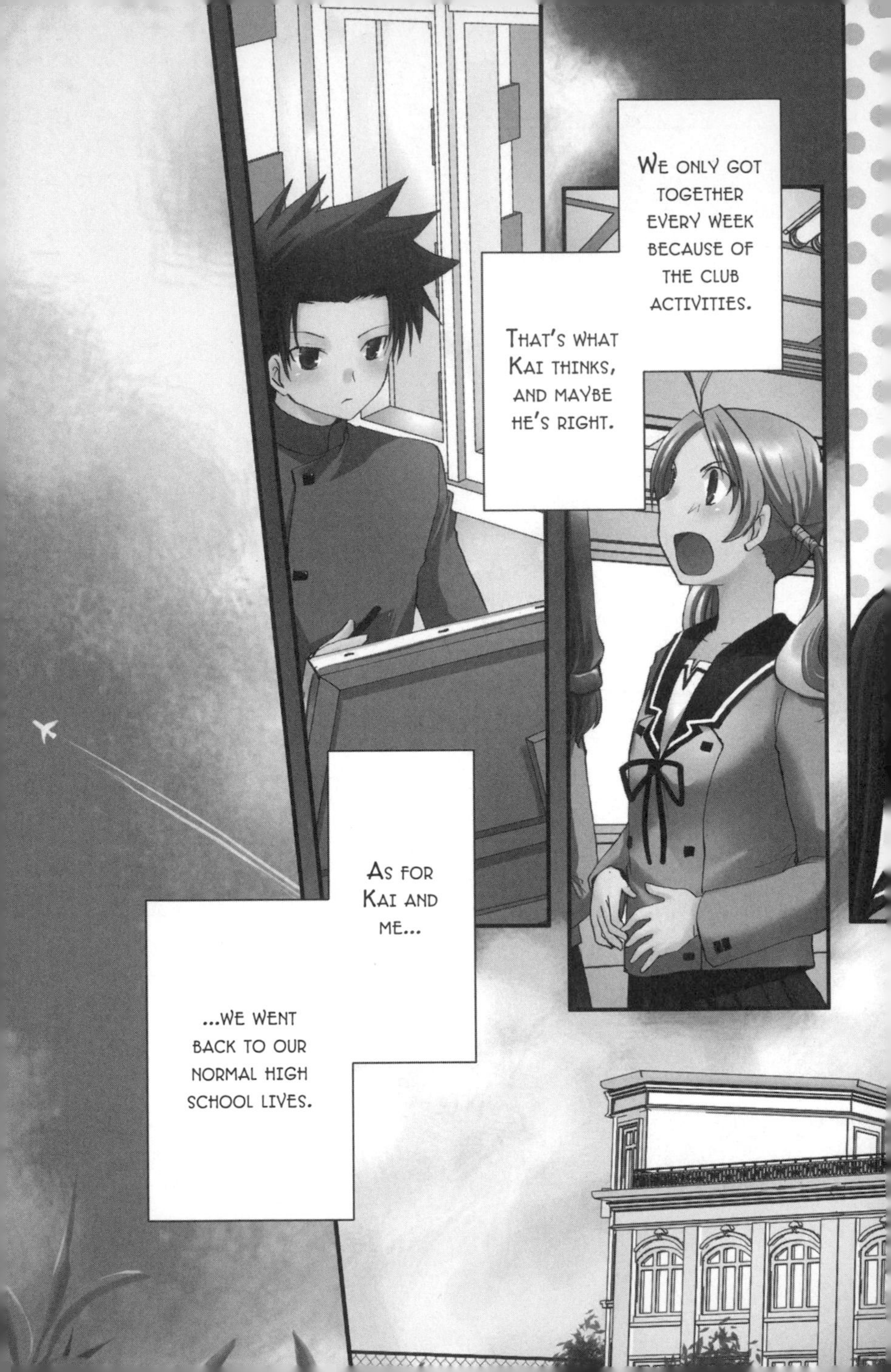
We only got together every week because of the club activities.
That's what Kai thinks, and maybe he's right.
As for Kai and me...
...we went back to our normal high school lives.

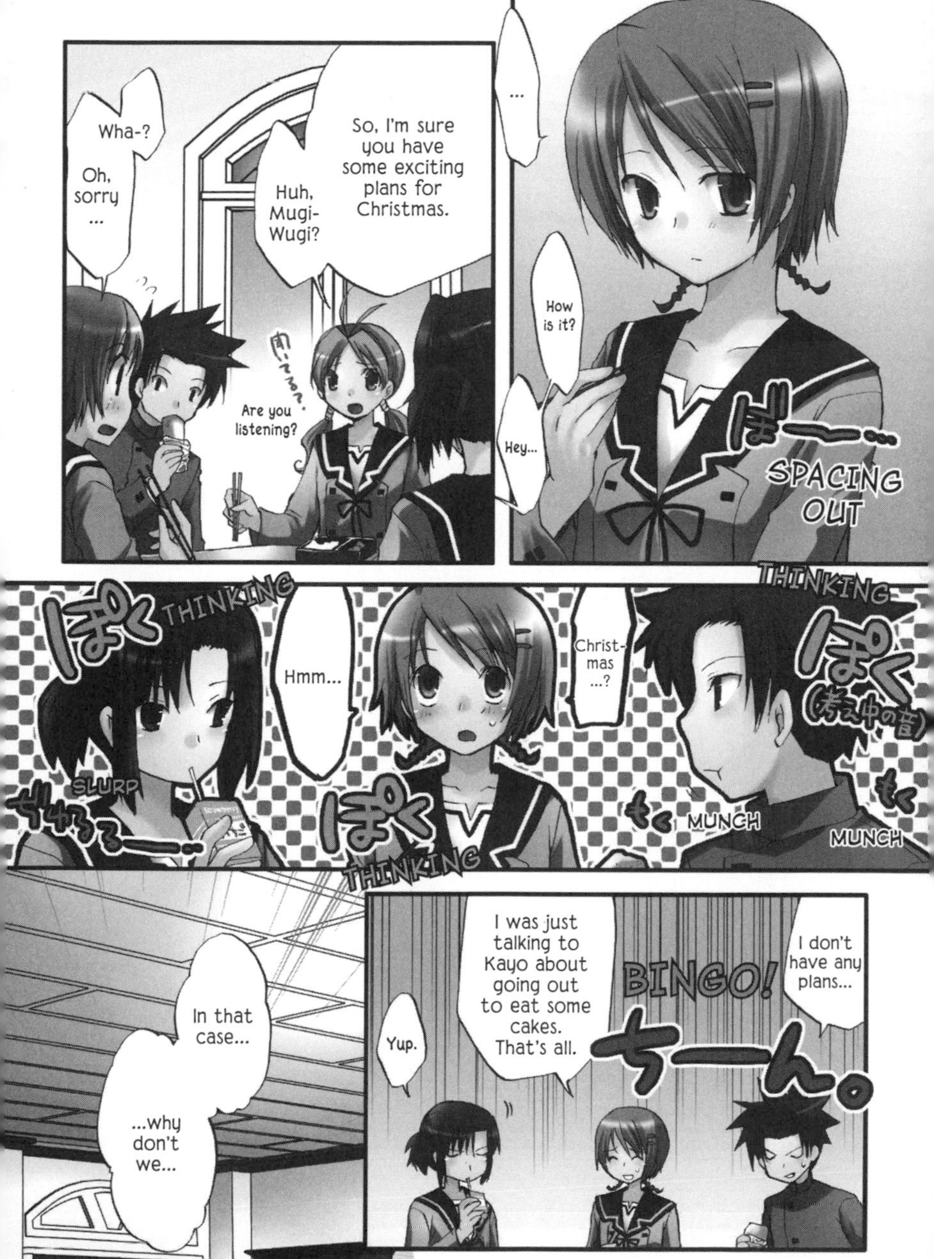
...
How is it?
Hey...
ぼ〜〜…
SPACING OUT
So, I'm sure you have some exciting plans for Christmas.
Huh, Mugi-Wugi?
Wha-?
Oh, sorry ...
聞いてる?
Are you listening?
THINKING
ぽく
(考え中の音)
もく
MUNCH
Christ-mas ...?
もく
MUNCH
ぽく
THINKING
Hmm...
ぽく
THINKING
SLURP
ぢゅるる〜〜…
I don't have any plans...
BINGO!
ちーん。
I was just talking to Kayo about going out to eat some cakes. That's all.
Yup.
In that case...
...why don't we...

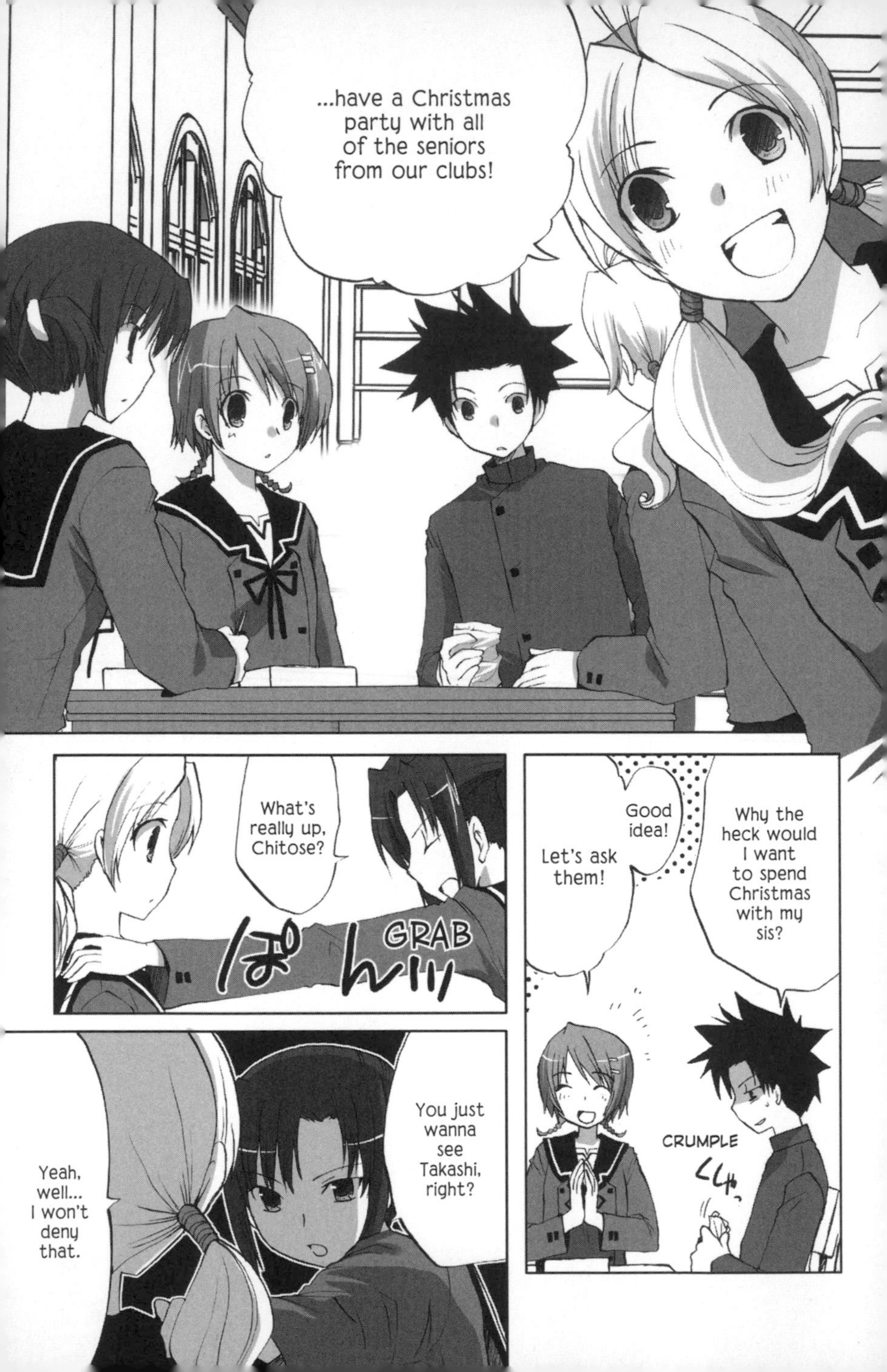
...have a Christmas party with all of the seniors from our clubs!
Why the heck would I want to spend Christmas with my sis?
Good idea!
Let's ask them!
CRUMPLE
What's really up, Chitose?
GRAB
You just wanna see Takashi, right?
Yeah, well... I won't deny that.

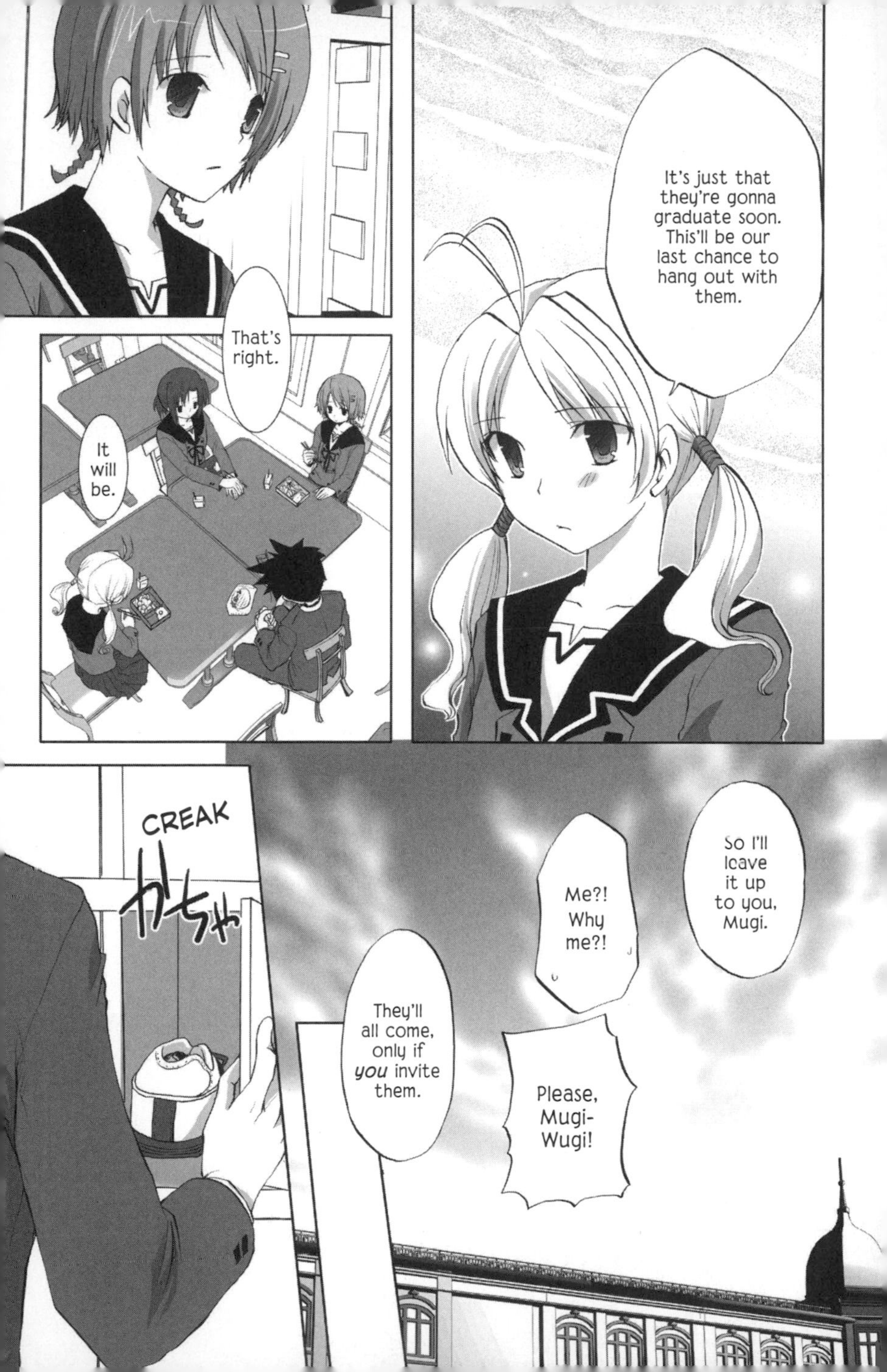
It's just that they're gonna graduate soon. This'll be our last chance to hang out with them.
That's right.
It will be.
So I'll leave it up to you, Mugi.
Me?! Why me?!
They'll all come, only if *you* invite them.
Please, Mugi-Wugi!
CREAK
かちゃ

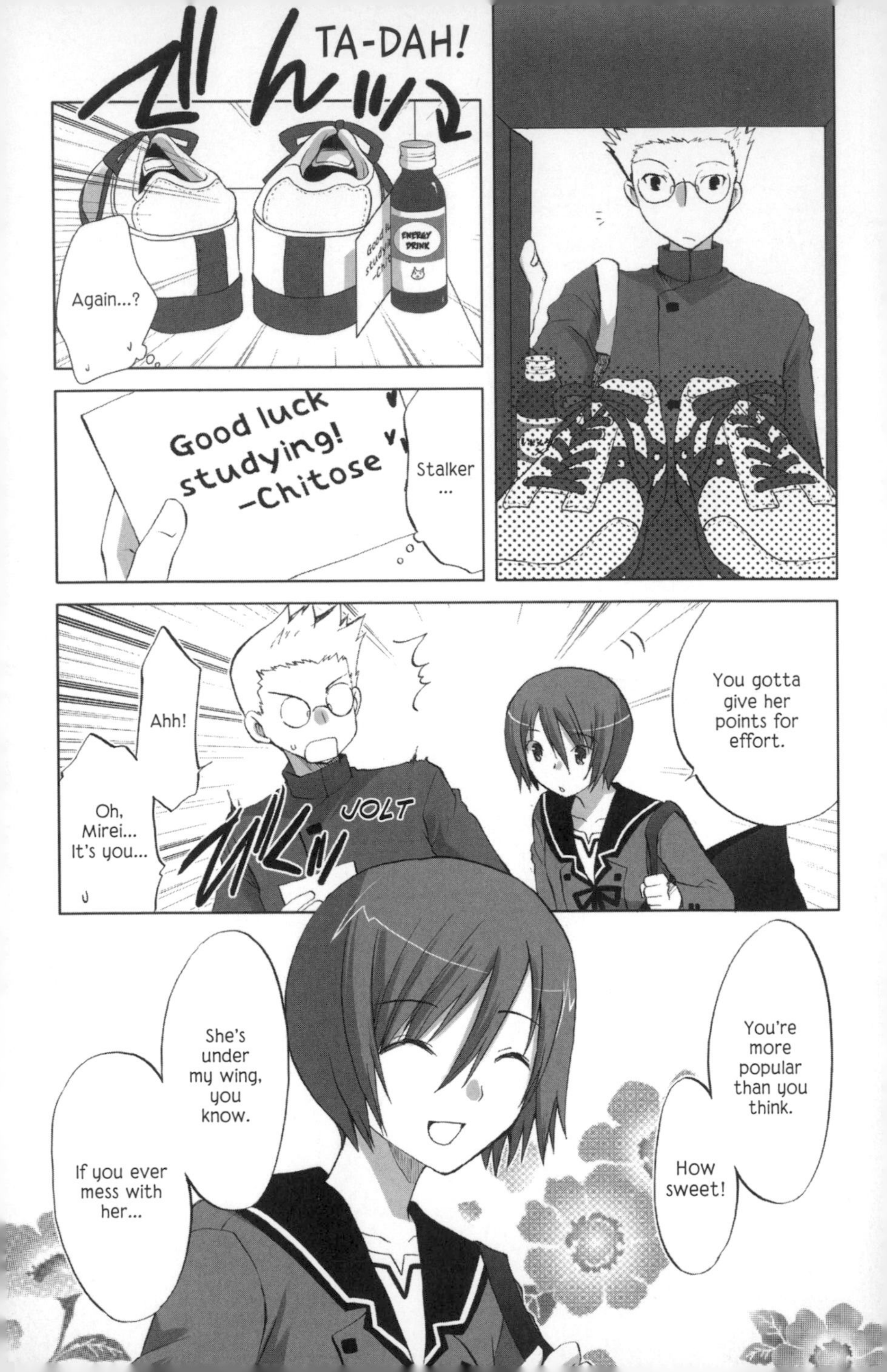
TA-DAH!
ENERGY DRINK
Again...?
Good luck studying! -Chitose
Stalker ...
You gotta give her points for effort.
JOLT
Ahh!
Oh, Mirei... It's you...
You're more popular than you think.
How sweet!
She's under my wing, you know.
If you ever mess with her...

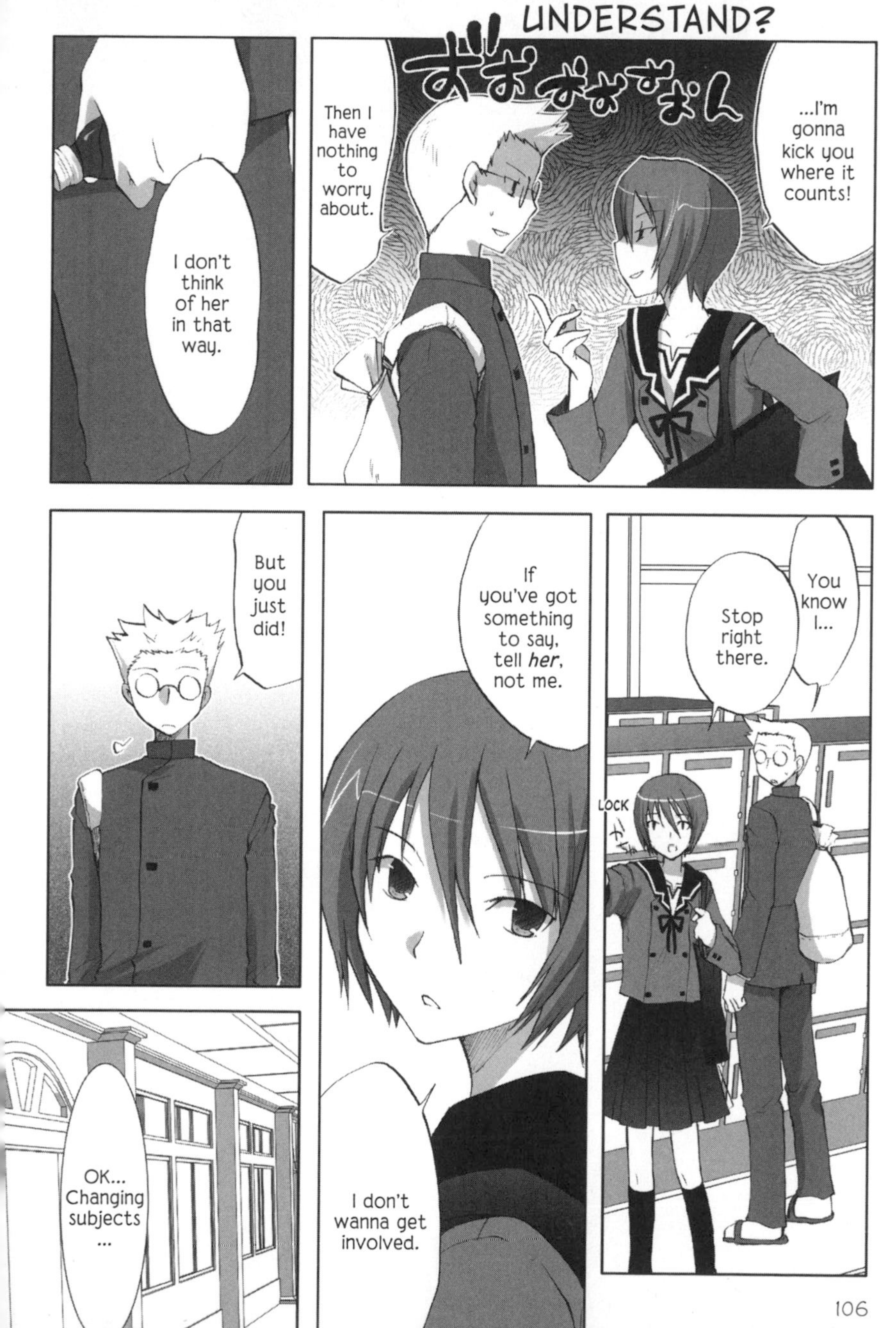
...I'm gonna kick you where it counts!
UNDERSTAND?
Then I have nothing to worry about.
I don't think of her in that way.
You know I...
Stop right there.
LOCK
If you've got something to say, tell *her*, not me.
I don't wanna get involved.
But you just did!
OK... Changing subjects ...

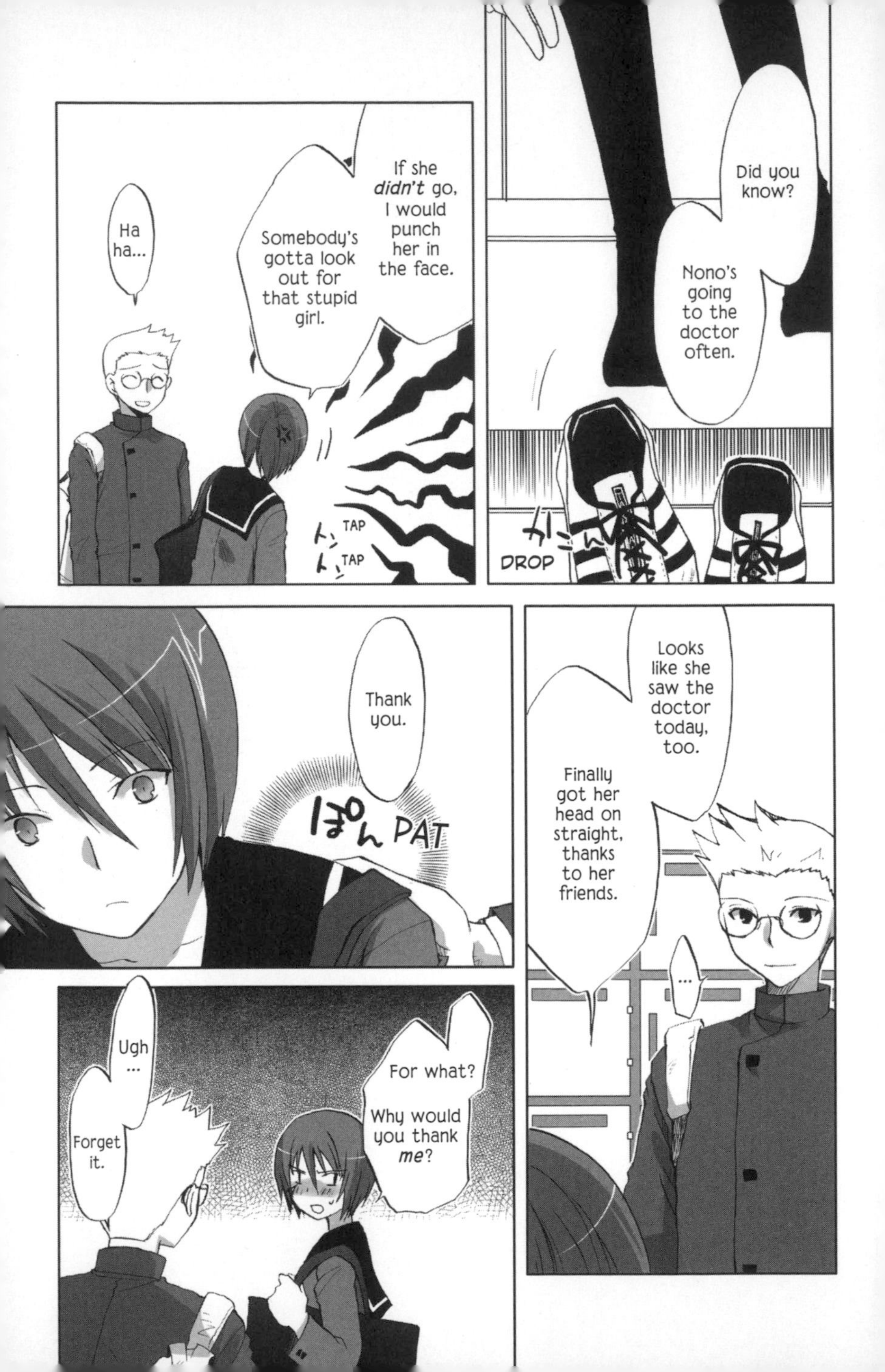
Did you know?
Nono's going to the doctor often.
DROP
If she *didn't* go, I would punch her in the face.
Somebody's gotta look out for that stupid girl.
Ha ha...
TAP
TAP
Looks like she saw the doctor today, too.
Finally got her head on straight, thanks to her friends.
...
Thank you.
ぽん PAT
For what?
Why would you thank *me*?
Ugh...
Forget it.

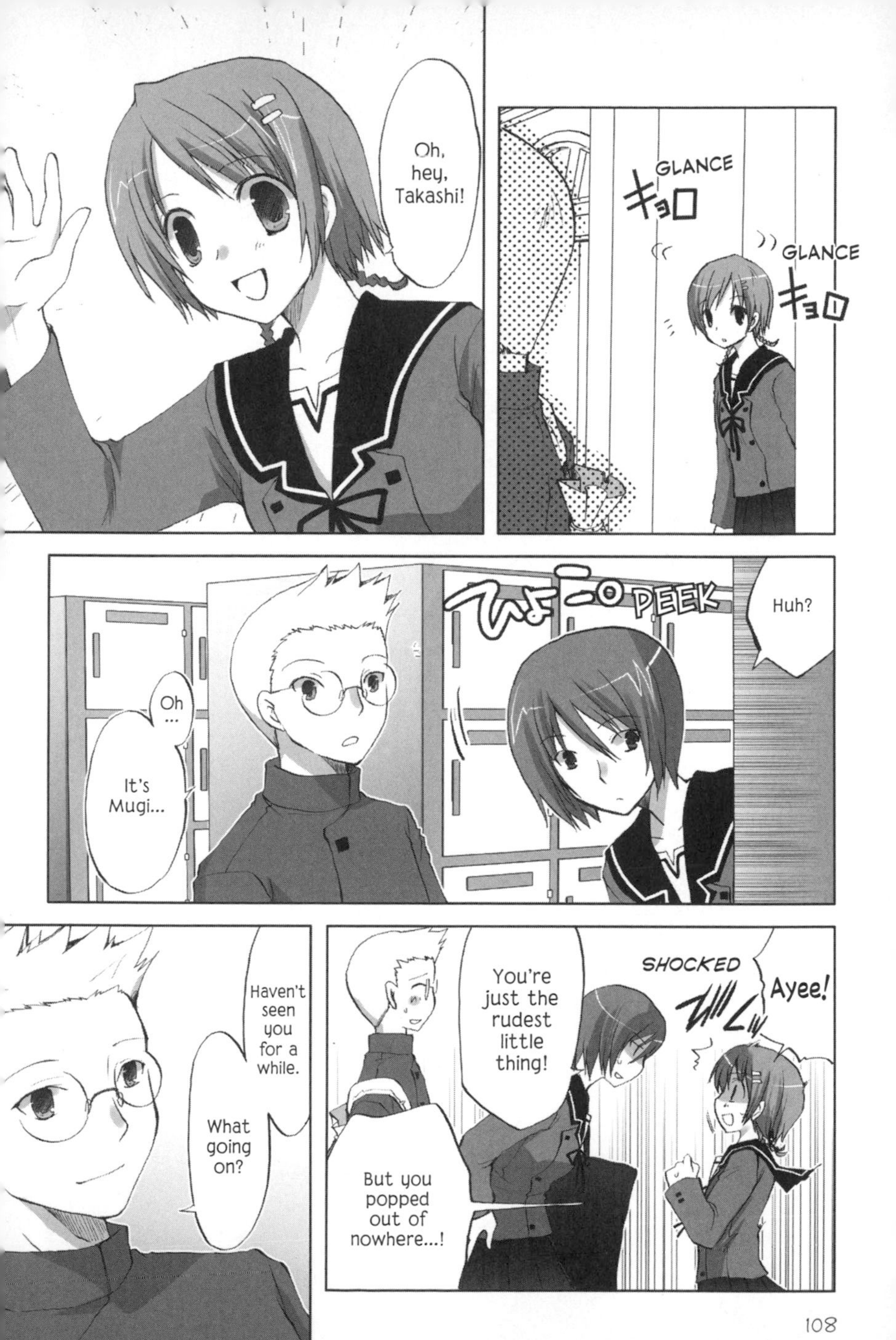
GLANCE
キョロ
GLANCE
キョロ
Oh, hey, Takashi!
Huh?
ひょこ PEEK
Oh...
It's Mugi...
SHOCKED
Ayee!
You're just the rudest little thing!
But you popped out of nowhere...!
Haven't seen you for a while.
What going on?

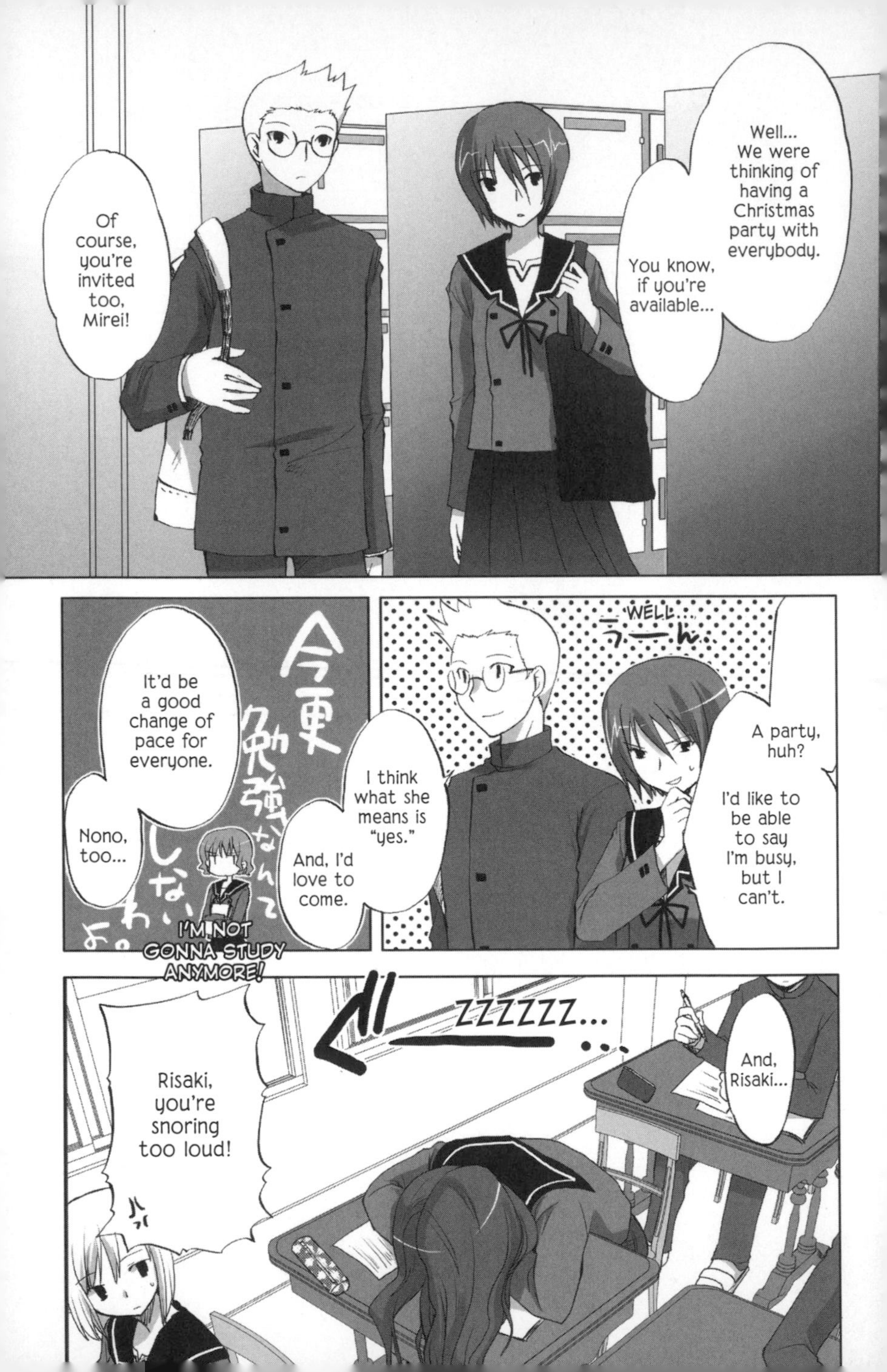
Well... We were thinking of having a Christmas party with everybody.
You know, if you're available...
Of course, you're invited too, Mirei!
うーん。
WELL...
A party, huh?
I'd like to be able to say I'm busy, but I can't.
I think what she means is "yes."
And, I'd love to come.
It'd be a good change of pace for everyone.
Nono, too...
今更勉強なんてしないわよ。
I'M NOT GONNA STUDY ANYMORE!
And, Risaki...
ZZZZZZ...
Risaki, you're snoring too loud!

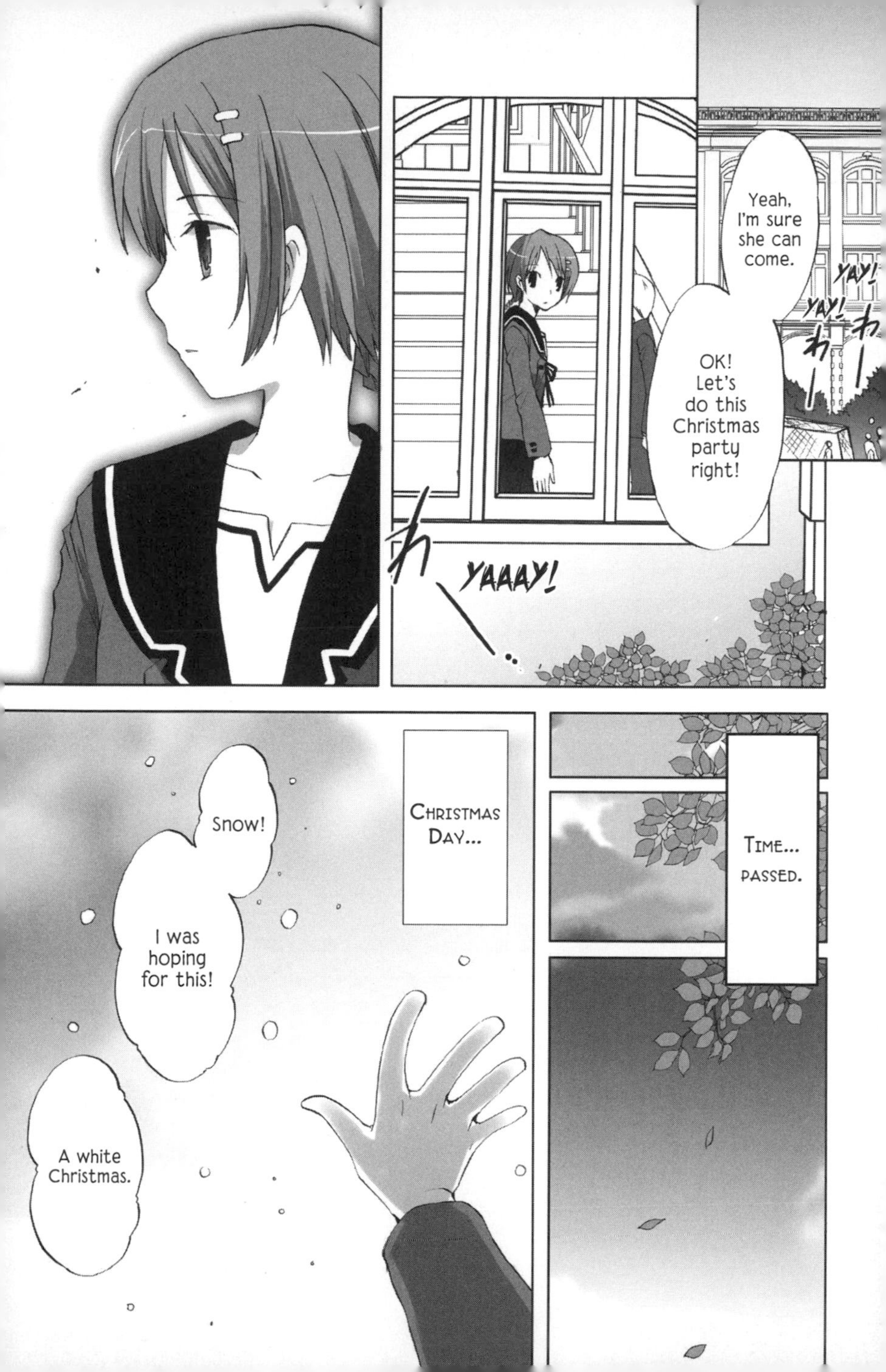

Yeah, I'm sure she can come.
YAY!
YAY!
わー
わー
OK! Let's do this Christmas party right!
わー
YAAAY!
Time... passed.
Christmas Day...
Snow!
I was hoping for this!
A white Christmas.

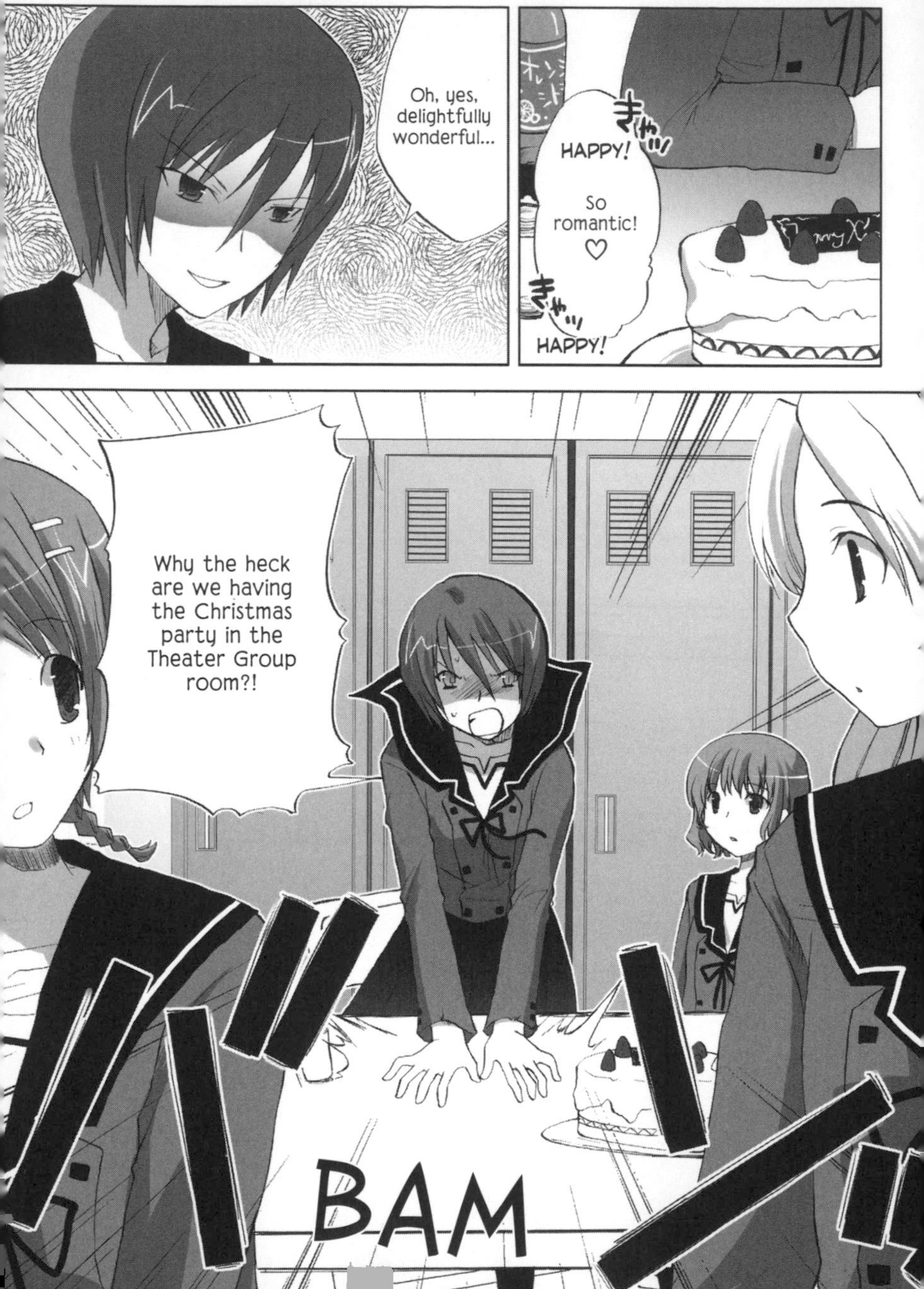
きゃっ
HAPPY!
So romantic! ♡
きゃっ
HAPPY!
Oh, yes, delightfully wonderful...
Why the heck are we having the Christmas party in the Theater Group room?!
BAM

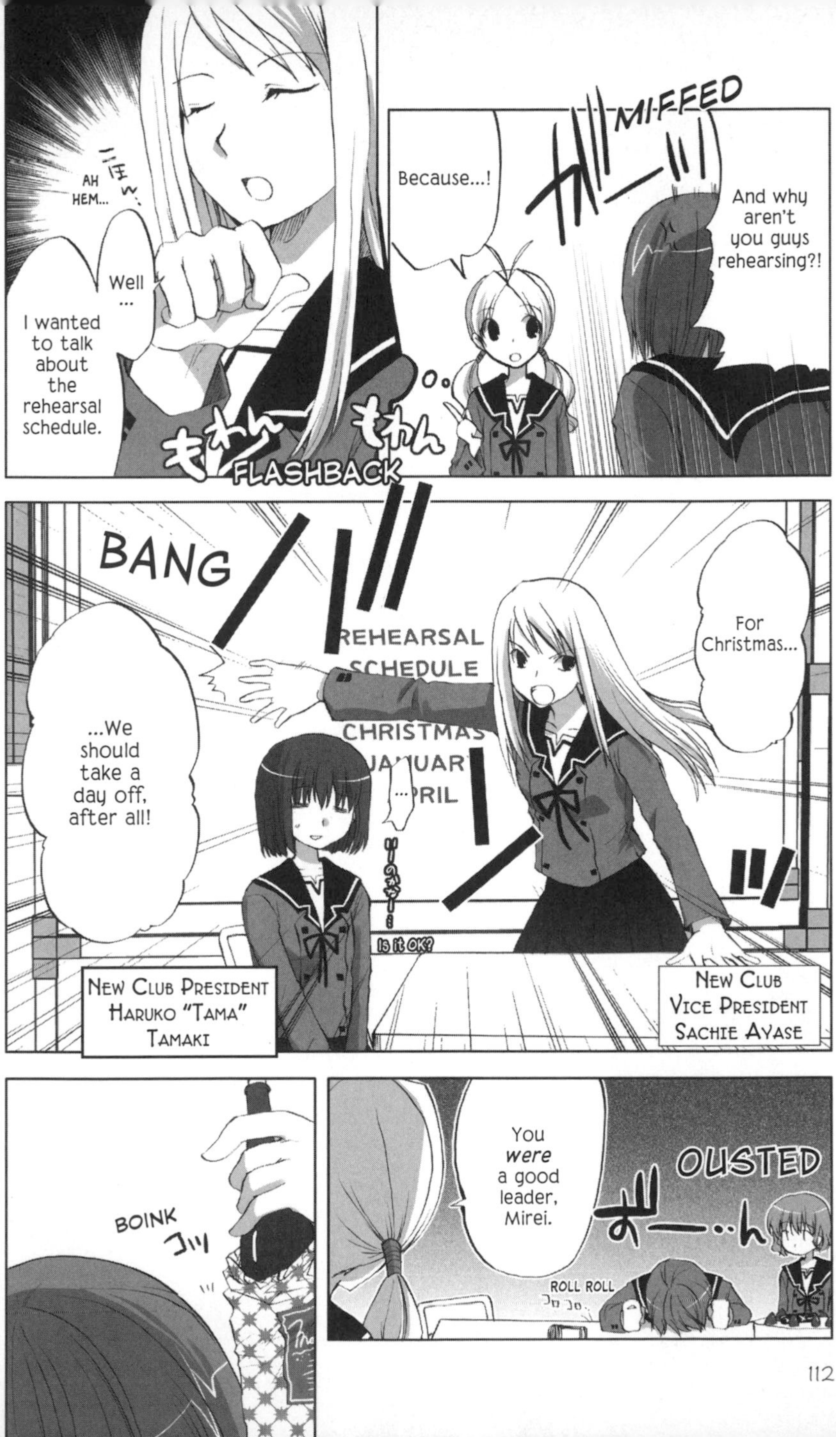
MIFFED
And why aren't you guys rehearsing?!
Because...!
AH HEM...
Well ...
I wanted to talk about the rehearsal schedule.
FLASHBACK
For Christmas...
BANG
REHEARSAL SCHEDULE
CHRISTMAS
JANUARY
APRIL
...We should take a day off, after all!
...
Is it OK?
New Club Vice President Sachie Ayase
New Club President Haruko "Tama" Tamaki
OUSTED
You *were* a good leader, Mirei.
ROLL ROLL
BOINK

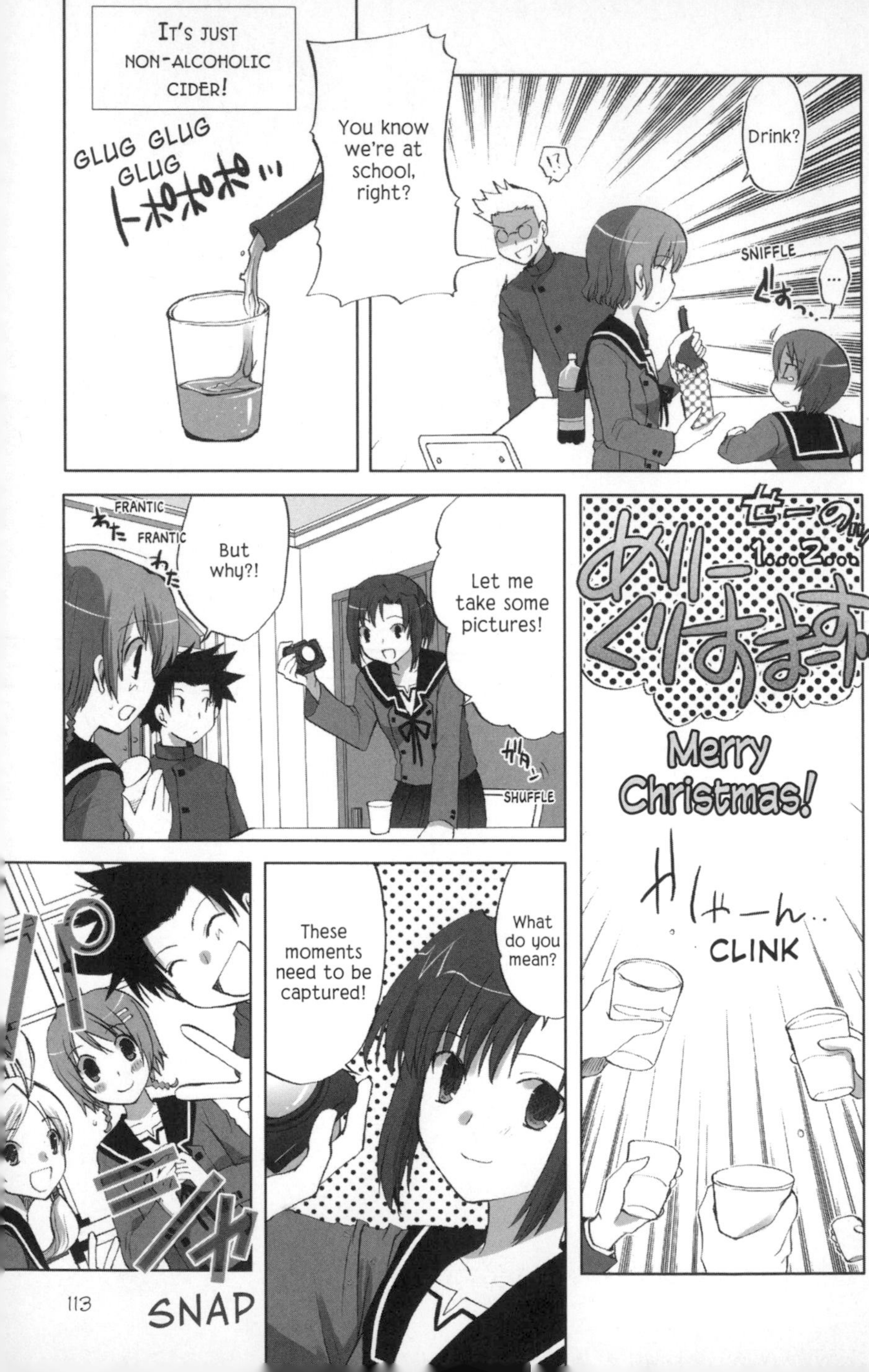
Drink?
!?
You know we're at school, right?
SNIFFLE
...
It's just non-alcoholic cider!
GLUG GLUG GLUG
1... 2...
Merry Christmas!
CLINK
Let me take some pictures!
SHUFFLE
But why?!
FRANTIC
FRANTIC
What do you mean?
These moments need to be captured!
SNAP

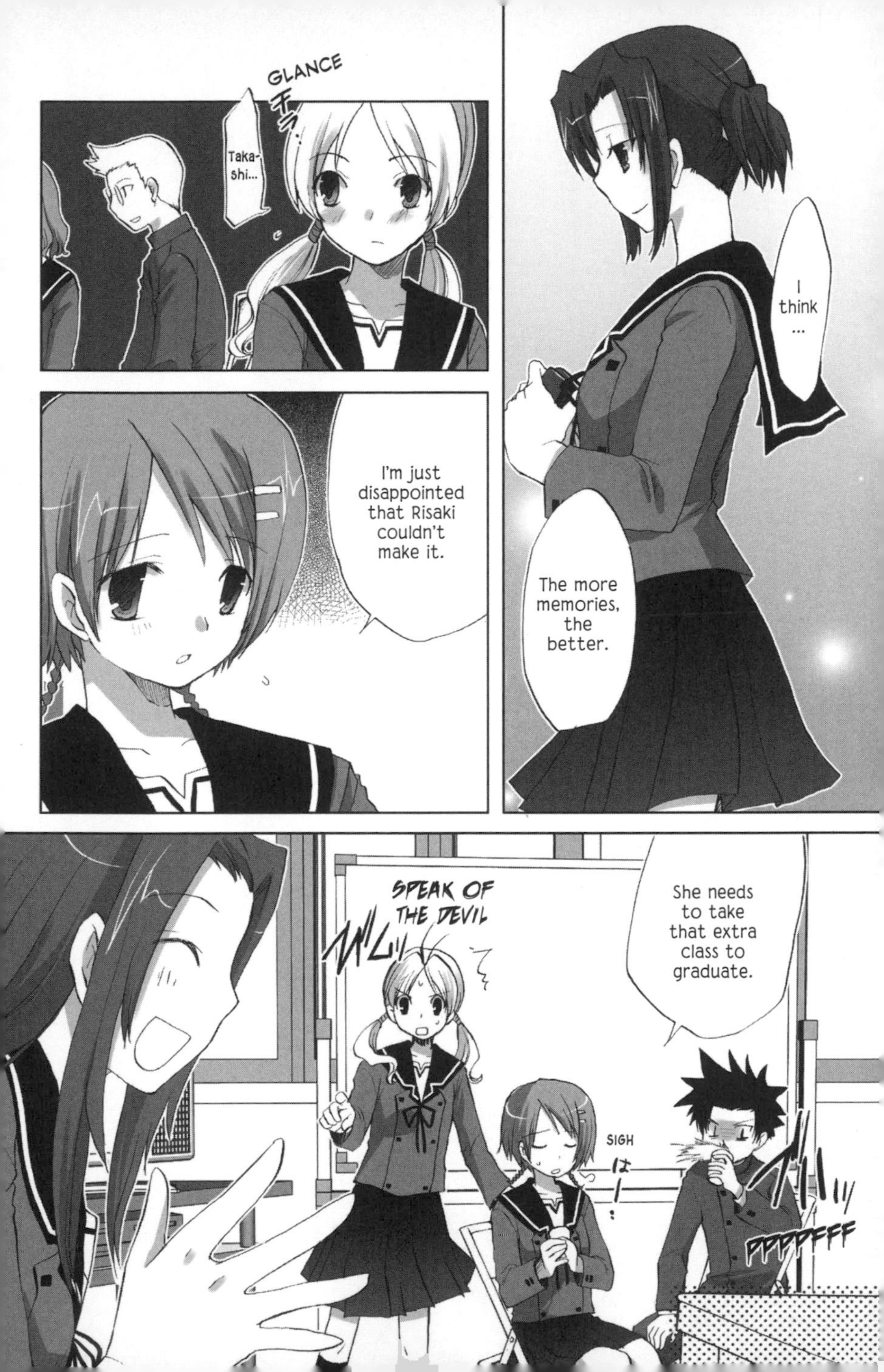
I think ...
The more memories, the better.
GLANCE
Taka-shi...
I'm just disappointed that Risaki couldn't make it.
She needs to take that extra class to graduate.
SPEAK OF THE DEVIL
SIGH
PPPPFFF

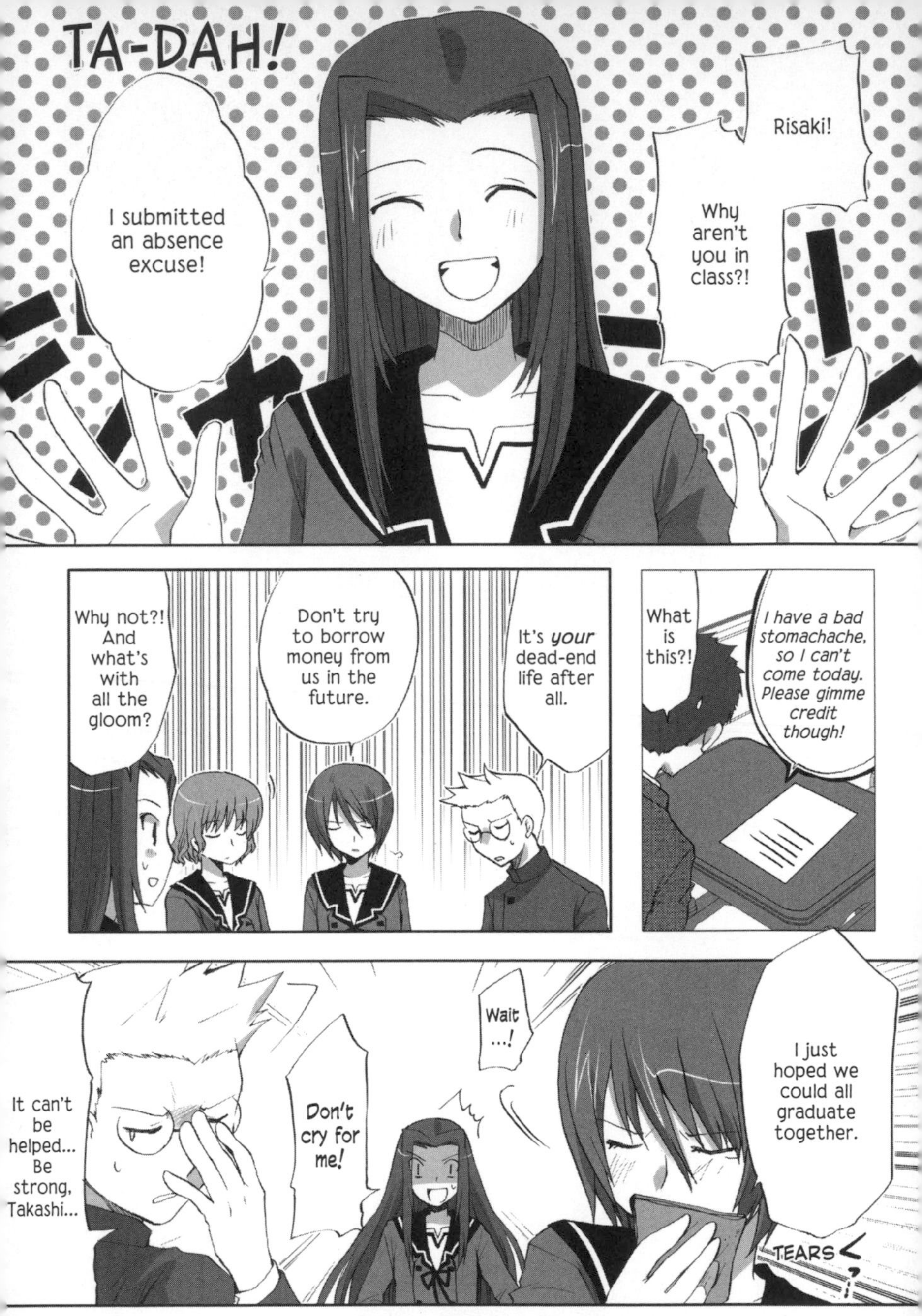
Risaki!
Why aren't you in class?!
TA-DAH!
I submitted an absence excuse!
I have a bad stomachache, so I can't come today. Please gimme credit though!
What is this?!
It's your dead-end life after all.
Don't try to borrow money from us in the future.
Why not?! And what's with all the gloom?
I just hoped we could all graduate together.
TEARS
Wait ...!
Don't cry for me!
It can't be helped... Be strong, Takashi...

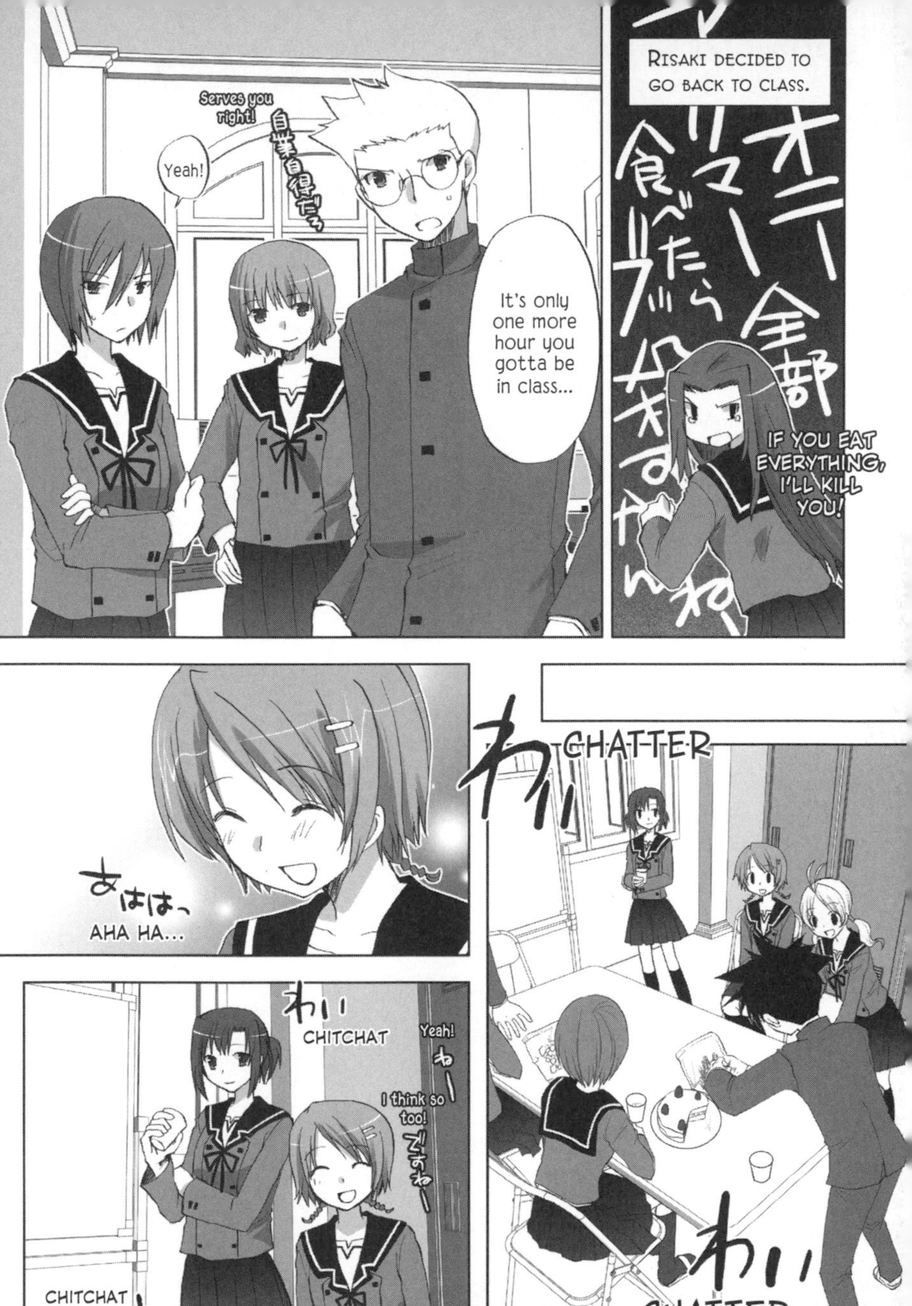
Risaki decided to go back to class.
If you eat everything, I'll kill you!
Serves you right!
自業自得だろ
It's only one more hour you gotta be in class...
Yeah!
わい
CHATTER
わい
CHATTER
あはは
AHA HA...
わい
CHITCHAT
Yeah!
ねー
I think so too!
ですねー
CHITCHAT
わい

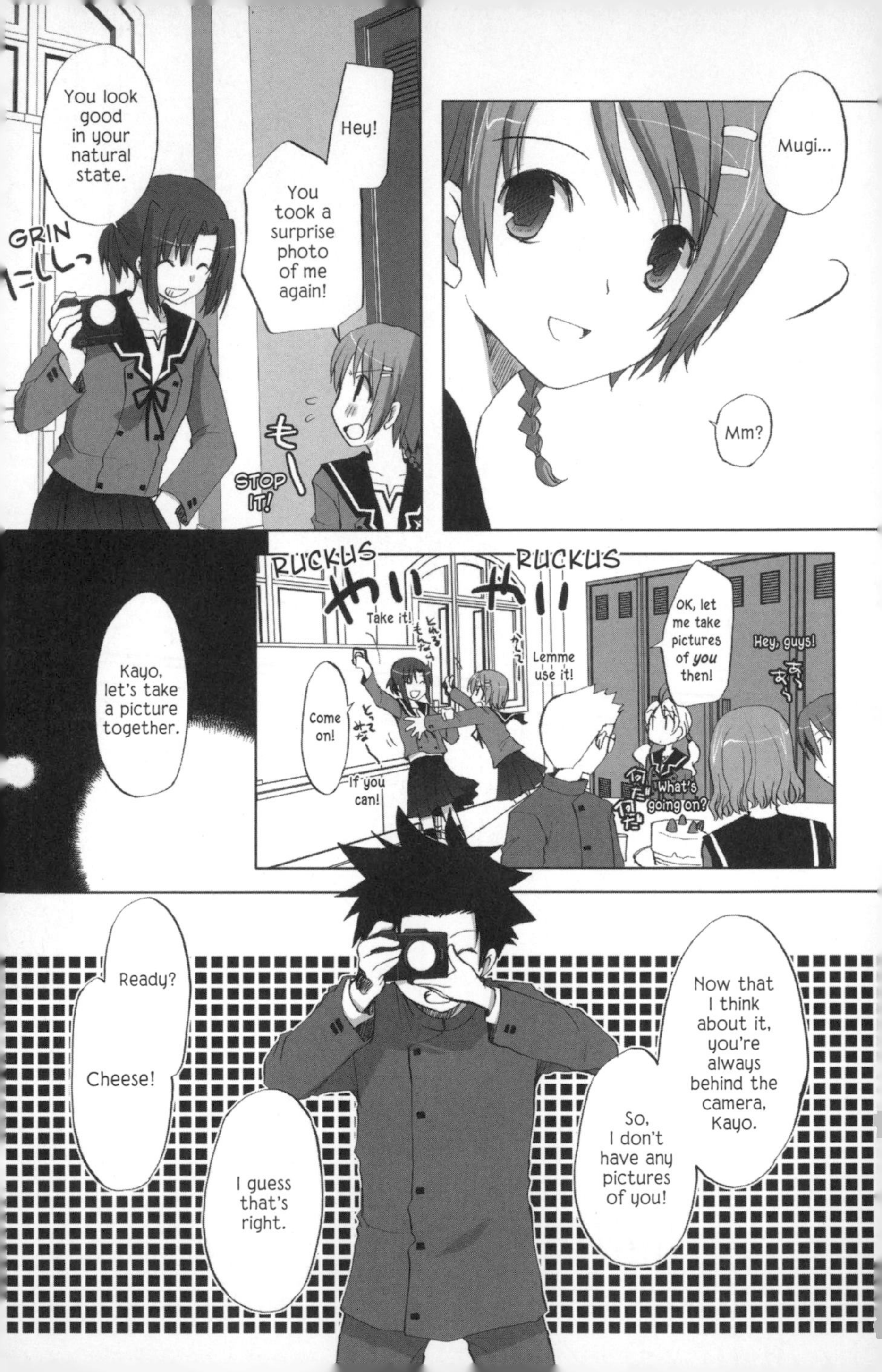
Mugi...
Mm?
Hey!
You took a surprise photo of me again!
You look good in your natural state.
GRIN
にしし っ
STOP IT!
RUCKUS
RUCKUS
Hey, guys!
OK, let me take pictures of *you* then!
Lemme use it!
Take it!
Come on!
If you can!
What's going on?
Kayo, let's take a picture together.
Now that I think about it, you're always behind the camera, Kayo.
So, I don't have any pictures of you!
I guess that's right.
Ready?
Cheese!

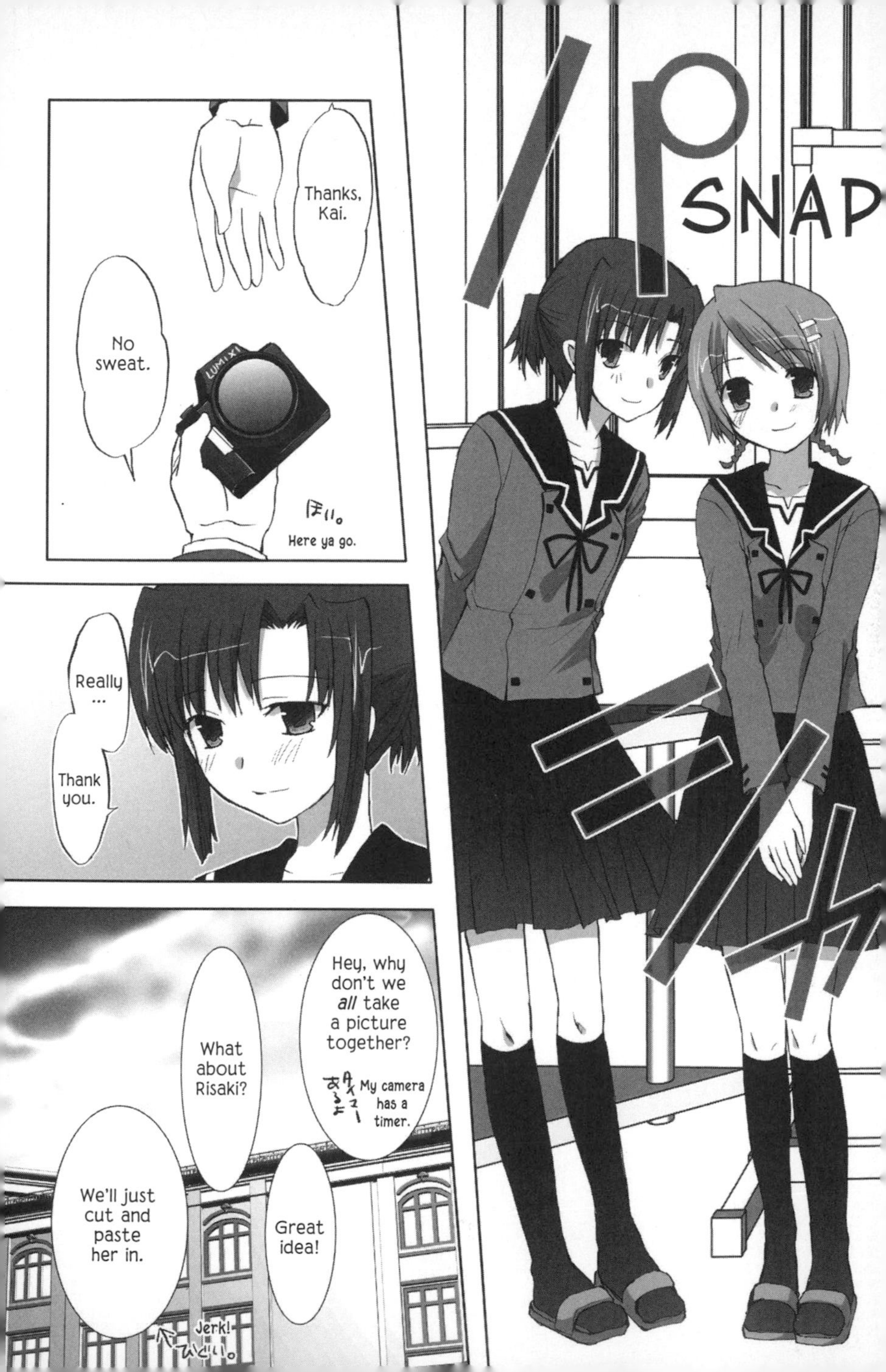
SNAP
Thanks, Kai.
No sweat.
ほい。
Here ya go.
Really...
Thank you.
Hey, why don't we *all* take a picture together?
My camera has a timer.
What about Risaki?
Great idea!
We'll just cut and paste her in.
Jerk!
ひどい。

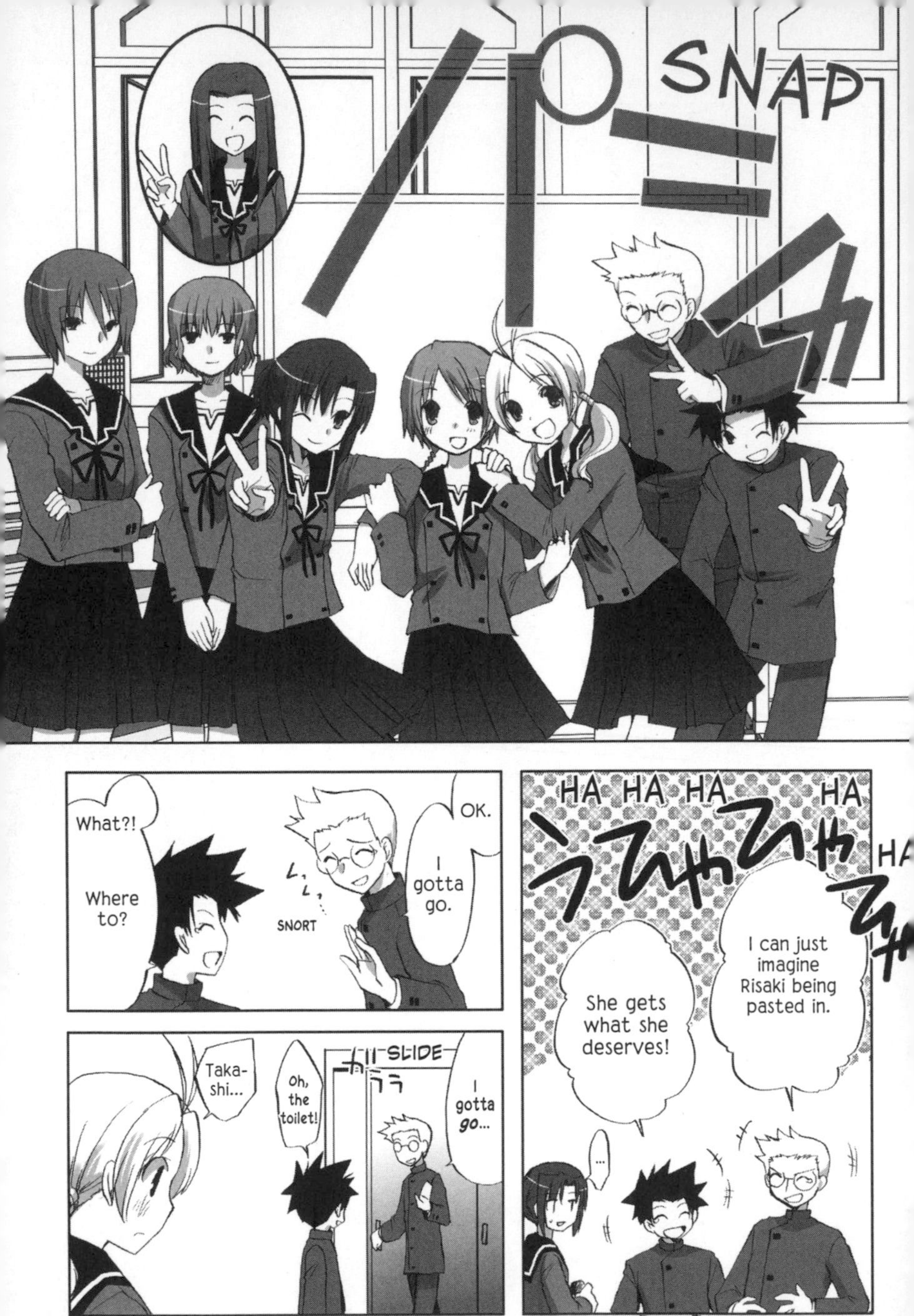
SNAP
OK.
I gotta go.
SNORT
What?!
Where to?
I gotta go...
SLIDE
Oh, the toilet!
Taka-shi...
HA HA HA HA HA
I can just imagine Risaki being pasted in.
She gets what she deserves!
...

Like old times...

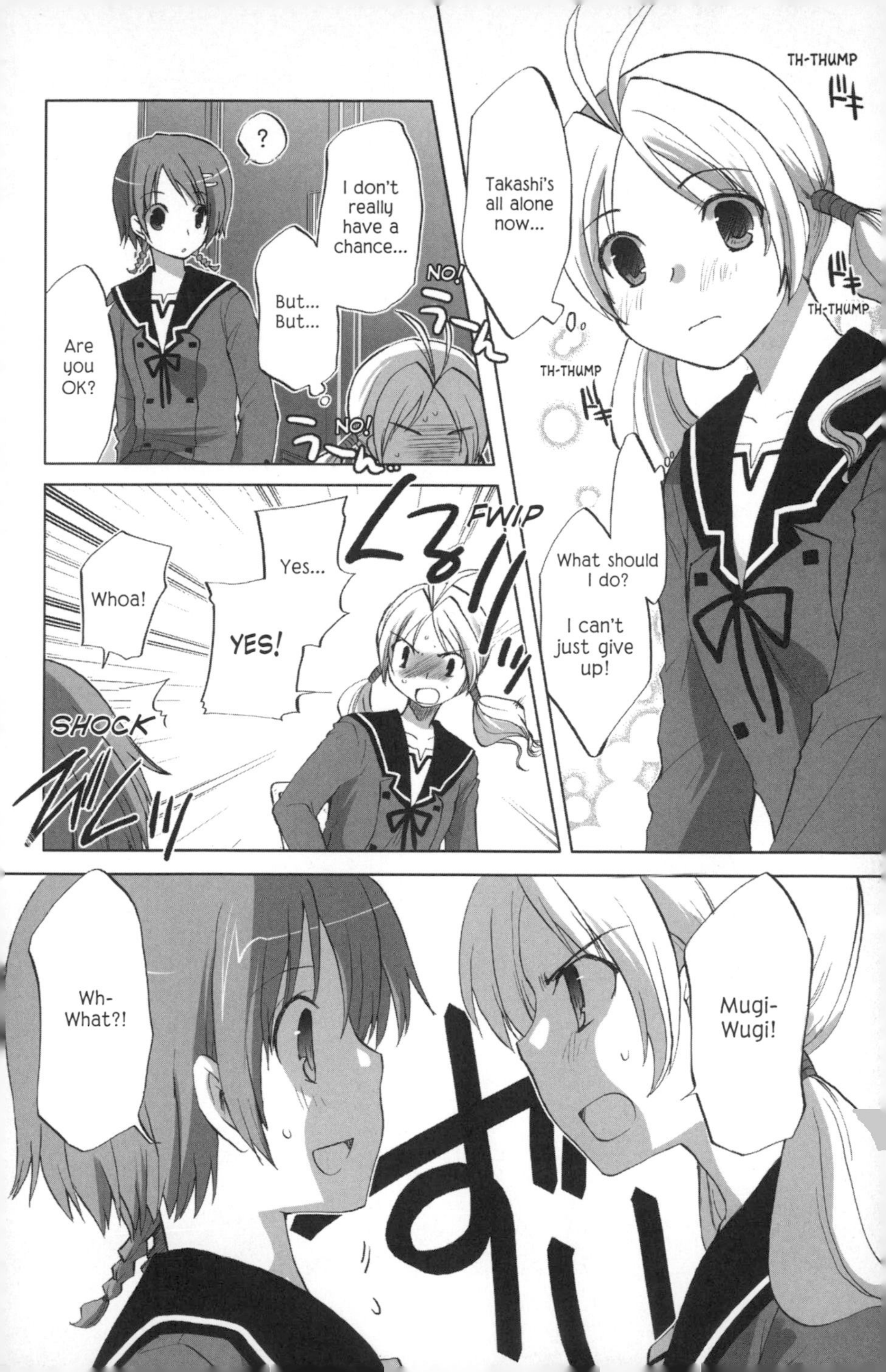
TH-THUMP
ドキ
Takashi's all alone now...
ドキ
TH-THUMP
TH-THUMP
ドキ
What should I do?
I can't just give up!
I don't really have a chance...
?
But... But...
NO!
NO!
Are you OK?
FWIP
Yes...
YES!
Whoa!
SHOCK
Mugi-Wugi!
Wh-What?!

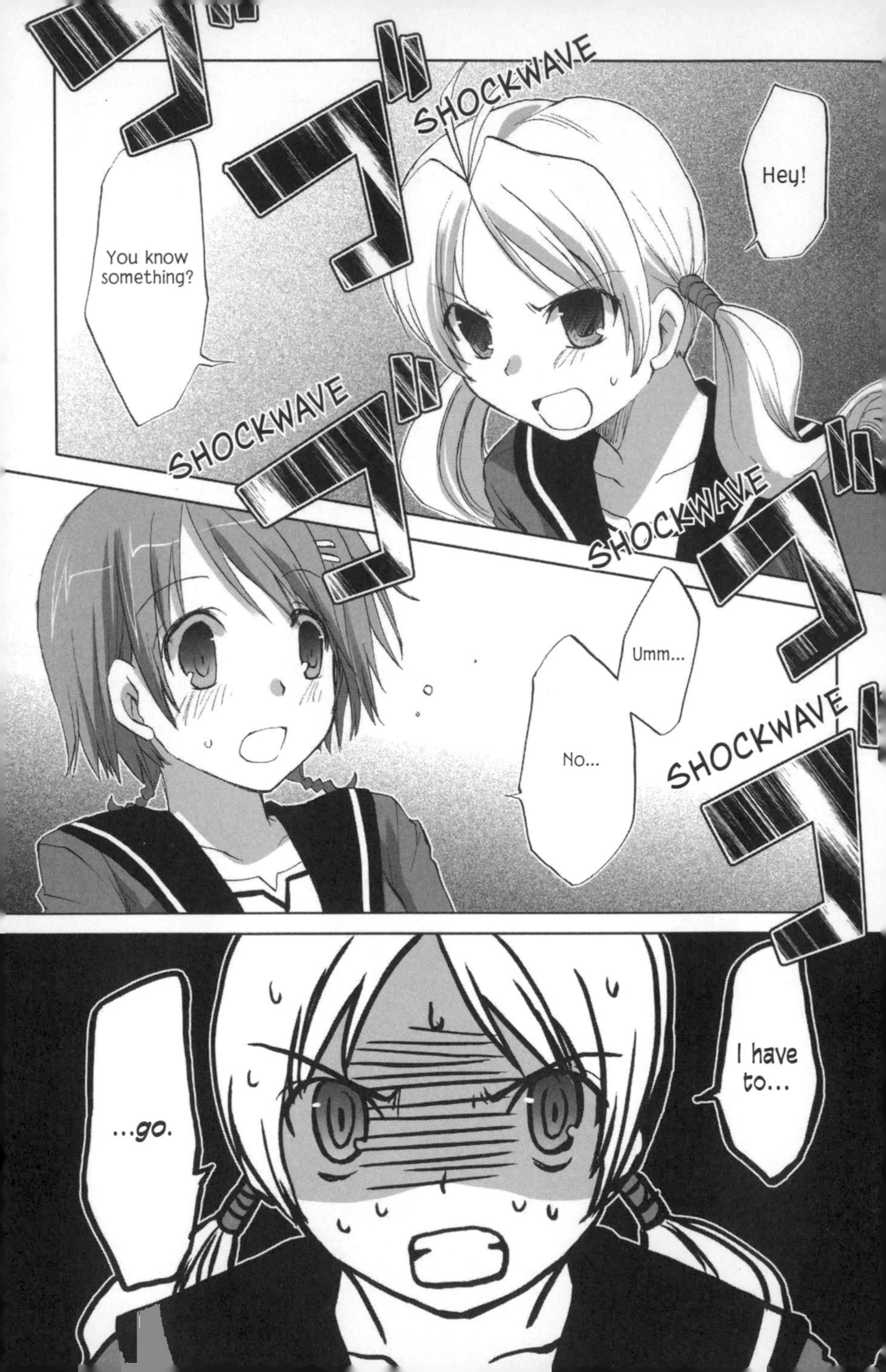
SHOCKWAVE
Hey!
You know something?
SHOCKWAVE
SHOCKWAVE
SHOCKWAVE
Umm...
No...
I have to...
...go.

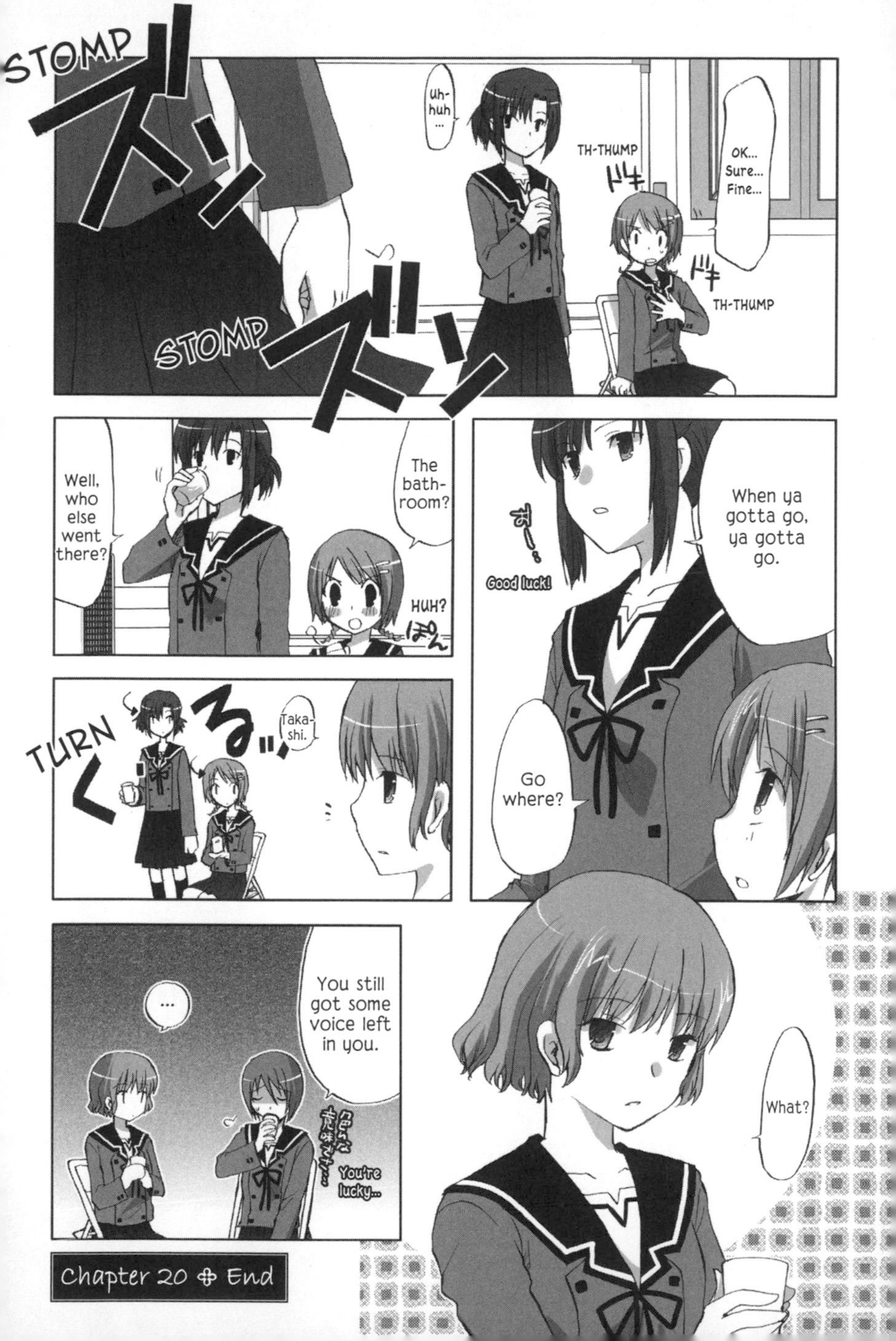
OK... Sure... Fine...
TH-THUMP
TH-THUMP
Uh-huh...
STOMP
STOMP
When ya gotta go, ya gotta go.
Good luck!
Go where?
The bathroom?
HUH?
Well, who else went there?
Takashi.
TURN
What?
You still got some voice left in you.
...
You're lucky...
Chapter 20 End

Best Friends Chapter 21

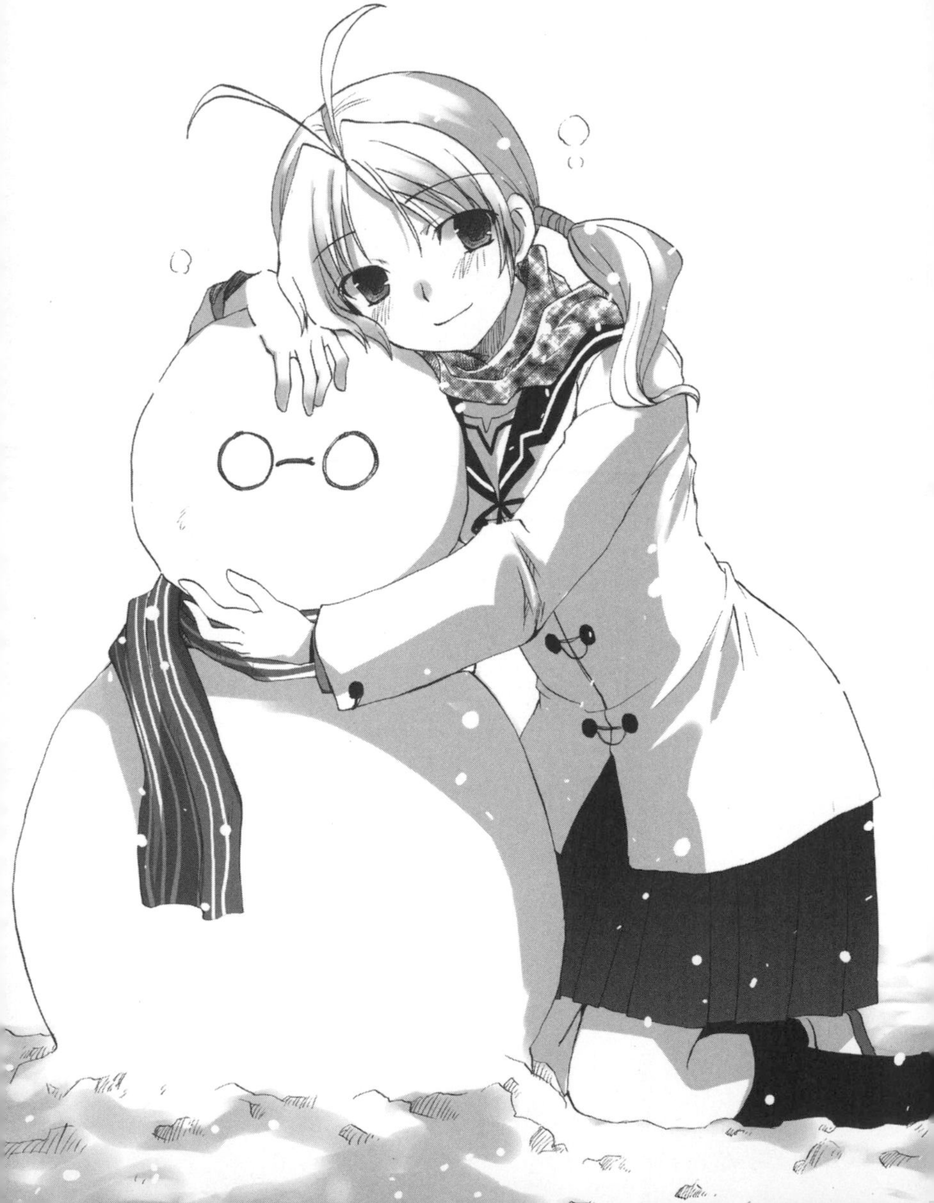

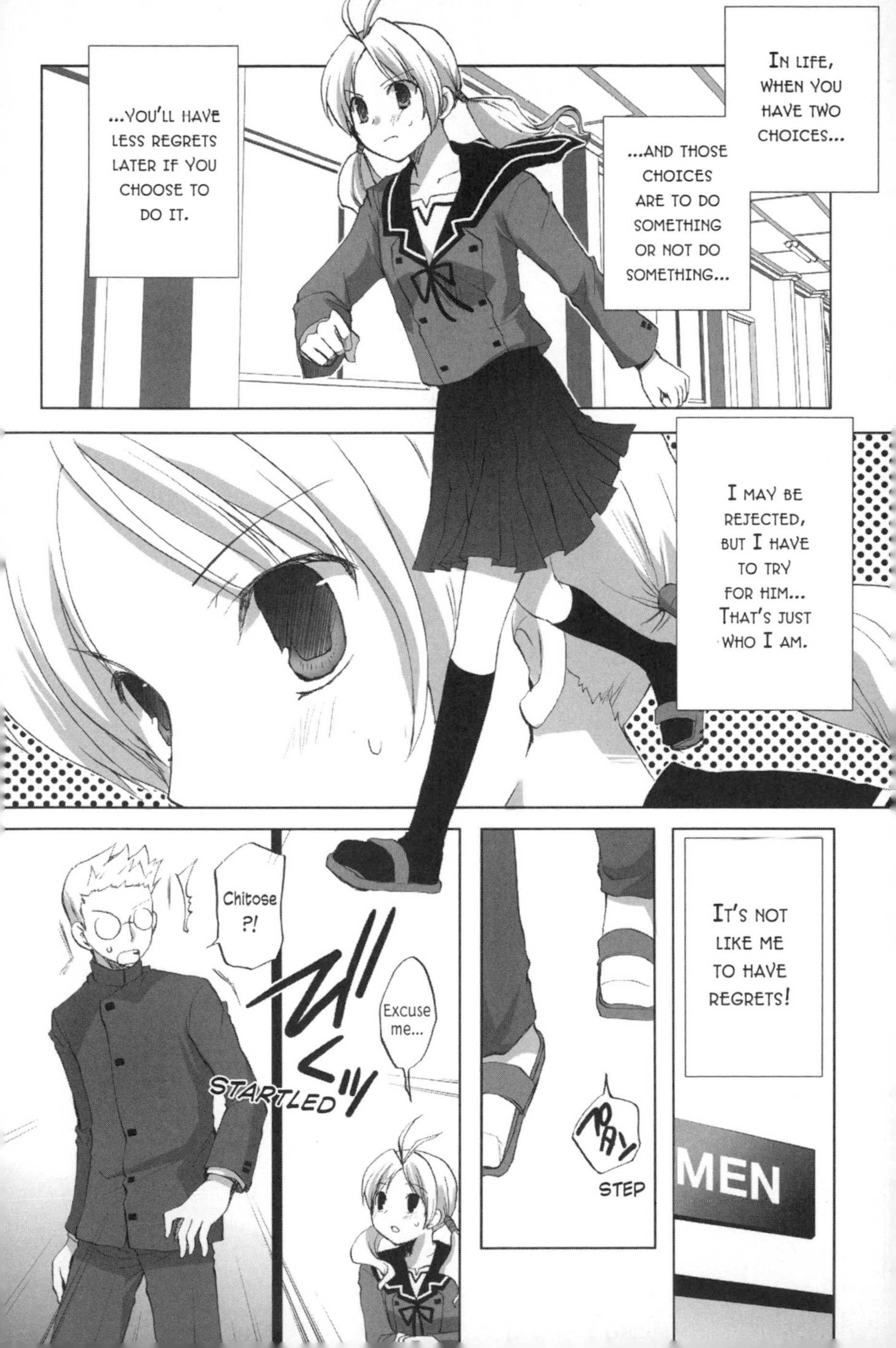
In life, when you have two choices...
...and those choices are to do something or not do something...
...you'll have less regrets later if you choose to do it.
I may be rejected, but I have to try for him... That's just who I am.
It's not like me to have regrets!
MEN
STEP
Chitose ?!
Excuse me...
STARTLED

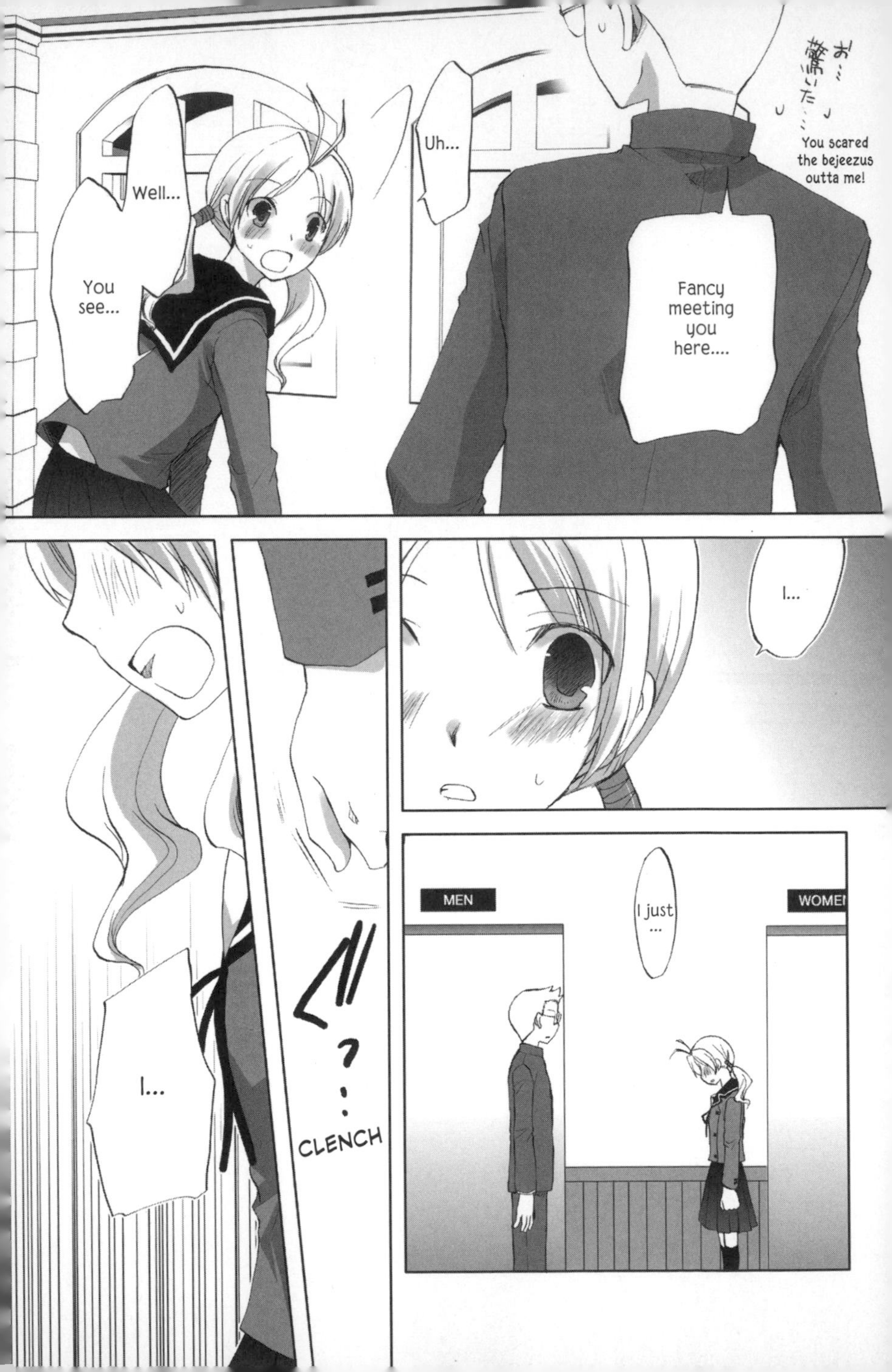

お…驚いた…
You scared the bejeezus outta me!
Fancy meeting you here....
Uh...
Well...
You see...
I...
MEN
WOMEN
I just ...
ぐっ
CLENCH
I...

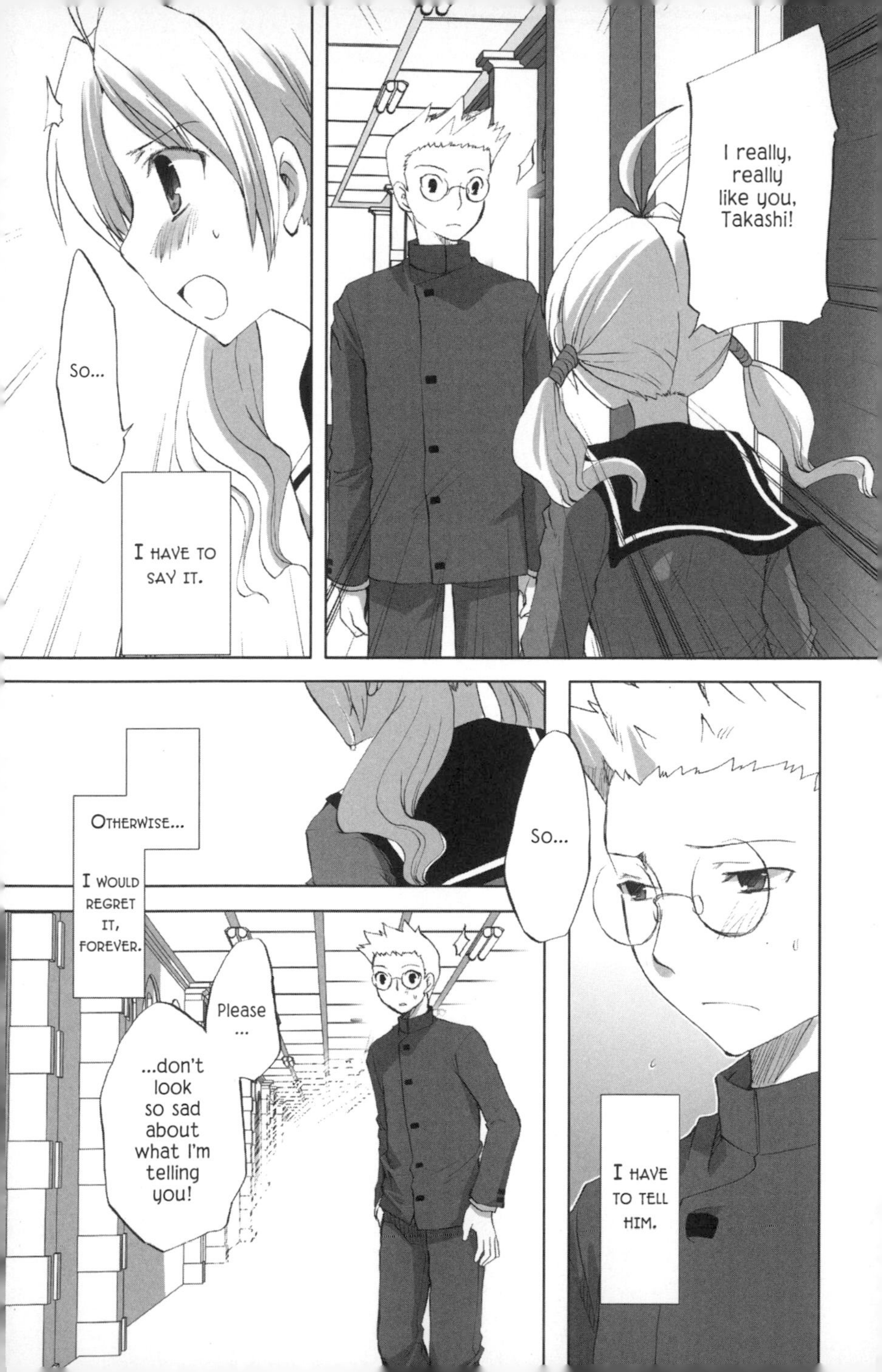
I really, really like you, Takashi!
So...
I HAVE TO SAY IT.
So...
I HAVE TO TELL HIM.
OTHERWISE...
I WOULD REGRET IT, FOREVER.
Please...
...don't look so sad about what I'm telling you!

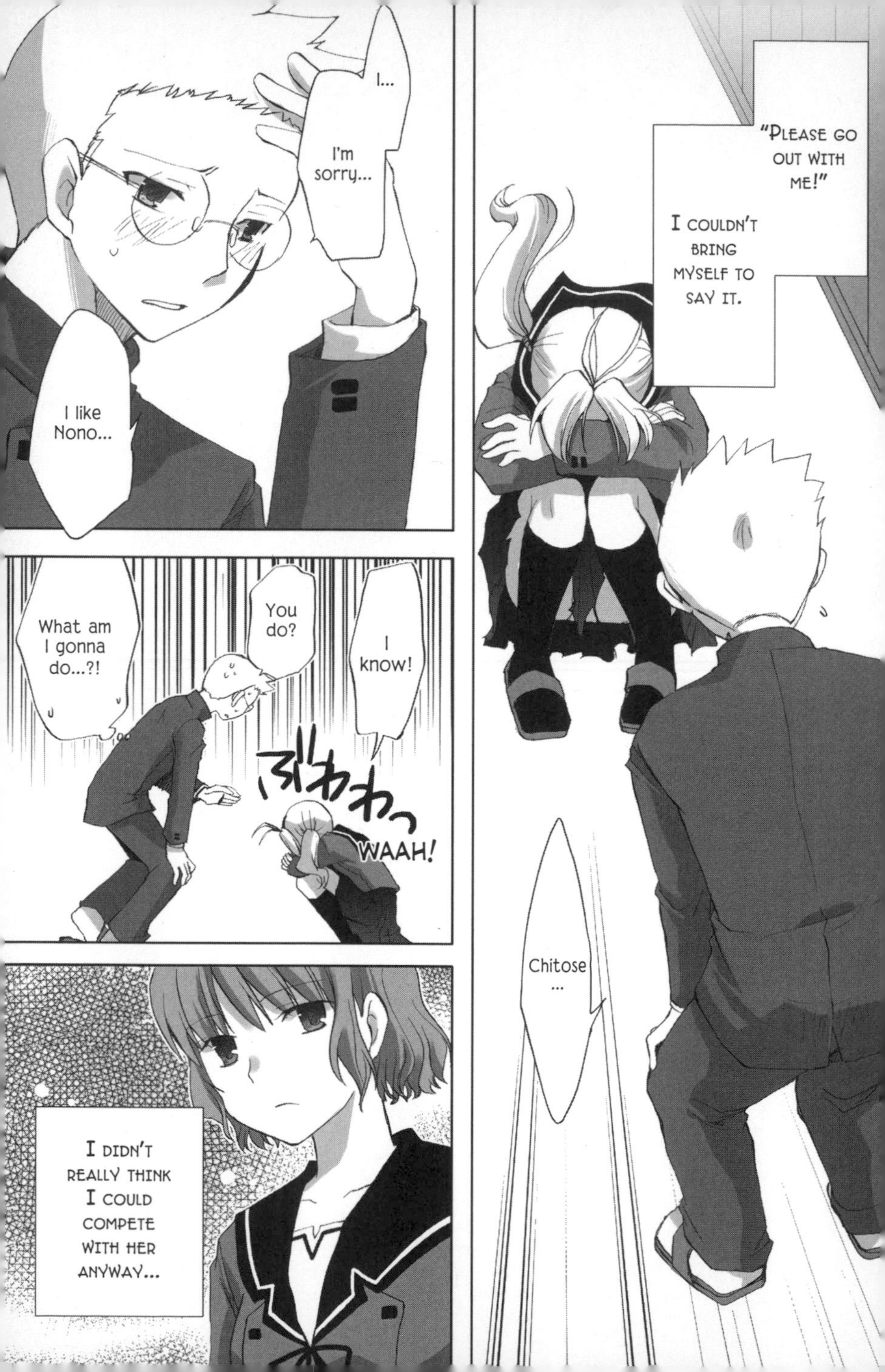
"Please go out with me!"
I couldn't bring myself to say it.
Chitose ...
I... I'm sorry...
I like Nono...
I know!
ぶわわっ WAAH!
You do?
What am I gonna do...?!
I didn't really think I could compete with her anyway...

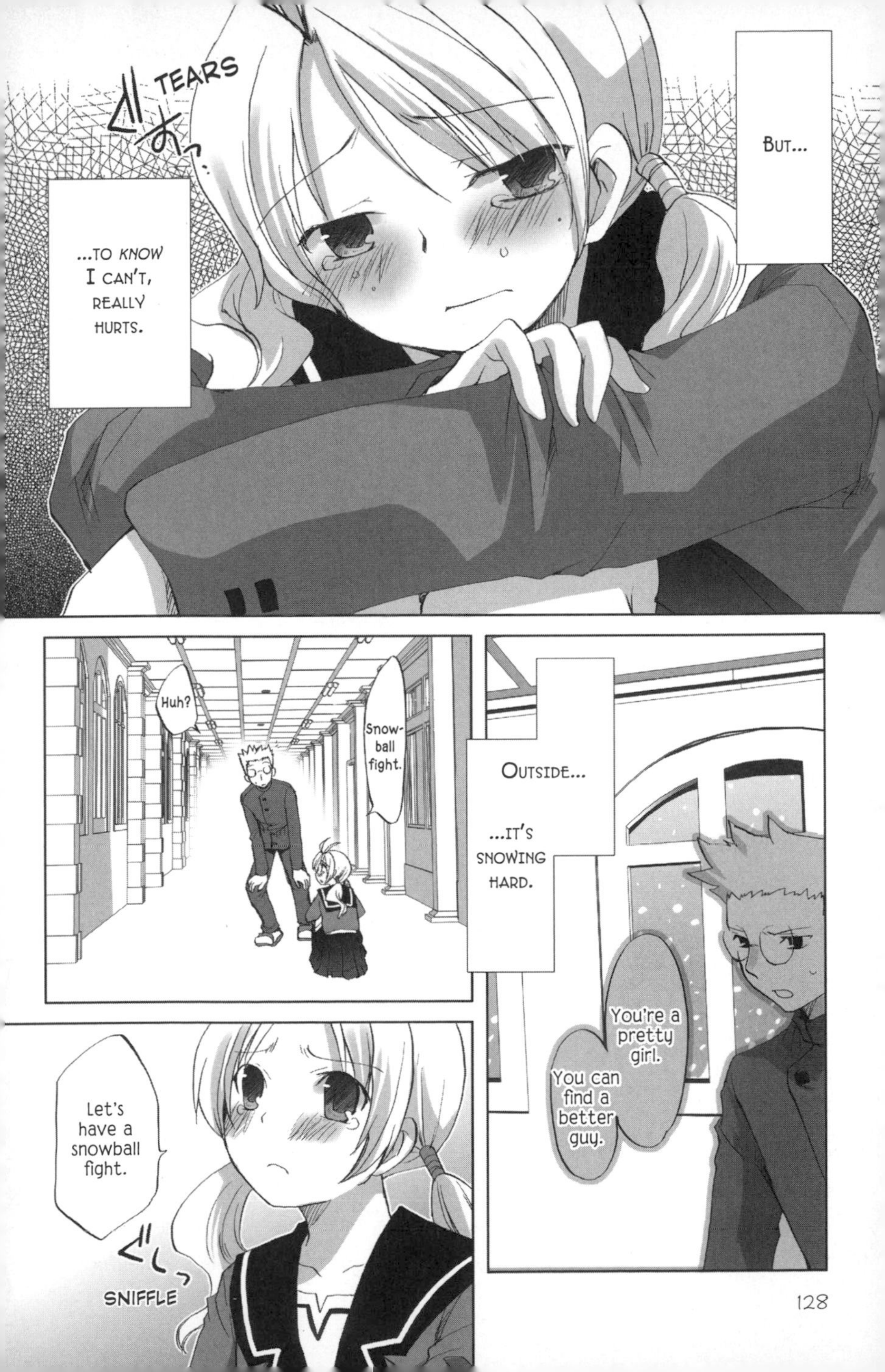
TEARS
But...
...to know I can't, really hurts.
Outside...
...it's snowing hard.
You're a pretty girl.
You can find a better guy.
Snow-ball fight.
Huh?
Let's have a snowball fight.
SNIFFLE

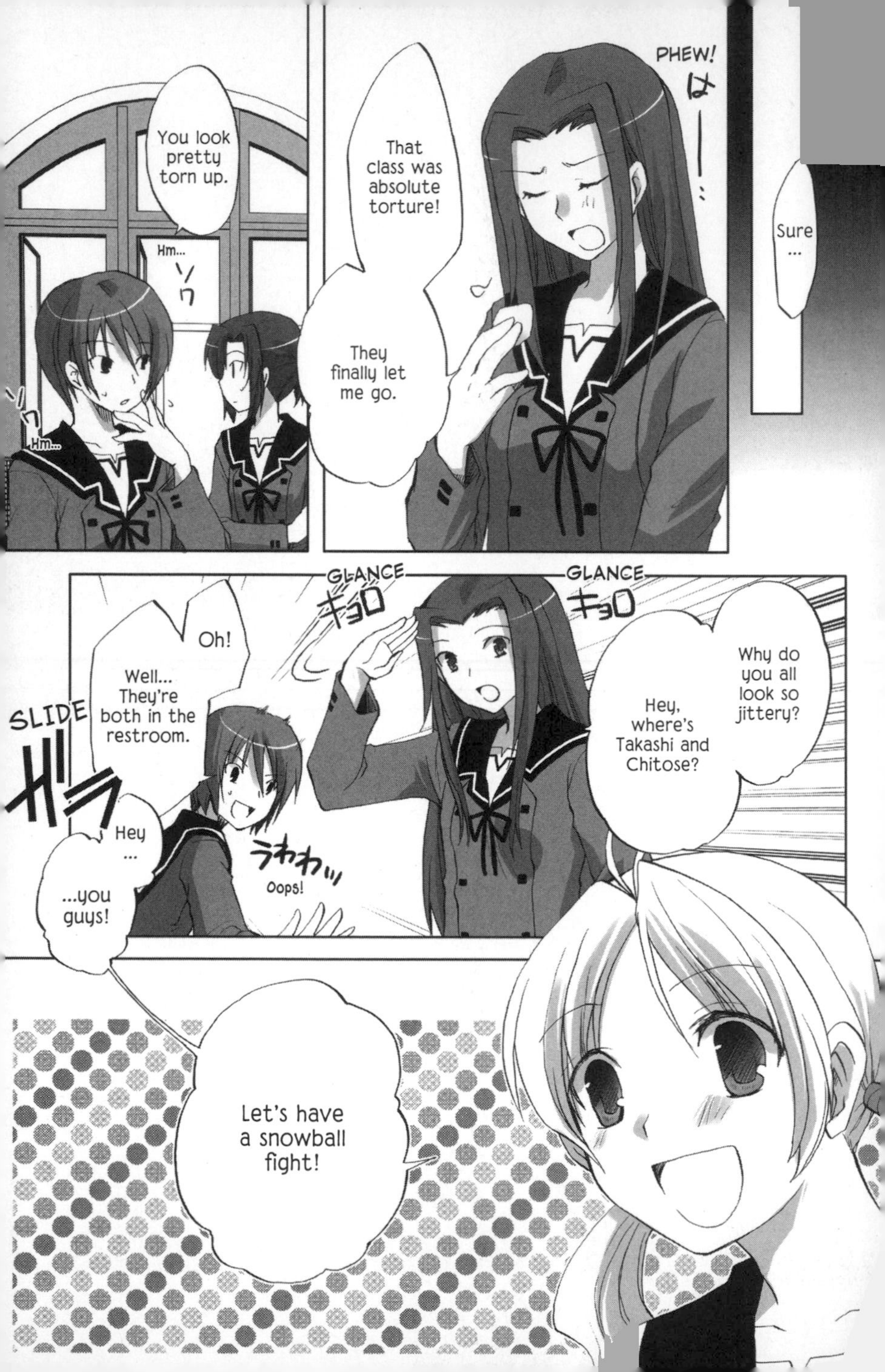
Sure ...
PHEW!
はー!
That class was absolute torture!
They finally let me go.
You look pretty torn up.
Hm...
ソワ
ソワ
Hm...
GLANCE
キョロ
Why do you all look so jittery?
Hey, where's Takashi and Chitose?
GLANCE
キョロ
Oh!
Well... They're both in the restroom.
うわわッ
Oops!
SLIDE
ガラ
Hey ...
...you guys!
Let's have a snowball fight!

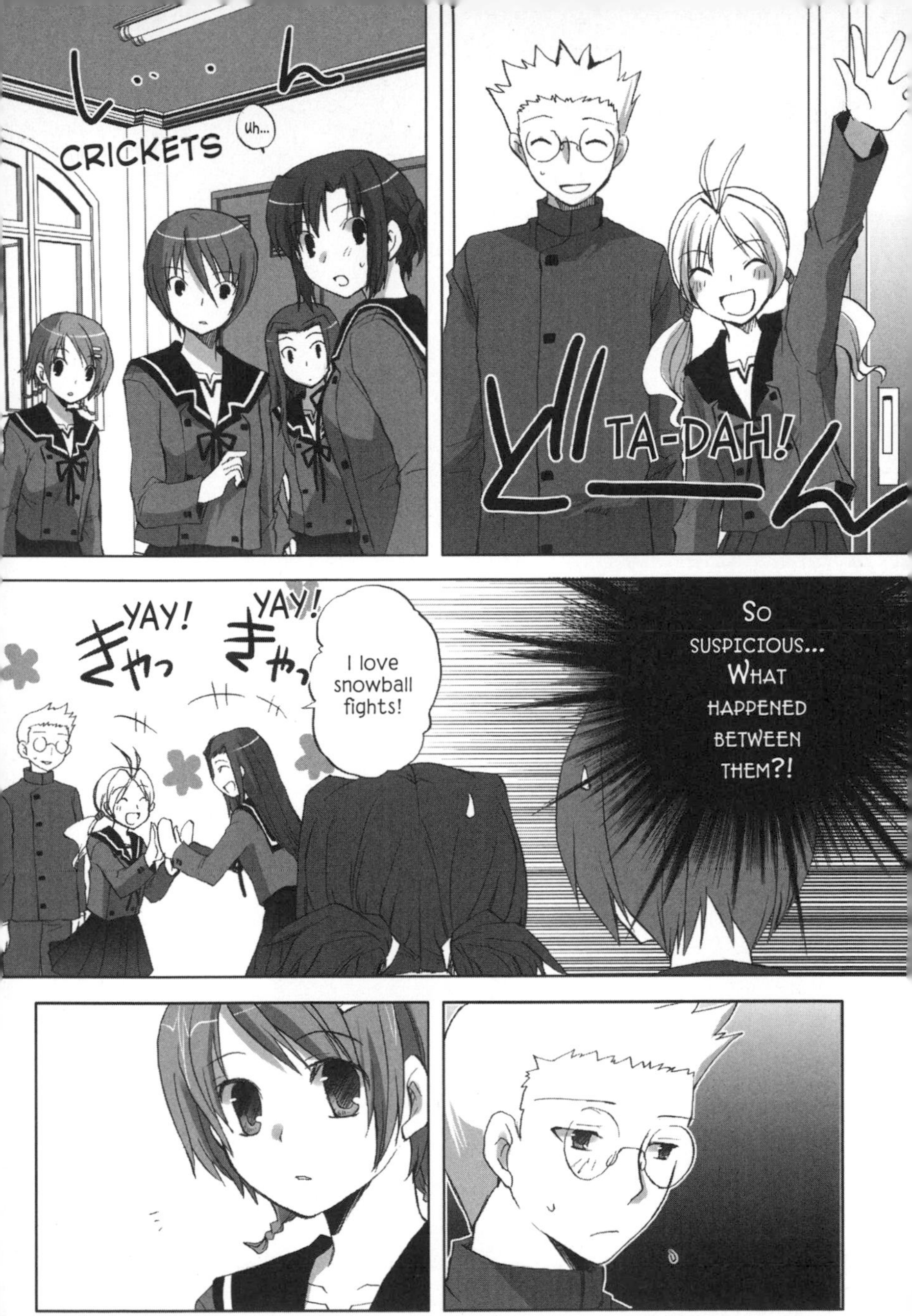

ど──ん
TA-DAH!
し…ん
CRICKETS
uh...
So suspicious... What happened between them?!
YAY!
きゃっ
I love snowball fights!
YAY!
きゃっ

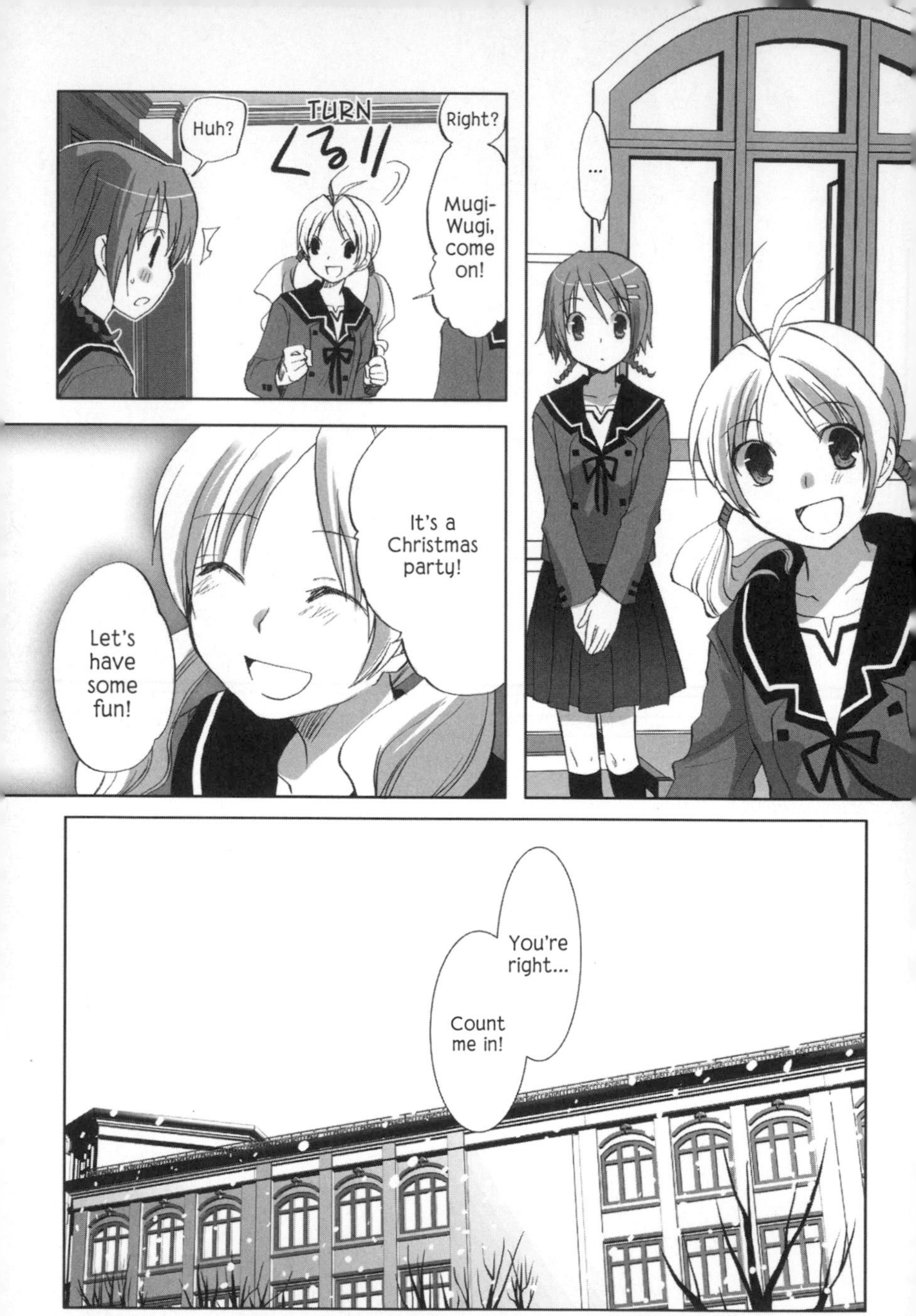
...
Right?
Mugi-Wugi, come on!
TURN
Huh?
It's a Christmas party!
Let's have some fun!
You're right...
Count me in!

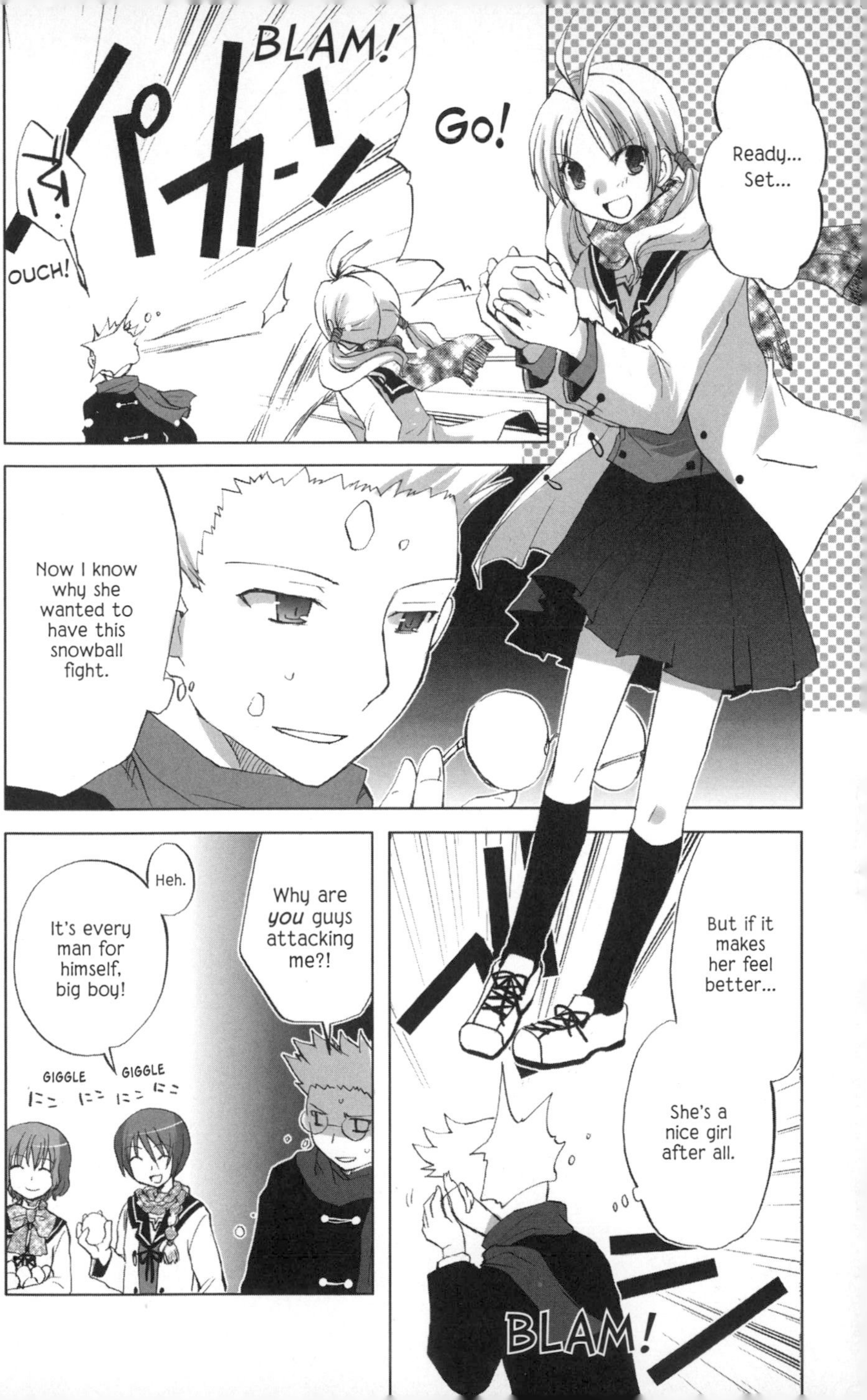

Ready... Set...
Go!
BLAM!
パカーン
OUCH!
Now I know why she wanted to have this snowball fight.
But if it makes her feel better...
She's a nice girl after all.
BLAM!
Why are *you* guys attacking me?!
Heh.
It's every man for himself, big boy!
GIGGLE GIGGLE
にこ にこ にこ にこ

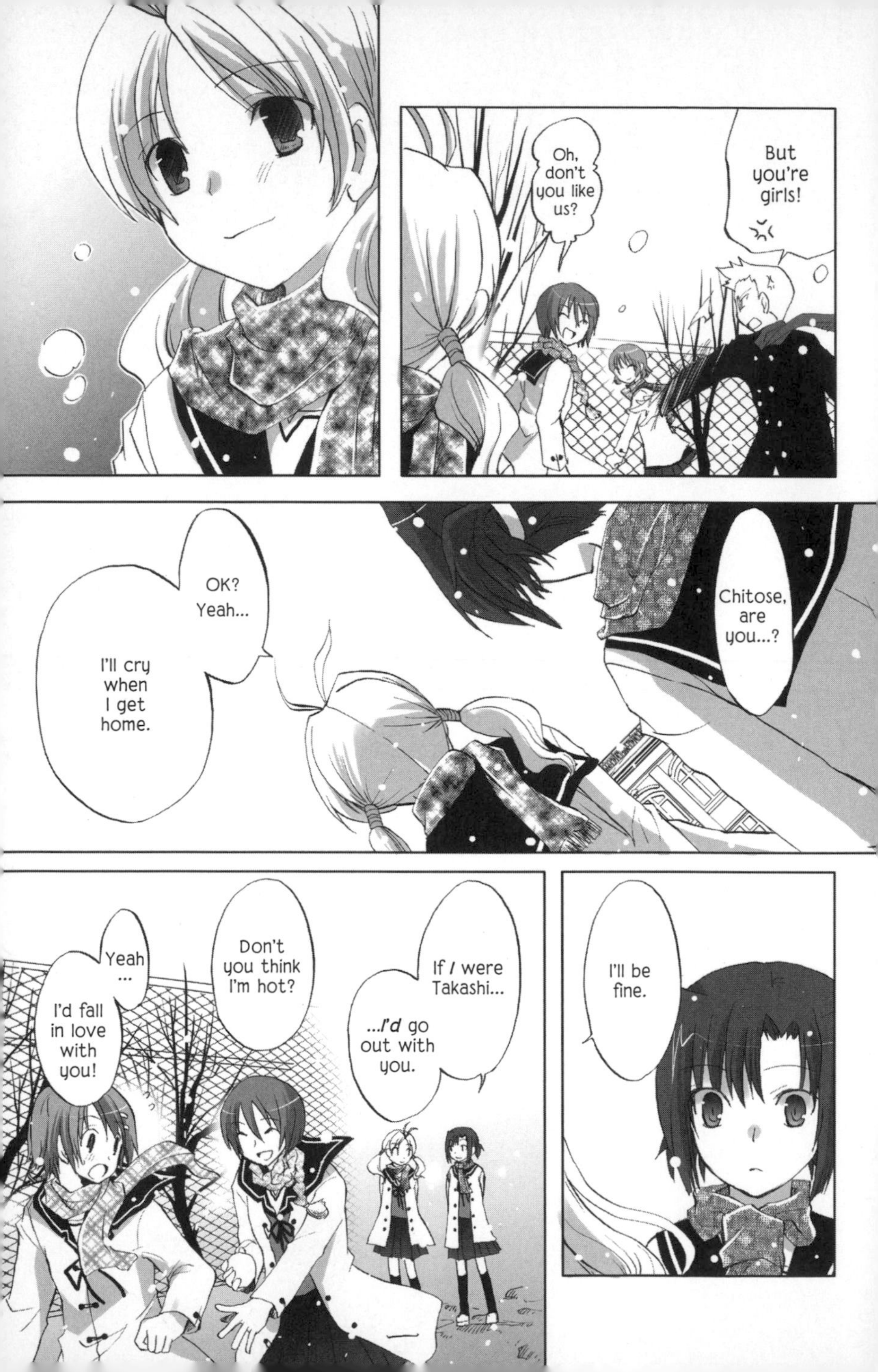
But you're girls!
Oh, don't you like us?
Chitose, are you...?
OK? Yeah...
I'll cry when I get home.
I'll be fine.
If *I* were Takashi...
...*I'd* go out with you.
Don't you think I'm hot?
Yeah...
I'd fall in love with you!

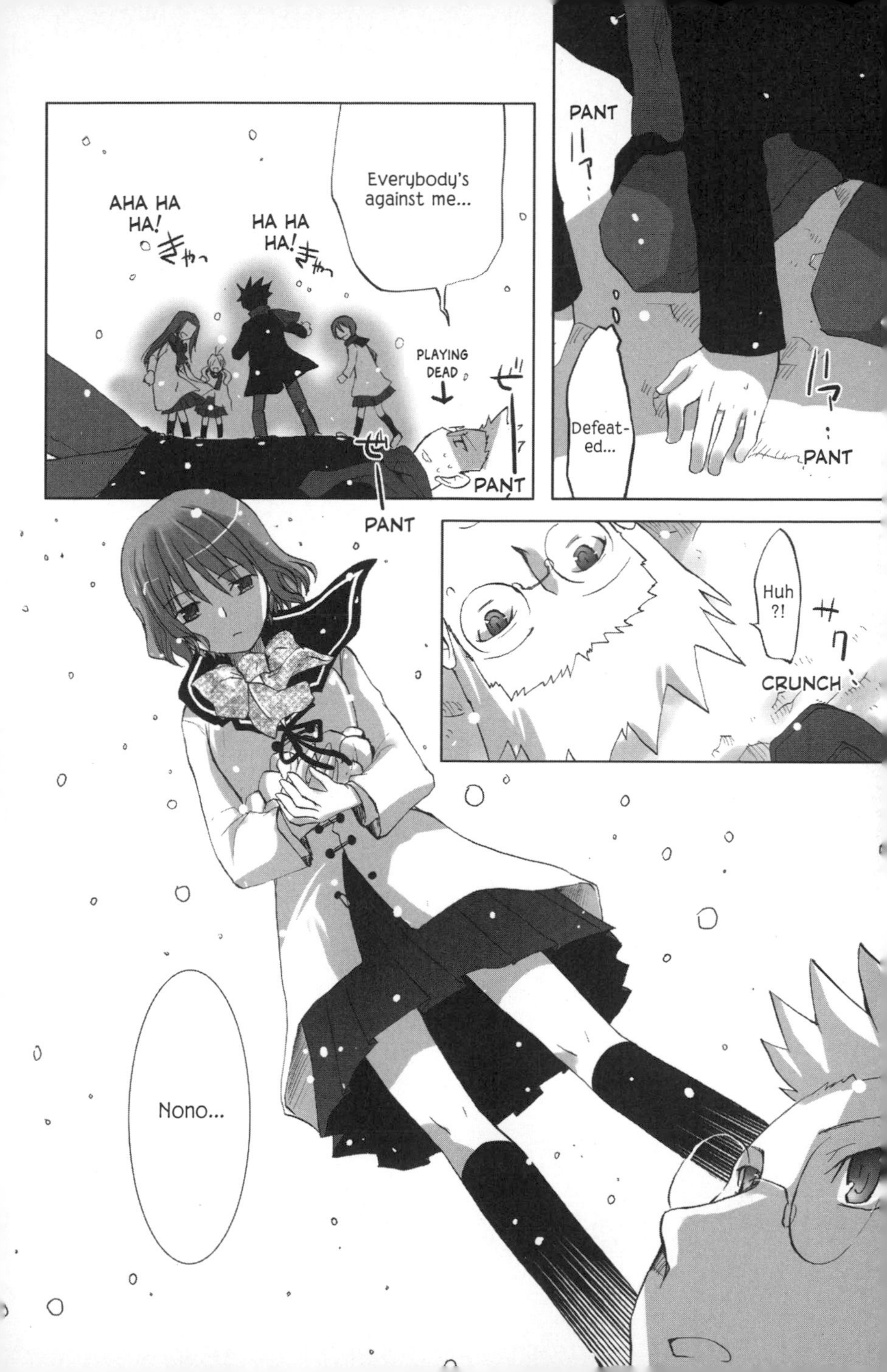
PANT
Defeat-ed...
PANT
AHA HA HA!
HA HA HA!
Everybody's against me...
PLAYING DEAD
PANT
PANT
Huh?!
CRUNCH
Nono...

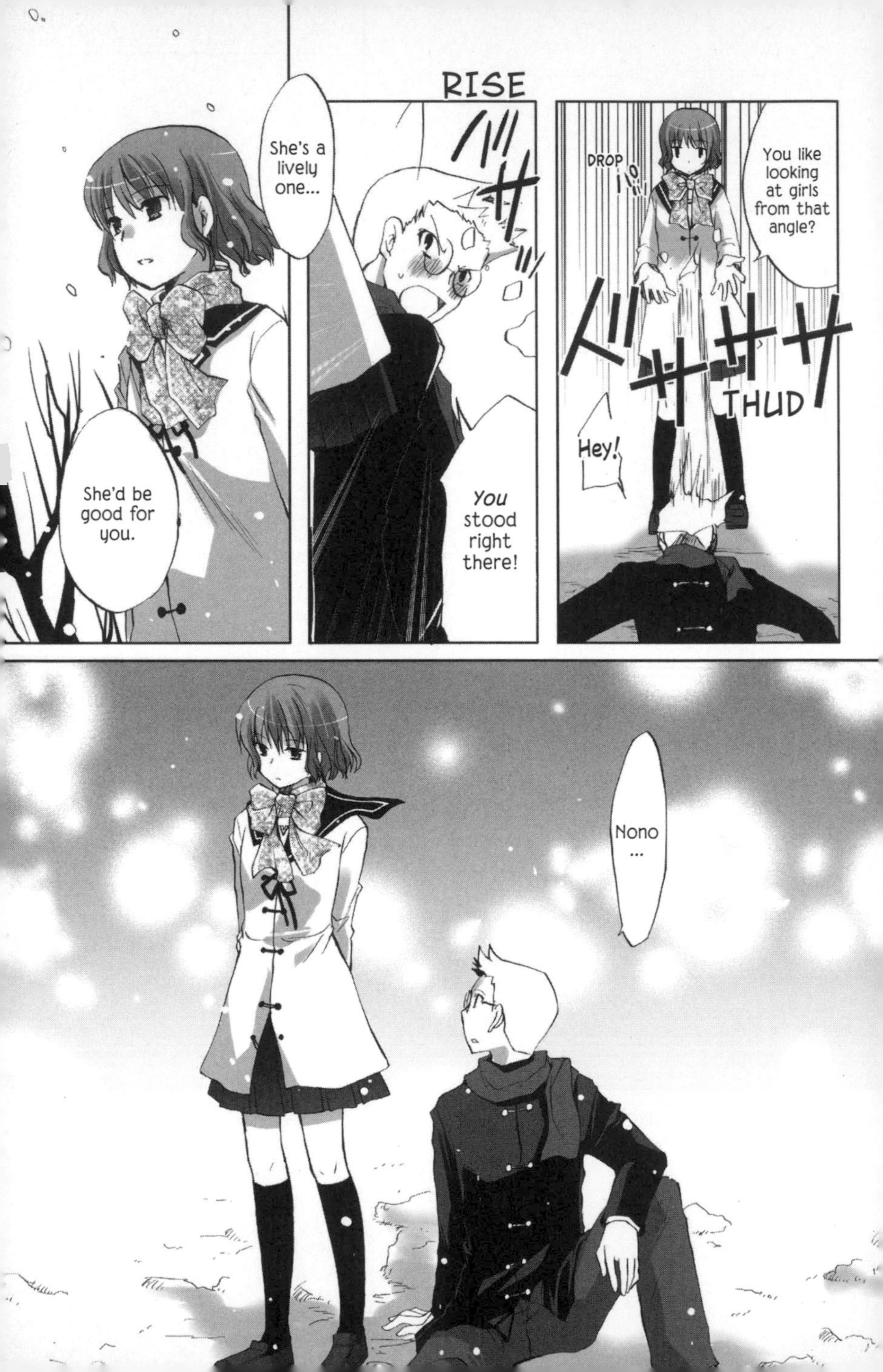
You like looking at girls from that angle?
DROP
THUD
Hey!
RISE
You stood right there!
She's a lively one...
She'd be good for you.
Nono ...

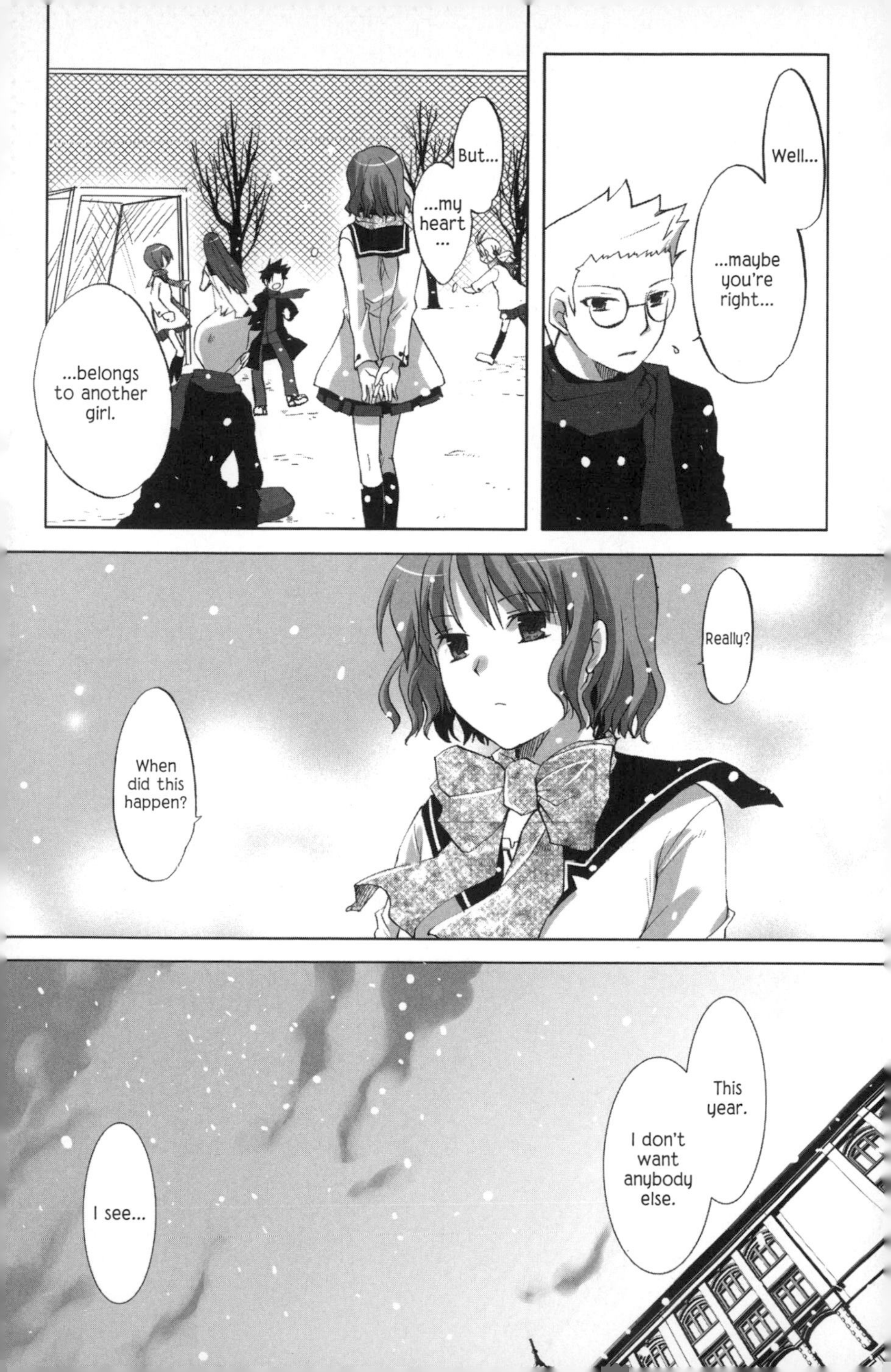
Well...
...maybe you're right...
But...
...my heart ...
...belongs to another girl.
Really?
When did this happen?
This year.
I don't want anybody else.
I see...

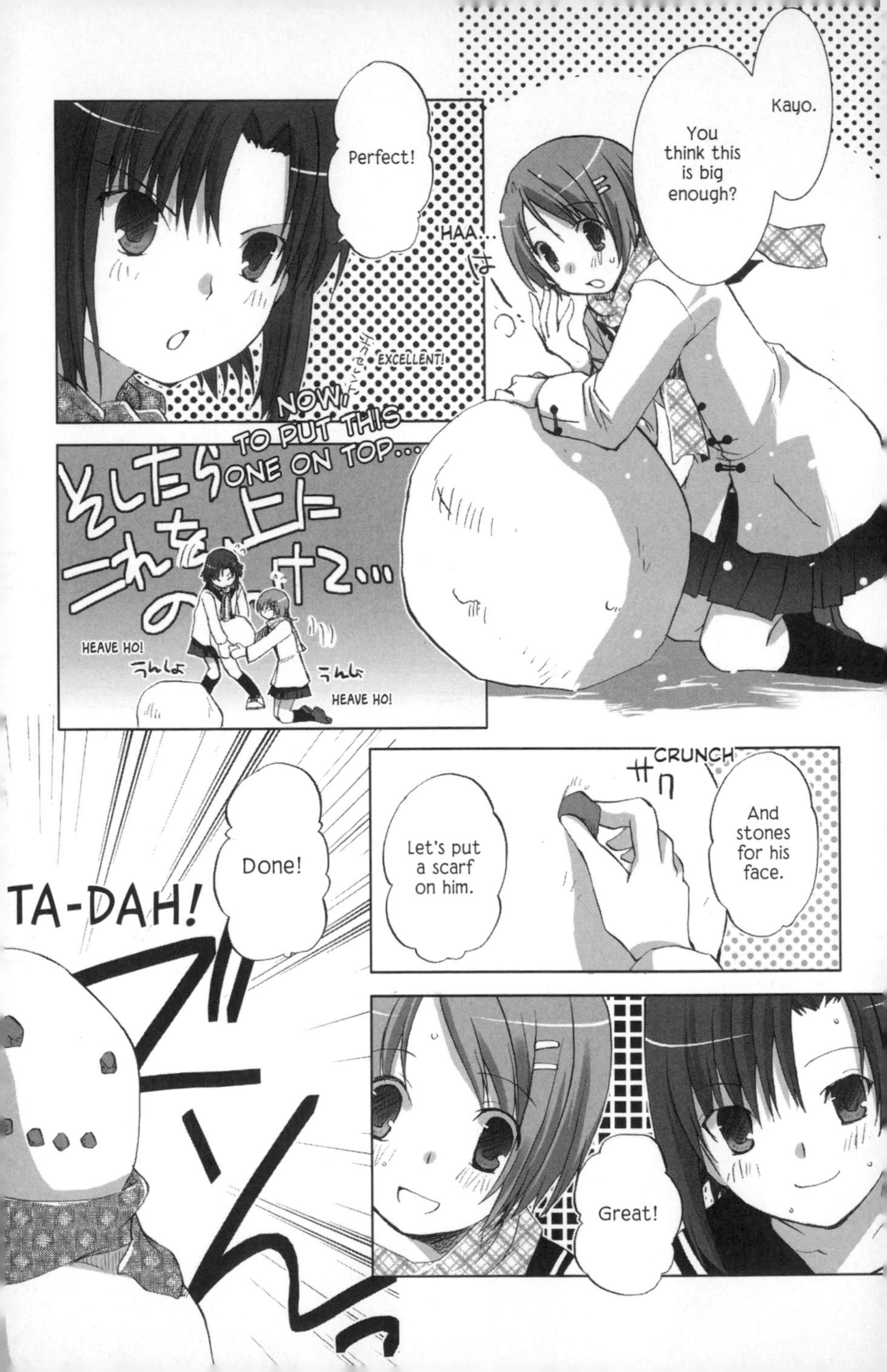
Kayo.
You think this is big enough?
HAA...
Perfect!
EXCELLENT!
NOW! TO PUT THIS ONE ON TOP...
HEAVE HO!
HEAVE HO!
CRUNCH
And stones for his face.
Let's put a scarf on him.
Great!
Done!
TA-DAH!

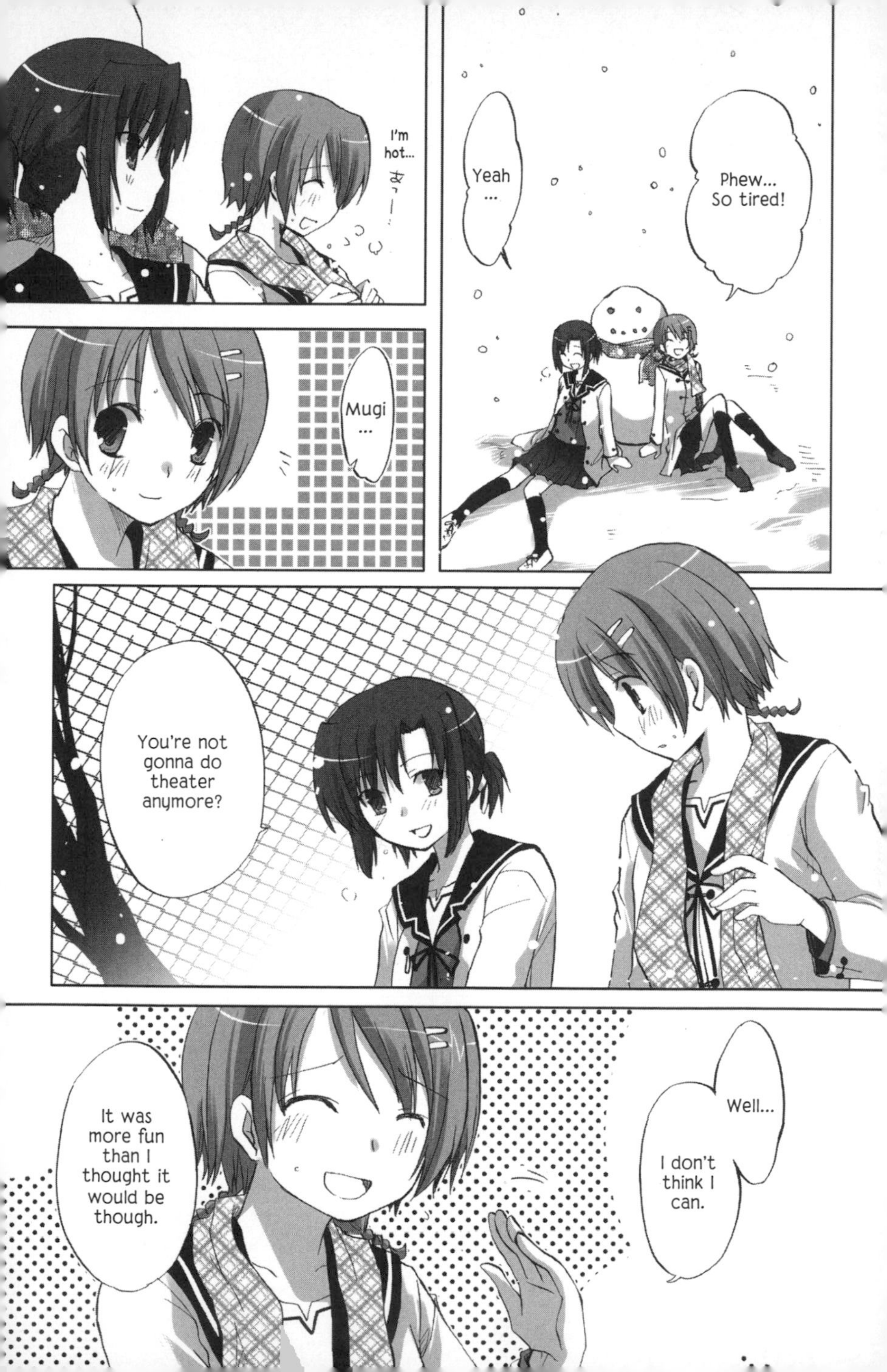

Phew... So tired!
Yeah ...
I'm hot...
あっー…
Mugi ...
You're not gonna do theater anymore?
Well...
I don't think I can.
It was more fun than I thought it would be though.

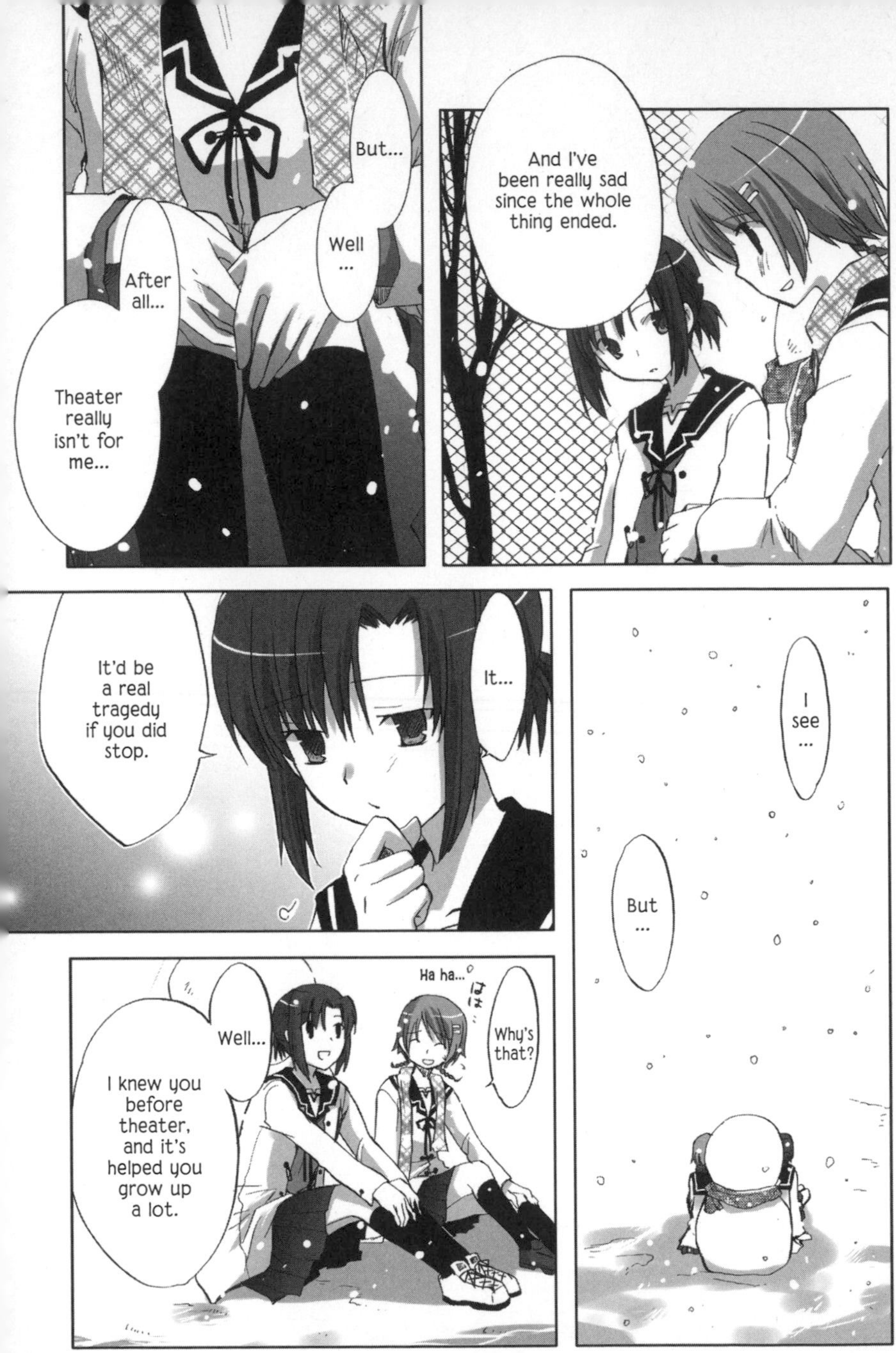

And I've been really sad since the whole thing ended.
But...
Well ...
After all...
Theater really isn't for me...
I see ...
But ...
It...
It'd be a real tragedy if you did stop.
Why's that?
Ha ha...
はは
Well...
I knew you before theater, and it's helped you grow up a lot.

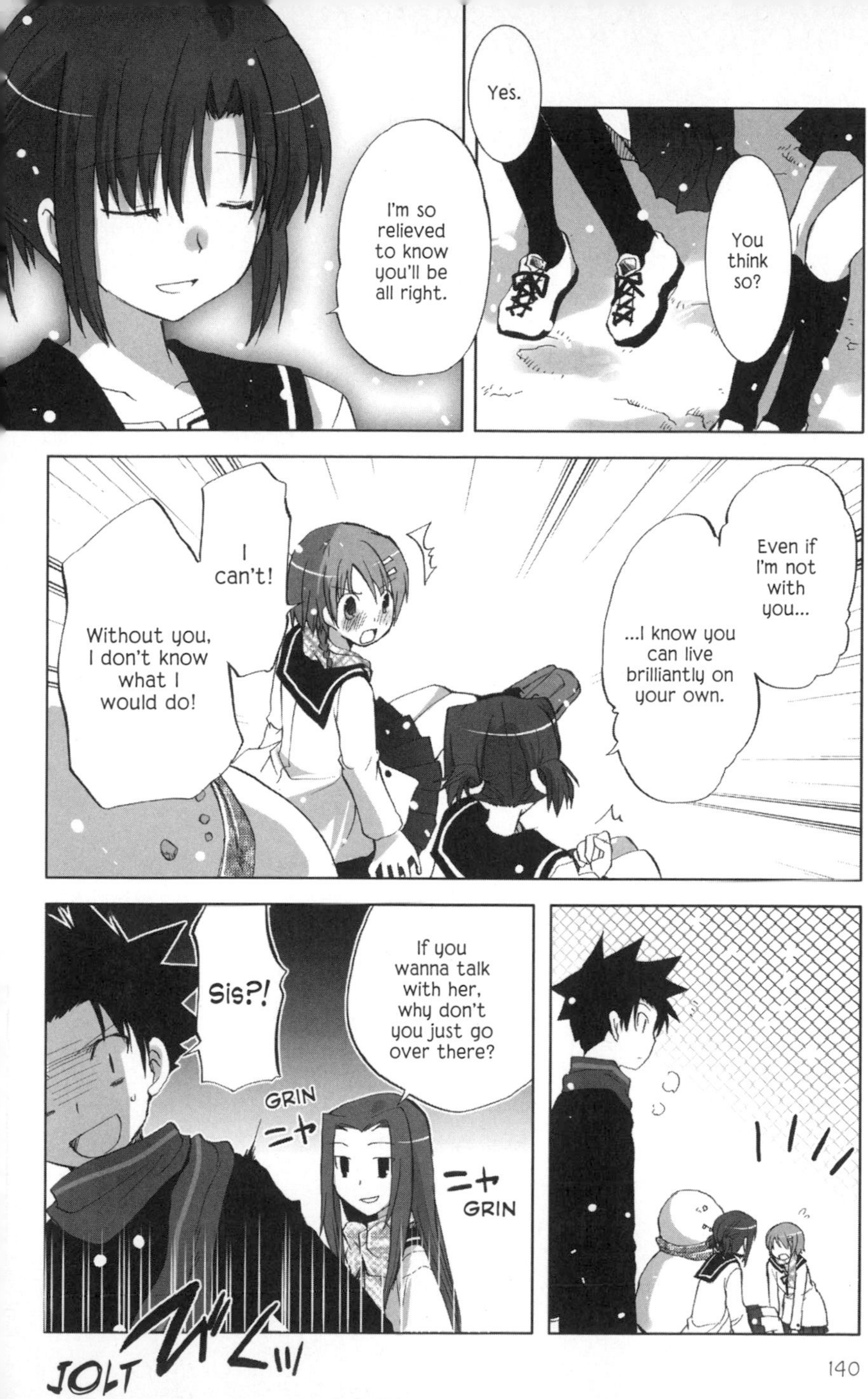
You think so?
Yes.
I'm so relieved to know you'll be all right.
Even if I'm not with you...
...I know you can live brilliantly on your own.
I can't!
Without you, I don't know what I would do!
If you wanna talk with her, why don't you just go over there?
GRIN
ニヤ
ニヤ
GRIN
Sis?!
JOLT

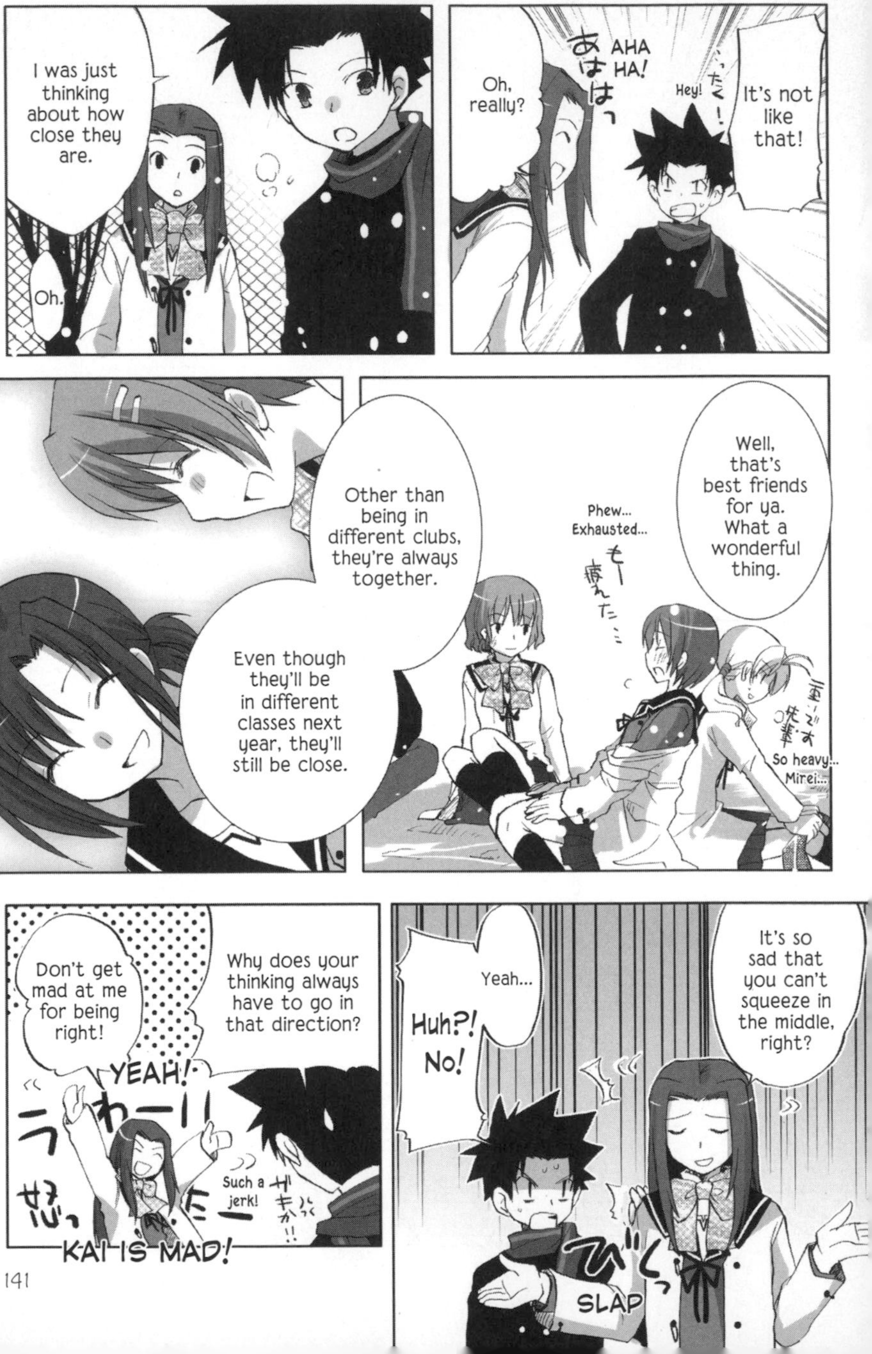
It's not like that!
Hey!
ったく!
AHA HA!
あはは
Oh, really?
I was just thinking about how close they are.
Oh.
Well, that's best friends for ya. What a wonderful thing.
Phew... Exhausted...
もー疲れた
So heavy... Mirei...
Other than being in different clubs, they're always together.
Even though they'll be in different classes next year, they'll still be close.
It's so sad that you can't squeeze in the middle, right?
Yeah...
Huh?! No!
SLAP
Why does your thinking always have to go in that direction?
Don't get mad at me for being right!
YEAH!
うわーい
Such a jerk!
ガキか
怒った
KAI IS MAD!

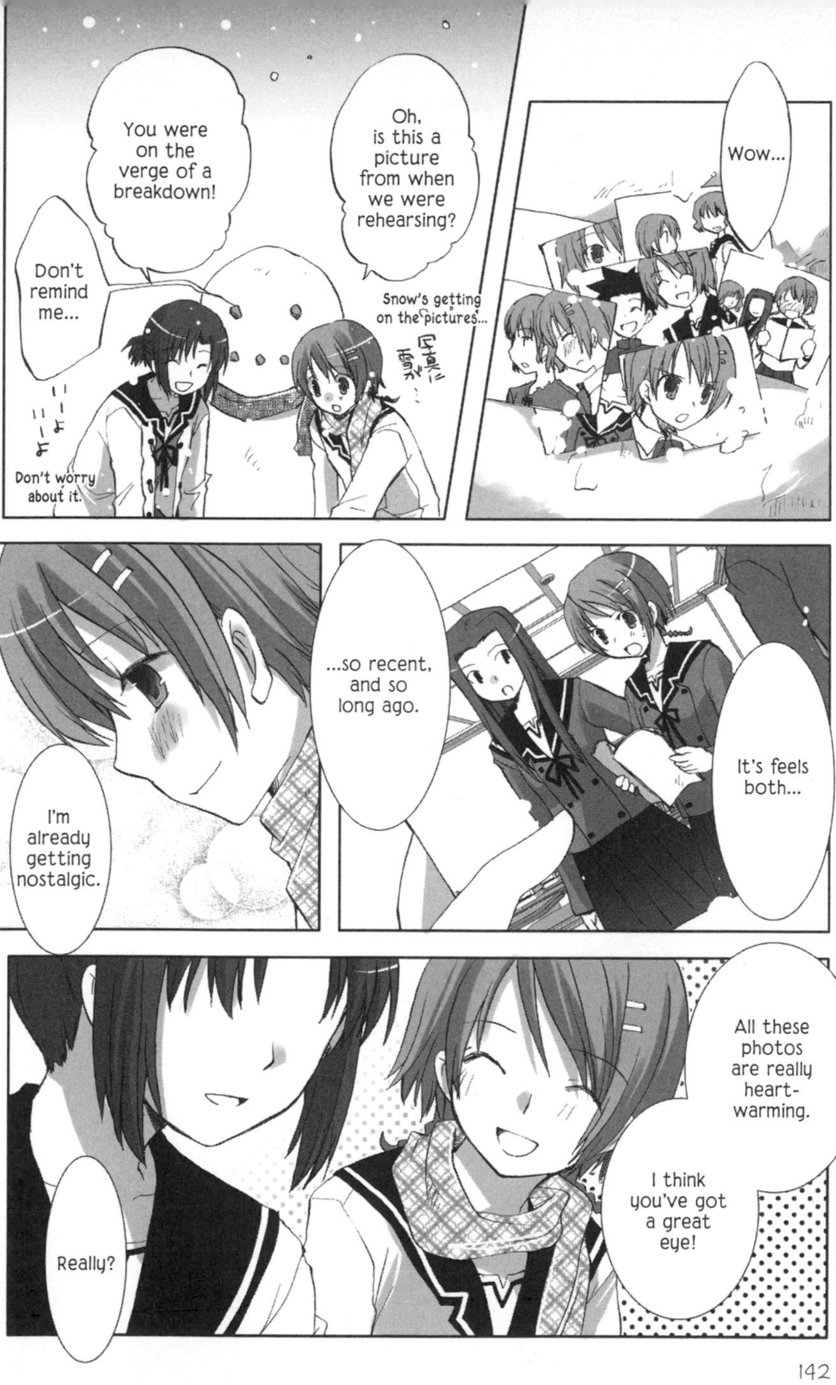
Wow...
Oh, is this a picture from when we were rehearsing?
You were on the verge of a breakdown!
Snow's getting on the pictures...
写真に雪が…
Don't remind me...
いーよいーよ
Don't worry about it.
It's feels both...
...so recent, and so long ago.
I'm already getting nostalgic.
All these photos are really heart-warming.
I think you've got a great eye!
Really?

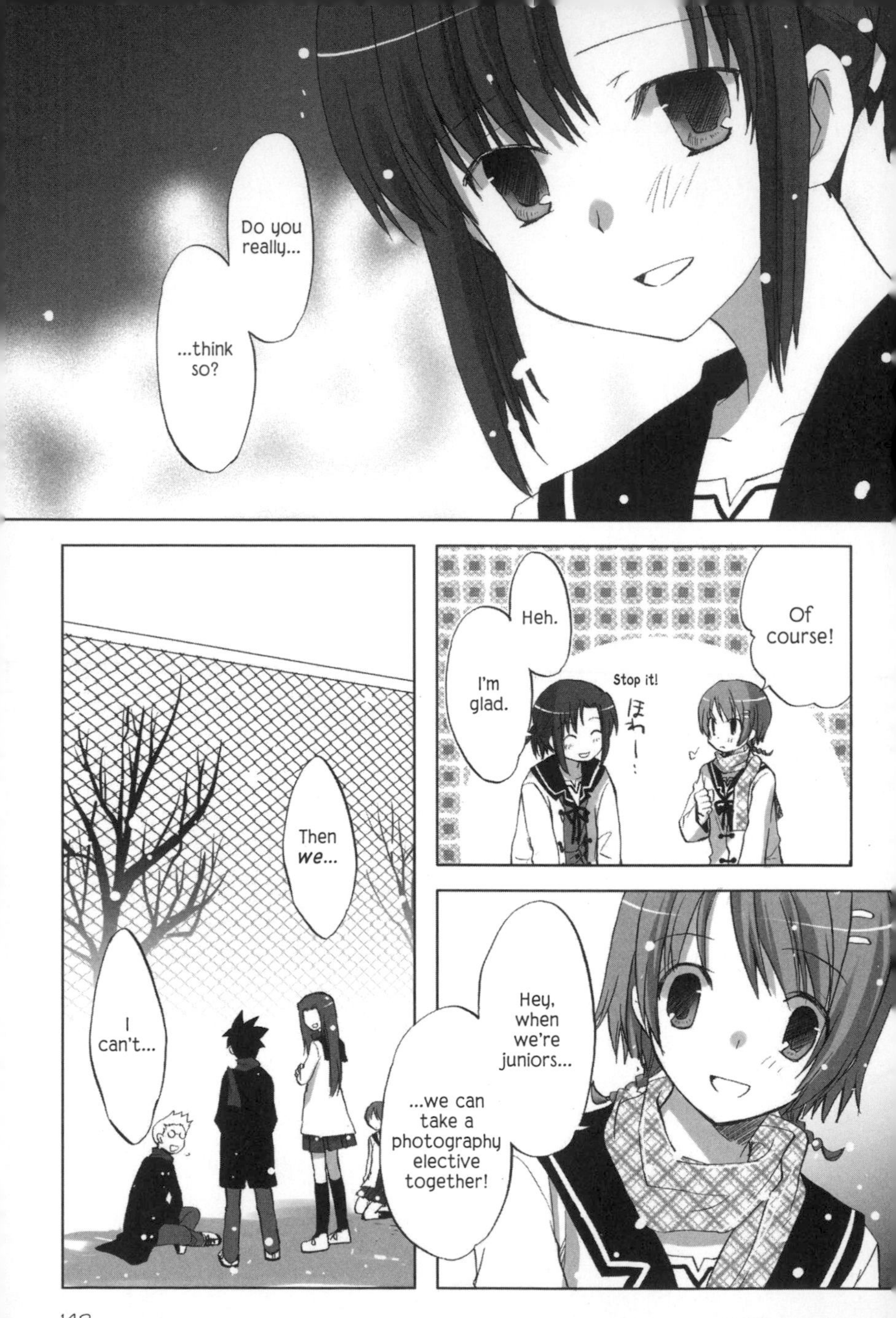
Do you really...
...think so?
Of course!
Heh.
I'm glad.
Stop it!
ほわー
Hey, when we're juniors...
...we can take a photography elective together!
Then *we*...
I can't...

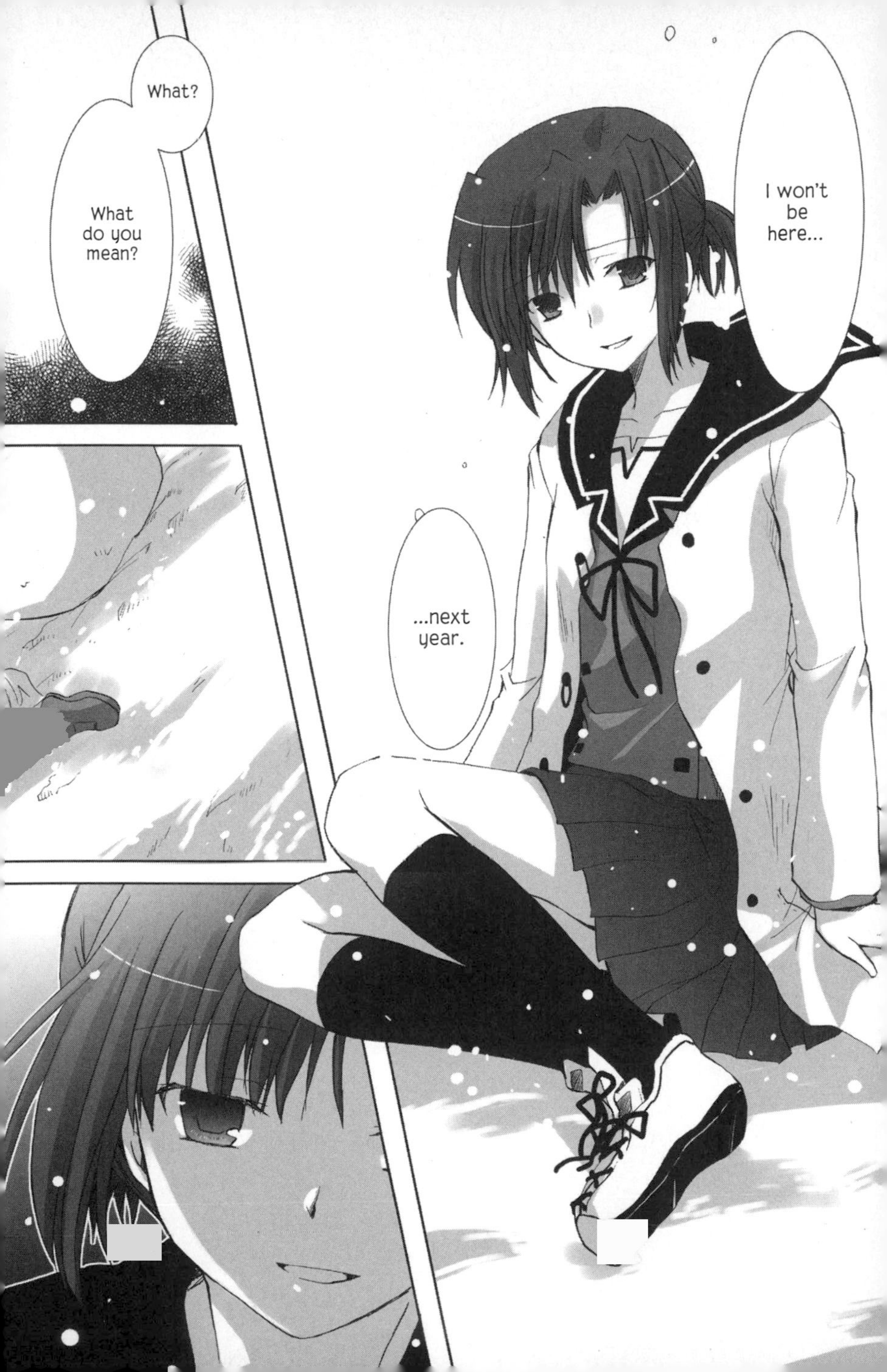
I won't be here...
...next year.
What?
What do you mean?

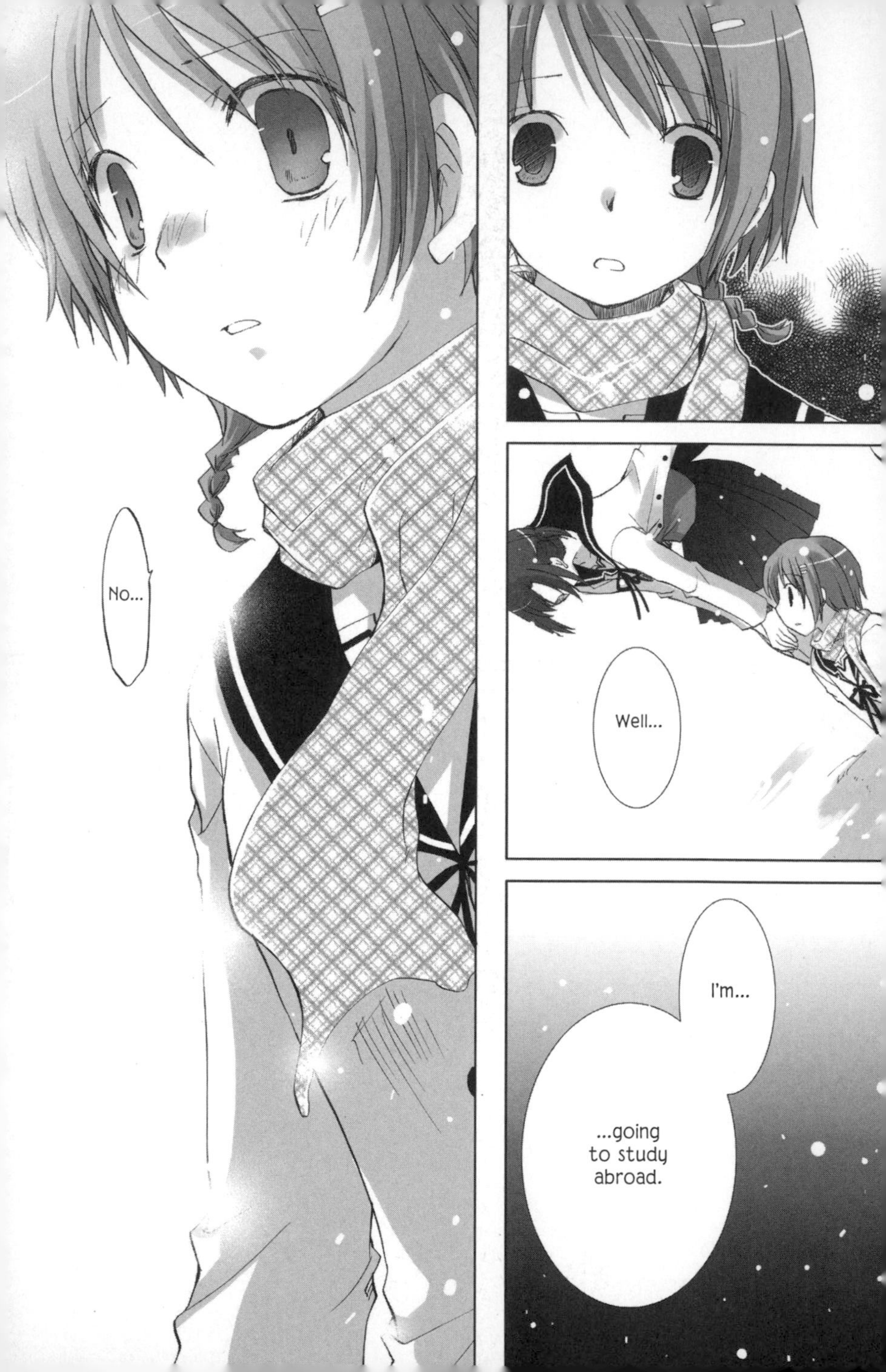
Well...
I'm...
...going to study abroad.
No...

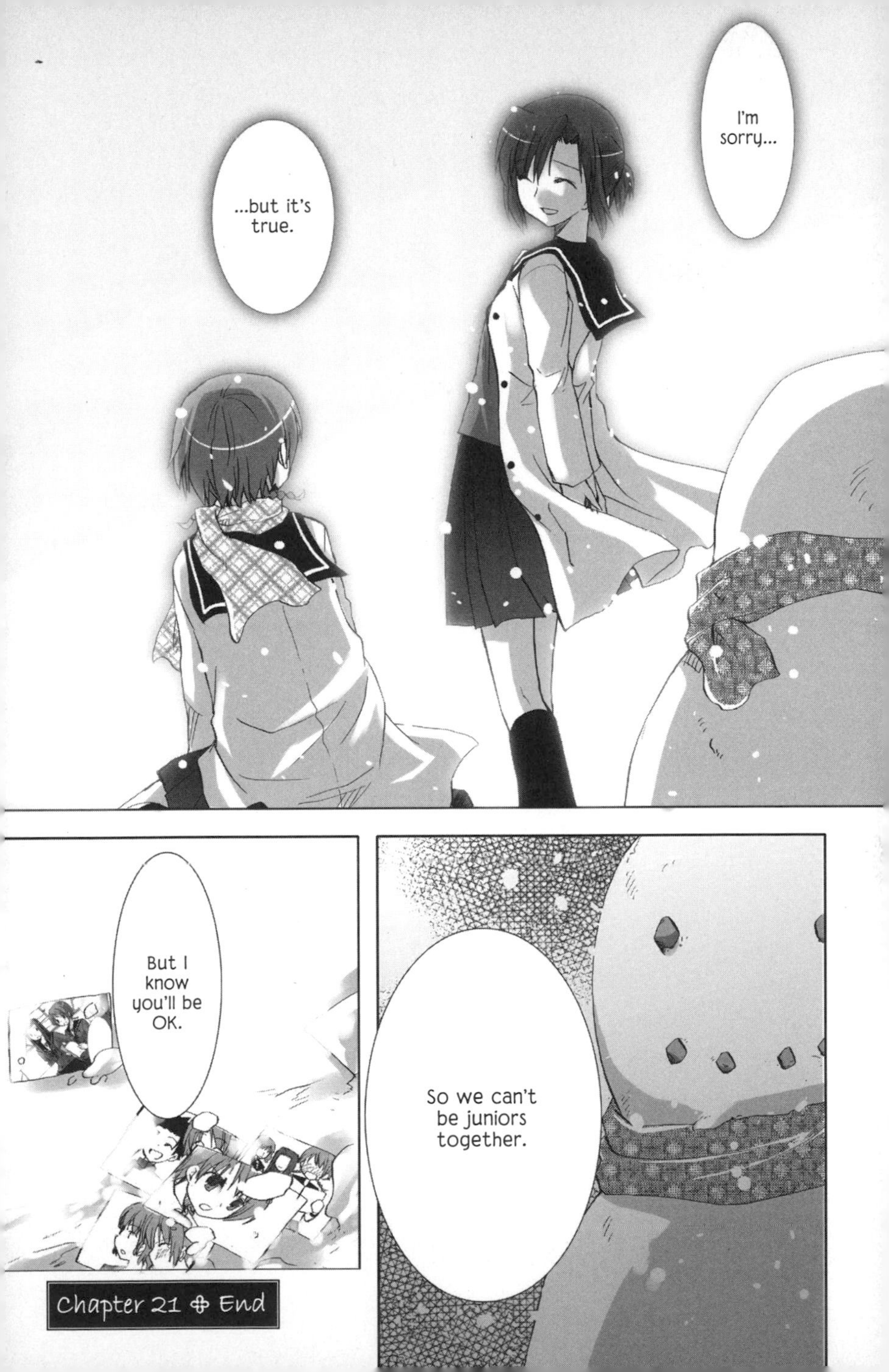
I'm sorry...
...but it's true.
So we can't be juniors together.
But I know you'll be OK.
Chapter 21 ✣ End

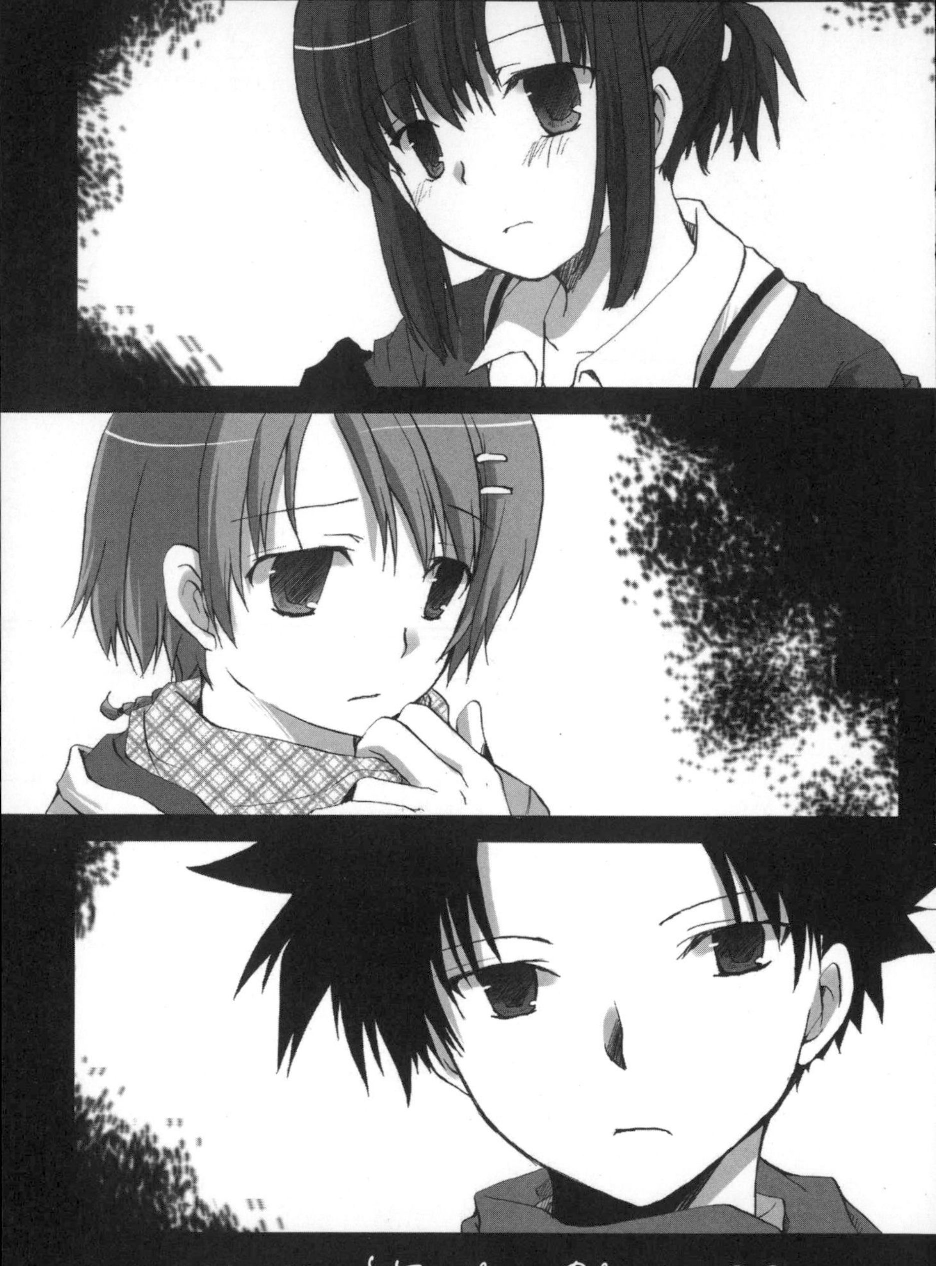

We Were Together Chapter 22

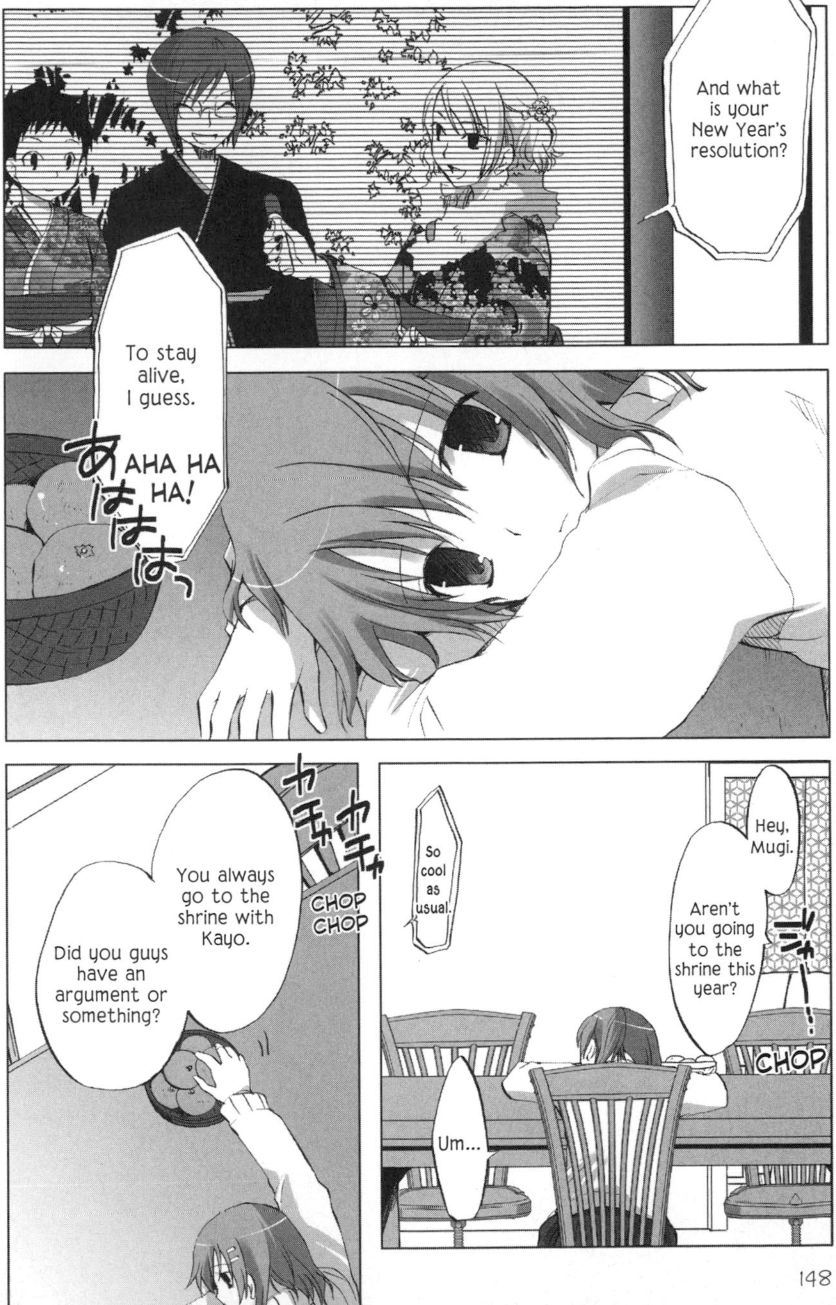
And what is your New Year's resolution?
To stay alive, I guess.
AHA HA HA!
Hey, Mugi.
Aren't you going to the shrine this year?
CHOP
Um...
So cool as usual.
CHOP CHOP
You always go to the shrine with Kayo.
Did you guys have an argument or something?

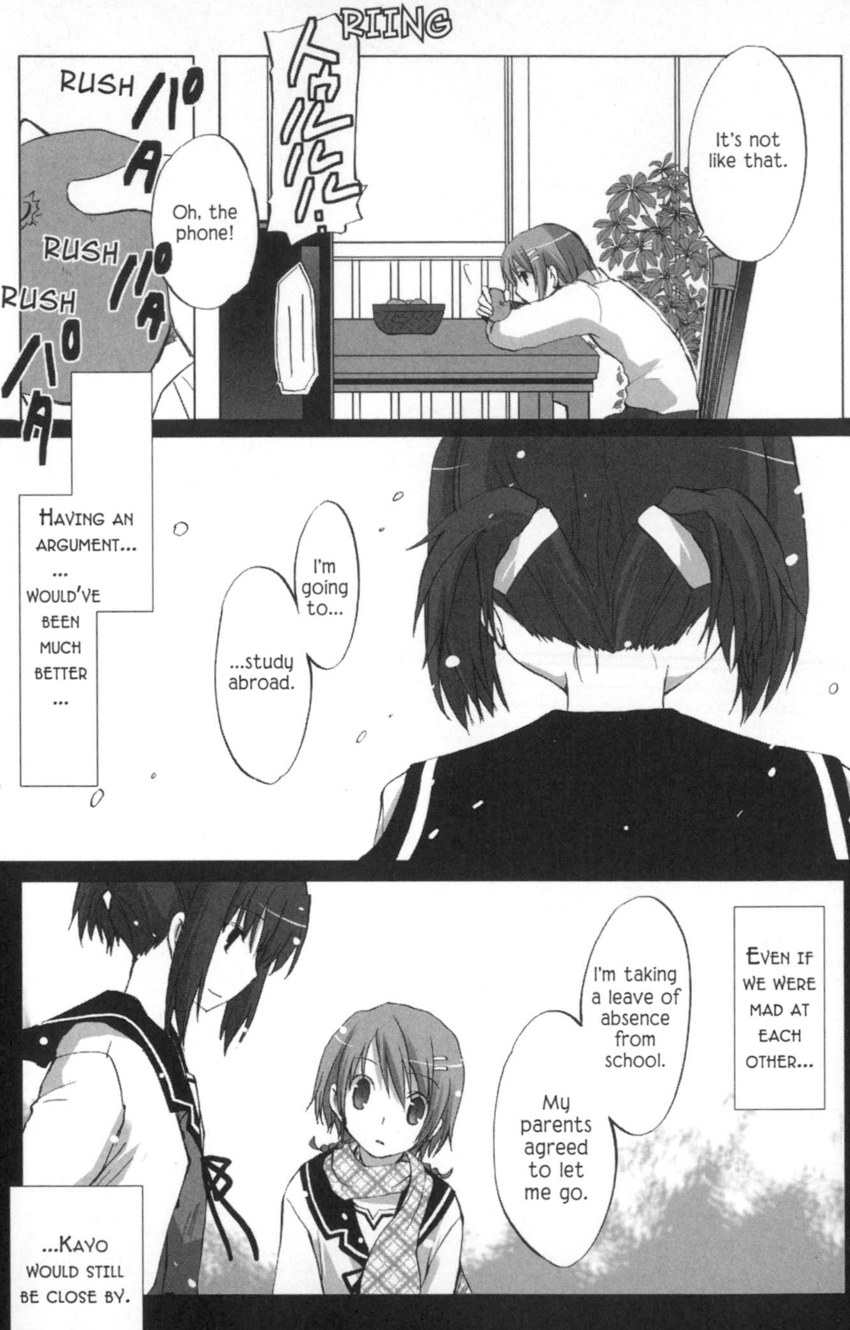
It's not like that.
RIING
Oh, the phone!
RUSH
RUSH
RUSH
I'm going to...
...study abroad.
Having an argument... ... would've been much better ...
Even if we were mad at each other...
I'm taking a leave of absence from school.
My parents agreed to let me go.
...Kayo would still be close by.

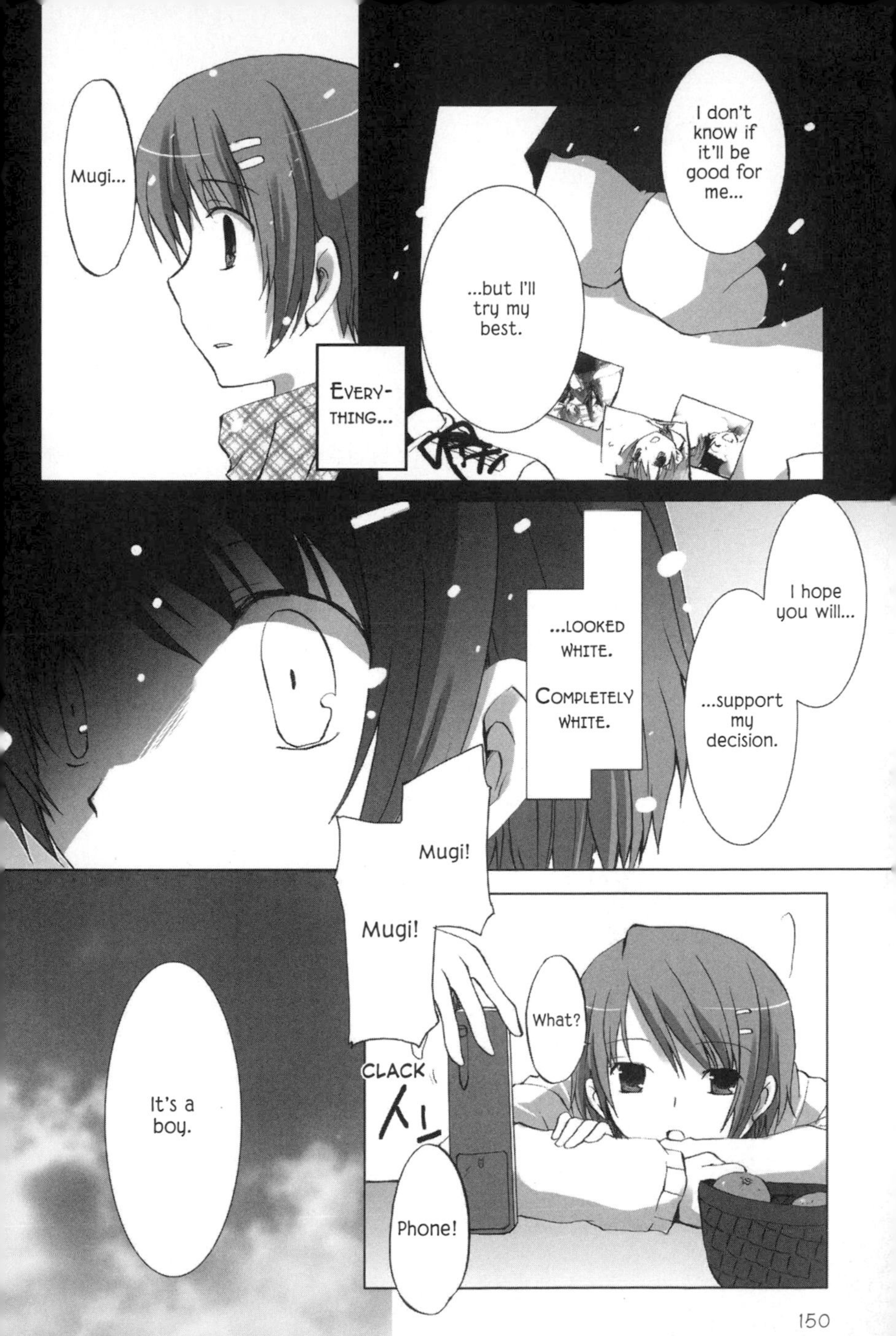

I don't know if it'll be good for me...
...but I'll try my best.
Everything...
Mugi...
I hope you will...
...support my decision.
...looked white.
Completely white.
Mugi!
Mugi!
What?
CLACK
Phone!
It's a boy.

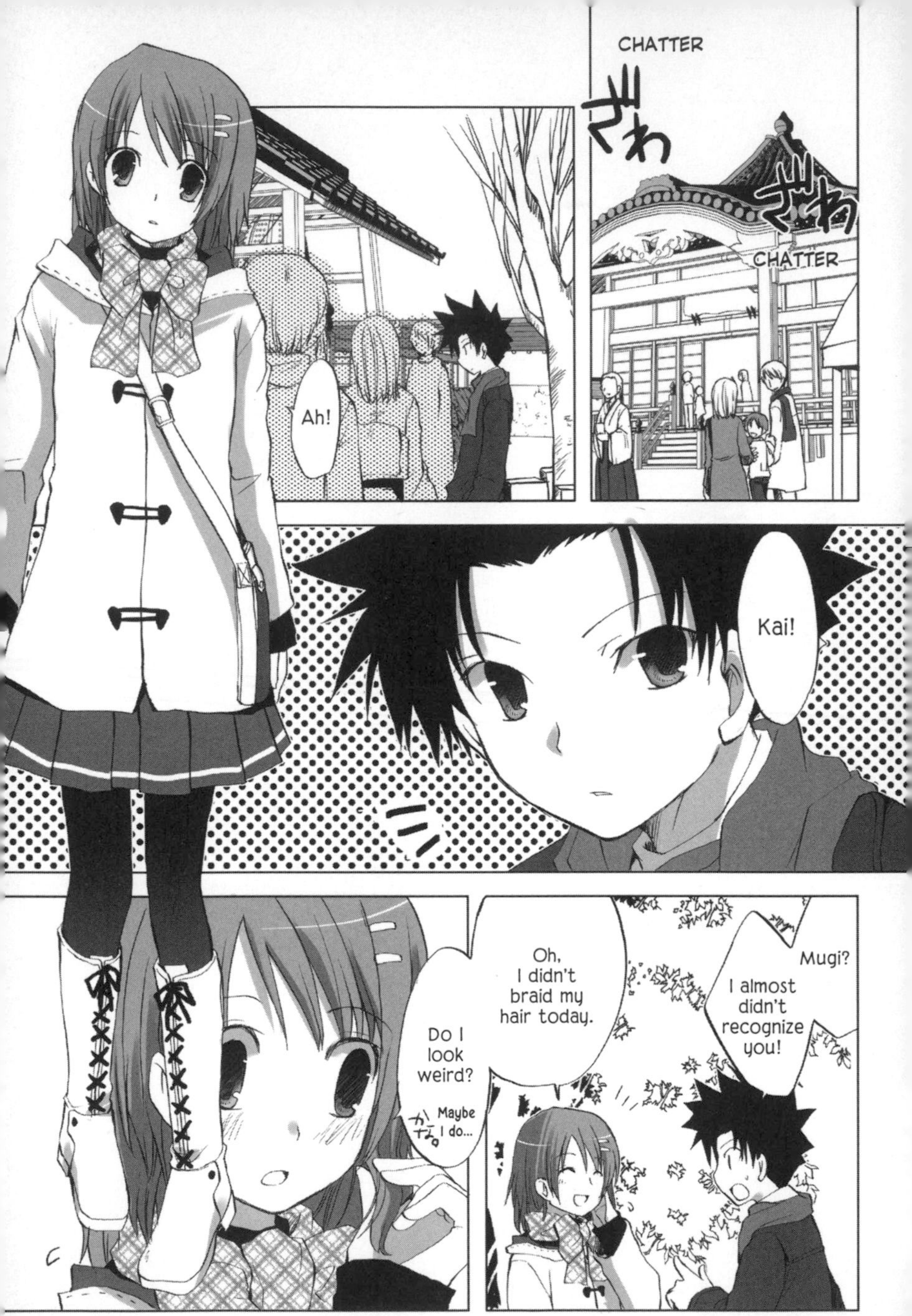
CHATTER
ざわ
ざわ
CHATTER
Ah!
Kai!
Mugi?
I almost didn't recognize you!
Oh, I didn't braid my hair today.
Do I look weird?
Maybe I do...

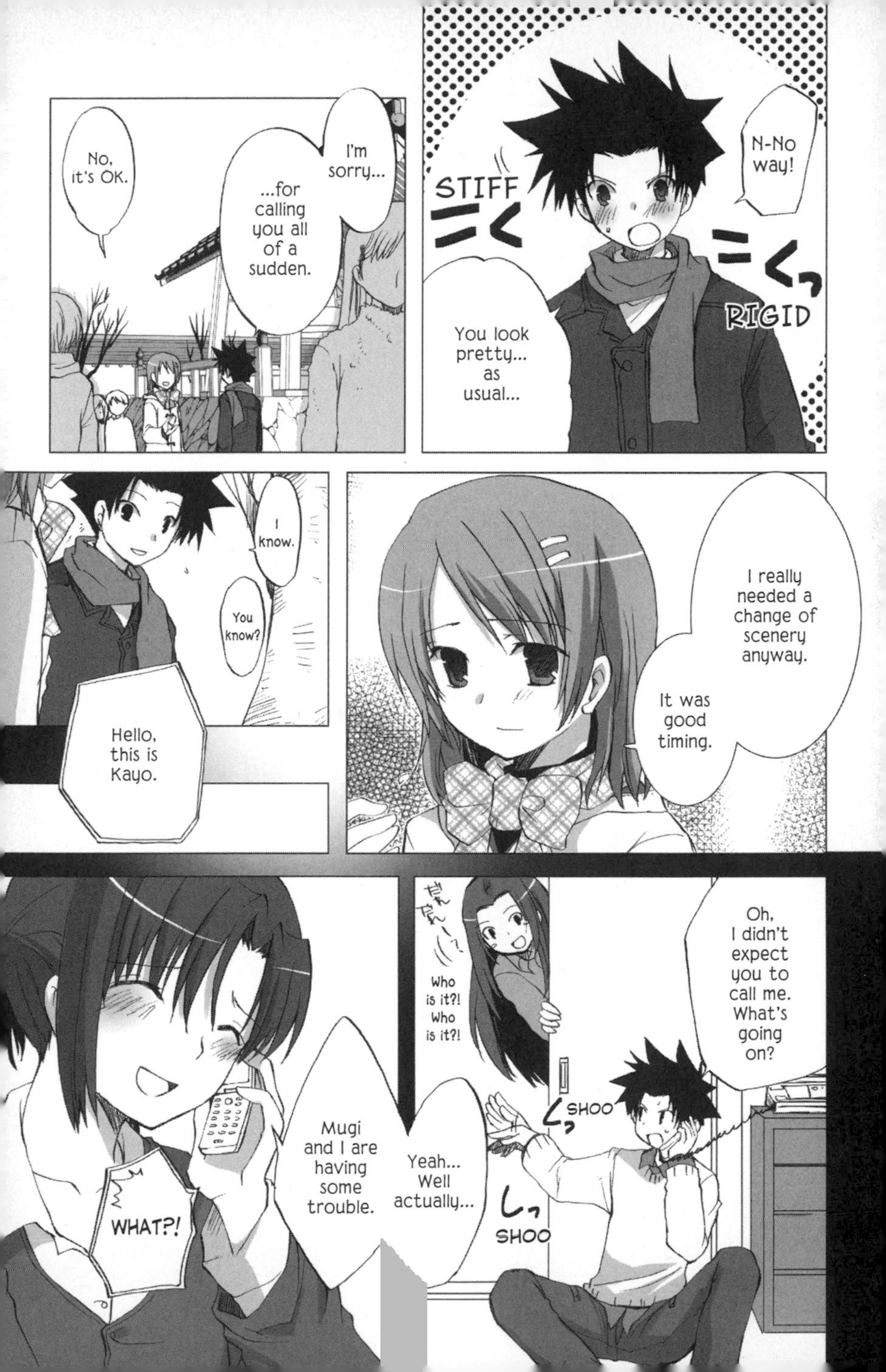
N-No way!
RIGID
STIFF
You look pretty... as usual...
I'm sorry...
...for calling you all of a sudden.
No, it's OK.
I really needed a change of scenery anyway.
It was good timing.
I know.
You know?
Hello, this is Kayo.
Oh, I didn't expect you to call me. What's going on?
Who is it?! Who is it?!
SHOO
SHOO
Yeah... Well actually...
Mugi and I are having some trouble.
WHAT?!

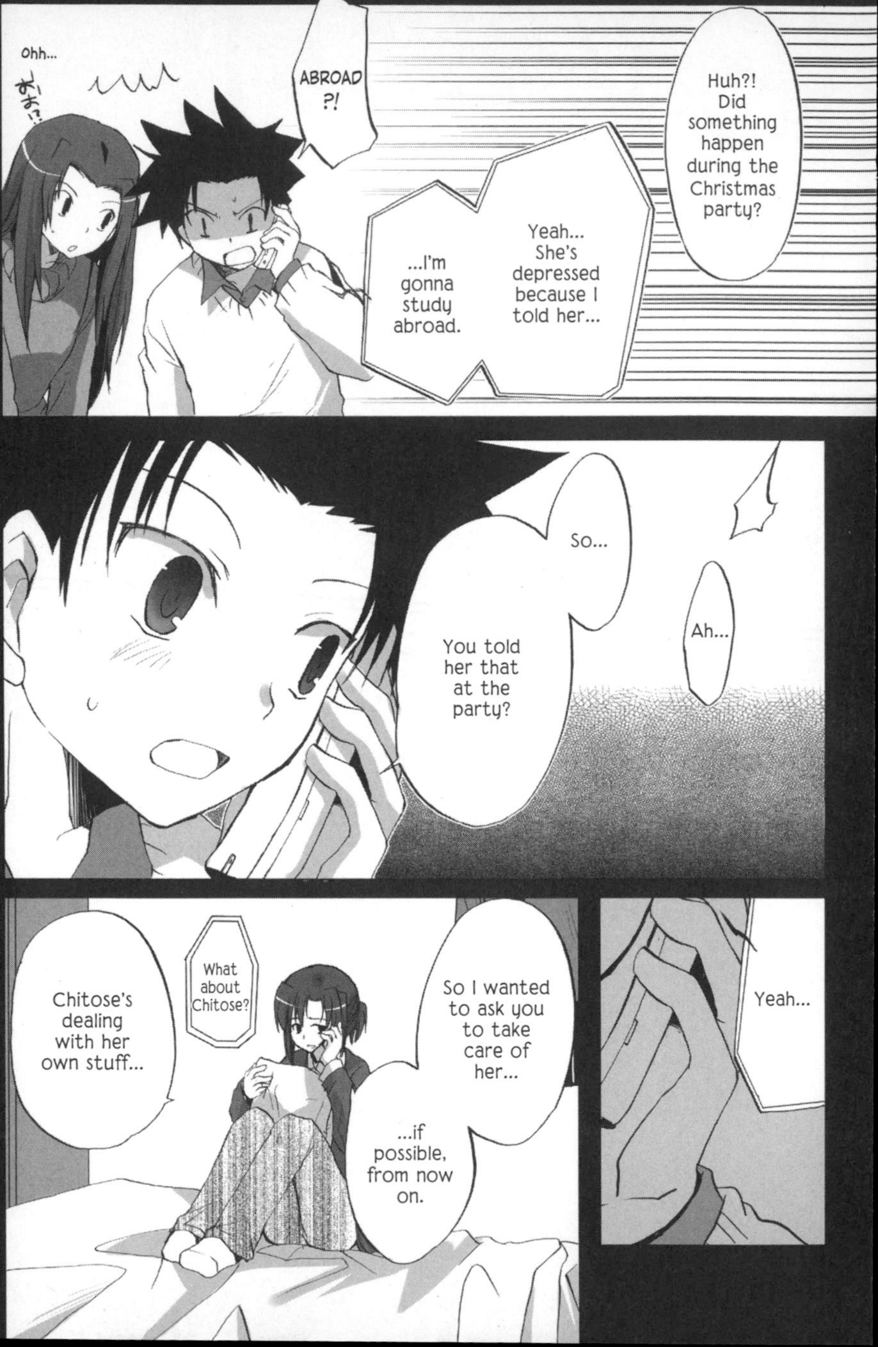
Huh?! Did something happen during the Christmas party?
Yeah... She's depressed because I told her...
...I'm gonna study abroad.
ABROAD ?!
Ohh...
Ah...
So...
You told her that at the party?
Yeah...
So I wanted to ask you to take care of her...
...if possible, from now on.
What about Chitose?
Chitose's dealing with her own stuff...

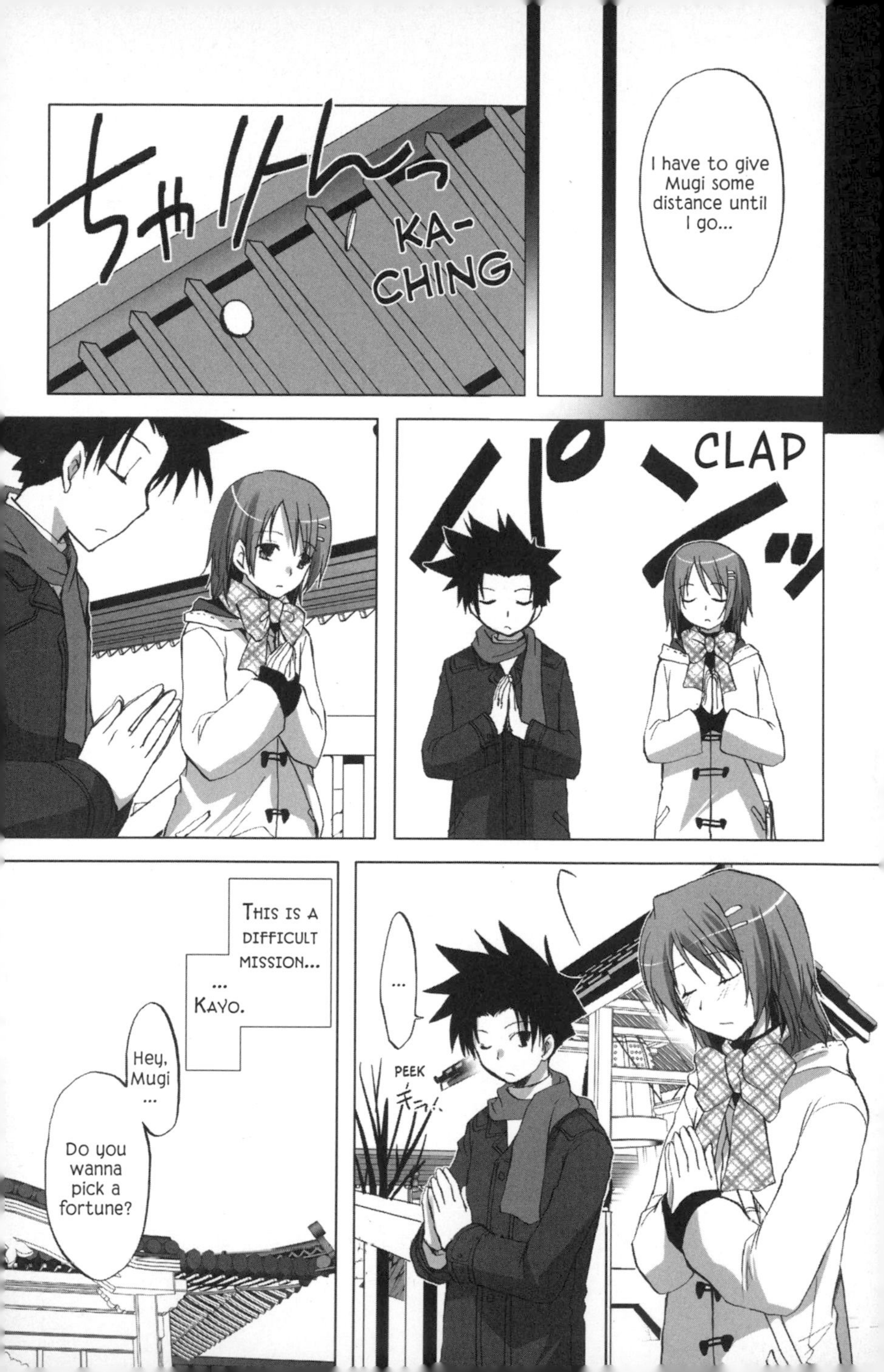

I have to give Mugi some distance until I go...
ちゃりんっ
KA-CHING
パンッ
CLAP
...
PEEK
THIS IS A DIFFICULT MISSION...
... KAYO.
Hey, Mugi ...
Do you wanna pick a fortune?

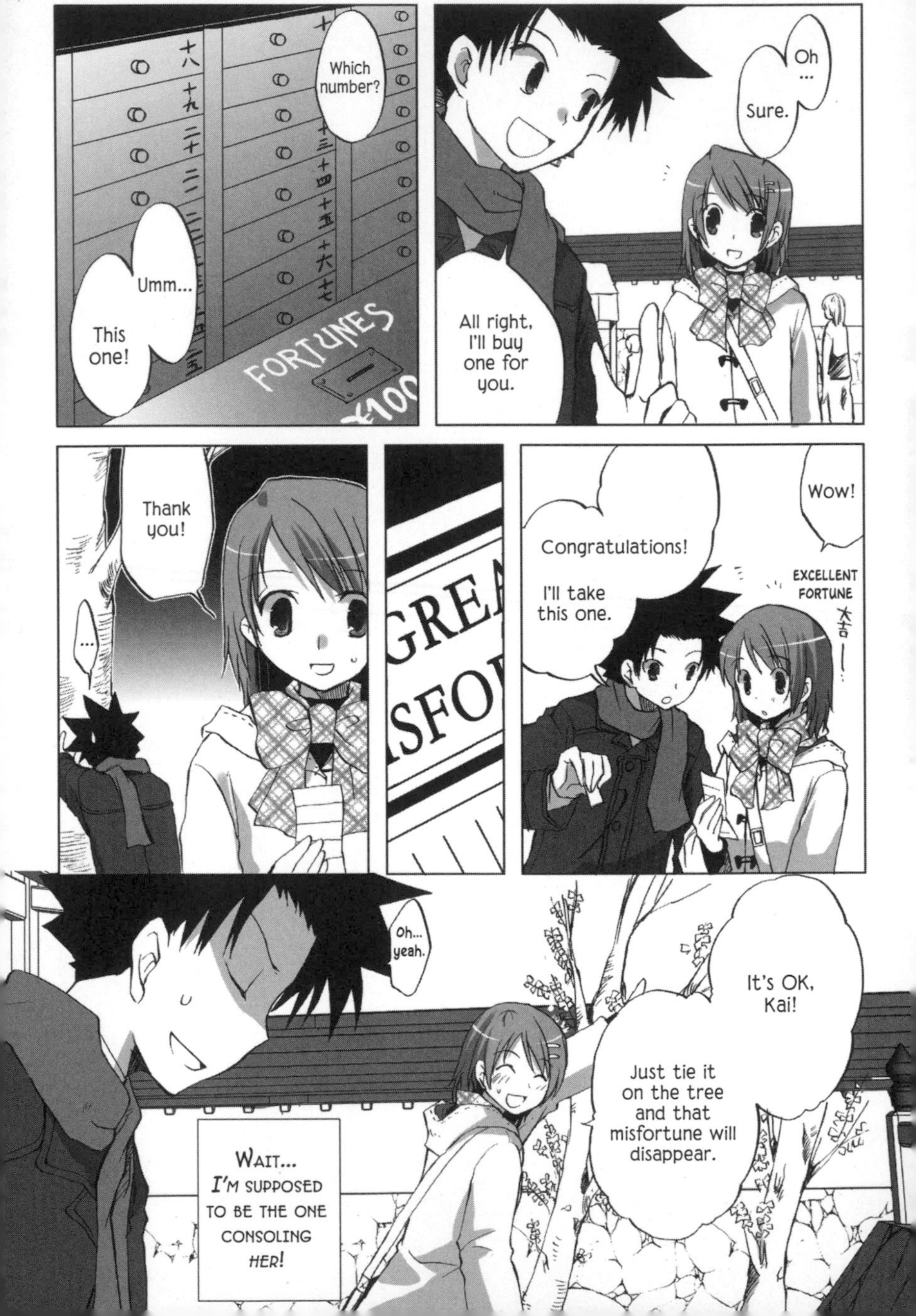
Oh ... Sure.
All right, I'll buy one for you.
Which number?
FORTUNES
¥100
Umm...
This one!
Wow!
Congratulations!
I'll take this one.
EXCELLENT FORTUNE
GREA
ISFO
Thank you!
...
It's OK, Kai!
Just tie it on the tree and that misfortune will disappear.
Oh... yeah.
WAIT... I'M SUPPOSED TO BE THE ONE CONSOLING HER!

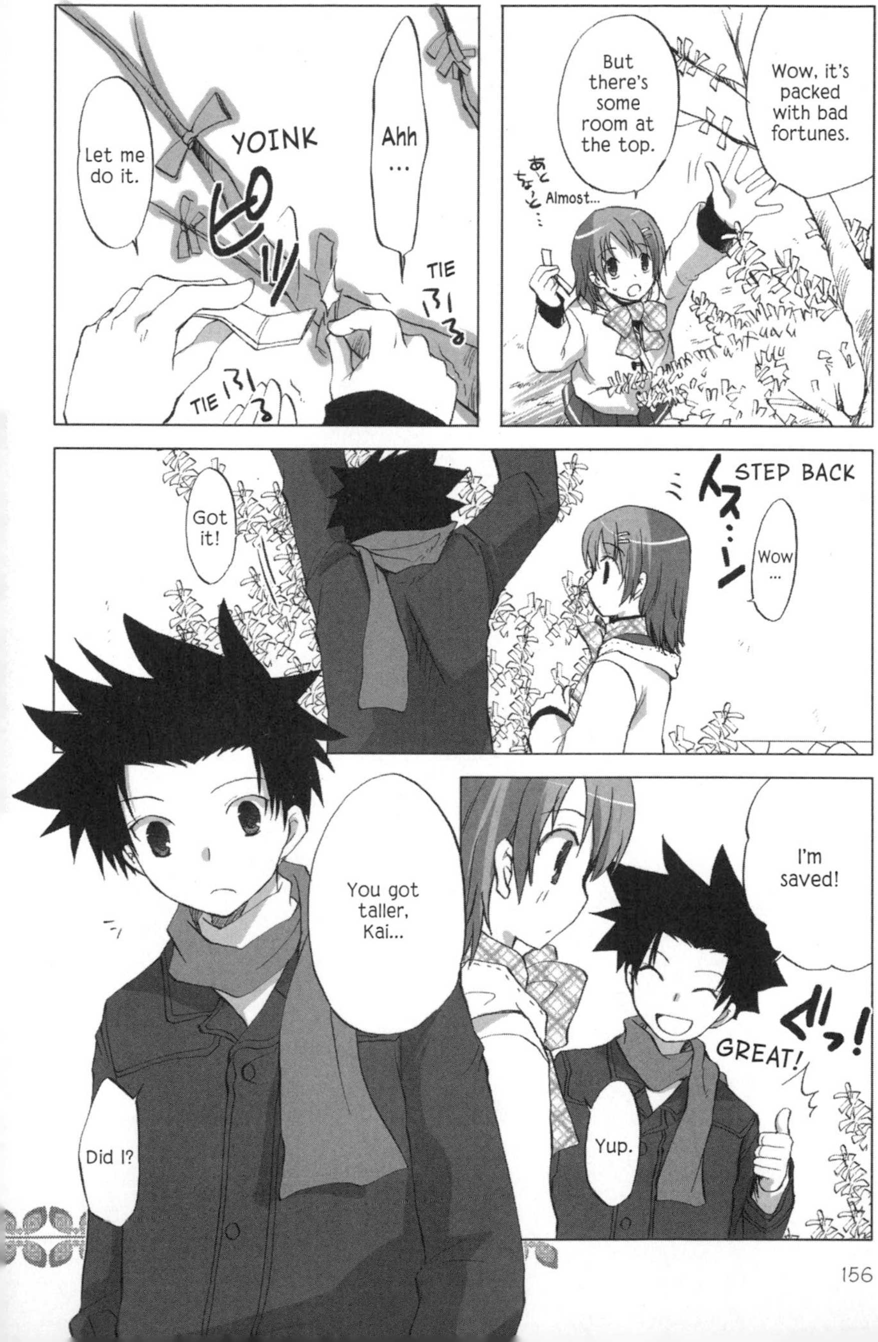
Wow, it's packed with bad fortunes.
But there's some room at the top.
あと ちょっと…
Almost...
Ahh ...
YOINK
Let me do it.
TIE ふる
TIE ふる
STEP BACK
Wow ...
Got it!
I'm saved!
GREAT!
Yup.
You got taller, Kai...
Did I?

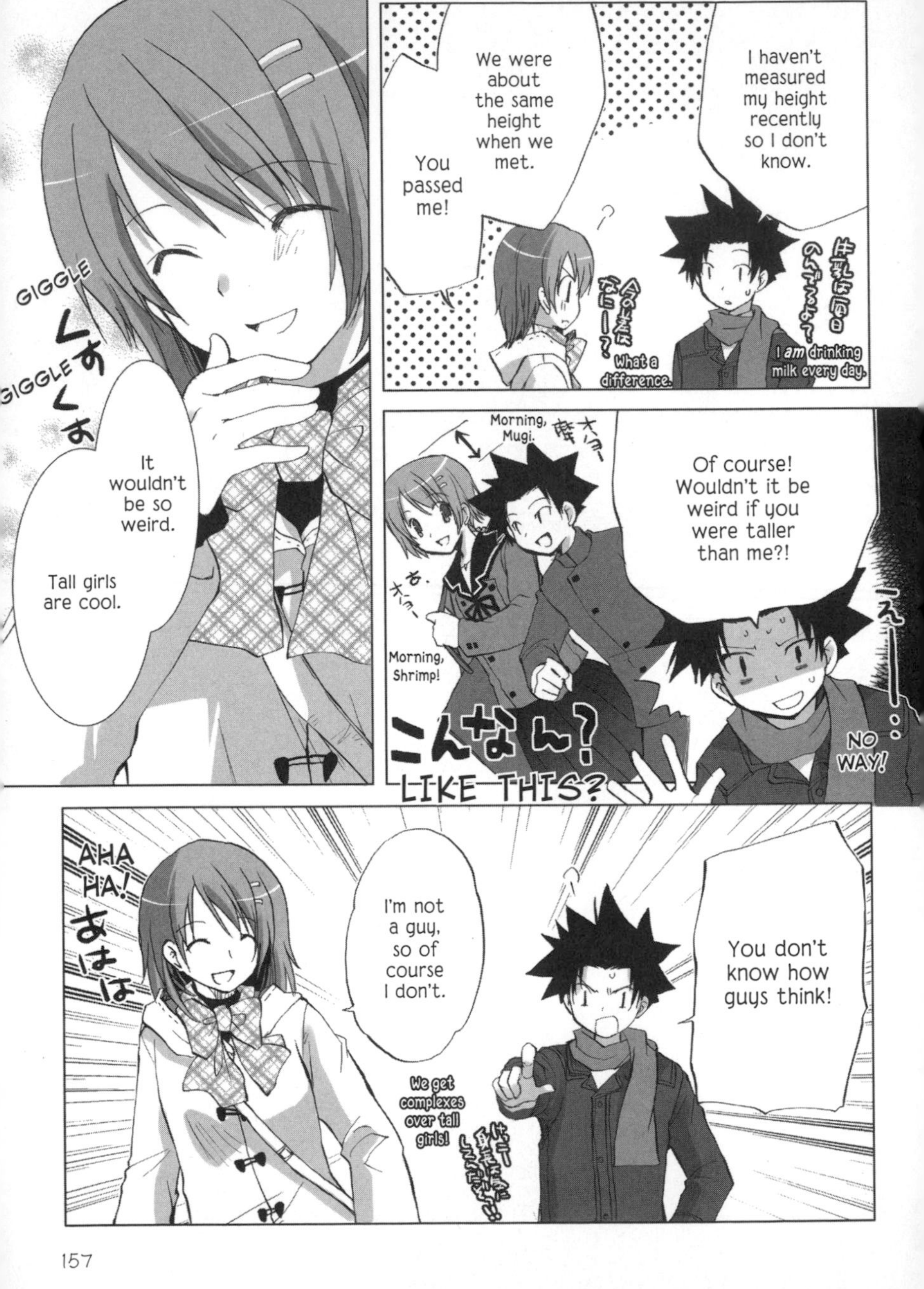
I haven't measured my height recently so I don't know.
牛乳は毎日のんでるよ？
I am drinking milk every day.
We were about the same height when we met.
You passed me!
今の差はなにー？
What a difference.
Of course! Wouldn't it be weird if you were taller than me?!
えー…
NO WAY!
Morning, Mugi.
Morning, Shrimp!
こんなん？
LIKE THIS?
くすくす
GIGGLE GIGGLE
It wouldn't be so weird.
Tall girls are cool.
You don't know how guys think!
We get complexes over tall girls!
I'm not a guy, so of course I don't.
あはは
AHA HA!

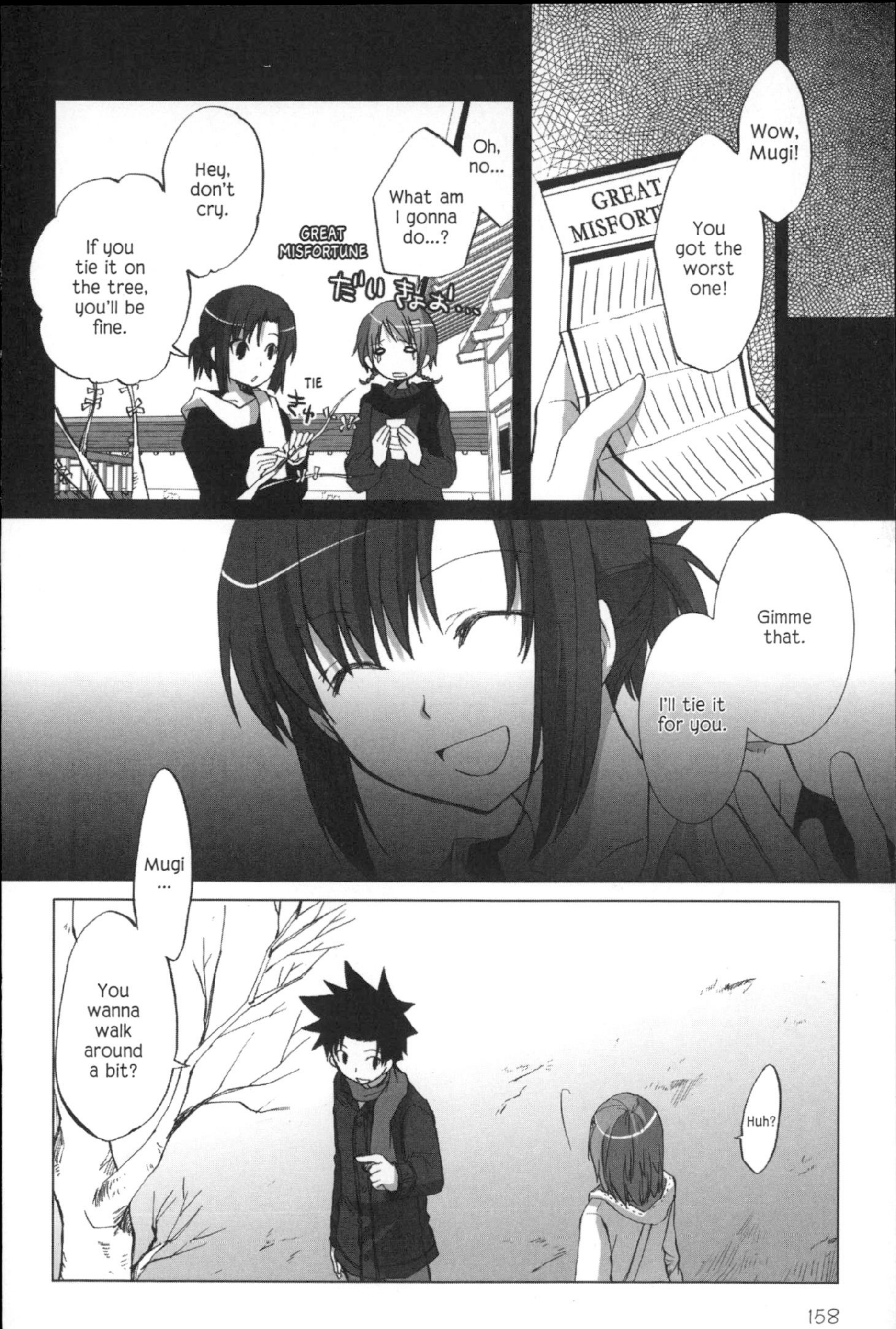

Wow, Mugi!
You got the worst one!
GREAT MISFORT
Oh, no...
What am I gonna do...?
GREAT MISFORTUNE
Hey, don't cry.
If you tie it on the tree, you'll be fine.
TIE
Gimme that.
I'll tie it for you.
Mugi...
You wanna walk around a bit?
Huh?

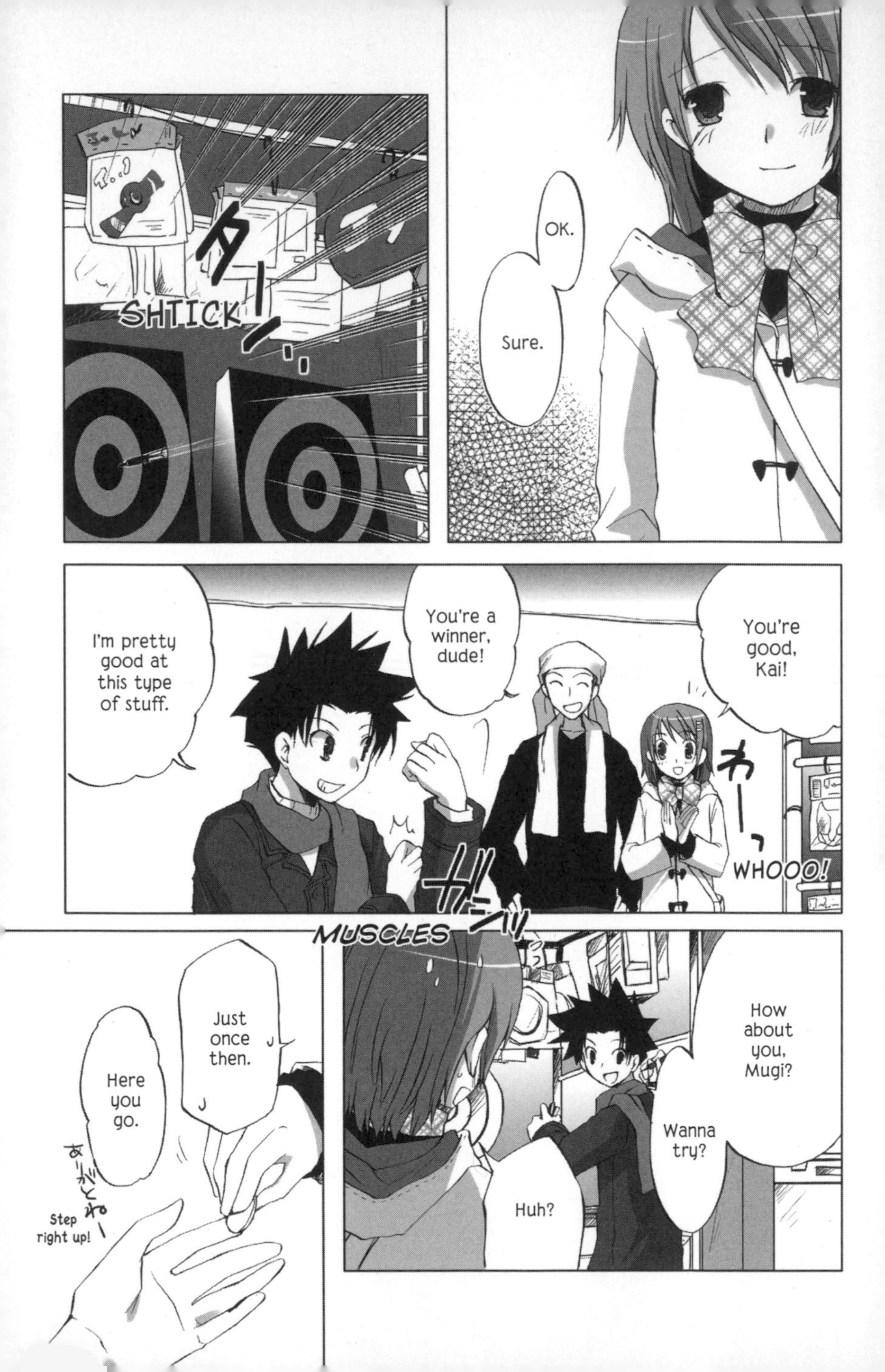
OK.
Sure.
SHTICK
You're good, Kai!
WHOOO!
You're a winner, dude!
I'm pretty good at this type of stuff.
MUSCLES
How about you, Mugi?
Wanna try?
Huh?
Just once then.
Here you go.
Step right up!

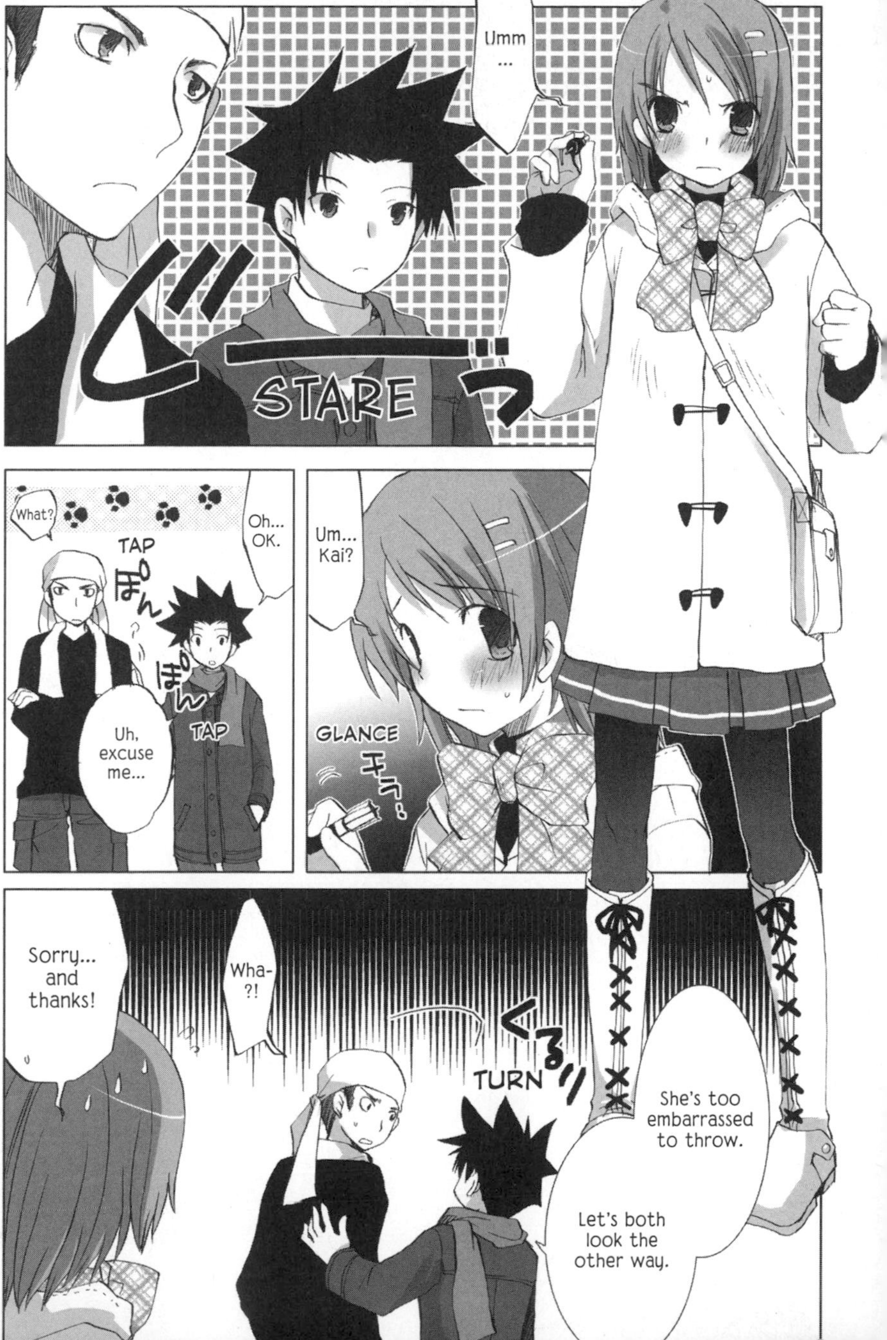
Umm
...
STARE
Um...
Kai?
GLANCE
Oh...
OK.
What?
TAP
TAP
Uh,
excuse
me...
She's too
embarrassed
to throw.
Let's both
look the
other way.
TURN
Wha-
?!
Sorry...
and
thanks!

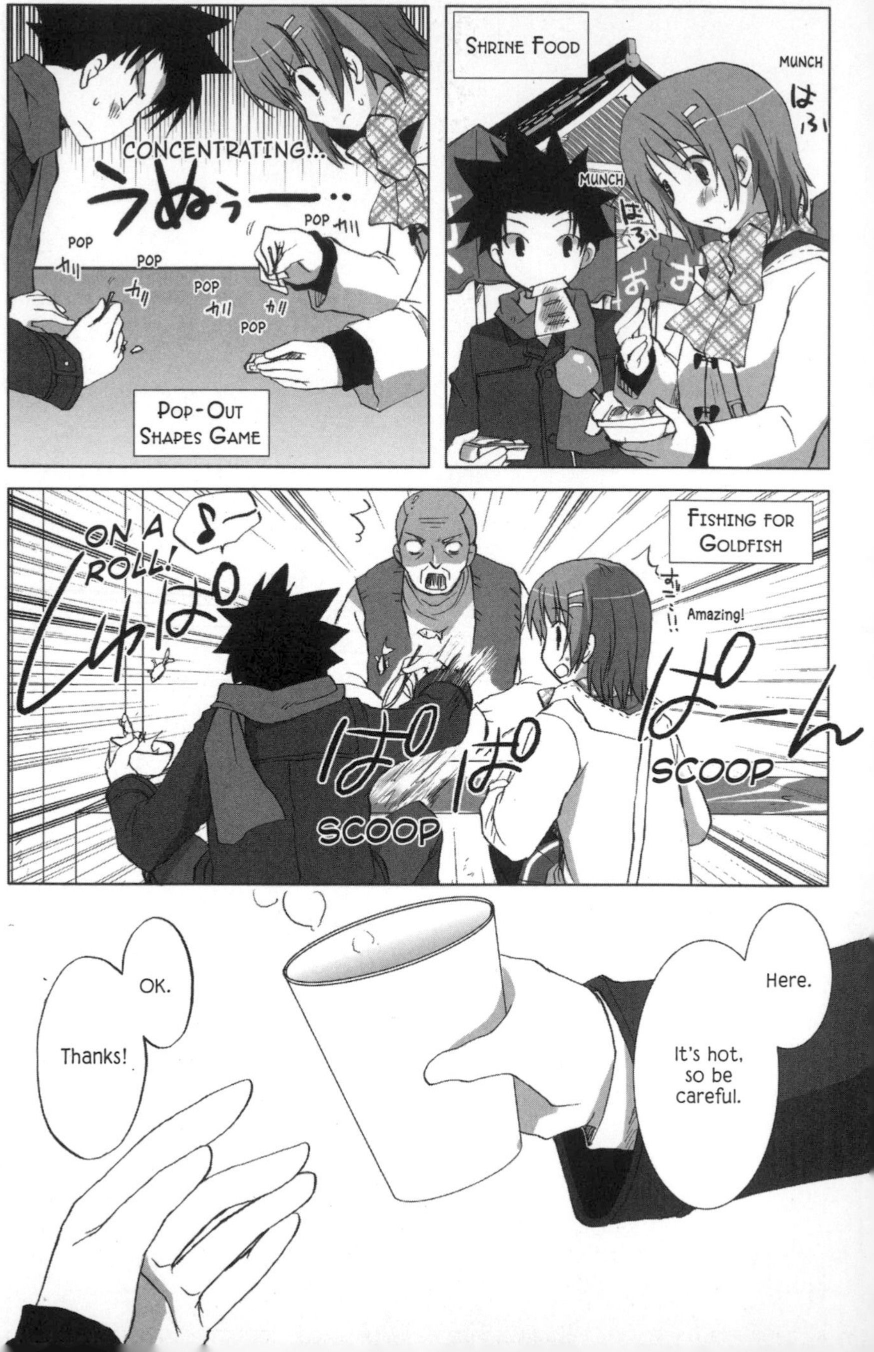
Shrine Food
MUNCH
MUNCH
CONCENTRATING...
POP
POP
POP
POP
POP
Pop-Out Shapes Game
Fishing for Goldfish
Amazing!
ON A ROLL!
SCOOP
SCOOP
Here.
It's hot, so be careful.
OK.
Thanks!

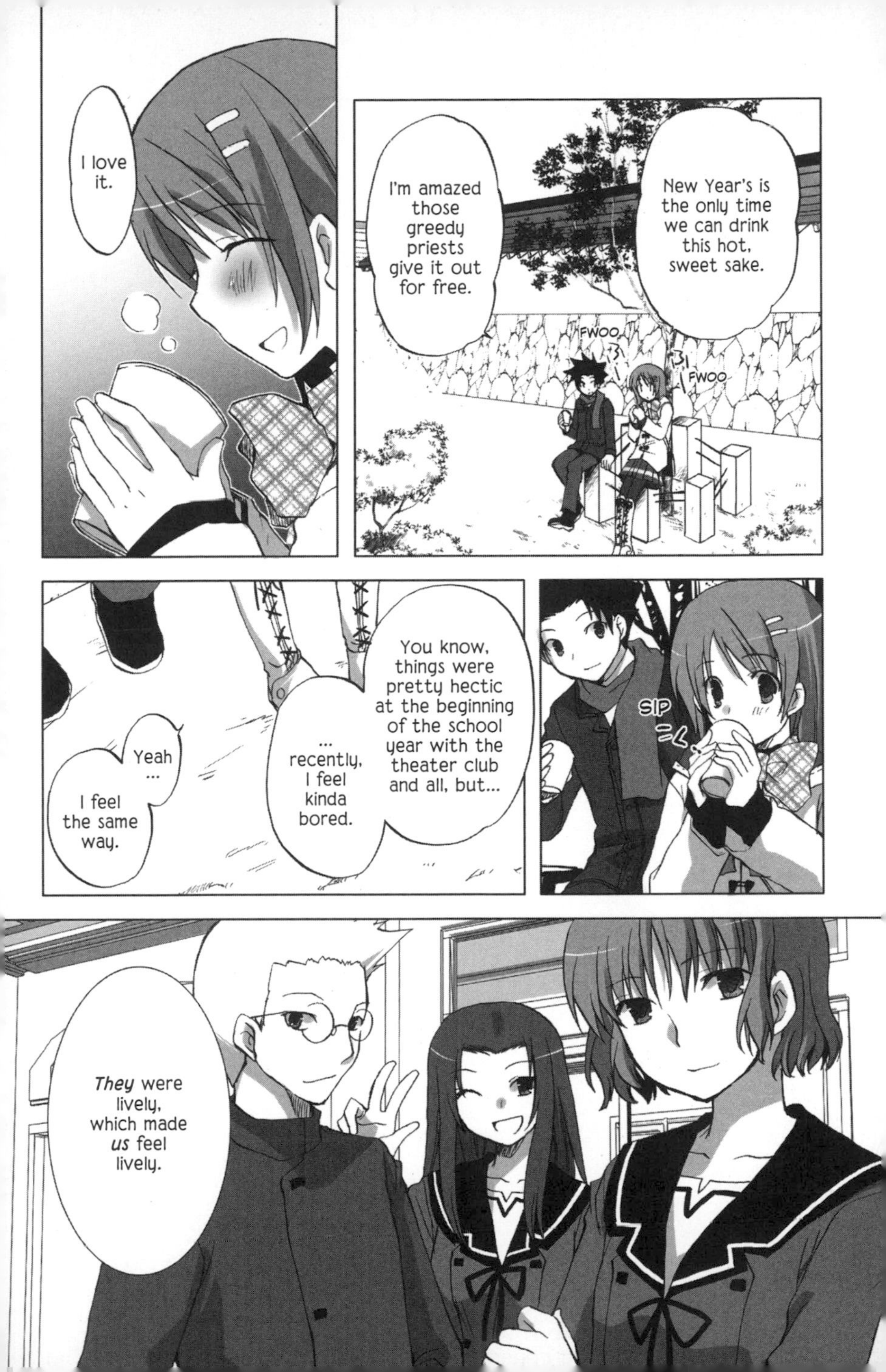
New Year's is the only time we can drink this hot, sweet sake.
I'm amazed those greedy priests give it out for free.
FWOO
FWOO
I love it.
SIP
You know, things were pretty hectic at the beginning of the school year with the theater club and all, but...
... recently, I feel kinda bored.
Yeah ... I feel the same way.
They were lively, which made *us* feel lively.

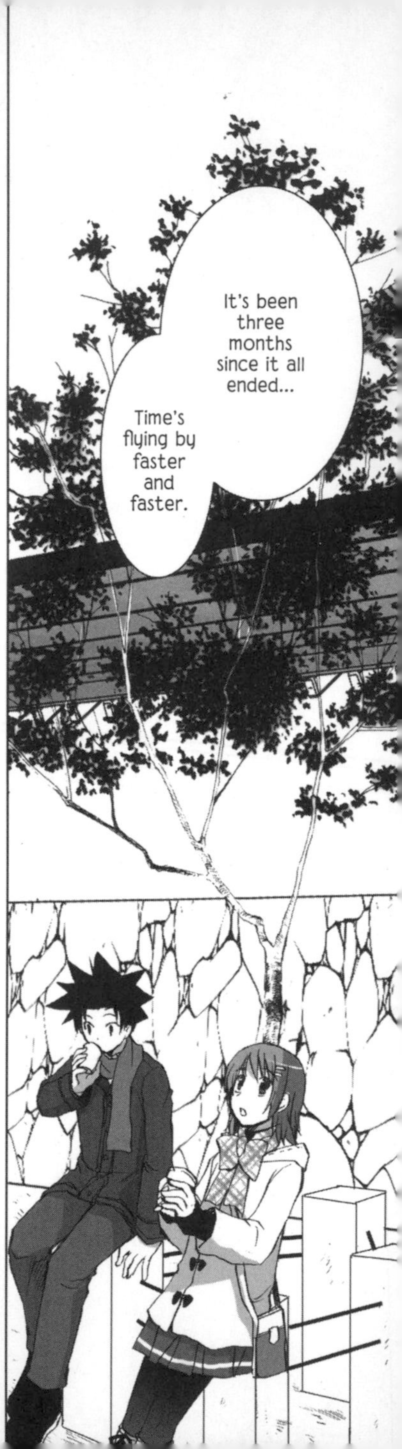
It's been three months since it all ended...
Time's flying by faster and faster.
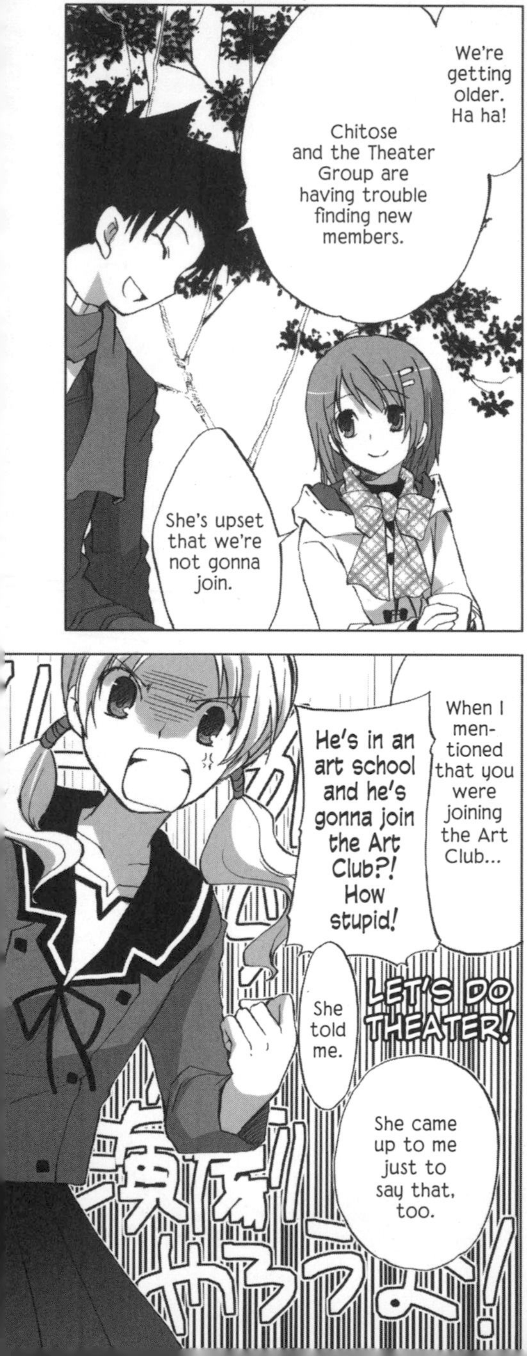
We're getting older. Ha ha!
Chitose and the Theater Group are having trouble finding new members.
She's upset that we're not gonna join.
When I mentioned that you were joining the Art Club...
He's in an art school and he's gonna join the Art Club?! How stupid!
LET'S DO THEATER!
She told me.
She came up to me just to say that, too.

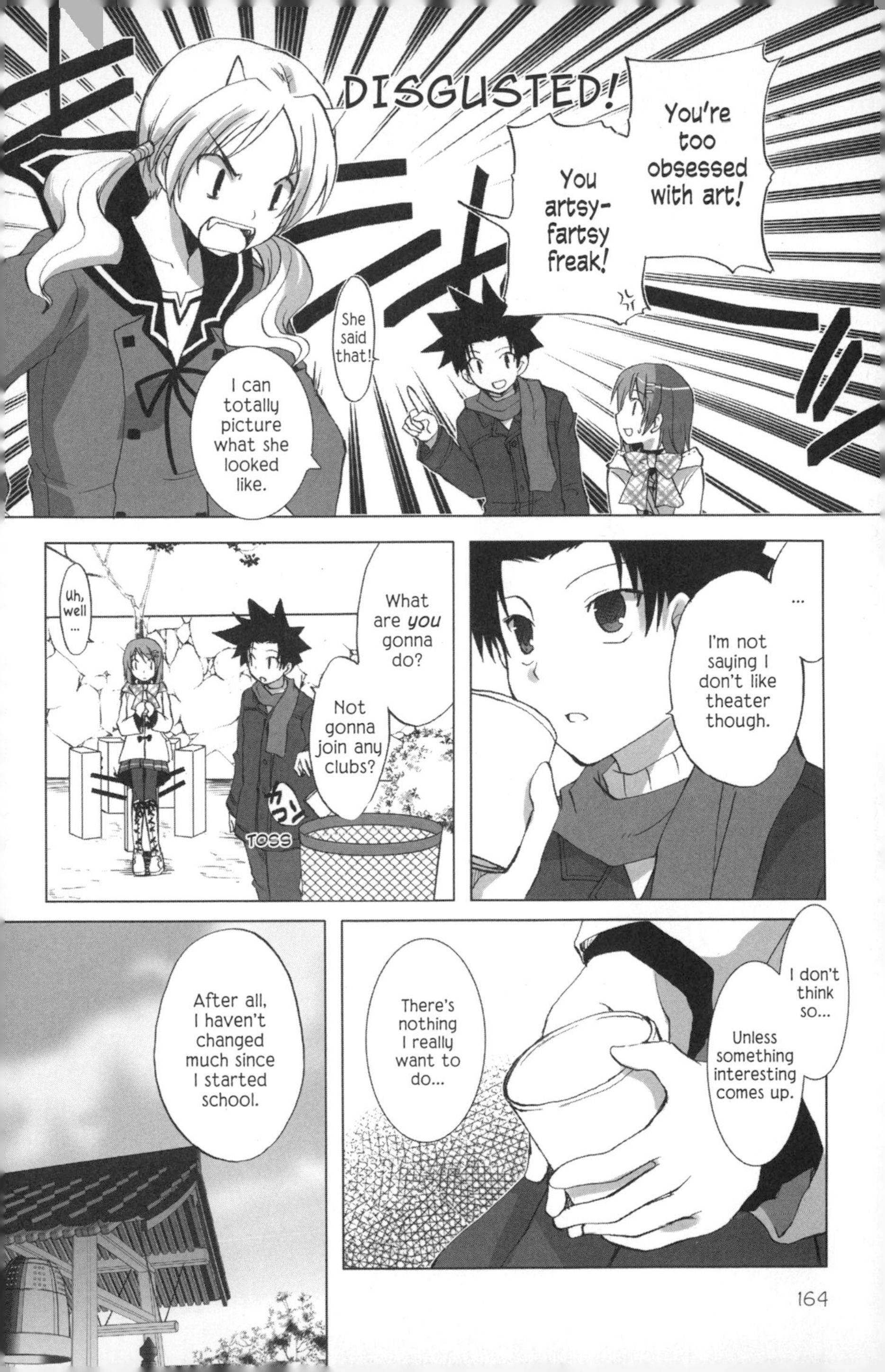
DISGUSTED!
You're too obsessed with art!
You artsy-fartsy freak!
She said that!
I can totally picture what she looked like.
...
I'm not saying I don't like theater though.
What are *you* gonna do?
Not gonna join any clubs?
Uh, well ...
TOSS
I don't think so...
Unless something interesting comes up.
There's nothing I really want to do...
After all, I haven't changed much since I started school.

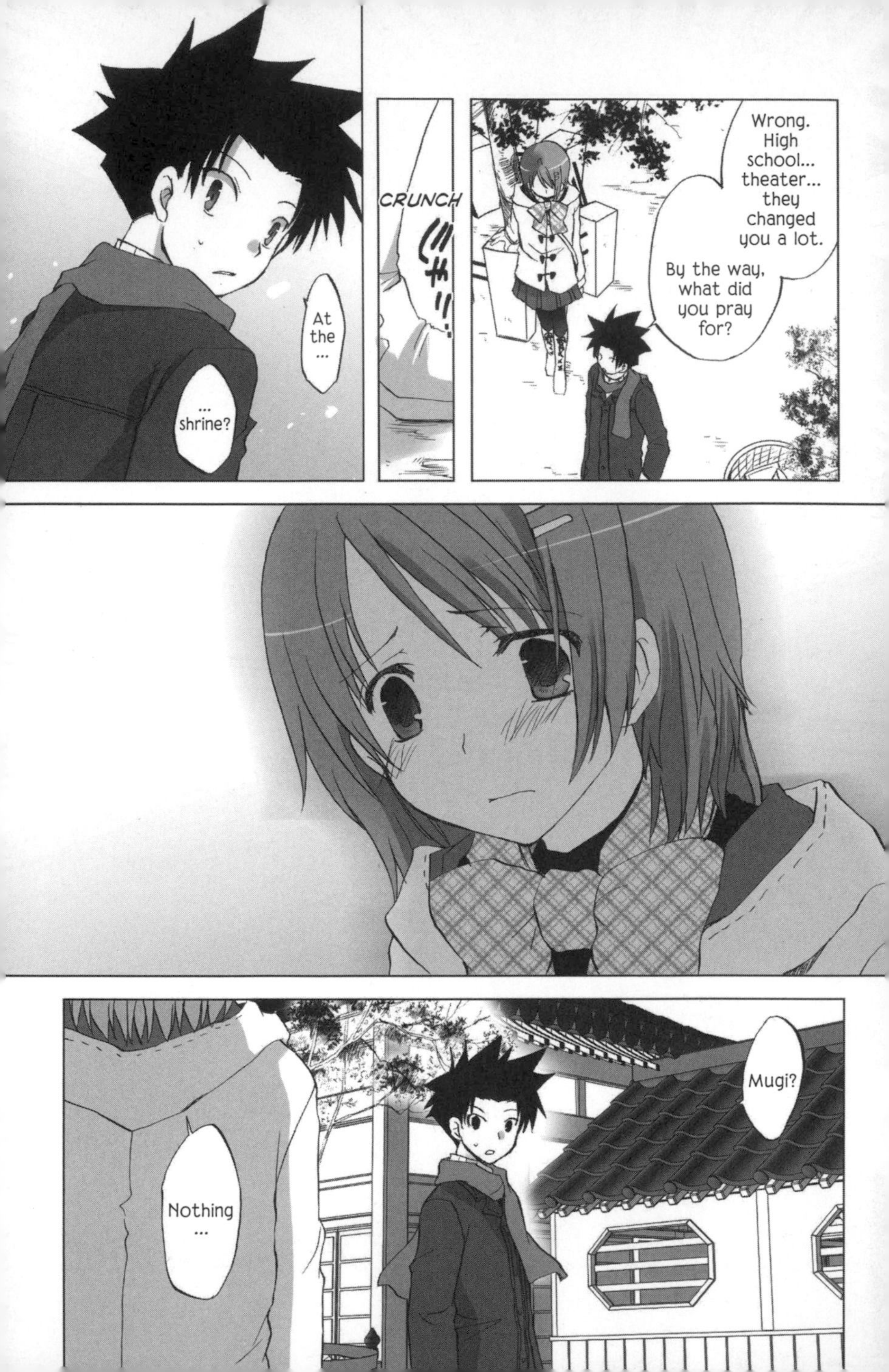
Wrong. High school... theater... they changed you a lot.
By the way, what did you pray for?
CRUNCH
At the ...
... shrine?
Mugi?
Nothing ...

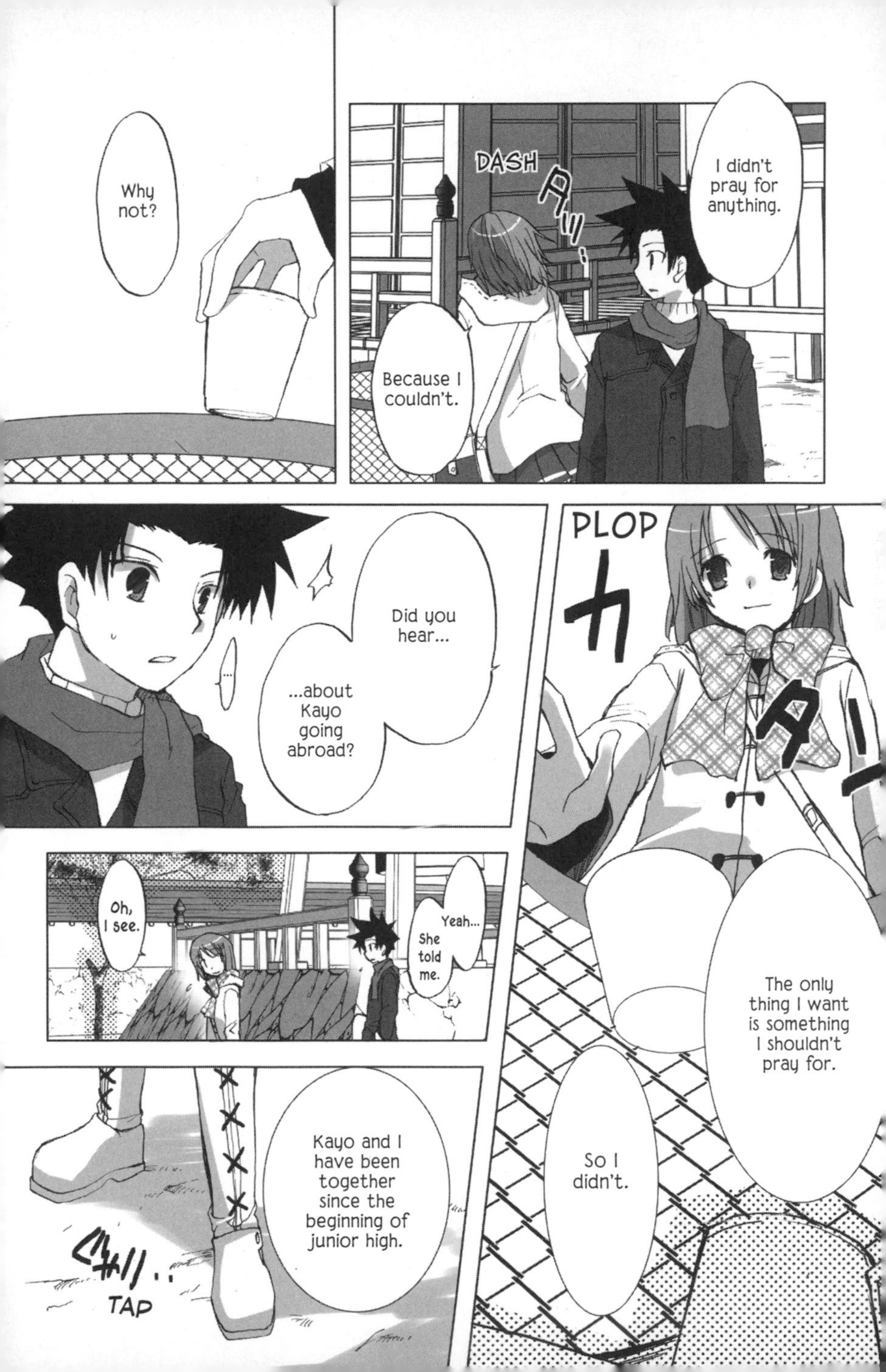
I didn't pray for anything.
DASH
Because I couldn't.
Why not?
PLOP
The only thing I want is something I shouldn't pray for.
So I didn't.
Did you hear...
...about Kayo going abroad?
...
Yeah... She told me.
Oh, I see.
Kayo and I have been together since the beginning of junior high.
TAP

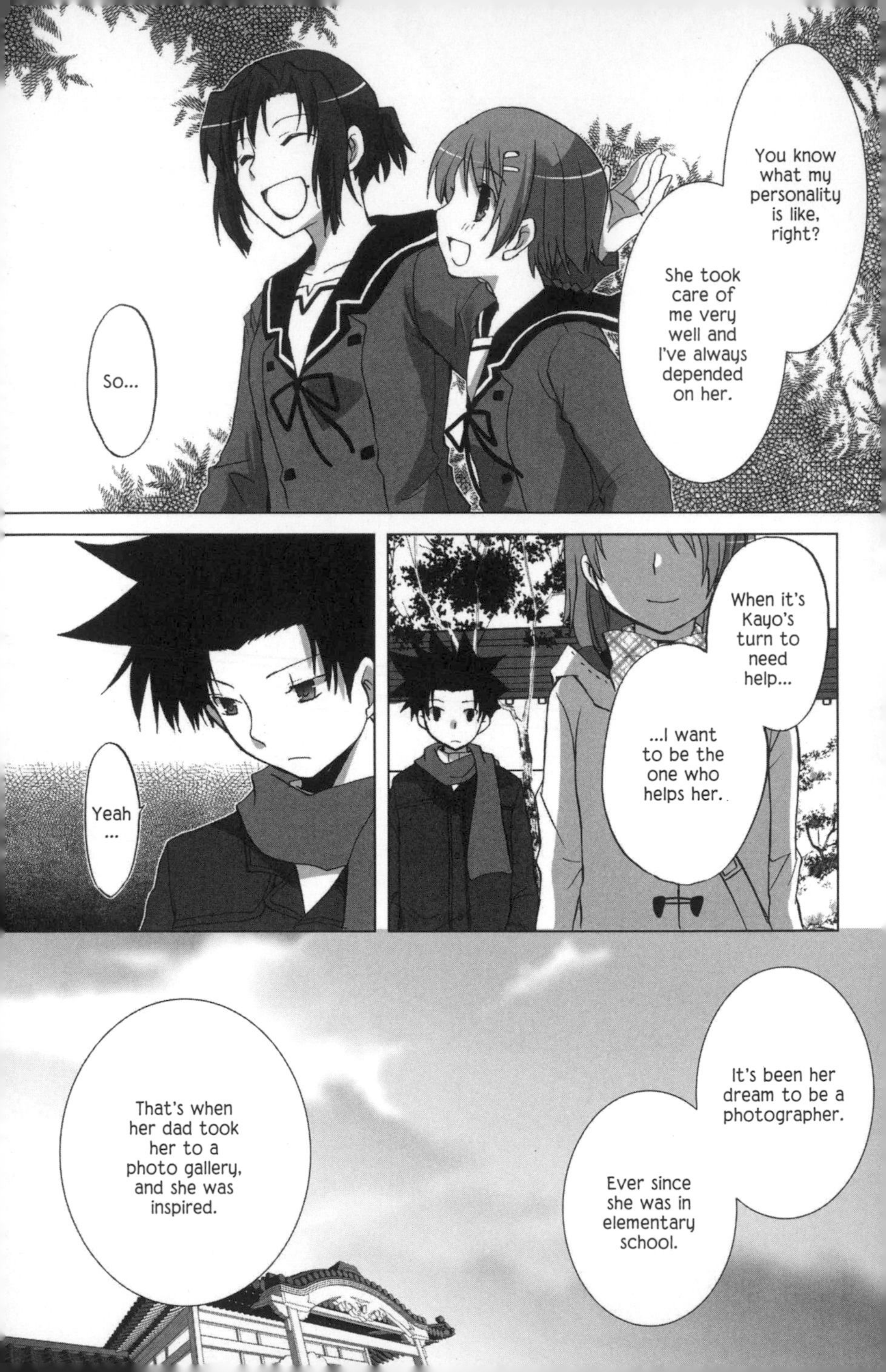
You know what my personality is like, right?
She took care of me very well and I've always depended on her.
So...
When it's Kayo's turn to need help...
...I want to be the one who helps her.
Yeah ...
It's been her dream to be a photographer.
Ever since she was in elementary school.
That's when her dad took her to a photo gallery, and she was inspired.

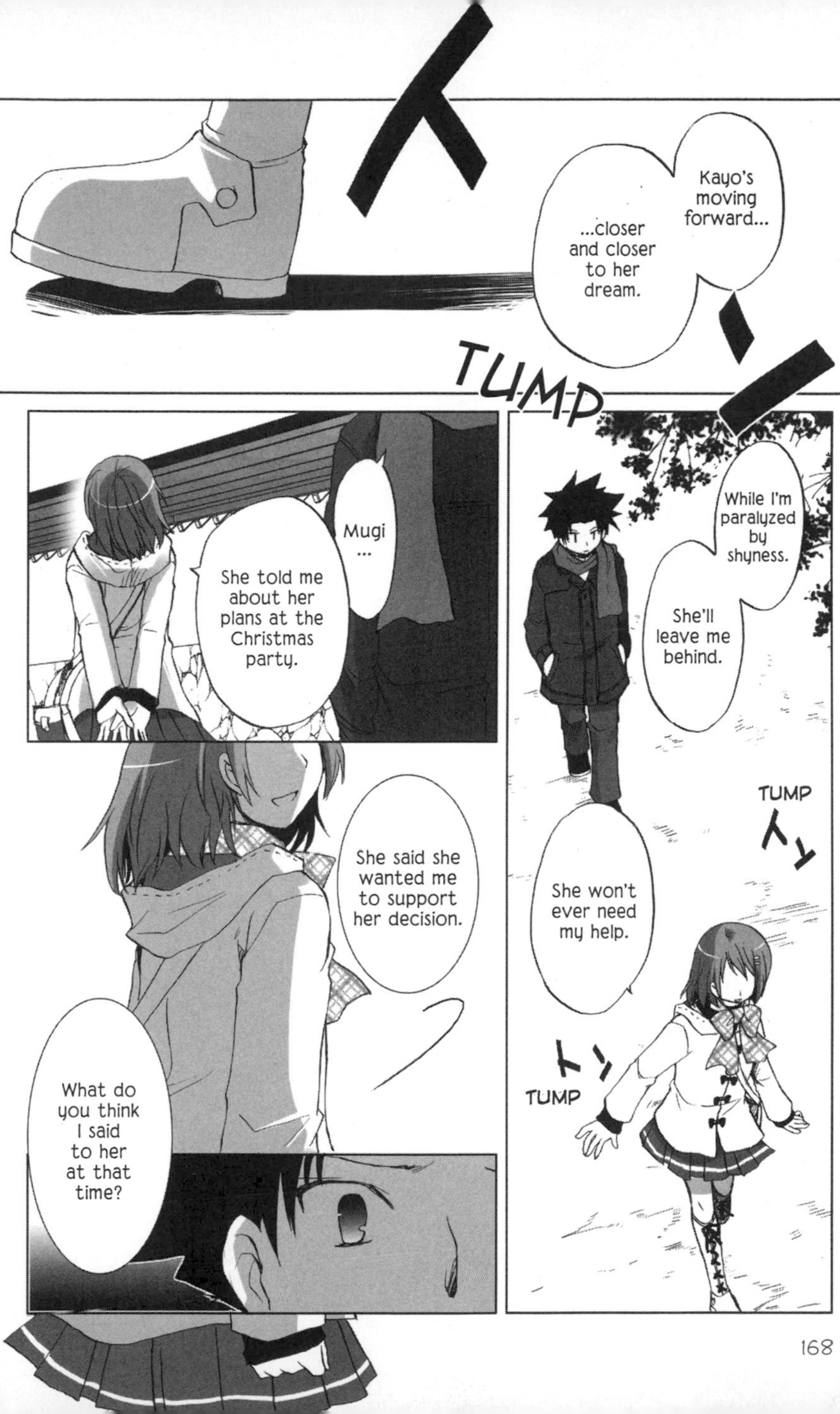
Kayo's moving forward...
...closer and closer to her dream.
TUMP
While I'm paralyzed by shyness.
She'll leave me behind.
TUMP
She won't ever need my help.
TUMP
Mugi ...
She told me about her plans at the Christmas party.
She said she wanted me to support her decision.
What do you think I said to her at that time?

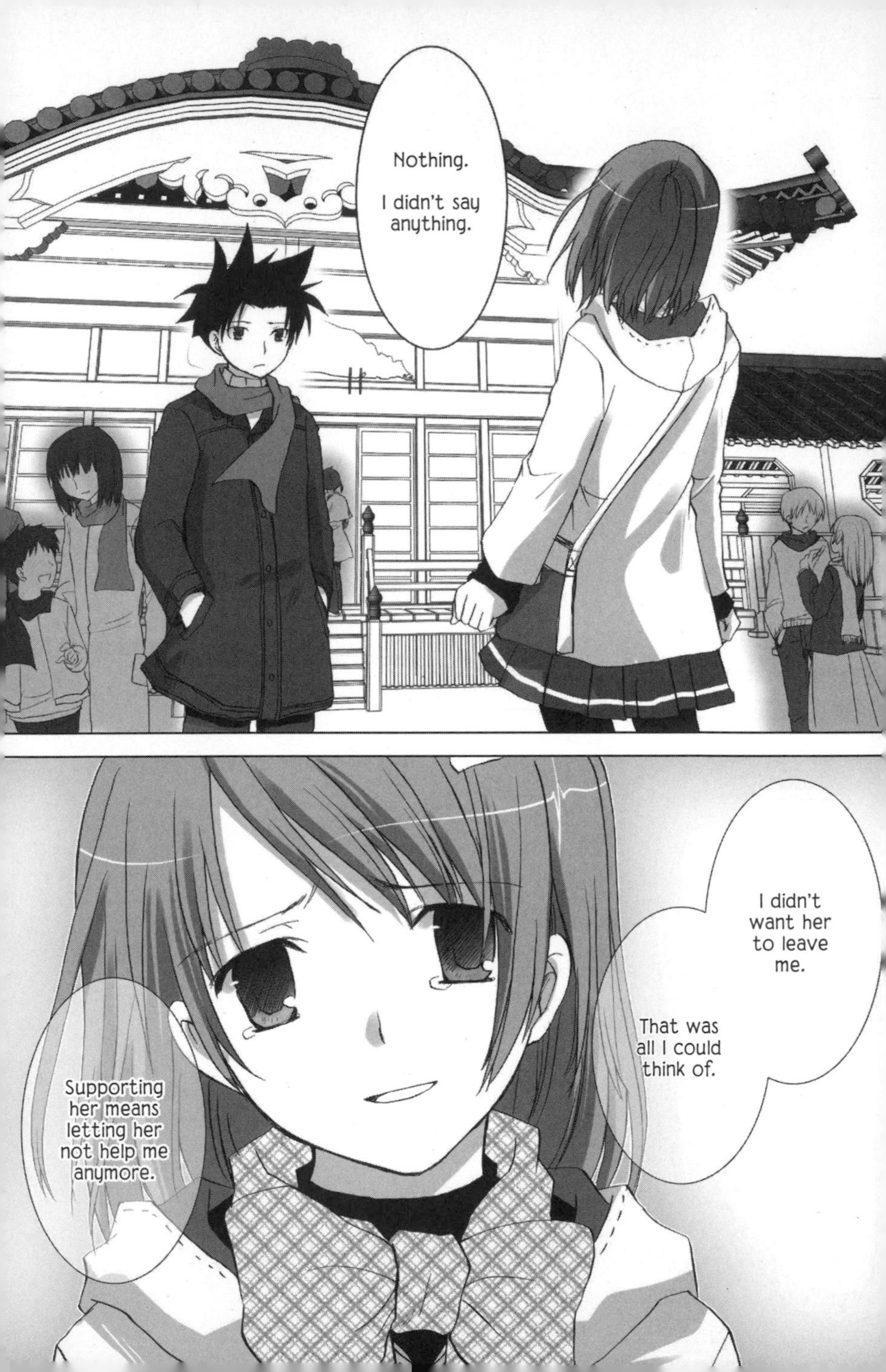
Nothing.
I didn't say anything.
I didn't want her to leave me.
That was all I could think of.
Supporting her means letting her not help me anymore.

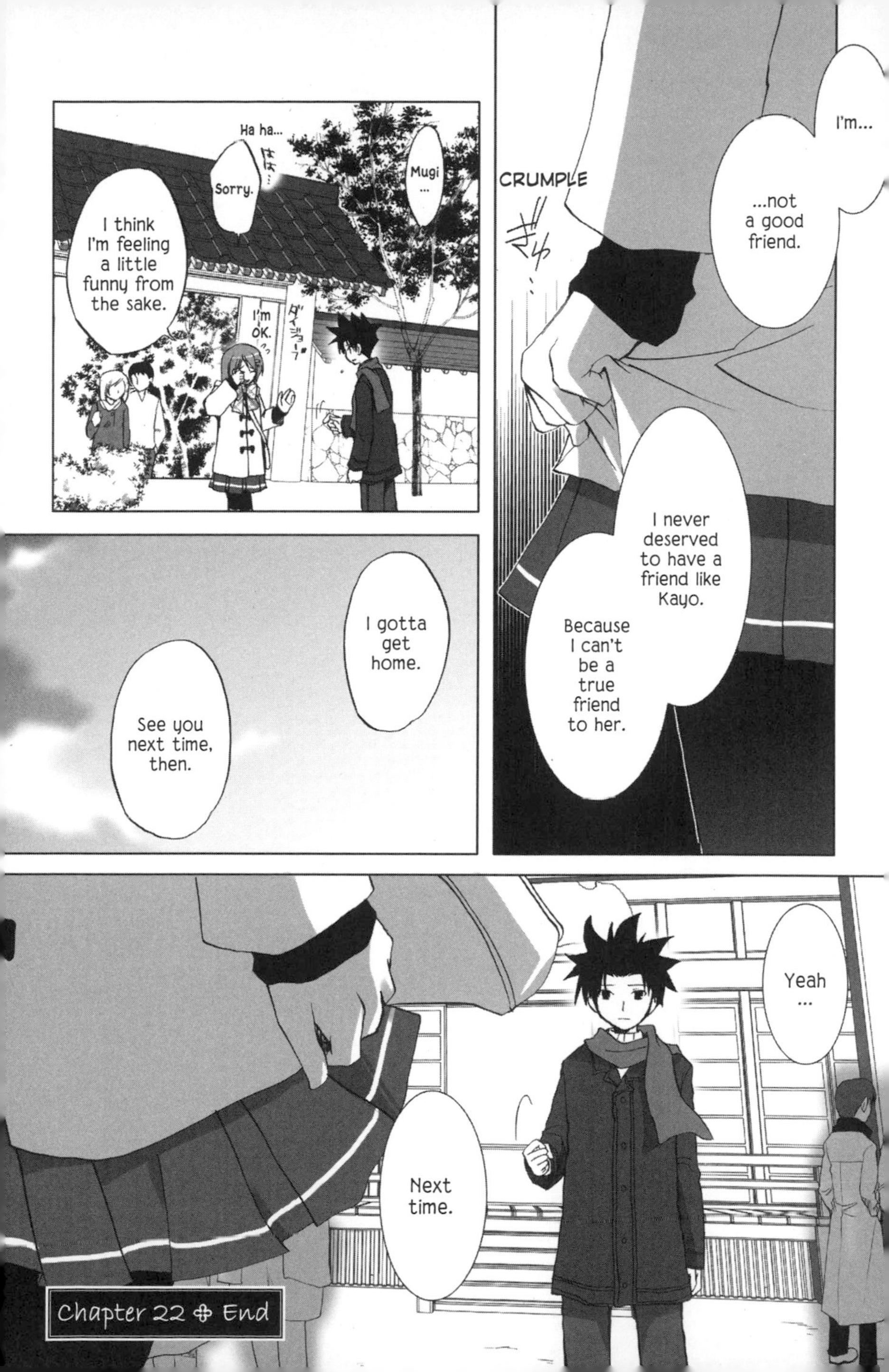
I'm...
...not a good friend.
CRUMPLE
I never deserved to have a friend like Kayo.
Because I can't be a true friend to her.
Mugi ...
Ha ha...
Sorry.
I think I'm feeling a little funny from the sake.
I'm OK.
I gotta get home.
See you next time, then.
Yeah ...
Next time.
Chapter 22 ✤ End

Hitohira Jr.

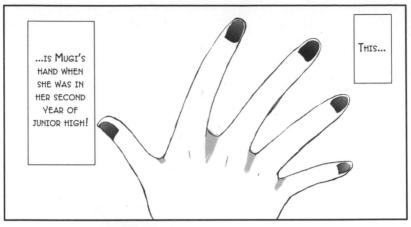

This...

...is Mugi's hand when she was in her second year of junior high!

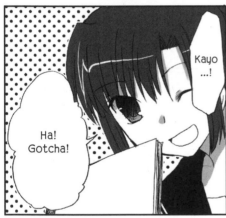

Kayo...!

Ha! Gotcha!

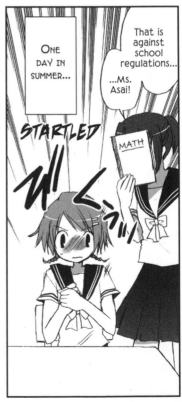

One day in summer...

That is against school regulations...

...Ms. Asai!

STARTLED

MATH

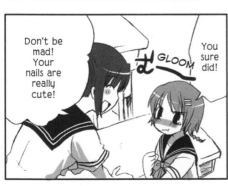

Don't be mad! Your nails are really cute!

GLOOM

You sure did!

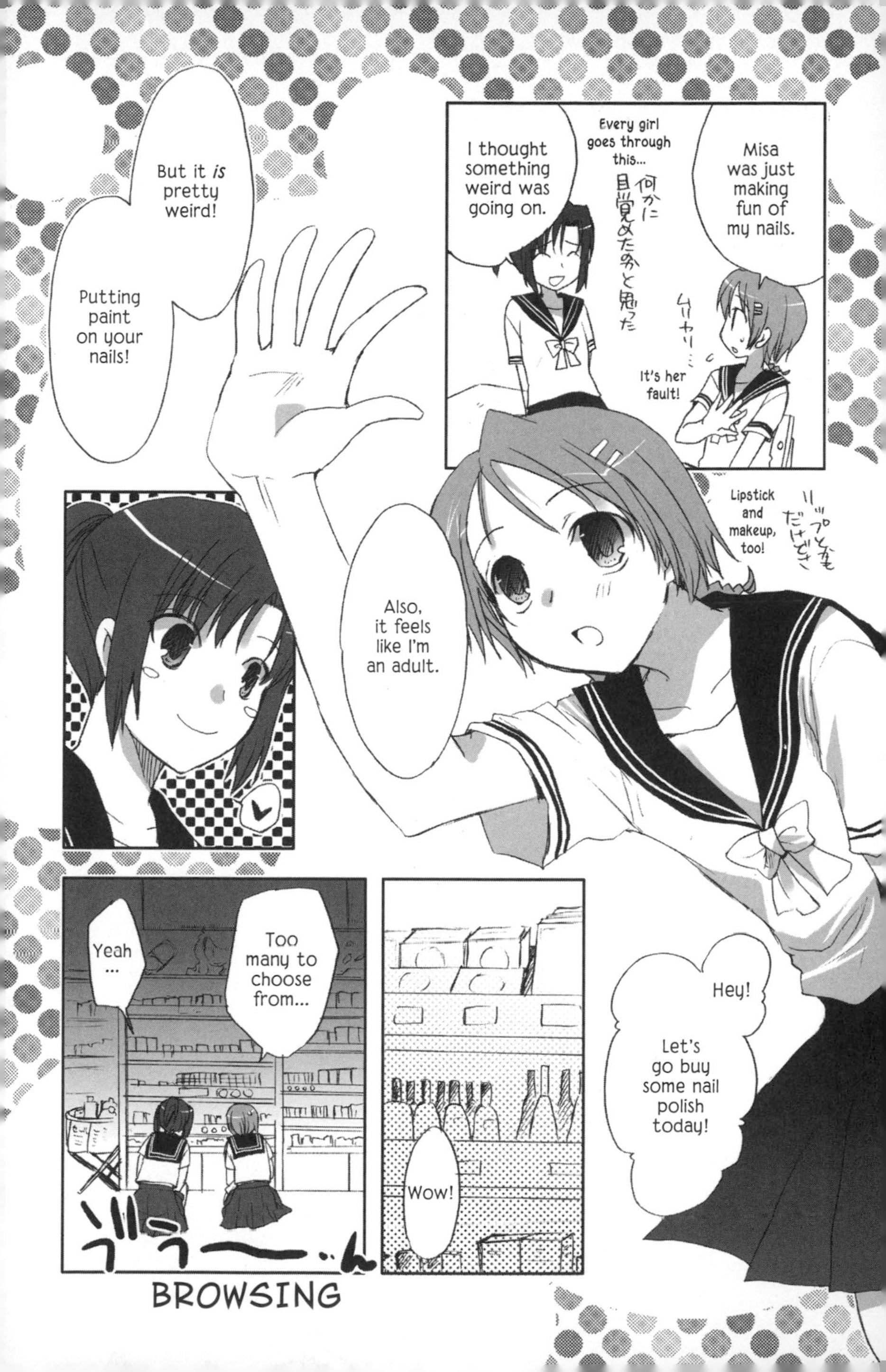
Misa was just making fun of my nails.
Every girl goes through this...
何かに目覚めた系と思った
I thought something weird was going on.
ムリヤリ...
It's her fault!
But it *is* pretty weird!
Putting paint on your nails!
Lipstick and makeup, too!
リップとかもだけどさ
Also, it feels like I'm an adult.
Hey!
Let's go buy some nail polish today!
Wow!
Too many to choose from...
Yeah...
ズラ〜〜ん
BROWSING

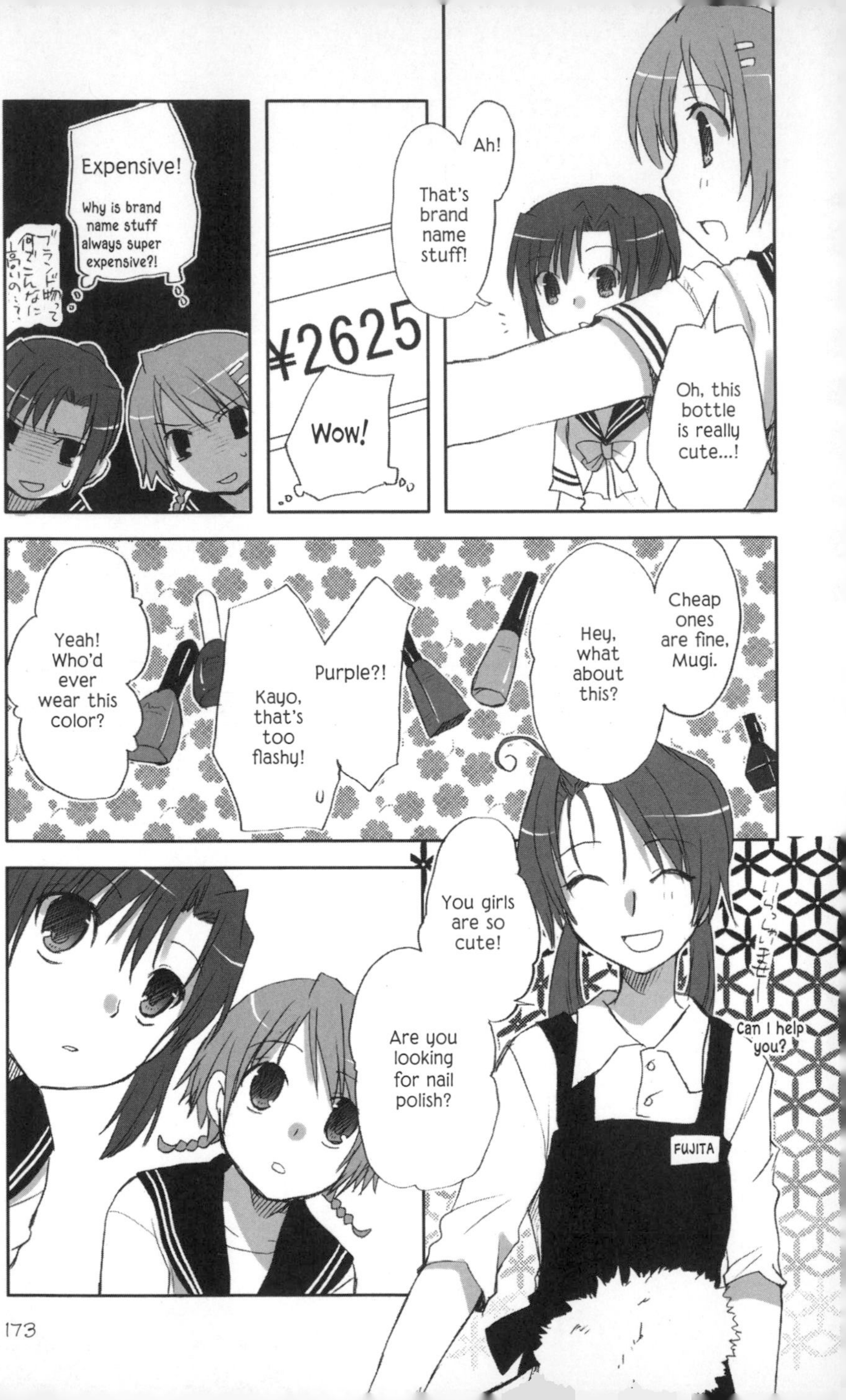
Oh, this bottle is really cute...!
Ah! That's brand name stuff!
¥2625
Wow!
Expensive!
Why is brand name stuff always super expensive?!
ブランド物って何でこんなに高いの…?!
Cheap ones are fine, Mugi.
Hey, what about this?
Purple?! Kayo, that's too flashy!
Yeah! Who'd ever wear this color?
いらっしゃいませー
Can I help you?
You girls are so cute!
Are you looking for nail polish?
FUJITA

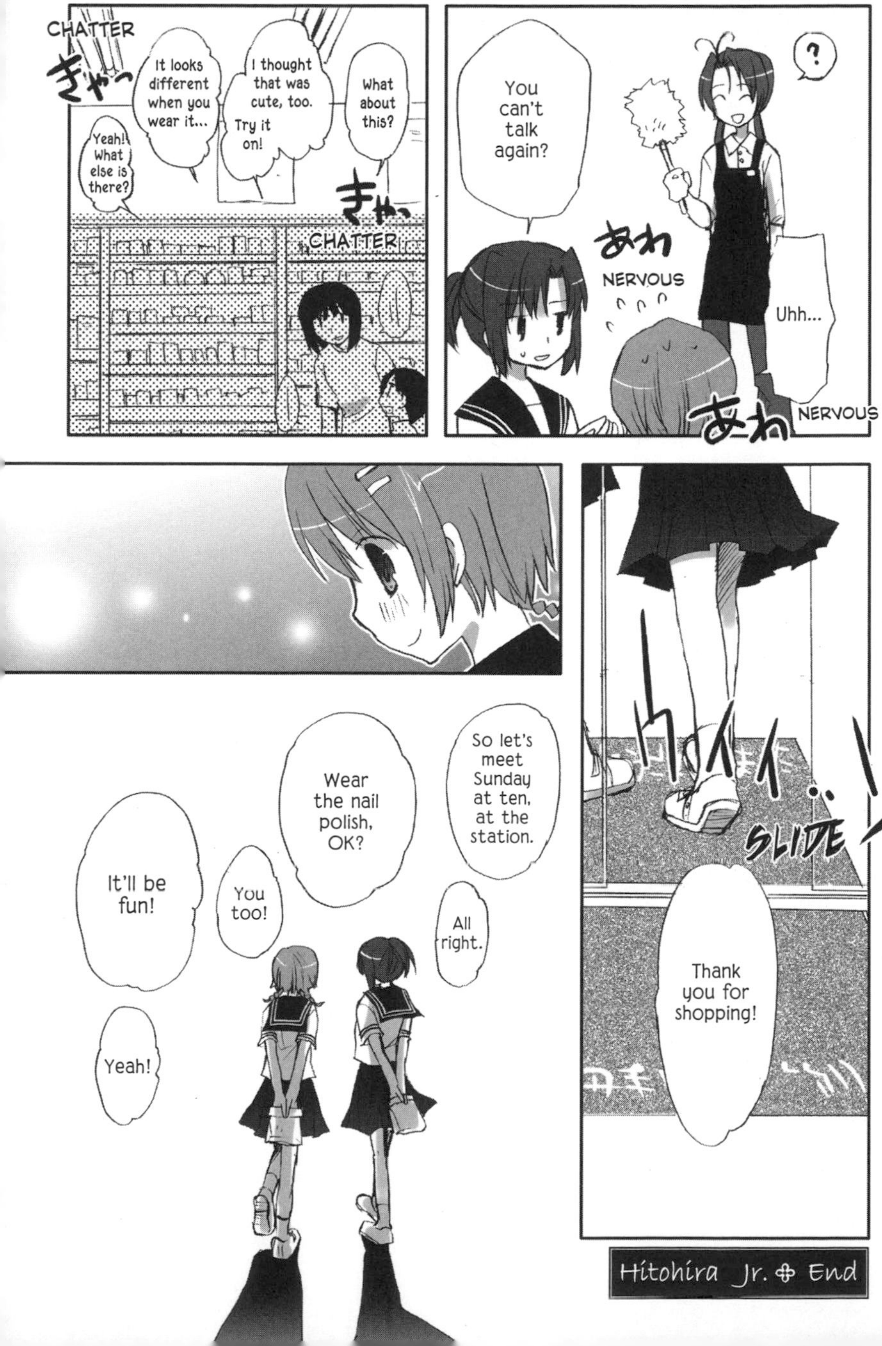
?
You can't talk again?
あわ
NERVOUS
Uhh...
あわ
NERVOUS
What about this?
I thought that was cute, too.
Try it on!
It looks different when you wear it...
CHATTER
ぎゃ～
Yeah! What else is there?
きゃ
CHATTER
SLIDE
Thank you for shopping!
So let's meet Sunday at ten, at the station.
All right.
Wear the nail polish, OK?
You too!
It'll be fun!
Yeah!

Hitohira Jr. ✤ End

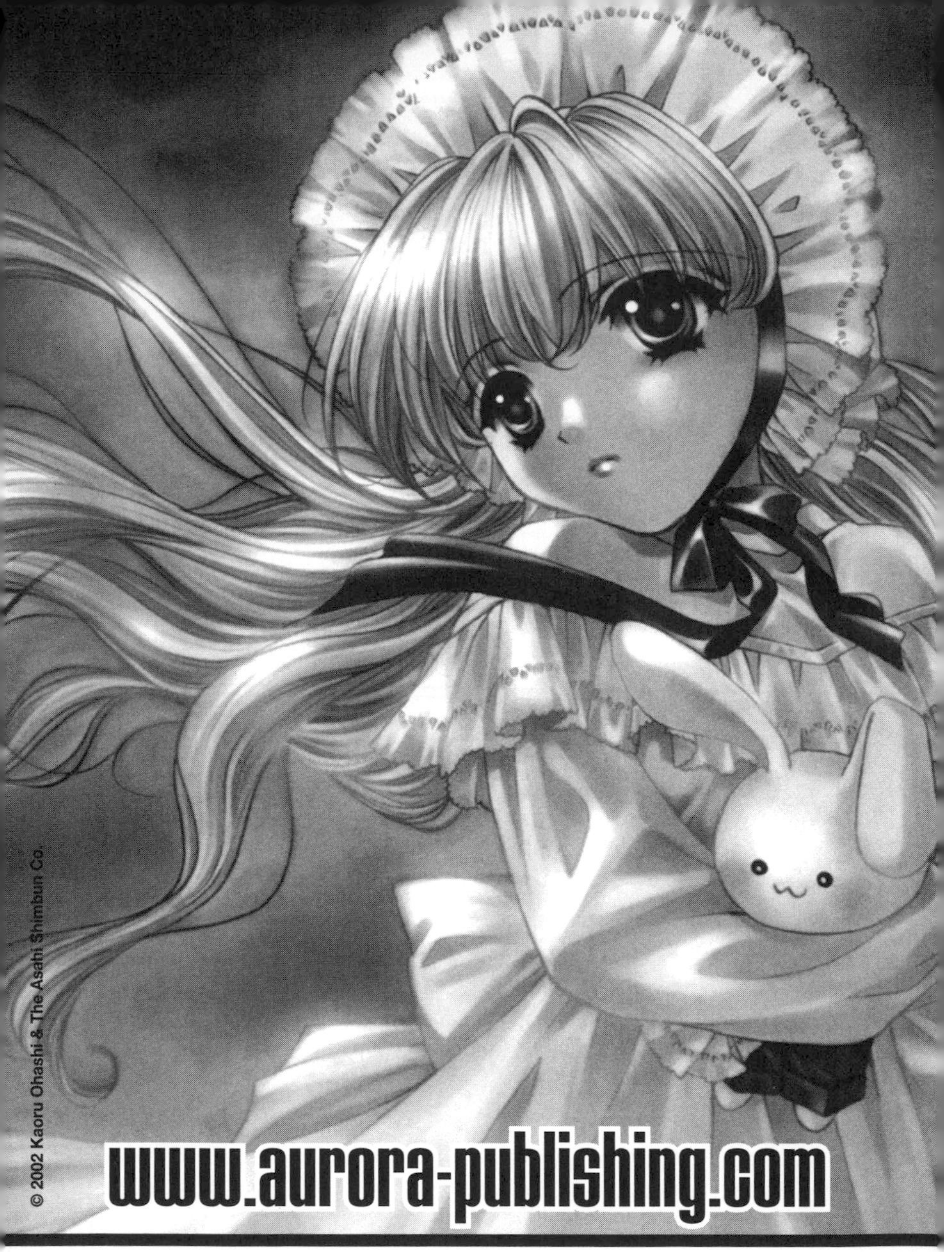
© 2002 Kaoru Ohashi & The Asahi Shimbun Co.
www.aurora-publishing.com

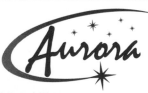

This is the back of the book
◄ ◄ ◄ ◄ ◄ **Turn over**

Hitohira 3

Hitohira • Volume 3
Story and Art by Idumi Kirihara

© Idumi Kirihara 2004. All rights reserved. First published in Japan in 2004 by Futabasha Publishers Co., Ltd., Tokyo as *Hitohira*. English version published by Aurora Publishing, Inc. Under license from Futabasha Publishers Co., Ltd.

Localization Supervision: Japan Visualmedia Translation Academy
Translation & English Adaptation: Maloosse Frootan
Lettering: Thea Willis

English Text © 2009 Aurora Publishing, Inc. All rights reserved.

Produced and Designed by Rod Sampson

Publisher: Nobuo Kitawaki

Published by Aurora Publishing, Inc.
www.aurora-publishing.com

Printed in Japan

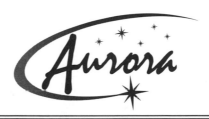